Transnational Citizenship

Transnational Citizenship

Membership and Rights in International Migration

Rainer Bauböck
Institute for Advanced Studies, Vienna

Edward Elgar
Cheltenham, UK • Northampton, MA, USA

Published by
Edward Elgar Publishing Limited
Glensanda House
Montpellier Parade
Cheltenham
Glos GL50 1UA
UK

Edward Elgar Publishing, Inc.
136 West Street
Suite 202
Northampton
Massachusetts 01060
USA

Reprinted 2002

British Library Cataloguing in Publication Data
Bauböck, Rainer
  Transnational Citizenship: Membership and
  Rights in International Migration
  I. Title
  323.6

Library of Congress Cataloguing in Publication Data
Bauböck, Rainer.
  Transnational citizenship: membership and rights in international
migration/Rainer Bauböck.
    p. cm.
  Includes bibliographical references and index.
  1. Citizenship. 2. Emigration and immigration. 3. Aliens—Civil
rights. 4. Immigrants—Civil rights. I. Title.
JF801.B384 1995
323.6'23—dc20
                                                            94–27375
                                                                CIP

ISBN 1 85278 942 5

Printed and bound in Great Britain by
Bookcraft, Bath

Contents

v

Preface

*Die Vaterlandsliebe wird schon dadurch
beeinträchtigt, daß man überhaupt keine
Auswahl hat. Das ist so, als wenn man die lieben
soll, die man heiratet, und nicht die heiratet, die
man liebt. (Bert Brecht, Flüchtlingsgespräche)*[1]

What does it mean to be a citizen? There are many possible answers that
come to one's mind. First, it means the opposite of being a subject, i.e. a
relation towards the state and its authorities in which people enjoy basic
rights. Second, it means also that people exercise control over governments
directly or indirectly by participating in political deliberation, by casting
votes on specific issues or by electing their representatives. Third, it means
that people are equals as members of an inclusive polity. There may be
large inequalities and wide cleavages in society but each citizen is counted
as one and as one only and all citizens are counted together.

We will obtain a quite different set of answers if our question is
understood to refer to citizenship in the international system of states. What
does it mean to be a citizen of a certain state? Responses to this question
will be more straightforward. It means being recognized as a member by
that state, i.e. not being a foreigner. And it means enjoying diplomatic
protection and the right to return when being abroad. As citizens of a state
we enjoy special rights and states control the access to citizenship in their
naturalization laws. My contention is that the answers liberal democratic
theory gives to the first question, challenge some of the answers
traditionally given to the second one.

A comprehensive analysis of citizenship has to take into account three
different aspects: (1) the rights and obligations attributed to citizens as
members of a polity, (2) the determination of individual membership, and
(3) the nature and shape of the polity itself. The first aspect describes what
a member of the community may legitimately do or expect to receive in a
society organized as a state and what can be legitimately expected from her
as a member. The second aspect concerns rules of admission to citizenship
as well as differences in the status of membership. The third aspect refers to
the changing shapes of the polity as a collective in space and time and to its
symbolic representation as a national community, as a population subjected

to a territorial sovereign, or as a society sharing democratic institutions and liberal rights.

Many theories of citizenship – and especially T.H. Marshall's pioneering essay of 1949 (Marshall, 1965) – have been exclusively concerned with the first question. Analyses of migration and migrants' insertion into a polity obviously have to start from the second question, but by doing so they often adopt a purely formal definition of membership – citizenship then becomes equivalent with the legal definitions of 'nationality'. Those who are not members may enjoy rights, but these are not regarded as rights of citizenship. Both approaches, the analysis of rights without regard to membership criteria, as well as the analysis of admission to membership which does not recognize the continuity between human rights, residence rights and citizenship rights, tend to take the third aspect as given and unproblematic. The polity is a nation, represented by a state, it is relatively stable over time and it is located in a specific territory with borders controlled by state authorities.

If we adopt the interpretation of the polity as an inclusive community or association of equal members that extends basic rights to everybody subject to its collective decisions, then the distinction between rights of aliens and citizens will become increasingly problematic. In a world of growing human mobility across state borders, liberal theory will have to develop new answers concerning the allocation of membership and rights. Although this may still serve as a starting-point we have to go beyond the dichotomy of, on the one hand, internal rights of citizenship in closed societies where individuals live a complete life (Rawls, 1993a) and, on the other hand, human rights which serve as a standard of justice in the international community of states (Rawls, 1993b). Citizenship will have to become transnational by reaching beyond boundaries of formal membership as well as territorial residence. However, as I will argue, this approach need not adopt a radically cosmopolitan perspective for which a global state is the target and end of history. In *cosmopolis*[2], membership would lose its quality of distinction: all would be members and therefore none could identify herself as a member. I will argue that transnational citizenship is the liberal democratic response to the question of how citizenship in territorially bounded polities can remain equal and inclusive in globalizing societies.

An analysis of citizenship rights could be conducted at four different levels.

(1) The first level is the descriptive one which identifies actual allocations of rights and the agents in decisions about these allocations: political actors within legislative systems, interest and pressure groups in civil society, those immediately affected by a right and general public opinion (see Elster, 1992, pp. 139–43). At this level, analysis is mainly

descriptive and empirical. It creates typologies and uses them to describe different distributions of rights.

(2) At a second level we could try to identify the general principles involved in these allocations (the principles already adopted and operating as well as those advocated as alternatives). This is only partly an empirical task, as it would involve the reconstruction of implicit norms from which actual allocations or political proposals for allocations could be consistently derived.

(3) At a third level, we can go further by exploring normative inconsistencies and conflict between the operative principles identified at the previous level on the one hand, and generally supported moral, political or cultural norms on the other hand.

(4) Finally, we may confront norms derived from analysing allocations of rights as well as from publicly supported general norms, with those that can be derived deductively from a philosophical moral and political theory. At this level the analysis will inevitably be itself normative and its purpose is to justify or criticize the use of norms in social practices.

The analysis of my book will be conducted primarily at the second and third level. Although this would make it possible in principle to refrain from normative judgement, I find it difficult to do so. Pointing out inconsistency or conflict between norms makes it almost imperative to develop one's own principles which might help to restore consistency or resolve conflict. This makes my approach open to charges that I deal with the fourth and philosophical level of analysis without developing it in a systematic way. I plead guilty to that charge. I will use different theories of justice and rights in an eclectic manner. I can account for this partly by saying that I have found none of them sufficiently elaborated or entirely convincing when applied to the problems I want to study. I feel, however, also unable to develop my intuitions concerning general normative principles into a fully elaborated theory. Given these shortcomings I believe it is better to make explicit my own normative judgement and to explain how it relates to different viewpoints in philosophical debates, on the one hand, and to what I perceive as liberal and democratic norms within contemporary polities, on the other hand.

When I first started to think and write about the idea of transnational citizenship some three years ago, I stated my hypotheses still in a rather crude and provocative way. I hope the argument of this book is less crude but still provocative enough to stimulate critique leading to further rethinking of these issues. Much improvement is due to discussions with a number of colleagues so large that I cannot acknowledge all my intellectual debts here. Some of those whom I am going to mention now will also feel that what I am writing is so much at odds with their own theoretical work that they do not really want to see their names associated with mine. I will mention them nevertheless, be it only to encourage them to state their disagreement: Joseph Carens, Stephen Castles, Jean Cohen, John Crowley, Thomas Faist, Ferenc Fehér, Ernest Gellner, Tomas Hammar, Agnes Heller, Zig Layton-Henry, Claus Offe, John Rex, Saskia Sassen, Volker Schmidt, Giovanna Zincone and Aristide Zolberg are among those who have influenced my ideas about citizenship or have discussed theirs with me. Special acknowledgements are due to my colleague Dilek Çinar who has never tired in her patient criticism and provided me with much useful information on naturalization rules. Apart from her, Andreas Schedler and Sonja Puntscher-Riekmann also read drafts or parts of the manuscript and gave me useful comments. I wrote my first papers about the subject of this book when I was a visiting fellow at the Centre for Research in Ethnic Relations at Warwick University in Coventry, UK, and would like to thank all colleagues there for their encouragement. Gertrud Hafner has provided invaluable support with the preparation of the typescript. Silvia and Anna Bauböck have helped to produce the index. Finally, I am grateful to Robin Cohen for permission to publish an extended version of a paper he had commissioned as the final chapter of this book.

NOTE

1.   'The love of one's country is already spoiled by the fact that you don't have any choice whatsoever. It's like having to love the one whom you marry, instead of marrying the one whom you love' (my translation).
2.   I have borrowed the term 'cosmopolis' from Onora O'Neill's discussion of transnational justice (O'Neill, 1991, p. 279). See also section 12.2.

PART I

Membership

1. Territorial Boundaries

Some people think of themselves as citizens of the world. They do not feel any deep attachments to a nation or state and they move with ease from one country to another. However, in order to do that they need passports which acknowledge them as citizens of a particular state. Being a cosmopolitan, not only in one's political opinions but also in one's life-style, is something which few can afford. Most ordinary people are citizens of separate states much more than they are citizens of the world.[1] Those who have to migrate in search of political protection or basic economic opportunities without belonging to the international elite in business, science, culture and sports experience this in the most dramatic way.

The international political system divides humanity into populations of different citizenship just as it divides the globe into different national territories. Transnational aspects of citizenship bridge these cleavages rather than level them out. They emerge in the crossing of territorial borders and in the extension of rights beyond membership of political communities. But even transnational citizenship does not dismantle these boundaries and create a single world state. Before exploring what sort of membership and rights characterize liberal democratic citizenship, it seems appropriate to ask first the fundamental question why there is this multiplicity of states and why it would even survive if this kind of citizenship were fully developed everywhere on the globe.

1.1. COSMOPOLIS IN POLITICAL THEORY

In social system theory, the long historical evolution of societal structures has been described as a transition from segmentary via hierarchical to functional differentiation. In some of its aspects the international system of states is obviously hierarchical, with economically and militarily powerful nations being able to dominate others by constraining their options in both foreign and domestic politics. There are also some elements of functional differentiation, especially in the field of international organizations. However, the basic structure of the system as a whole is one of segmentation. Thus, there seems to be something profoundly premodern about this structure.

The historical process from which global segmentation has emerged is well known. During the 19th and 20th centuries, the break-up of empires in the North and the decolonization of the South have led to a remodelling of international politics according to the originally European system of independent nation-states. The model of the nation-state has been adopted all over the world. Together with capitalist economics and modern science and technology it has been the most successful invention of Western civilization. However, while the economic and technological revolutions have created new forms of global interdependency, the 'nationalization' of the state system has re-emphasized the separateness of sovereign political units. Even capitalism triumphant on a global scale has not led to the simultaneous emergence of a global political structure where goods, money and people can move freely and laws can be enforced beyond small territories.

One explanation for this is that the nation-state model which made possible the establishment of European political and economic hegemony in the world had the potential of being emulated by those subjected to that very hegemony. Just as oppressed cultural and ethnic minorities of the older European states could raise their own claims to nationhood against imperial rule that turned national (Anderson, 1983, chapter 6), external peripheries subjected by colonialism could also emancipate themselves by national mobilization. However, for late-comers the economic opportunities for industrial development within the national frame became and smaller and smaller over time. Western nation-states had drawn their resources for economic development from both inside and outside. Colonial expansion was an important part of their success story. When former colonies became independent nations their economies had already been transformed to serve the needs of international trade towards the North. What could they benefit from political emancipation without economic development? Elites certainly could gain a lot by distributing among themselves the spoils of political rule. But why has there been so much popular support for national independence even where there was little prospect of improving living conditions? And why was the socialist dream that the impoverished masses of the colonies would eventually unite with the exploited working classes of the metropolis doomed to failure in each single case?

There is little doubt today that the segmented structure of the international political system has become an obstacle rather than a necessary operational basis for the global economy. The persistence of this structure and its accelerated further segmentation which we are witnessing in Central and Eastern Europe today cannot be easily explained as long as one does not take into account an autonomous dynamic of politics which is not simply functional for the economic processes of globalization.

Neo-Marxist historical analysis has certainly paid more attention to political structure than orthodox Marxist traditions. However, in Immanuel Wallerstein's world system analysis it is still the long chains of commodity production which are the determining causal factor in globalization. States control relations of production in various ways by regulatory legislation and taxation but they do this in order to promote capital accumulation (Wallerstein, 1983, chapter 2). On the international level, the state system forms a political superstructure of historical capitalism shaped by the relations between centre and periphery. The concept of the nation expresses the interregional and intraregional rivalry between states fighting for a better rank within this system (Wallerstein, 1988, pp. 106, 112). In this view, the structure of the global state system is hierarchical in the core/periphery relation and functionally differentiated in the international division of labour. Its segmentation into formally equal and sovereign nation-states is understood as a political ideology masking economic relations of dependence. At the same time this ideology also serves as a powerful resource for challenging and changing the international rank order of states. However, without a proper account of the political autodynamics of nation-building, it is difficult to understand how ideology could upset the functional imperatives of a global capitalist system.

In contrast with monocausal economic explanations of modernization, contemporary social system analysis has emphasized the process of functional differentiation of social subsystems, each of which operates with its own internal code of communication. In Niklas Luhmann's version of system theory, the relative autonomy of subsystems has been described as *autopoiesis* in analogy with the basic self-referentiality of nervous systems discovered in the biology of cognition by Humberto Maturana and Francisco Varela (1980). Yet this analysis of the political system has hardly helped to explain the persistent segmentation of the international state system. Luhmann uses the concept of society to denote the 'unity of the totality of the social'. There is no social environment for society. 'Society is the autopoietic social system par excellence. Society operates by communication, and whatever operates by communication is society' (Luhmann, 1984, p. 555, my translation). World society thus becomes a theoretical postulate rather than a historically contingent possibility. At the same time, Luhmann remains sceptical with regards to the possibilities of self-description of world society (Luhmann, 1984, pp. 585–7). Interaction systems of society such as the economic and the political ones can produce their own self-descriptions. Society itself, however, can no longer be understood as an interaction system but only as the unity of these functionally differentiated systems.

In a modified version of system theory it could be possible to reconstruct the notion of society and its boundaries towards other societies from the perspective of different subsystems (Kittel, 1993). This conceptual strategy would have to abandon the idea that society is nothing but a theoretical construct for the ultimate unity of everything social as distinguished from the non-social world. Instead, each functionally differentiated social subsystem produces its own specific description of society. These descriptions will contain specific core institutions of the respective system such as markets for the economy or states for the political system. However, any such description will also contain an image of society as a set of individuals. In this perspective, society is not the unity of subsystems, but still *societas* in the original sense of the word, a collective of interdependent and interacting human beings. While it seems to me possible to accept Luhmann's claim that individuals constitute the internal environment rather than the basic elements of functionally differentiated *social subsystems* (Luhmann, 1984, pp. 286–9, 346–8), I find the theoretical decision to eliminate individuals as the basic elements of *society* deeply problematic. In the present context the point of this distinction between subsystems and society[2] is that we can then realize that each social subsystem generates its own description of society as a set of individuals to which it constantly refers in its internal operations.

The descriptions of society produced by different subsystems need not be identical. Seen from within the economic system, boundaries of societal membership no longer distinguish a specific society from an environment constituted by other societies. The modern market economy is not structured into segmentary units which we can identify as separate societies. The set of individuals which constitute society from the point of view of the economic system is unlimited (although of course not infinite). Modern economic society is composed of individuals who interact in (more or less) open markets in order to realize individual (rather than collective) preferences. For that reason modern society can indeed be seen as global if one intends to describe the social unit encompassing all the actors involved in communication within the economic system.

The situation is very different if one turns to the political system as the reference point from where to determine the boundaries of societies. There is an international community of states with its own rules of interaction partially·codified in international law, and a range of political organizations operating at the global level. However, this is obviously not a functionally differentiated subsystem of a single global society. This international system remains subdivided into essentially similar political units called states. Seen from the perspective of states, the social units which they organize are *different societies* and not just regional sections of a single global society, in much the same way that nation-states themselves are organized as *different polities* rather than as federal provinces of a world state.

Social system theory of Luhmann's kind has been criticized for merely developing a sophisticated terminology but not providing sociological explanation. This charge would still hold against a modified version in which the common-sense idea that societies are composed of individuals as basic agents is readmitted into the theory. Such a theory could account for the observation that functionally differentiated social subsystems generate their own descriptions of society and its external boundaries. But this does not yet explain *how* these images of society are constructed and *why they are different* for the two dominant subsystems. Why is there no world state or world federation of states at the horizon of modernity? Is there just a time lag in political modernization and globalization compared to economic development? Is the nation-state an anachronistic survival of early modernity which will eventually be overcome? Or, alternatively, is the contemporary proliferation of the number of states inherent in the very dynamic of political modernization?

I will not try to answer fully such questions in this book. In all that follows I take the existence of separate states with distinct territories as given. My focus will be on the consequences of this structure for political membership of increasingly mobile populations. However, it seems appropriate to ask first whether this given feature of our political world will be a permanent one also for the foreseeable future. The predicaments of people who are deprived of citizenship because they do not fit into the structure of the nation-state system, and the dilemmas involved in extending citizenship beyond its national constraints, would be real and pressing ones even if one could assume that global citizenship will eventually replace the present national forms. But we might then at least be confident that further modernization will provide a solution. Second, as far as the normative aspects of my analysis are concerned, one could also ask whether this segmentation itself can be regarded as morally justified, desirable or at least acceptable. If global citizenship were genuinely desirable or even morally imperative as a goal for liberal democratic politics, this would resolve many dilemmas of normative reasoning. We would know what to strive for even though not necessarily how to get there. However, both teleological assumptions about historical progress towards global citizenship and normative arguments in favour of it have been strongly contested in the history of political theory. In the following pages I will briefly review the pertinent premises of major schools of political thought, and present my own sceptical argument about the possibility and desirability of a global superstate.

The 'realist' tradition which dominates research on international relations has consistently seen states as individual actors in the international arena. Just as classical social contract theory and contemporary methodological individualism view society as composed of autonomous individuals making their own choices and pursuing their own interests, so international politics is constituted by the essentially self-interested actions of states. The difference between national society and the international community of states is that the latter cannot escape from a Hobbesian state of nature. International agreements and coalitions remain strongly constrained by the fundamental goals of national politics. States are always each other's potential enemies. There is no world sovereign to whom they could surrender their natural autonomy in exchange for peace and protection, and the power distribution of international politics makes the emergence of such a global authority highly improbable. Realist thinking has always rejected speculations about a historical tendency towards the emergence of global political actors. However, the same frame of reasoning makes it difficult to explain the process of state formation in the modern age of nationalism. In this view, separation should be just as unusual as fusion. How, then, to explain the dramatic increase in the number of formally independent states? In the reordering of European borders after World War I the principle of national self-determination was still constrained by the realist notion of a minimal threshold of viability for sovereign states in terms of population, territory, economic resources and military power. Why have these constraints been so widely ignored in the formation of new states since 1945?[3]

Realist accounts of the international state system usually are suspicious of normative arguments. Realists have sometimes tended to think of morals and politics as two worlds entirely apart. 'Far more characteristic of the realist position, however, is the view that action on behalf of the national interest is itself an ethical imperative. The preservation of the state's security, well-being and institutional integrity is the condition for the realization of other values, without which no civilized existence is possible at all' (Hendrickson, 1992, p. 215). In a more universalistic perspective, realists have not only assumed a basic moral justification for national interest but also for the segmented structure of the international state system as a whole. The coexistence of independent states has been seen as a pluralistic structure, allowing for legitimate diversity and for the development of checks and balances against tyranny and war. Realism has been 'identified in European history with the defence of the state system and with the refuge from oppressive power that a system of independent states permitted' (Hendrickson, 1992, p. 217).

This latter idea seems to be borrowed from liberal thought, which is concerned with the autonomy and rights of individuals rather than of states. In contrast with realists, their distaste for nationalist ideology has turned many liberals into advocates of cosmopolitan ethics. Yet this need not imply a plea for a world state. I can imagine four reasons which could lead liberals to prefer a plural and segmented world of states to a world state. First, developing liberal democracy within a state may depend to some degree upon competition with other democratic states. Second, totalitarian regimes can sometimes only be weakened by outside pressure or overthrown by outside intervention − a world government turning totalitarian will not face any external opponents. Third, the possibility of emigration can create internal pressure against a slackening of liberal and democratic standards or for the restoration of democracy (Hirschman, 1970, 1978). Fourth, the possibility of secession and the creation of new states may defuse certain internal conflicts which could otherwise fuel protracted civil war. Taken together, these four arguments make a strong case that internal standards of liberal democracy might be easier to sustain within a pluralistic structure of world politics.

However, this conclusion may be premature. Versions of liberalism which have been called 'neoliberal' in Europe or 'libertarian' in the USA have asserted that the task of liberal regimes is to maintain and to maximize negative individual freedom. Equal negative freedom consists in the absence of interference by others with those choices and actions that do not themselves interfere in a similar way. The state monopoly of legitimate force has been defended as indispensable for maintaining negative liberty in a society. However, for libertarians, any state interference beyond the protection of physical security and the enforcement of property rights and valid contracts is by definition unjust, as it restricts the sphere of voluntary agreement between autonomous individuals.[4]

In Robert Nozick's libertarian theory, just states emerge from voluntary protective associations. One would assume that any voluntary association must guarantee the rights of collective secession and individual exit. However, as Nozick explains, the minimal state that can be justified is a *dominant* protective association which holds a *de facto monopoly* in a certain territory This monopoly comes about because maximally competing voluntary protective associations cannot provide their services within the same territory, i.e. they cannot effectively protect their clients. Continuous violent conflict would be the result (Nozick, 1974, pp. 16–17).[5] However, by extension of the same argument, a subdivision of territories between dominant protective agencies will presumably make for a much less stable situation and worse protection than a single dominant protective association for all territories of the world. Even if one disregarded the incentives for each protective agency to invade the territory of another one in order to protect their clients more effectively against potential threats from neighbours, there remains the unresolved problem how to protect individuals who move into the territory of another association.

The rights of emigration and secession figure prominently in Nozick's 'framework for utopia', but they refer to voluntary associations within a minimal state rather than to this state itself (Nozick, 1974, chapter 10). Presumably, libertarians would still support these rights within a given world of many different and more than minimal states. Yet their approach seems to make it difficult to accept such a structure of the world in the first place.

Less radical models of neoliberalism do acknowledge the social demand for scarce public goods other than mere internal security. The production and distribution of these public goods requires political authority which may legitimately tax property and income and interfere with some forms of negative individual freedom. Generally, neoliberals of this kind have favoured a market model of democracy. For them the democratic quality of politics lies in the availability of choice. Citizens are seen as consumers who choose among politicians and programmes. They exercise control not by active political participation but by choosing a different ruling personnel next time. Joseph Schumpeter has summed up this approach in his famous formula: 'the democratic method is that institutional arrangement for arriving at political decisions in which individuals acquire power to decide by means of a competitive struggle for the people's vote' (Schumpeter, 1950, p. 269). I will assume for the moment that in a liberal theory 'the people' is not an ethnic group or nation but rather the general population within a given state territory. While the libertarian notion of maximum negative liberty should lead to *preferring* a world state, this conception of democracy would *allow* for creating it by making possible an indefinite extension of the territorial scale of rule without thereby abandoning its democratic legitimation. Why should political elites not compete for power on a global scale? The communication technology which is necessary to make known their profiles and views to a world audience is already there. A corresponding technology which would allow for world-wide delivery and aggregation of votes could presumably be created.

So in the minimal model of liberal democracy defended by neoliberals there is little that would obstruct its extension to ever larger territories and populations. This should even be seen as advantageous as it opens a greater space within which people can communicate, move and more generally make their own choices with no other restrictions than those imposed by institutional safeguards for an equal liberty for all. The liberal arguments against world government which I have outlined above require a more extensive interpretation of what freedom entails. The right of secession involves a genuinely collective choice, and the right of emigration means that individuals have an opportunity not only to choose political leaders and programmes but also to choose politically organized societies of which they want to be members. Both kinds of rights cannot be easily accounted for in libertarian theory.

The argument for a world state can of course also be made from a very different point in the ideological spectrum. Instead of being welcomed as a desirable frame for the extension of individual liberty, it can also be seen as an imperative necessity and precondition for the elimination of collective threats to humanity as a whole which appear to be insoluble within a segmented system of sovereign states. The contemporary globalization of issues of security and ecology provide the most obvious illustrations.[6]

In contrast with other types of arms, nuclear weapons are not designed as means of internal coercion and oppression. The nuclear proliferation and arms race are obviously an outcome of the structure realists accept as given, i.e. of national strategies by states acting independently from each other in the pursuit of their fundamental interests of security or domination. However, the fact that a world state would probably eliminate this particular threat to human survival does not imply that the threat in itself will also help in bringing about that solution.[7] As the world now realizes again after the dissolution of the Soviet Union, nuclear weapons are a powerful backing for claims to sovereignty and independent standing in the global political system. Given a situation in which a (growing) number of states already possess nuclear weapons, the only available path towards disarmament seems to be negotiating for it among sovereign and independent states. Uniting states into a world federation and establishing a single world monopoly of legitimate force is not a means towards the end of radical disarmament, but the other way round: disarmament would have to take place within the given multiplicity of states before there could be any realistic possibility for the formation of a world government.

Some ecological threats and disasters are truly global in scale and many of a more regional nature clearly transcend the coping capacity of nation-states. In contrast with nuclear armament, issues such as ozone depletion or greenhouse warming not only require global policies but should also create some common interest among states and government to seriously address the problem. However, at a second glance it often turns out that in the absence of global enforcement agencies collective action dilemmas are hard to resolve. Each individual state can gain economically from free-riding on the ecological self-restraint of others. Furthermore, interests in specific ecological policies, capacities to implement them, and effects of non-action are distributed highly unequally between countries. As the examples of desertification in Africa or of unsafe nuclear power plants in Eastern Europe demonstrate, the most disastrous effects of inaction are usually concentrated in countries which either lack necessary resources or have short-term priorities which override ecological concerns.

The argument that global ecological policies would be easier to implement within a world state is certainly coherent. The structure of the prisoners' dilemmas, which presently impede effective reform, probably also suggests that strengthening supranational agencies in this field would be a better strategy than merely relying on intergovernmental co-ordination as must be done in disarmament. However, even if ecological issues are of utmost importance for the future of humanity, it is far from obvious that world government would be sufficiently legitimated because of this reason alone. Ecological fundamentalists who argue that only global dictatorship would be powerful enough to enforce the necessary changes should alert us to realize that while some ecological problems might indeed require global governance, other equally essential values and political targets such as certain individual liberties, democratic participation or social redistribution might be easier to sustain within a framework of separate states.

Such conflict of values is generally difficult to resolve. Some normative theories postulate a priority of certain values over others. The conflict between the values of liberty and life which lurks behind these issues is probably the most controversial one.[8] One (deceptively) simple way to avoid this dilemma seems to be offered by the utilitarian paradigm. Why should we not just register individual preferences in matters such as arms control, ecological reform, or free movement, and then look for that political structure which would maximize the chances for the greatest possible number of individuals to get their preferences realized?[9]

At first glance one would assume that the utilitarian approach would naturally incline towards a cosmopolitan view. If there are global problems of collective choice and the utilities or preferences of each human being are to be weighted equally, how could we then be in favour of parcelling out political authority, needed to resolve these problems, into separate states? Frequently, applied utilitarianism (especially in national economics) has simply taken the existence of states and state populations as a basic given. Consistent utilitarians, however, should identify first the range of all who might be affected by some decision or action and then aggregate all preferences within that population. Yet despite its appeal to analytical rigour and its assertion that moral issues can be resolved by calculation, utilitarianism might come up with very different answers to the question whether a structure of politically independent states is superior to world government. It all depends on preferences attributed to individuals which can never in fact be calculated, where there is no institutional setting in which such calculation becomes explicit. This is, for example, the case in markets and in voting systems and here utilitarian analysis can operate fairly well. It is not so in moral and political issues when individual preferences do not expose themselves in similar ways in order to be counted. Utilitarians may well defend a world segmented into nation-states, on the grounds that most people have strong patriotic sentiments and that only independent states can preserve and develop the particular national cultures which they feel attached to.[10]

A different strategy for resolving the dilemma might look for intermediate but stable solutions halfway between a world of completely sovereign states and a single world government. Liberal arguments for plurality and concerns with global security and ecological sustainability can be reconciled in various ways. One which seems particularly attractive is the Kantian idea of a world confederation of states. Kant seems to suggest a confederation rather than a federation (Kant, 1984, second article).[11] A confederation is a model of voluntary association the individual members of which are states. They may leave when they so decide and new ones may be admitted if they are accepted by the present members of the confederation. This model presupposes that states do not abandon their sovereignty and do not merge into some larger unit, just as individual persons are assumed to retain their basic autonomy when joining a voluntary association. That idea is perfectly compatible with the realist notion of taking states rather than individuals, social groups, corporations or organizations as the basic agents in international politics. The model of federation, on the other hand, would allow for a diminution of sovereignty and an eventual transformation of states into administrative regions within larger units. Both models have been successfully tested in history and the European Union is about to decide whether to follow the first or the second road. However, there is no indication of a dynamic along either path of overcoming segmentation at the global level. Given the diversity of interests between states, the fusion of all states into a single federation was ruled out by Kant, not as a future possibility but as unattainable by peaceful means. The less demanding model of confederation might not be much easier to accomplish but it can at least be justified normatively on Kantian grounds. An obligation of states to seek peaceful and friendly relations with all other states which refrain from threatening and unfriendly action in their external policy would be perfectly sufficient as a basic principle. Only a state in a globally dominant position in which it is stronger than any coalition of other states could consistently reject this. If no state is in such a position and all are vulnerable by hostile actions of others, each state has rational reasons to act according to this principle if only the normative criterion of universalizability of basic principles (or maxims, in Kant's terminology) is accepted. If all states acted along these lines, a global confederation would result. However, there is a paradox involved in this line of reasoning. An association can only remain voluntary within an environment where some potential members are not included, or at least not included permanently. If everybody who could be a member joins and never leaves again the association loses its test criterion for voluntariness. Conversely, as long as an association remains truly a voluntary one it cannot, and ought not to, prevent changes in the composition of its membership. On a global scale where it would have to encompass all states, the model of confederation could be stable over time only if it turned into a federation denying the right to secession.

The realist school of thought in international relations has assumed the segmented structure of world politics as given in its basic premises, and liberal theorists have often hesitantly accepted it as insurmountable. It is the republican tradition which has fully embraced this structure as something both built into the very nature of politics and also desirable for the common good of human beings. This tradition goes back to Aristotle for whom the multiplicity of Greek city-states and their different constitutions was a starting-point for finding the best constitutional mix within any single one (Aristotle, 1981). However, the essential idea that republicanism has contributed to the problem we are discussing is not that of interstate plurality and competition, but the inherent boundedness of political space. Only within the confines of the ancient city walls and the national borders of contemporary states can political decision-making become an affair for a public composed of citizens and oriented towards a notion of their common good. Different thinkers stressed either the exclusivity of republican politics within an environment formed by other states or the internal communality which can only be created by political participation. Machiavelli and Carl Schmitt emphasized the former aspect and Rousseau and Hannah Arendt the latter one. Nevertheless, though weights may be different, internal homogenization and external exclusion go inevitably hand in hand.

This becomes especially clear in Arendt's writings. Her insistence that political freedom requires a bounded public space deserves being quoted at some length. Arendt has been frequently misunderstood as naively trying to revive the tradition of the classical Greek *polis*. However, she refers to this tradition in a way which is quite different from more recent communitarian and Neo-Aristotelian authors like Michael Walzer (1983, 1987) or Alasdair MacIntyre (1981, 1989). These writers try to show that any normative argument can only claim validity when it is formulated within a tradition (MacIntyre) or refers to the shared cultural understandings of a particular political community (Walzer).[12] Arendt's concerns – which are essentially those of the whole republican tradition – are more universalistic. She wants to examine general conditions and forms of human action and the specific qualities of the political in human life rather than the cultural specificity and relativity of political values and conceptions of the common good.

This is how Arendt characterizes the boundaries of the Greek *polis*: 'The law of the city-state was neither the content of political action ... nor was it a catalogue of prohibitions .... It was quite literally a wall, without which there might have been an agglomeration of houses, a town ... but not a city, a political community. Without it a public realm could no more exist than a piece of property without a fence to hedge it in; the one harboured and inclosed political life as the other sheltered and protected the biological life process of the family' (Arendt, 1958, pp. 63–4). The metaphor of the law as a fence reappears in Arendt's characterization of contemporary citizenship: 'A citizen is by definition a citizen among citizens of a country among countries. His rights and duties must be defined and limited, not only by those of his fellow citizens, but also by the boundaries of a territory. ... Politics deals with men, nationals of many countries and heirs to many pasts; its laws are the positively established fences which hedge in, protect, and limit the space in which freedom is not a concept, but a living political reality. The establishment of one sovereign world state ... would be the end of all citizenship' (Arendt, 1970, pp. 81–2).

Of course Hannah Arendt does not only describe boundaries in modern politics, but also criticizes them. Mass society, in her view, has largely eliminated the necessary internal boundaries which protect the political space and separate it from the private realm and the sphere she calls the social one. It contains within itself the seeds of totalitarianism (Arendt, 1967), one of whose manifestations is imperialism: the elimination of territorial political boundaries by conquest and domination. So probably Arendt did not wish to rule out the eventual formation of a world state, but she clearly saw this possibility as either a result of, or as paving the way for, the victory of totalitarianism.

Arendt's approach does not allow for the exclusion of entire *social groups* from politics as was the case in Greek democracy. However, as Agnes Heller pointed out, one major difficulty with accepting Arendt's views is that they imply the exclusion of so many *issues* which have become genuinely political ones under modern conditions (Heller, 1991, p. 336). Her argument for bounded citizenship could have been much stronger had she only seriously discussed contemporary conditions for democratic legitimation of political decisions on such matters as electoral representation, public education, regulation of labour markets, or social redistribution. Instead of understanding the importance of such issues for modern politics as a result of a *mutual* interpenetration of social and political spheres, she could only perceive it as a symptom for the 'rise of the social' and a corresponding decline of the truly political activity of public speech and action.

1.2. TERRITORIAL CONSTRAINTS OF POLITICS

My own view is that normative statements about the best or most desirable global order of political communities should be based on an account of what modernity implies for politics with respect to both societal structures and post-traditional legitimation. A cosmopolitan model of a world state seems to me as much out of gear with the basic dynamics of modern politics as a republican model of self-contained communities forming sovereign units within an international political system.

Among the basic features which characterize political modernity are the following: (1) a growing territorial rigidity of state institutions and boundaries, (2) the overcoming of structural barriers of communication which limited the extension of public space and restricted the size of densely organized political societies in premodern eras, (3) a growing interdependency within a global system due to an exponential increase of externalities of policies implemented at any level below the global one, (4) the legitimation of political authority and the exercise of political power by referring to the imputed will or interests of society, imagined as a large and inclusive community (rather than as a particular gender, class or group). I take features (2) and (3) to be rather evident. The hypotheses of territorial rigidity (1) and of community-based legitimation (4) might need explaining.

Modern state bureaucracy has created forms of social control and surveillance that no ancient tyrant could have dreamt of. We can think of this structure as consisting of two different elements, an institutional 'hardware' and a set of 'softwares' or programmes applied by these institutions. The software must be flexible and complex in order to deal with a highly mobile society, in which individuals constantly move spatially as well as between social positions in a way totally inconceivable in agrarian society. However, this software can only operate within a hardware that is rigidly fixed with respect to territory.

Nomadic societies which had developed state institutions, such as the Mongol empire, could move their basic political institutions in space with ease. The locus of government was where the headquarters of the emperor's army happened to be. Sedentary agricultural societies organized territory in a different way. The fight for territory and the fortification of its boundaries became the essential target of government. However, the territory conquered was structured politically only in a very loose manner, essentially by military occupation. Conquest by some different ruler hardly changed the spatial organization of society and its institutional infrastructure. The state really permeated society and reorganized it territorially only during the age of European absolutism.[13] The new territorial rigidity of state institutions and boundaries has become indispensable precisely in order to cope with enhanced internal mobility of people, goods and services in a capitalist market economy. This does not imply that external borders are necessarily more stable than in earlier historical eras, nor does it mean that they are policed to suppress all external movements of people and goods which are not commissioned or controlled by the state (although this was certainly a major function of borders under absolutism). In the age of capitalism, imperialism and nationalism modify borders again and again. The difference is that now any change is much more dramatic. It means a deep rupture for societal structures. Even if the state apparatus performs roughly similar functions in each nation-state, historical events which bring a territory under the rule of another state or lead to the creation of a new one have the inevitable consequence of political reorganization of society. In this sense, the building of nation-states is a truly revolutionary business, not just a reshuffling in the ruling personnel of a political class.

The first three features of political modernity mentioned above cannot sufficiently explain the persistent segmentation of the international state system. In my interpretation the first feature does explain why state power is territorially organized rather than floating around in a global social space like information, goods, money or people. It suggests that modern state bureaucracy operates within a hierarchical structure, the lowest level of which is inevitably local. Nevertheless, this requirement could be perfectly met in a centralized or federalized world state. Such a state would furthermore clear the way for an unimpeded and less conflict-ridden development of the expansive second and third features. Political space would finally become congruent again with societal spaces which have been dramatically extended by the use of communication and transportation technologies. Externalities of state action would become reinternalized within a single political structure in which higher authority could overcome the multiple collective action dilemmas of the present interstate system.

It is the fourth feature of political modernity which is the decisive obstacle. In some utopian vision one can certainly imagine humanity to form a single political community, and a corresponding world government which would have to justify its political decision with respect to the imputed will or interests of humanity rather than of particular populations. There is no *conceptual* inconsistency in this vision. It is therefore not the criterion of legitimation as such which explains segmentation, but its available interpretations within the conditions of modernity. If we accept the basic features outlined above as limits even to reasonable normative and utopian thinking, and if we can show that political community cannot be congruent with humanity in any interpretation within these constraints, then the combination of the four features will sufficiently explain both the increasing interdependency and the persistence of segmentation in the global political system.

I have refrained from formulating the legitimation requirement of modern politics in terms of democracy. Conceiving of democracy as an essential characteristic of political modernity would be a spurious claim twice over. First, the Athenian model of democracy which has most profoundly inspired modern European political thought is premodern in its origins. It seems that despite all efforts to get rid of the classical antique conception of democracy as 'rule by the people' (Schumpeter, 1950), this is still the essential meaning underlying the concept even in its contemporary use (Held, 1987, pp. 170–85, Sørensen, 1993, pp. 3–16). Second, modernity has been characterized by novel forms of tyranny, namely totalitarianism, as much as by the novel regimes of liberal democracy.

All four features are pertinent for democratic as well as for totalitarian regimes and for the many variants in between. However, the democratic idea is by no means an accidental ingredient of political modernity. It provides one possible interpretation of the fourth feature: the idea of a people as a community of citizenship which in some mediated way participates in political deliberation of those laws that are collectively binding for its members. There are, however, rival interpretations for the political definition of society as an 'imagined community' (Anderson, 1983). One is the nation as a community of culture, history and future destiny. Another one interprets the people also as a biological community, i.e. a 'race'. A third one invokes the community of the proletariat as the only truly universal class whose emancipation will liberate society as a whole. What all these ideologies share in common is the idea that political legitimation requires an inclusive concept of society. In these perspectives politically organized societies are self-reproducing and complete. In contrast with antique or feudal conceptions of the polity, the later modern ones do not restrict membership to an elite or class or gender which, in their social reproduction, depend vitally on the functions performed by their excluded opposites.

Internal inclusiveness of this sort still allows for radical exclusion of 'the other' in non-democratic ideologies. For nationalism, the outsiders are those who belong culturally to an alien nation. Although nationalism has been rarely formulated as a universalistic principle (Gellner, 1983, p. 2), its universal application leads straightforwardly into a world of independent states. In pre-World War II racism some of the excluded are genetically inferior and incapable of either belonging to the nation or forming one themselves. For the communist interpretation of Marxism, the members of ruling classes have to be politically excluded at least temporarily until their material power as a class has been broken and they have been resocialized as individuals into the new egalitarian society. In contrast with nationalism, the racist and the communist view might aim at some homogenized society of the future which would span the whole globe. Their practical implications, however, invariably reinforce the segmentary logic of nationalism both in the partial realization of their own projects as well as in the orientation towards which popular resistance to these ideologies is driven.

Liberal democratic forms of political legitimation have basically contradictory implications. Modern democracy offers more than libertarians accept as justifiable.[14] Citizenship is not only about negative liberties. Political legitimation requires positive freedom and rights. In contemporary democracy, citizens acquire claim-rights towards the state which far exceed those of mere protection against violence. There can be no democratic legitimation of political authority without institutionalized forms of political participation in civil society beyond the electoral process and without basic rights to protection against existential risks in market economies. This is not only true for the 'advanced' industrial societies of the West but even more so for the poorer and exploited countries of the global South. Explaining the implications of such rights for the territorial organization of political power and membership will be a recurrent theme in this book. For the moment I will just state my central hypothesis, which consists of two apparently contradictory statements.

A comprehensive concept of citizenship which contains individual as well as collective rights, civil and political as well as social rights can only be institutionalized within communities bounded both territorially and in terms of membership. In this way democratic citizenship reinforces the territorial segmentation of the global political system. At the same time, communities defined by the range of allocation of these rights reach beyond nation-states. In this way, democratic citizenship questions the existing forms of segmentation, extends the spaces of politically organized society and creates a complex map of overlapping memberships.

Some basic features of citizenship rights will be examined in the second part of this book. For the first part we have now gained a starting-point for analysing the meanings of citizenship as membership in a political community. Historical analysis has provided us with good reasons to assume a subdivision of the global political system into a plurality of states as given and as persistent. Normative arguments have shown that a political programme to replace this structure with a single world state will be difficult to justify for liberal and democratic approaches. Using Albert

Hirschman's terminology we can sum up these arguments in the formula that liberal democracy depends on opportunities of exit and voice and that *both* require territorially bounded political authority. At the same time society as described from the perspective of such a political system can no longer remain wholly confined within these boundaries.

Contemporary nation-states are confronted with economic, ecological or information systems that escape their political control. Furthermore, they abandon elements of their external sovereignty by forming collective systems of national security, international political organizations and by accepting a growing body of international law. Rather than driving states towards the establishment of a global political authority, these phenomena lead to *disjunctures of globalization* 'between, on the one hand, the formal domain of political authority liberal democratic states claim for themselves and, on the other hand, the ways in which international, regional and global power structures condition the actual practices of states' (Held and McGrew, 1993, p. 264). Held and McGrew discuss a non-exhaustive list of disjunctures of globalization which comprises international security structures and power politics, the world economy, internationalization of the state and international law. I propose to add disjunctures of political membership to this list. These arise between the sets of persons formally recognized as citizens of a state and those who are, or who ought to be, covered by basic rights in liberal democracies. There are internal as well as external disjunctures of this kind (see Held, 1991a, Held and McGrew, 1993, p. 265). Internal ones concern, for example, the rights of minors who are excluded from active political citizenship while being more and more recognized as individual rights-bearers in other spheres of society. Another issue in this field is collective rights of women or of different minorities against social discrimination perceived to diminish their status as equal citizens. My book will mainly deal with external disjunctures of membership, i.e. with the exclusion from formal citizenship of groups and individuals who are in a social position from where they can appeal to membership in a political community. Immigrants have today become a paradigmatic case for problematic exclusion of this kind.

I have chosen the term 'transnational' in order to characterize three kinds of developments, which expand citizenship beyond the national frame but still do not add together to 'global citizenship as the political counterpart of the world economy' (Turner, 1990, p. 213): first and foremost, a clash between normative principles of liberal democracy and current forms of exclusion from citizenship at the level of nation-states; second, the emergence of interstate citizenship in certain regions of the world – the most significant development being that of European Union citizenship; and third the evolution of human rights as an element of international law with some, although still rather powerless, enforcement mechanisms.

NOTES

1. Hannah Arendt thought of this as a feature of the human condition:'For men cannot become citizens of the world as they are citizens of their countries' (Arendt, 1958, p. 257).
2. This strategy would follow contemporary authors such as Anthony Giddens (1984) in their search for a middle course between the *Scylla* and *Charybdis* of all sociological theory: agentless structuralism on the one hand and reductionist individualism on the other.
3. For some speculations on this issue see Bauböck (1992c, 1993c).
4. In contrast with anarchist libertarians, neoconservative ones strongly oppose direct participatory democracy which could adopt self-imposed laws curtailing their individual members' autonomy. Robert Nozick's radical version appears to be critical even of representative democracy, although he admits that it could develop within a minimal state without violating the side-constraints of libertarian justice (Nozick, 1974, chapter 9). The general focus of libertarian critique, however, has not been the democratic process itself but social redistribution as its potential outcome.
5. It is interesting to note that the most anti-consequentialist of all normative political theorists clearly bases his argument on consequences at this decisive point. Nozick justifies the minimal state as opposed to competing voluntary protective associations by comparing the consequences of both situations for the well-being of individuals. This is why I think it legitimate to extend the argument to evaluating in a similar way the consequences of a single minimal world state as compared to a multiplicity of territorial protective associations. For those who think this interpretation is unwarranted, it should not be too difficult to construct a Nozickean hypothetical history of how such a global minimal state would come about starting from a plurality of geographically separate ones.
6. 'The existence of a multiplicity of states with nuclear or thermonuclear armaments violently generalizes the problem of security, forcing upon these states an endless hectic causal analysis of a complex and largely inscrutable field, whether their active responses at any given time exacerbate or mollify its dangers. The Hobbesian (and putatively rational) solution to this predicament is the creation of a single world government (or universal empire), furnishing security for all by removing the capacity for harm from any: except, of course, itself' (Dunn, 1991, pp. 39–40).
7. '[E]ven if nuclear weapons have made the construction of a universal empire rational for human beings, they have also set formidable obstacles in at least one of the potential paths towards its construction. In a world with at least two great nuclear powers, universal empire can scarcely, any longer, be a commonwealth by acquisition' (Dunn, 1991, p. 40).
8. For a general statement on the role of these two values in a dynamic concept of justice see Heller (1987, chapter 3).
9. Classic act-utilitarianism as formulated by Jeremy Bentham differs from liberalism in being little concerned with safeguards for individual liberties if overriding them will maximize utility within a collective. John Stuart Mill was the first utilitarian to introduce some important reservations: 'I regard utility as the ultimate appeal on all ethical questions; but it must be utility in the largest sense, grounded on the permanent interests of man as a progressive being' (Mill, 1972, 'On Liberty', p. 79). Contemporary rule-utilitarians have extended this argument by maintaining that actions are morally right if they conform to rules the general following of which would maximize overall utility.
10. This is basically the reason given by Henry Sidgwick for preferring the 'national ideal of political organization' to the cosmopolitan one at least in the short run (Sidgwick, 1897, p. 308).
11. Kant sharply poses the problem that there is no Hobbesian solution to the international state of nature in which states would give up their wild (lawless) liberty ('*ihre wilde (gesetzlose) Freiheit*') and accept the coercive laws of a peoples' state ('*Völkerstaat*') which would grow to encompass finally all peoples of the earth. The positive idea of a world republic has to be replaced with the negative surrogate of a world confederation of states as an attainable second-best solution (Kant, 1984, p. 20, my translations).

12.   Communitarians share with utilitarians the idea that the overriding normative principle in politics is the realization of the common good. They sharply disagree on the question whether this common good can be simply computed from individual preferences and whether any aggregate of individuals can serve as a reference set for this calculation.

13.   'To a considerable extent, the absolutist state arose as a result of a laborious and eventually successful fight for the formation and territorial unification of a geographical unit' (Hirschman, 1978, p. 96).

14.   This is to say I think of libertarian utopias as being profoundly anti-modern. It is not by chance that they so often start with early modern accounts of liberty such as Hobbes's or Locke's, and seem to go beyond them only in their analytical style but not in their implicit substantive descriptions of society.

2. Attributed Membership

Citizenship is a kind of membership as well as a bundle of rights. The relation between both aspects is central to the argument of this book that liberal democratic citizenship extends beyond legal membership and opens access to this membership. The first part of this chapter will present an initial conceptual analysis of these two aspects. In the second and third parts I examine the attribution of citizenship to persons at their birth and the rationales behind the two dominant principles of territory and descent.

2.1. NOMINAL AND SUBSTANTIAL CITIZENSHIP

Citizenship is a relation between individuals and states. We can analytically separate two different aspects of this relation. The first one is the classification of individuals into groups of different state membership. In this way we distinguish French citizens from German or Italian ones. Legal scholars describe citizenship as a relation between a state and its members in which persons are assigned a legal status.[1] Apart from the specification that citizenship is a legal status, this relation is regarded as empty of any particular content.[2]

The second aspect is the particular nature of the relation itself and the characterization of both individuals and states implied in it. We can, for example, describe this relation as a transaction of rights and obligations. This makes citizenship different from other relations between individual and state such as subjecthood or national membership. With respect to the individual this description refers to citizenship as a particular kind of status. It would distinguish full or active citizens from other groups of the population who do not enjoy all the rights and/or do not have to comply with all the obligations of citizenship (such as minors, foreigners, prisoners, severely mentally disabled persons, etc.). Finally, citizenship in this sense also implies a description of the state. Citizenship is not a privilege granted by some autocratic sovereign. There must be institutional guarantees for certain basic rights. In T.H. Marshall's analysis this requires at least an independent judiciary, a parliament emerging from free elections, the public provision of school education, legal regulation of labour contracts and some welfare policy (Marshall, 1965, pp. 78–80).

I will call the first aspect *nominal citizenship*.[3] In juridical language it is frequently referred to as nationality. This is an unfortunate terminology. First, it identifies membership in a nation with the legal relation between individuals and a state although the former often describes cultural affiliation which need not be relevant for the latter. Second, 'nationality' is also used to characterize membership in particular kinds of national groups which have not acquired full statehood but some sort of regional or cultural autonomy within a state. In pluri-national states an individual's nationality will therefore differ from her citizenship in name as well as in meaning.

The concept of nominal citizenship points to the ordering of individuals into parallel sets labelled by the name of a state.[4] A nominal order of citizenship can be characterized by two features. First, I will call such an order *complete* if in it all individuals are related to a state. In an incomplete order, some individuals are *stateless*. Second, a nominal order is *discrete*, if in it no individual is related to more than one state. In a non-discrete order some individuals are *multiple citizens*. Completeness and discreteness of an international order of citizenship have been adopted as targets in international declarations and conventions, especially since World War II.[5] Principles of citizenship acquisition and the rules derived from them can be tested to determine how well they comply with these allocational meta-norms.[6] When doing that one should be aware that the avoidance of statelessness and multiple citizenship have not always been concerns of citizenship regulations. They could only become such concerns under several historical preconditions: first, the emergence of an inclusive conception of national citizenship which enlists whole state populations as citizens; second, increased international mobility so that states frequently have to deal with citizens of other states; and third, an international order in which states generally respect other states' responsibility for their citizens.

This same order generates the irregularities which then are made the object of international co-ordination. In a mobile world, national citizenship laws necessarily come into conflict with each other. When national sovereignty extends to the determination of membership, states can adopt their own specific laws and rules of citizenship acquisition. Irregularities could only be avoided if rules were uniform across states, if they were mutually compatible in their application to identical cases and if jointly they would cover all populations. A spontaneous order of citizenship which emerges from unco-ordinated decisions by individual states cannot meet all these requirements. More concretely, sovereign states cannot be denied the right to attribute citizenship to those who meet their own internal criteria even if the same persons are also citizens of another state. Similarly, states still cannot be forced to refrain from involuntary expatriation (which for the sake of terminological clarity I shall call denaturalization),[7] or to adopt those as their own citizens who have not been recognized as citizens by other states.

We can imagine the allocation of nominal citizenship as similar to an international political map with the important difference that the 'territories' of citizenship are neither all seamlessly connected to neighbouring ones nor completely disjointed from them: there are stretches of no-man's-land inhabited by stateless persons and regions of dual citizenship for which two states simultaneously claim sovereignty.

Figure 1: The allocation of nominal citizenship – dual citizenship and statelessness as irregularities

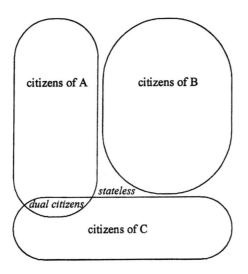

A nominal order is not a hierarchy. In this sense nominal citizenship is different from a *rank order* of citizenship as a social status. Labelling people living in France as French, Italian or Moroccan citizens does not tell us whether all French citizens are equal amongst themselves, or whether Italian or Moroccan citizens in France are equal among each other and equal with French ones. In a way a nominal order is egalitarian, because each person is characterized by a name and a name only. But obviously a nominal order does not exclude a hierarchical one on top of it. Equality may be due only to a lack of relevant information. If we add some more facts and contrast native French citizens with Italian citizens who enjoy special status as members of the European Union and with Moroccans who don't, and if we further add the distinction between long-term resident Moroccans, new legal arrivals and illegal immigrants, we will get a rank order of citizenship.

Yet even this hierarchical order contains little information. It does not tell us in which respect French citizens rank higher than Italian and Italian higher than Moroccan ones. Any comparison that establishes a more than purely nominal equality or any distinction that implies a difference of rank must specify a criterion. With regard to citizenship, this criterion lies obviously in those aspects of membership that establish a relation between individuals and states which is socially and politically consequential for both sides. This brings us to the second aspect mentioned in the beginning which I will call *substantial citizenship*. I will argue that in a modern and liberal view the basic elements of substantial citizenship are generalized rights within a political community.

This term is sometimes used in a different way when it is contrasted not with nominal but with (merely) *formal citizenship*. The idea is that it is not only the label of membership which is formal, but also most of the rights. Anatol France's famous remark about the beauty of the law which prohibits the rich and the poor alike to sleep under the bridges of Paris explains well what is meant by merely formal equality. In this view, substantial citizenship would be achieved only where there is some appropriate form of social equality so that equal rights can translate into (roughly) equal social opportunities. I want to postpone for the moment discussing which kind of social equality is necessary for fully developed citizenship. The important point here is that citizenship is membership in a polity rather than in a society. The status of members in a polity is defined by their rights and obligations, not by their descent, their wealth, their talents or their merits. Rights and obligations are the very substance of political membership even when they appear to be merely formal. Certainly, descent, wealth, talents and merits will translate into different ranks in most polities. But this already presupposes that specific rights are attached to them. Political systems differ in the degree to which social inequalities imply different rights and thus unequal political membership. Only in stateless societies was it possible to eliminate virtually all effects of social hierarchy from politics. Citizenship of the ancient city-state as well as in the modern age means not abolishing all inequality of political status, but narrowing its accepted range by establishing both lower and upper thresholds. The lower threshold is one of basic rights which are equal for all citizens, the upper threshold is built of constraints on the accumulation of political power.

Citizenship is therefore a substantial form of equality in the public-political sphere which results from blocked translation[8] of social inequalities into political ones. Whether the persistence of social inequality outside the political sphere contradicts equal citizenship depends on the scope of its rights. If in a libertarian minimal state citizenship were reduced to property rights and negative liberties of free speech, assembly, religious opinion, etc., those sleeping under the bridges and those living in palaces would be indeed substantially equal as citizens. Where citizenship has come to mean more than this and includes some idea of democratic government under popular control, it will be essential to prevent the owners of palaces from buying political influence and to provide those sleeping under the bridges with accommodation so that they become able to act as autonomous persons in the public sphere. Unrestrained social inequality is incompatible with the idea that citizens are equally entitled to participate in political deliberation and to run for political office. What is different between these libertarian and democratic ideas of citizenship is not the 'substance of citizenship' – in both cases this substance is equal rights – it is rather which and how many rights citizens enjoy.

The absence of substantial citizenship in this broader sense means one of two things: either that membership in a polity is not based on *equal* rights, or that a class of people is without *any rights*. The first case is exemplified by hierarchically organized systems of rule where individuals belong to different estates or castes and membership in the polity is only a mediated one; the second case is illustrated by slavery. In Orlando Patterson's words, slavery means social death (Patterson, 1982). In the citizenship context I would suggest speaking rather of political death. Slaves have no status whatsoever in a polity because they cannot have either rights or obligations. In this respect slaves were different from women, lower classes or resident foreigners who had also been excluded from citizenship but who had been assigned some rights and obligations (different from those of citizens).

While slaves are completely deprived of substantial citizenship (see van Gunsteren, 1992, pp. 54–7), stateless persons are similarly excluded from nominal citizenship. The rights of foreigners can be based both on recognizing them as regular resident members of society and on recognizing them as members of another state with whom peaceful relations are entertained. Protecting foreigners will thus be a normal obligation accepted by states even where these foreigners do not enjoy the same rights as citizens. In contrast with slaves, stateless people and refugees who have been *de facto* deprived of their citizenship might be seen as bearers of human rights, which put states under an obligation to protect them. But their predicament is that, in order to be able to claim these rights effectively, they must first be admitted as regular residents of a state. Under the Geneva Refugee Convention, states are obliged not to send them back where they will be persecuted, but they are not similarly obliged to admit them into their territory in the first place. Thus slaves who are totally excluded from substantial citizenship lack the capacity to enjoy rights while the stateless lack the ability to claim rights.

After comparing the positions of the two kinds of outcasts we can now ask how the nominal and substantial dimensions of citizenship relate to each other in their modes of inclusion. Seen from the perspective of the state, the nominal distinction between its own citizens and those of other states is not only one of difference but also of priority. Thus the minimal interpretation of substantial citizenship, which seems closely attached to the purely nominal understanding, is that each state is specifically responsible for its own citizens. Is there a corresponding minimum from the perspective of the individual? On the one hand, being a citizen of any state certainly makes a difference when compared with statelessness. If citizenship were just an empty shell, statelessness would be no existential threat. On the other hand, it is not possible to specify a core set of rights that must be attached to any nominal citizenship. A regime may deprive citizens of all their rights and yet these people will be seen as that country's citizens in the international arena. In cases of crimes against humanity, other states may be entitled to intervene against such a regime. But they will not normally argue that the victims had been deprived of their citizenship and now ought to be regarded as if they were their own citizens. The example given by the Swedish diplomat Raoul Wallenberg who, in 1944 distributed Swedish citizenship certificates to Jews in Budapest in order to save them from being transported to the concentration camps, is still an exceptional one. The case of the French and German Jews who had been denaturalized before they were sent to the gas chambers, might be quoted as proof that even this century's most tyrannical regime had in a cynical way recognized the obligation to protect its nominal citizens. But what this example shows is of course the converse: because these Jewish German and French citizens were destined to be treated as if they were non-human they had to be turned into non-citizens first. And once their citizenship had become a purely nominal one it could also no longer contain the right not to be deprived of it arbitrarily. This is the paradox hidden behind the innocent claim of legal positivism that citizenship is nothing but a formal relationship between states and individuals void of any content.[9]

As I have already pointed out above, some progress has been made after World War II at least at the level of international norms. Article 15 of the Universal Declaration of Human Rights postulates everybody's right to a citizenship and that nobody shall be deprived arbitrarily of his or her nationality nor be denied the right to change it. This general norm is concretized in international conventions such as those on the legal status of refugees and stateless persons or against racial and gender discrimination. Whereas before all substantive human rights depended for their effective implementation on nominal citizenship, now the latter has itself become the object of a substantial human right.

From a purely juridical point of view this must still seem paradoxical. How can there be a right to something which in itself does not contain any specified right?[10] Yet this right is indeed a fundamental one which gives a minimal substance to nominal citizenship. In the international political system of independent states, any guarantee for human rights presupposes the general recognition that each and every individual human being has a right to be recognized as a member of at least one of the sovereign units of this system. If human beings can fall out, or be pushed out, of state membership there will be no conceivable guarantee for their human rights. On the one hand, an international system in which this human right to nominal citizenship is respected has taken an important step beyond a Hobbesian state of nature. A complete nominal order can only be achieved if states are not completely free in the choice of their members. On the other hand, such a human right to nominal citizenship will be necessary only as long as sovereignty lies essentially with individual states. If there were a global authority within a federation of states of which *individuals* could be members (and not just states as today in the UNO) there would be no reason for guaranteeing an individual right to state membership. Human rights would then still have to be enforced against state governments, but a human right to nominal citizenship would become entirely dispensable. Statelessness could then be freely chosen and this would presumably also extend possibilities for states to deprive citizens of their membership with impunity. The task of protecting basic human rights for those without nominal citizenship would fall upon global agencies. Stateless persons would not only be under their mandate but would enjoy the right to international protection because they would themselves be members of the international political community. Although arrangements of this sort might seem attractive to cosmopolitans, I am sceptical that they would improve global compliance with human rights.

I will further analyse tensions between the nominal and substantive aspects of citizenship in later parts of this book. In this and the following chapters my concern will be with the criteria for the allocation of nominal citizenship, i.e. the acquisition and loss of citizenship by individuals. This is another aspect where substantial issues inevitably enter the analysis. We can abstract from the content of citizenship in terms of rights and obligations when looking at a static distribution of nominal citizenship. But the rules which govern individual entries or exits and the transmission of citizenship from one generation to the next, are themselves deeply embedded in specific concepts of political community. It is ideas about the ties and relations between members of political communities which shape the principles, rules and practices of allocating nominal citizenship.

Henry Sidgwick identified the three fundamental principles for determining nominal citizenship. 'There are two obvious alternatives, (1) Birth, and (2) Consent: and the first subdivides again into two, according as "birth" is understood to mean either "birth from parents who are members" or "birth within the territory"' (Sidgwick, 1897, p. 230). I adopt this classification with the minor addition that territory and descent might also become a relevant criterion after birth when citizenship is acquired because of residence or ethnic and family ties.[11] So the three principles underlying the manifold rules of national legislation are those of territory, descent and consent. The first two will be discussed in this chapter. What they share in common is that both are mechanisms of attribution rather than choice.[12] Birth in a territory as well as descent from citizen parents are understood to determine a person's citizenship in an objective manner, independently of her consent. In their pure form, these principles cannot provide rules for naturalization. However, as I will try to show, there are rules of admission to a new citizenship after birth which are closely related to these principles although they invariably incorporate elements of consent.

The principle of consent raises much more fundamental questions of political theory which will be addressed in chapters 3 to 7. It is a principle that makes citizenship self-referential. First, the image of the polity is that of a community based on rights and obligations to which each member has consented (or could rationally consent). Second, this political community is understood to be an association where each member has consented in some appropriate way (or could rationally consent) to her membership. Third, what those who have become members by consent share as members of the community is that they are ruled with their own consent.

Self-referentiality of this sort is often self-defeating when its implications are carried to their logical extremes. Although I defend a version of citizenship that invokes the democratic principle of consent, I will try to show that ultimately the allocation of membership in liberal democracy cannot be made fully consensual. Rules of exit and entry ought to emphasize individual choice between different options of membership. But the available options of political membership for individuals are broadly determined by biographical and social facts such as place of birth, current or former residence, family ties, ethnic affiliations, etc. While there is some scope for consent when individuals change their membership, democratic polities cannot decide about the composition of their *demos* in a consistently democratic way. Dynamic norms of liberal democracy tend to make membership ever more inclusive and comprehensive within the boundaries of state territories. But the shape of these territories and the composition of populations within them have to be generally taken as contingent outcomes of historical processes. Territorial self-determination by popular vote is no universalizable principle of democracy (see chapter 7).[13]

My analysis in these chapters (as in the rest of the book) will be largely ideal-typic. It is guided by the following questions. In which way does each principle allocate individuals to states? Which image of the collective of citizens of a state does it support? Which general political norms does it correspond with? In order to be applied to individual cases the three principles must be translated into more specific rules. National citizenship laws invariably contain a complex set of rules which refer to at least two, but mostly all three, basic principles. Nevertheless, such laws may be strongly characterized by one single principle which operates as the dominant one. I shall not present a historical or comparative analysis of citizenship laws[14] but will try to focus on the general relation between principles and the most frequent rules. The following table sums up the main points of the analysis in this chapter.

Table 1: Principles for the attribution of nominal citizenship

determining principles	rules of transmission	rules of admission	concept of the people
residence	*ius soli*	domicile	population
descent	*ius sanguinis*	family membership	ethnic nation

2.2. TERRITORY AND RESIDENCE

We started our enquiry with the observation that the international political system divides populations into groups of citizenship in a similar way as it divides the earth into state territories. A first answer to the question how nominal citizenship is allocated in this system could be that both kinds of division are not only similar but that the latter determines the former. In this interpretation a citizen is an inhabitant of a state territory. I will call this the *principle of residence*. In order to be applied in the actual determination of citizenship this principle has to be translated into rules. The simplest rule would be to turn into a citizen everybody who lives in the territory and to deprive anybody of citizenship who leaves the territory.

This rule is obviously not workable. Sovereignty gives states the right to the exclusive use of natural resources found in the territory. But people are not tied to territory in this way. They can move around and cross borders. Determining nominal citizenship merely by the territory in which one happens to be at the moment would make for a very unstable relation between individuals and states. Such instability would be quite incompatible with the basic features of modern bureaucratic states outlined in the first chapter. States would then be reduced to the administration of territories. Their 'software' could only process populations which are permanent residents. Anybody would be able to escape their control by simply moving into another state. If control over territory also implies the right to control population movements across borders, this could be prevented by simply closing frontiers. However, any other policy, be it some form of controlled migration or completely open borders, would lead to an automatic change in the size or composition of the citizen-population.

A simple rule of residence would be problematic also from the individual citizen's perspective. The rights of substantial citizenship correspond to fundamental interests and needs. But people cannot shift all their fundamental interests in space in the same way as they move their bodies. They will need physical protection, food and accommodation where they happen to be. However, being abroad they will also wish to know that back home their houses are not confiscated and that they will be readmitted when returning. Territorial movements of people and territorial shifts of their interests are completely synchronized only in nomadic societies. In modern societies territorial mobility involves movements in space and time between relatively stable locations and long periods of residence. Basic interests and identities of people on the move are still related to social networks which remain fixed in the locations of the sending and the receiving area. In such a world the only category of people whose fundamental interests move along with them are refugees. If citizenship were strictly determined by one's present territorial location, there would be no more tourists and all migrants would be like refugees.

Within a territorial frame of citizenship, the relation between state and population can be stabilized by two criteria: birth in the territory and permanent residence. The first rule makes a lifelong citizen of everybody who is born in the country. This is the rule of *ius soli* which is characteristic for the Anglo-American legal tradition. The second rule would recognize as a citizen anybody who has established a household in a state territory or lived there for a certain time. This has been referred to as the domicile principle (Grawert, 1973) or *ius domicili* (Hammar, 1990, p. 76). While the first rule derives citizenship from the beginning of a person's life and is thus past oriented, the second rule can been seen as more future oriented. Having lived in a country for a long time or maintaining a home there are good indicators that residence has become permanent. The most radical formulation of *ius domicili* in history is perhaps that of the French Constitution of 1793: 'Tout homme né et domicilié en France, âgé de vingt et un ans accomplis, tout étranger âgé de vingt et un ans accomplis, qui est domicilié en France depuis une année, y vit de son travail, ou acquiert une propriété, ou épouse une française ou adopte un enfant, ou nourrit un vieillard; tout étranger enfin qui sera jugé par le corps législatif avoir bien mérité de l'humanité est admis à l'exercise de citoyen français.'[15]

A pure rule of *ius soli* will determine nominal citizenship in an unequivocal manner and satisfy both criteria of completeness and discreteness. Given that there are no more inhabited but stateless territories and that the structure of the state system is perfectly segmentary, *ius soli* will lead to a corresponding distribution of citizenship. Everybody's place of birth lies in one state and in one state only. But its very simplicity makes this an inflexible rule. Babies born on board of an aeroplane flying over US territory become US citizens. Pregnant Mexican mothers cross the border into the USA illegally to deliver there because their child's citizenship will eventually allow them to re-enter the USA. A child born in country A of two parents who are both citizens of B will, according to this rule, still be a citizen of A even after her parents' return to B. So pure *ius soli* turns into citizens those who were born in a country by chance[16] or because of their parents' merely temporary stay and deprives of citizenship those who happen to have been born abroad.

A number of European states, among them France, Spain and Belgium have adopted a modified principle which is called *double ius soli*: a child born in the territory is a citizen by birth if a parent of the child has been born in the territory as well. Here the parent's birth in the country indicates that the child will grow up and reside permanently in the country as well. A second rationale for *double ius soli* is that it interrupts the intergenerational transmission of citizenship acquired by descent among emigrants living permanently abroad. Of course, in contrast with simple *ius soli* this rule is not a self-sufficient one. It leaves open the definition of citizenship among the first generation born abroad which is then usually determined by *ius sanguinis*. However, birth in the territory is often also made relevant for these children by facilitating their naturalization compared to persons born outside the territory, or even giving them a right to automatic or optional acquisition of citizenship (see section 4.1).

Ius domicili is a more flexible rule which for that same reason can lead to apparently contradictory results. Generally speaking, permanent residence is not a sufficient criterion for the determination of citizenship in all possible cases. Children below the age corresponding to the residence criterion and persons who have not stayed long enough in any country to become that state's citizen would remain stateless if this rule were strictly applied to them. Apart from leading to statelessness, *ius domicili* may also produce multiple citizenship. If the residence criterion is used only as a rule for acquiring but not also as one for losing citizenship, it would lead to a potential accumulation of citizenships by staying in a country for the prescribed time of residence and then moving on to the next one. Multiple citizenship or statelessness will also result if criteria for admission and expatriation are not exactly symmetric. State A may admit some person to citizenship after ten years of residence while B, the state of her previous citizenship, may still regard her as a citizen living abroad after that time or, alternatively, may have already expatriated her after five years. There is neither a natural way of determining a threshold for permanent residence, nor an international authority which could override the sovereignty of independent states and impose such a standard criterion.

Combining the two rules can alleviate the problems which would result from an exclusive application of either *ius soli* or *ius domicili*. As only *ius soli* meets the basic criterion of producing a complete nominal order it must serve as the master rule. *Ius domicili* can then be used to correct the allocation of citizenship by *ius soli* when there is a permanent discrepancy between place of birth and country of residence.[17] The master rule of citizenship must always be one for *automatic transmission* of citizenship from one generation to the following, i.e. determination at birth. A modifying rule regulates *secondary admission*, i.e. a change of previous citizenship (including the admission of stateless persons). Rules of admission may or may not operate automatically. In most cases they do not – admission depends upon voluntary applications by the individuals who want to become citizens.[18] However, as the German scholar Rolf Grawert observed, taking voluntary domicile in a country could be regarded as a more legitimate ground for making somebody a citizen than the mere chance factor of birth in the territory (Grawert, 1973, p. 224).[19]

The combination of *ius soli* and *ius domicili* does not logically exclude the irregularities of statelessness or multiple citizenship, but it allows an avoidance of them in most cases if this is intended by all states concerned. However, even the combination will not completely satisfy the 'fundamental interest' criterion for all individuals. If only citizenship gives individuals a right of indefinite abode, host states can easily manipulate residence permits so that some immigrants are not allowed to stay long enough to become citizens.

The principle of residence in the determination of individual citizenship correlates with one specific interpretation of the collective of all citizens. The image of this collective is that of a resident population. Territorial sovereignty gives every state a basic right to enact laws in this territory. Diplomats and temporary visitors may be exempted from certain laws but the rest of the population living in the territory is generally equally subjected to them. The residence principle turns this subjection to the law into the foundation of citizenship. It would be a conceptual mistake to think of *ius soli* and *ius domicili* as defining populations in geographical instead of political terms. Territory only serves as a proxy for determining who can be rightfully subject to laws because the scope of state legislation is delimited by territorial borders. As we will see later on, the decisive advantage of the territorial principle compared with the other two is that it minimizes the potential incongruities between the population over which territorial sovereignty can be rightfully exercised and the collective of those formally recognized as citizens.

The historical origins of this principle are pre-democratic. Feudalism organized society so that populations were tied to the land and 'represented' by their local lords. The final victory of the king as the internal sovereign unified the territory and transformed feudal serfdom, in which the relation of individuals to state authorities was a mediated one, into absolutist subjecthood. The basic justification for *ius soli* determination of subjecthood is that the sovereign's control over territory stretches to anybody born within it. While subjecthood became thus universal and equal within a state, citizenship was still a particular and privileged status. Jean Bodin has given a lucid analysis of this initial discrepancy. In his definition, a citizen is a free subject who is subordinate to a sovereign. While subjecthood is clearly defined territorially, citizenship is an inherited status. Slaves and serfs are subjects, but not citizens because they are not free.[20] Citizens are not necessarily equal in political status among themselves. They enjoy different privileges awarded by the sovereign but in Bodin's view this does not affect their common citizenship. He polemicizes against Aristotle's definition of citizenship as ruling and being ruled in turn, and against the view that citizenship could be described as a specific list of rights and obligations. The essential transaction implied in the relation between the citizen and the sovereign is loyalty and obedience of the free subject to his sovereign prince on the one hand, and the granting of protection, justice and defence by the prince on the other hand (Bodin, 1981, I.6, pp. 173, 180).

Serfdom, slavery and aristocratic privilege were overcome and equal subjecthood turned into substantial citizenship only after a long series of liberal reforms and democratic revolutions. Citizenship based on the principle of residence appears to be an enrichment of subjecthood with rights rather than an extension of privilege to the population as a whole. Territorial sovereignty remains the starting-point which determines the state's population. Residential citizenship defines every member of the population as a (potential) citizen. Substantial citizenship is then only a subsequent result of a social contract in the pre-Hobbesian late medieval tradition, concluded between the sovereign and the people rather than among the citizens themselves. It is not the citizens who constitute themselves as a 'commonwealth' or 'civil society' and who institute the sovereign. The latter is already there and by exercising his authority, determines who are the citizens.

Is this an outdated interpretation no longer relevant for contemporary liberal democracy? One should hesitate to dismiss it out of hand. What all citizens of the same state share with each other is essentially being subject to legislation in their state, while their rights have been historically contingent achievements won within this basic relation of dependence. Still, rights which enable citizens to regain autonomy inside the iron cage of bureaucratic rule will be essential for any vision that puts some positive value on citizenship. Peter Schuck and Rogers Smith, who make a strong argument for a move towards the principle of consent in the allocation of US American citizenship, nevertheless concede that ascribing citizenship on a territorial principle 'can be defended by appealing not to any presumed natural order but simply to the realities of existing national authorities and actual, interdependent communities. ... Because it insures that all persons can claim protection from the government that most directly asserts power over them, territoriality also resonates to human rights concerns' (Schuck and Smith, 1985, p. 39).

Is this not a more plausible explanation for political integration of societies at the level of contemporary liberal democratic states than the claims of national or popular sovereignty, which conceive of the unity of the people as either preceding state power or emanating directly from its exercise? How can we seriously maintain the former when all claims to common ancient descent and present cultural community of national populations have been exposed as ideological chimeras? How can we pretend that state authority emerges from the collective will of the people when there is no substantial direct democratic participation in either agenda-setting or decision-making?

The residential conception of citizenship would still be an unattractive one if it were based only on this sceptical interpretation of Western democracy. However, there is a normative aspect tied to this same notion of citizenship which has come to distinguish contemporary democracy from both ancient republican and early modern forms of political rule. This is the *norm of inclusiveness*. I take this to be the basic *liberal* norm of citizenship.

The liberal tradition has not given a coherent account of what the rights of citizenship ought to be. There is a minimalist view of rights essentially formulated by Hobbes and later somewhat extended by Locke and the natural rights philosophy of enlightenment. The utilitarian critique of natural rights (Bentham, 1987) has eroded even this narrow common ground for a liberal conception of citizenship. Libertarians have restated the natural rights paradigm but reversed the classical argument. While Hobbes and Locke were concerned that an accumulation of citizens' rights would undermine political authority, modern libertarians have held the opposite view that extended rights of citizenship would require too much political authority for their enforcement and that this would lead to intolerable restrictions of individual liberty. They have therefore added to a strictly minimal set of rights the quest for a corresponding minimal state. In contrast with this approach, contemporary liberal egalitarians such as John Rawls (1971, 1993a) and Ronald Dworkin (1977, 1985, 1986) have formulated normative theories of justice, that live up to the institutionalized modes of political legitimation in contemporary Western democracies and support the provision of a comprehensive and complex bundle of basic rights.

Liberalism's general contribution lies not in specifying rights but in consistently arguing against the exclusion of relevant populations from whatever rights appear to be justified. From Hobbes's insight that in the state of nature all human beings are roughly equal in strength and abilities (Hobbes, 1973, XIII, p. 63) to Bentham's felicific calculus in which each counts as one and as one only, the major thinkers of liberalism have always supported an inclusive view of the population whose rights or well-being ought to be the principle target of politics. Certainly, many have supported exceptions from their own principles and advocated the exclusion of propertyless classes or of women when discussing practical politics. Some liberals, such as John Stuart Mill, managed to overcome in their work hegemonic views of racism or sexism while at the same time promoting exclusion based on class and education.[21] I do not want to vindicate either the theories or the political proposals of liberal thinkers as genuinely supportive of inclusiveness. I only maintain that the principles developed by virtually all currents of liberalism could be interpreted consistently as a demand for ever more inclusive forms of citizenship by those social movements that found themselves deprived of it.

While liberals have been at odds with each other about what the rights and obligations of substantial citizenship ought to be, there is much more agreement that nominal citizenship – and whatever rights and obligations have come to be connected to it – should be distributed as widely as possible among the population. In contemporary liberal democracies, inclusion into nominal citizenship has reached levels where many think that there is no more deficit to overcome. Demands for further extension often seem to focus entirely on substantial aspects within a given frame of common nominal citizenship. The so-called new social movements of feminists, ethnic and 'racial' minorities, environmentalists and others mostly take for granted that they organize people of common citizenship – or, as far as they reach beyond borders – people who are citizens of their respective states. Their demands are frequently about collective rights and the legal and political recognition of difference. This brings them into conflict with proponents of classical liberalism who have often parted ways with those struggling for enriching citizenship with such new qualities.

However, there are still groups of people for whom inclusion into nominal citizenship matters at the level of already given rights. The residential concept of citizenship provides an adequate frame for voicing their complaints against exclusion. These are immigrants and their children who do not obtain the citizenship of their country of residence. Restrictive rules for naturalization and *ius sanguinis* regulations can be opposed on traditional liberal grounds. The norm of inclusiveness also supports a broader view that citizenship rights should be distributed equally within a resident population independently from their status of nominal citizenship. The principle of residence thus provides a rationale for *immigrant citizenship*.

2.3. DESCENT AND FAMILY MEMBERSHIP

The second principle for determining citizenship is descent. Its basic rule is *ius sanguinis*: citizens are those whose parents have already been citizens. According to this principle, territory and people are two separate fields of sovereignty none of which can be derived from the other. The people of a state are not identical with its population but are a self-reproducing human group.

The principle of descent has been the most widely adopted one for the determination of citizenship. Whereas *ius soli* has a background in feudalism and absolutism, *ius sanguinis* goes back to the roots of democracy in ancient Greece. In Athens until the early 5th century the status of a free member was often acquired by fiat. Aristocratic clan chiefs bestowed citizenship on many foreigners in order to enlarge their political clientele. A strict requirement of hereditary citizenship became a safeguard against this abuse only in 451 B.C. under Pericles. This can be seen as a necessary (although certainly not sufficient) precondition for the unfolding of Athenian participatory democracy (Bruschi, 1988, pp. 137–8). The principle of descent was a political instrument in order to determine a stable core of citizens who would share in the business of ruling. It did not lead to a narrow conception of the *demos* as a community of descent. The *polis* was a community founded above all on a common law. This distinguished it clearly from the generally smaller extended lineages of the clans and the much broader Hellenic cultural community. Only modern nationalism has developed an ideology which collapses these three different forms of community into a single one and sees the political form of the nation as a naturally given *telos* of its pre-political forms as a community of descent and culture.

The instrumental attitude of ancient Greek democracies towards the principle of descent is documented in Aristotle's demographic explanation for varieties and changes of citizenship rules:

> In many constitutions the law admits to citizenship a certain number even of foreigners; in some democracies the son of a citizen mother is a citizen, and in many places the same applies to illegitimate children. Lack of population is the usual reason for resorting to laws such as these, But when, after making such persons citizens because of a dearth of legitimate citizens, the state has filled up its numbers, it gradually reduces them, dropping first the sons of slave father or slave mother, then sons of citizen mother but not father, and finally they confine citizenship to those of citizen birth on both sides (Aristotle, 1981, 1278a, p. 185).[22]

For the ancient republics, the purpose of a citizenship principle was to create a stable internal order which was neither meant to be inclusive nor universalizable across a number of states. The requirement of a complete nominal classification of all individuals across all states combines these two criteria. In this respect a principle of descent has obvious shortcomings when compared to birth in a territory. If one adopted Aristotle's standard rule that 'for practical purposes a citizen is defined as one of citizen birth on both his father's and his mother's side' (1275b, pp. 171–2) all children born to parents of different citizenship would remain stateless. Only a rule which chooses one of the parents as the sole transmitter of citizenship and is uniformly adopted in all countries would lead to a nominal order of the same kind as *ius soli*. Until the mid-1970s, *ius sanguinis* countries had come quite close to this. Almost everywhere citizenship was inherited from the father only.[23] Since then, the demand for equal treatment of women has prompted revisions in many countries[24] so that now citizenship is mostly transmitted by either the father or the mother. While Aristotle's rule produces statelessness in cases of mixed parentage, this new rule does not meet the requirement of discreteness as it produces dual citizenship. *Ius sanguinis* transmission by parents of different citizenship has in fact been one of the major causes for the contemporary increase of dual citizenship in Europe (Hammar, 1990, p. 110).

A second difficulty with *ius sanguinis* already noted by Aristotle is that it can lead to an infinite regress. If citizenship is strictly derived from descent, then all previous generations with the sole exception of original colonists or founders must also have been citizens. This raises 'the puzzle of how a great or great-great-grandfather's citizenship can itself be determined' (Aristotle, 1981, 1275b, p. 172). 'The ascription of citizenship on the basis of descent works fine as a means of reconstituting and replenishing an existing citizenry, but it cannot serve to constitute the citizenry in the first place, for it presupposes an existing body of citizens' (Brubaker, 1992, pp. 277–8). Aristotle's solution is to refer back to his substantial definition of citizenship: if the forefathers had participated in the constitution in the required manner, they were citizens. In a republican tradition, *ius sanguinis* citizenship does not need an *Ahnenpaß* [25] recording every citizen's descent back into a distant past. Once this is accepted *ius sanguinis* is no longer a completely self-sustaining rule over time, but refers implicitly to either residence or consent somewhere back in the line of the generational sequence.

Ius sanguinis has been in fact often combined with *ius soli*. There are two ways of doing this: both criteria can be required cumulatively or they can be applied alternatively. In late medieval and early modern times the cumulative combination was used to enforce further restrictions in the transmission of citizenship. This is expressed in Bodin's formula for nominal citizenship: a citizen by birth is a free subject of that state where he was born either of whose parents is a citizen (Bodin, 1981, I.6, p. 161). Alternative application has the opposite effect of extending inclusion either beyond descent or beyond territory. *Ius soli* replaces the master rule of *ius sanguinis* for births in the territory when there are compelling reasons for attributing citizenship but the latter principle cannot be applied. And conversely, as *ius soli* can never be applied outside the territory, *ius sanguinis* has always been used in order to allocate citizenship there.

The first of these combinations is relevant for children born stateless or of uncertain origin. Most national laws provide today for the automatic attribution of citizenship in these cases in order to avoid the generation of statelessness inherent in a pure principle of *ius sanguinis*. The second combination exists in virtually all contemporary laws based on *ius soli*. Those born in the country become citizens because of territorial birth, but children born of citizen parents abroad acquire citizenship *iure sanguinis*. If this double standard became universalized, it would generate multiple citizenships for all children born abroad. Children acquire one citizenship by descent and another one by birth in the territory. This is not just a theoretical possibility but in fact a second major source for acquisition of dual citizenship at birth.[26]

A number of states have made the attribution of citizenship for children of emigrants conditional in different ways by combining it with the principle of territorial residence and birth. A frequent requirement is that parents must themselves have been born or resident in the country of origin, or that the children will only retain a citizenship acquired by birth abroad if they take up residence in their parents' country of origin later in their lives.[27] Both are precautions against an endless transmission of nominal citizenship among populations who have lost all contact with the country whose members they are supposed to be.

From the perspective of state interests, the rationale behind *ius soli* allocation inside the territory and *ius sanguinis* allocation outside may be the attempt to maximize the overall number of citizens. From the point of view of the first generation born abroad who have strong social ties to two states this will be usually both justified and beneficial. On the other hand, in *ius sanguinis* states which radically prohibit dual citizenship, the transmission of an emigrant citizenship by *ius sanguinis* might become an obstacle for the acquisition of the citizenship of one's country of birth because of the other combination mentioned above: only if the child does not acquire her parents' citizenship will she have to be made a citizen of her country of birth.

In ancient city-republics and early modern states, the principle of descent was not intended to create a complete nominal order relating all individuals to states. Its task was to determine legal membership in a self-reproducing political and social class within each state. The interpretation of the principle has changed dramatically in the age of nationalism since the French revolution. In nationalist thought cultural community, territorial population, and lineages of descent which had been vastly different in size and composition ever since the emergence of states in human history, became imagined as three appearances of a single essence: the people. By implication, the supreme task of national politics was to make boundaries and composition of the three coincide. This could be achieved in different ways: by assimilating a culturally heterogeneous population living in a given state territory, by uniting different territories inhabited by a supposedly culturally homogeneous population into a single state and finally by population transfers, i.e. driving out of the territory resistant minorities or 'bringing back home' ethnic and linguistic relatives. In this way both culture and territory could be restructured to conform with the nationalist ideal. It seems to be more difficult to change politically the lineages of descent reaching back into the past. However, this task was willingly carried out by national historiography inventing long traditions (Hobsbawm and Ranger, 1983) and ancient origins of nations that served to legitimate present political targets.

At the same time nationalism took its conception of the people also from the democratic revolutions against the old order of estates. In the nationalist vision the people became identical with a total territorially organized society, encompassing the bourgeoisie, peasantry and the nascent working class. The national concept of the people was thus much more inclusive than older definitions of the citizenry. Yet this is not the inclusiveness of liberalism derived from individual equality and autonomy. It is the inclusiveness of a pre-political and self-reproducing collective. In contrast with the civic corps of ancient city-republics or the third estate under absolutism, the nation was imagined as preceding the state, not as identical with the state or dependent upon a sovereign. While the principle of residence implies a demand for inclusive citizenship for all living under a common political rule, the principle of descent can be manipulated to create internal boundaries of citizenship different from those of territorial sovereignty. It allows the members of the nation to be clearly distinguished from others who happen to live within the same state.

Ius sanguinis means transmission of citizenship by the family. It is a mechanism for the generation of legal membership which relates the family (rather than the individual) as the basic unit to the nation as an imagined super-family, a community of descent. Two different interpretations can be given of the role of the family for the reproduction of the nation. The first is the narrowly biological one. Here the simple fact of birth from parents who are members of the nation makes the child a member, too. In this interpretation it does not matter whether the child is born abroad and never enters the territory of the nation-state. It also does not matter whether the child is raised by its natural parents or brought up in a family of different national affiliation. This conception of the nation as an intergenerational community of genetic relatives corresponds in a way to the strict interpretation of *ius soli*, where the mere chance factor of birth in a territory is sufficient to establish lifelong citizenship. Both express a completely passive and objectivist notion of citizenship.

There is a second interpretation available for the reproduction of the nation by *ius sanguinis*. This is a culturalist one. The family is the institution of primary socialization. It is here that the child learns the national language, religion and essential cultural values. Transmission of citizenship by the family in this view means entrusting parents with educating children to become conscious members of the nation as a cultural community. This corresponds to a primordialist theory of ethnic and national identities which are presumably formed in early childhood and can only be superficially altered by later secondary education.[28] One can object that it was not the modern nuclear family but compulsory elementary school which became the most important instrument for cultural homogenization and nation-building. Certainly, basic social abilities and features of personality are shaped by early socialization in the family. But it is difficult to accept that these are traits of *national* character and that a basic cultural knowledge is shared by all those whose parents happen to be regarded as members of the same nation.

The nationalist description of the people can be characterized as an *ethnos* in contrast with a resident population or with a *demos* that is constituted by sharing in political rule. An ethnic nation is imagined as a community of shared history and future destiny. It may be seen as emerging from a social compact, but in Edmund Burke's stark formulation this is 'a partnership not only between those who are living, but between those who are dead, and those who are to be born' (Burke, 1987, p. 118). The ethnic people turns into a nation by exercising, or aspiring for, sovereignty within a state. There is a strong emphasis on choice and autonomy in the narratives about the transformation of ethnic communities or 'peoples' into nations, but it is a purely collective choice: the people wills itself to be a nation and thereby becomes autonomous in the political realm. However, it was already autonomous from the state before in its biological and cultural self-reproduction and it retains this basic pre-political autonomy in its independence from any particular form of constitution or government. The political norm supported by the principle of descent is that of *collective autonomy*. This must not be confused with a Kantian notion of positive freedom or individual autonomy *within* a collective which consists in giving a law to oneself to which all affected can rationally consent.[29]

In some national traditions, such as the French or the US-American one, the origins of the nation have been ascribed to the foundational political acts of democratic and anti-colonial revolutions rather than to common ethnicity and descent. Even within these 'political nations', nationalist and nativist currents have invariably invented their own exclusionary and pre-political cultural and ethnic traditions. However, it is a significant fact that countries with a hegemonic ethno-national tradition have generally adopted *ius sanguinis* for their citizenship laws. From this it does not follow that the predominance of *ius soli* indicates a stronger liberal and democratic tradition. In the case of Britain and its former colonies it was rather the imperial legacy that interpreted citizens as subjects of the Crown (Dummett and Nicol, 1990). In North America and Australia this tradition was reinforced by the countries' origins as nations of immigrants where *ius sanguinis* would have excluded the majority of the population.

So far I have discussed only generational transmission by descent but not admission after birth. If *ius sanguinis* is the master rule, are there any corresponding secondary rules consistent with the principle of descent? The most obvious one is extension of citizenship to those who become new members of families already composed of citizens. Until recently, marrying a citizen led to automatic acquisition in many countries. Where transmission of citizenship followed the male line of descent only, the corresponding rule of admission by marriage was that the wife became a citizen automatically, while a foreign husband had to apply or to wait for a few years after marriage in order to acquire his wife's citizenship. Equalization of gender treatment has brought a change in these rules, too (see section 4.1). The same rule of family entry holds in the case of adoptions. Here regulations differ widely between countries. In some cases birthright overrides family entry and the child's citizenship is determined by his or her circumstances of birth, in others it acquires the adopter's citizenship automatically, on decision of the authorities, or through facilitated naturalization. The family is relevant in other rules of citizenship acquisition, too, which combine the principles of descent with those of residence and consent. Often summary naturalizations of families are encouraged by the law or by administrative practice. Spouses and minors[30] will be granted naturalization even when they have not been in the country for the generally required time.

Even in the most inclusive interpretation, when citizenship can be inherited from either parent, *ius sanguinis* is still a strongly exclusive rule. The admission rule of family entry allows for a little more flexibility by at least accepting those who, while not themselves of national origin, can become members by joining the basic reproductive unit of the community of descent. However, this is a far less efficient corrective than the rule of permanent residence is for *ius sanguinis*. Where there are large groups of non-nationals in the country and where there is little intermarriage, a substantial number of the population will remain excluded from citizenship. Moreover, for nationalists intermarriage with foreigners will always be regarded as a double-edged sword: it might increase the stock of the national population but it will also dilute the homogeneity of the people.[31]

These exclusionary effects of *ius sanguinis* are of course the major point of liberal critique. *Ius sanguinis* operates symmetrically in the reproduction of both membership and non-membership. Whoever is born of non-citizen parents inherits her or his parents' status as aliens. It is this intergenerational transfer of non-membership which makes a strict rule of *ius sanguinis* incompatible with liberal democracy. First-generation immigrants are often either not interested in acquiring the citizenship of their host country, or are able to compensate for their lack of citizenship rights there by reorienting towards their home countries. The fundamental interests of subsequent generations born in immigrant families are much more strongly located in the country where they have grown up. Depriving them of this country's citizenship and forcing upon them the citizenship of their parents' countries can only be justified in an anti-liberal view of the individual as a passive member of a collective of destiny and descent.

Ferenc Fehér and Agnes Heller have pointed to the etymological roots of the word *naturalization* (Fehér and Heller, 1994). It can be understood to define the receiving group as a natural one and to require that new members change their nature. Yet if our nature is the sum of all features about our body and character which we cannot change at will, naturalization will be only possible for those who already share a common nature (e.g. by belonging to the same ethnic or language group). So exclusion seems to be implied in the very term used for voluntary acquisition of citizenship. However, frequently the meaning of the term naturalization appears to have been closer to the residential principle. In France and England from the 14th to the 18th century the native-born are seen to be *natural* subjects of a sovereign and naturalization signifies a *natural* way of obtaining a similar status by residing permanently in a country, acquiring property and obeying its laws. In these legal traditions, naturalization first meant an extension of certain rights and privileges rather than a change in global status and identity (Grawert, 1973, pp. 67–8). Both interpretations of naturalization are incompatible with the idea that membership primarily depends on an act of conscious choice on the part of the immigrant.

Is there anything that can be said in defence of the principle of descent from a liberal democratic perspective? There is one essential advantage in the 'naturalization' of citizenship inherent in this principle: it makes political membership independent from the exercise of political power. Territorial citizenship may change indirectly with a change in the state territory. It thus depends on the exercise of effective sovereignty. The residential criterion may even be manipulated directly by shortening or lengthening waiting periods or defining additional residence requirements such as sufficient income or stable employment (see section 4.1). As the introduction of strict *ius sanguinis* in Periclean Athens illustrated, one rationale for citizenship by descent is to immunize membership against arbitrary decisions by authorities.

However, the principle of descent immunizes citizenship not only against political manipulation but also against demands of social justice. For most people their membership in a family is a more natural and more essential fact than their attachment to a particular territory where they have been born and raised. This could well be an anthropological feature characteristic for human beings as nomadic animals during most of the species' history. Once it has been established for some time, birthright citizenship by descent acquires the same naturalness as family membership. One consequence of this is that we generally do not regard the allocation of citizenship as a political issue which is to be evaluated by standards of social justice.

Let me consider for a moment the implications of this parallel between family and state membership. John Rawls has emphasized in his theory of justice that being born into a family which has the resources to develop the child's capacities is a morally arbitrary circumstance. Inequality of this sort between families is at odds with the principle of fair equality of opportunities (Rawls, 1971, p. 301). However, Rawls, as most others who have considered this problem, shies away from the consequence of abolishing the family in the name of social justice (p. 511). Also, few would go along with a utilitarian proposal to increase overall happiness by redistributing some children from poor families with too many offspring to rich ones with fewer children. Both ideas show limits of social justice where it confronts a kind of 'natural order'. The only road that seems open is some form of redistribution of material assets between families, which in itself clearly will not sufficiently guarantee equality of opportunities.

Reasoning about the allocation of citizenship on a global scale mostly reveals a strikingly similar argumentative pattern. Nobody 'deserves' to be born as a citizen of a rich or of a poor country. Apart from strict libertarians, most moral philosophers would see in the unequal resources tied to inherited citizenship at least a problem that should be addressed by norms of social justice. However, few would ever consider either abolishing the nation-state or redistributing individuals (rather than powers and material resources) among states as proper remedies to correct this global injustice. There are important arguments against both kinds of proposals. I have considered some against the former in the previous chapter and I will discuss the latter in the final chapter of this book. What is worrying about conceiving of citizenship in analogy with family membership is that this does not even permit the issue to be raised. Apart from unworkable solutions, that approach also forecloses less demanding policy options, such as a redistribution and equalization of citizenship rights among the territorial population of a single state. The argument for a principle of descent as a safeguard against political manipulation of membership is therefore at best an ambiguous one.

What can be said in defence of this principle is that there are historical circumstances under which the norm of collective autonomy can acquire convincing force. Let me re-emphasize that this notion of autonomy implies independence of the people as a collective both from consent of the individuals who compose it and from governments which rule it. When government turns tyrannical, when it disintegrates in a state of civil war or when it is taken over by invaders from outside, the idea that peoples exist independently from government and can retain their unity even against warring factions will inspire popular resistance. Because it is imagined as self-reproducing, an ethnic nation can continue to exist even after it has been collectively expelled or after its state has been wiped off the political map. How else should the Kurds or the Palestinians keep alive their claim to become self-governing other than by defining themselves – for the time being – as communities of descent? Of course one may think of this as a 'necessary illusion'. What keeps these and other people fighting for statehood is not their common ancestry, but their present shared hardships as refugees or discriminated minorities and their hopes for future self-governance. In this way they can retain their autonomy against a present government only by aspiring for a future one. Furthermore, they can remain autonomous without a government which they can recognize as their own only as long as they develop a political underground society which organizes individual consent. The very idea that collective autonomy can have any meaning at all if it is not translated into some form of individual consent is an absurd and dangerous myth. It has seduced a number of nationalist movements, which started with the overwhelming consent of those whom they represented and continued into the downward spiral of terrorist self-isolation.

A related case is when *ius sanguinis* is applied in order to restore a continuity of national statehood which had been interrupted by foreign occupation or annexation. The reconstitution of the three Baltic republics provides a contemporary example. The new citizenship laws divide resident populations into those who had already been citizens of the interwar republics and their descendants on the one side, and others who had immigrated after annexation on the other side: in Latvia and Estonia the latter now have to meet residence and language requirements before being admitted to citizenship (Brubaker, 1992, see also sections 5.1 and 7.3).

Apart from populations who have no state they can recognize as their own, there are also ethnic diasporas which have a state that accepts responsibility for their fate. 'In times of trouble, the state is a refuge for members of the nation, whether or not they are residents and citizens' (Walzer, 1983, pp. 41–2). In two special cases, states have attributed to their diaspora minorities a kind of virtual or dormant citizenship with important policy consequences. Israel has done this with respect to Jews everywhere in the world and Germany has made similar commitments towards groups it regards as ethnic Germans in Central and Eastern Europe. There are many more cases where diaspora groups receive special protection and will be accepted as priority immigrants,[32] without the far-reaching implications of the Israeli Law of Return and the German Basic Law which give any such immigrant automatic access to citizenship because of his or her assumed co-ethnic descent. Whether or not such forms of ethnic citizenship can be legitimated by other than nationalist criteria, will depend on the assessment of the situation of these minorities and on the indirect effects of exclusion for other immigrants produced by such priority rules.

For David Hendrickson the right of both Germany and Israel 'to practise favouritism in their naturalization policy seems incontestable, for both might plausibly claim compelling state interests in justification. Such discriminations in favour of particular racial, cultural, or religious groups derive their force from the family resemblance to the right of return to one's own country' (Hendrickson, 1992, p. 222). In my view the appeal to state interests in justifying unequal treatment of individuals because of their origins is very different from that to the universal human right of return. There are also two different ways how to argue the 'family resemblance' between the latter and preferential admission of co-ethnic foreigners. One is to draw a parallel between individual and collective rights of return. In this perspective, Germans and Jews are ethnic or religious groups who are collectively entitled to return to the territory where they had come from generations or centuries ago. However, the territory of almost every modern state has been the homeland of some other ethnic groups at some point back in history. This is a nationalist principle which inevitably leads to conflicting but equally legitimate claims to territories resolvable only by war (see section 7.2). The second family resemblance is that between the individual right of return and the individual right to protection by a state. The obligation of states to unconditionally accept their own citizens as immigrants derives from the latters' lack of protection as aliens subject to the territorial sovereignty of another state. This is the one parallel which seems to hold for both Germans and Jews. Where minorities do not feel sufficiently protected by the citizenship of their state of residence and do not possess the citizenship of another one, they may need the virtual citizenship of a state which can be actualized in immigration. Of course there is a fundamental difference between both cases: the task of protecting Jews was resolved by founding a new state. The dynamics of state-building implied that in this case immigration became free for everybody claiming Jewish ancestry and not just for those who come from states where Jews are persecuted. In the German case the state was already there and it developed into a country of immigration for people from many different origins. In this context, indiscriminate preferential admission for ethnic Germans because of their origins rather than because of their collective discrimination must be seen as much more problematic.

There is one more justification for citizenship transmission by descent. While the principle of residence supports different forms of immigrant citizenship, the principle of descent backs up *emigrant citizenship*. Its effect is that those who have left their country do not lose their original citizenship automatically because they are then subject to the laws of a foreign sovereign. They retain their right to return and to be reinstated as full citizens. *Ius sanguinis* allows even those who are born abroad to become citizens of their parents' country. In many *ius sanguinis* countries there is also facilitated or optional readmission for former citizens who have been naturalized abroad. The importance of emigrant citizenship will certainly fade away over the generations, and an indefinite transmission of a legal status that ties individuals to states where their forefathers have come from will then become a questionable achievement.

However, for the first generation of emigrants, citizenship defined by origin is a strong protection against denaturalization. If citizenship rested completely on a principle of residence a state might be entitled or even obliged to denaturalize anybody who has left the country for good. If consent is taken into account such a harsh rule can be modified in different ways. One would be to expatriate only those who have left voluntarily and who have committed themselves to a foreign sovereign. Such commitment might be inferred either from merely being a legally resident foreigner, or from applying for naturalization, from entering military service or occupying a public office in the foreign state. In a liberal perspective continued residence abroad can never be sufficient grounds for denaturalization, because this would lead to statelessness and thus to a fundamental loss of protection for this person's basic human rights. When toleration of dual citizenship has been established as a liberal principle, not even naturalization abroad will justify denaturalization. However, as I will explain in chapter 5, the principle of consent may be used in the following way: naturalization plus a longer period of residence abroad may be interpreted as *prima facie* evidence that an emigrant is no longer interested in her citizenship of origin. A liberal state of origin is certainly not obliged to conserve membership status for those who neither need it nor want it. Nor should it be entitled to do this against the emigrants' will. This is an argument for asking immigrants who have been naturalized abroad after some years of residence there whether they want to renew their old citizenship, and to denaturalize those who tacitly or expressly renege this offer of renewal. In a liberal perspective, citizenship by descent may thus provide a basic rationale for emigrant rights but it has to be strongly modified by elements of residence and consent even in this regard.

NOTES

1. See Makarov (1962), quoted in (de Groot, 1989, p. 12).
2. De Groot characterizes citizenship in this legal sense as an 'empty linkage concept' ['*leerer Koppelungsbegriff*'] (de Groot, 1989, p. 13).
3. The German term '*Staatsangehörigkeit*', as it is commonly used, describes fairly well the nominal concept of citizenship, although the word *Angehörigkeit* itself is full of ambiguous connotations such as emotional belonging, family membership or voluntary affiliation. The original root of the word *hörig* characterizes subjection and dependence. In German the terms *Staatsbürgerschaft* and *Staatsangehörigkeit* are synonyms. However, they could be given different meanings in order to distinguish substantial from nominal citizenship.
4. As de Groot points out the *nominal* concept of citizenship is a form of naming persons which has certain parallels with the usage of family names: they indicate that an

individual *belongs* to a family but at the same time the name is a personal attribute of the individual which she has a *right* to carry (de Groot, 1989, pp. 12–13).

5.　　Article 15 of the 1948 Universal Declaration of Human Rights proclaims a human right to nominal citizenship. The 1966 UN Covenant on Civil and Political Rights only insists in its Article 24, paragraph 3 that every child has the right to acquire a nationality. In 1961 the United Nations adopted the Convention on the Reduction of Statelessness. The 1963 Convention on the reduction of cases of multiple nationality and military obligations in cases of multiple nationality was only signed by a relatively small number of member states of the Council of Europe.

6.　　I will suggest later that in a liberal democratic perspective an international order of citizenship ought to be complete but not necessarily discrete, whereas the normative background assumptions of national sovereignty often have led to the opposite conclusion.

7.　　Often 'denationalization' is used instead of denaturalization (see, for example, Schuck and Smith, 1985). I want to avoid this term because it implies that what is taken away is 'nationality' rather than citizenship.

8.　　Michael Walzer has called this 'limited convertibility of social goods' (Walzer, 1983, pp. 17–20) or 'blocked exchange' (Walzer, 1983, pp. 282–4). I prefer the term translation. First, it is not obvious in most cases who are the agents and what are the objects of exchange when social status leads to political power. If the wealthy ones exercise political power, do they always pay for that power and do they receive the power from the people they dominate in exchange for distributing some of their wealth? Second, translation seems to be a more appropriate term because it alludes to a difference in languages or codes of communication between the political and the social spheres. Translation is blocked when institutionalized patterns of communication that establish dominance in one sphere do not lead to isomorphic patterns in another one.

9.　　This view is not shared by all legal scholars. Criticizing de Groot, Jessurun d'Oliveira insists that 'The sense and purpose of possession of a nationality and of grant and deprivation of nationality lies in the normative entailment of rights and duties' (d'Oliveira, 1992, p. 2, see also d'Oliveira, 1990, pp. 116–9).

10.　　De Groot takes this position and maintains that Article 15 is illogical and contains a dubious human right. He thinks it would have been better to specify a right to diplomatic protection and to a country where one can live without the threat of expulsion (de Groot, 1989, p. 15).

11.　　Sidgwick dismissed the criterion of residence as a fundamental one. He insisted that mere local habitation is not sufficient to determine membership: 'the inevitable result would be either to dissipate the sentiment of nationality which we have recognised the importance of maintaining, or to hamper intolerably the intercourse between nations' (Sidgwick, 1897, p. 230). While I do not share his concerns about the sentiment of nationality, I agree that the criterion of residence provides a workable rule only when combined with those of birth and consent.

12.　　Following Rogers Brubaker (1989c), I prefer to use the term attribution instead of ascription for characterizing these principles. Strict *ius sanguinis* and *ius soli* are certainly rules of ascription. Nevertheless, the citizenship they ascribe is never entirely ascriptive in the sense that gender or 'race' are. One cannot change one's descent and one's place of birth but one can change a citizenship acquired by these criteria. The great majority of citizens never test its non-ascriptive character by trying to change it. However, there are always some rules for new acquisitions or loss of membership after birth. Where such opportunities for change exist, citizenship could be called attributive instead of strictly ascriptive.

13　　What it can achieve is to confirm the end of colonial rule when the oppressors have already been defeated or renounced their claims, or to legitimize partition when states are already about to break apart.

14.　　See for example Grawert (1973), de Groot (1989), de Rham (1990), Brubaker (1989a 1992).

15.　　'Every man born and resident in France who has completed his 21st year of age, every foreigner who has completed his 21st year of age and has been resident in France for one year and lives from his labour or acquires a property or marries a French spouse or adopts a child or nourishes an aged person; finally every foreigner who will be judged by the legislative body to have rendered humanity good services is admitted to the exercise of French citizenship' my translation.

16. Peter Schuck and Rogers Smith criticize US ascriptive citizenship by *ius soli* because it 'significantly constrains governmental control over membership and can even compel the state to provide protections to those, most notably illegal aliens, whose entrance to the country it has actively endeavored to prevent' (Schuck and Smith, 1985, p. 21).

17. A peculiar combination of *ius soli* and *ius domicili* exists in the Netherlands. A child born in the country of alien parents is attributed citizenship if one of the parents was an ordinary resident at the time of the birth and that parent's mother (i.e. the child's grandmother) had also been a resident in the country at that parent's birth. This rule serves the same purpose as double *ius soli* (de Groot, 1989, p. 206).

18. Article 44 of the French *Code de la Nationalité*, which will be discussed more extensively in chapter 4, was until the recent reform a rare case of automatic admission. It combined *ius soli* (birth in France from alien parents, themselves not born in France) and *ius domicili* (five years of residence) with an element of consent (the possibility to reject automatic naturalization at majority).

19. Quoting the scholars of international law, Wengler and Verdroß, Grawert even discusses *imposing* citizenship on domiciled foreigners by forcing them to choose between leaving the country or applying for naturalization (Grawert, 1973, p. 224).

20. As for women, Bodin does not categorize them with slaves and serfs, but gives his opinion that they ought to be kept out of all public offices as far as possible so that they can devote themselves passionately to their task as spouses and housewives (Bodin, 1981, III.8, p. 570).

21 One can even agree with Carole Pateman that the classic ideas about the social contract were inherently exclusionary in gender terms (Pateman, 1988).

22. It must be emphasized that Aristotle is writing about a shortage of people for public offices reserved for citizens, not about a general lack of populations who perform the economic functions. A similar explanation has been given for the introduction of *ius soli* and the general liberalization of naturalization laws in 19th century France. This was the only European country with demographic stagnation during that time. However, in political debates the decisive factor was not the economy which could well be filled with foreign immigrants but army recruitment. The Napoleonic mass army relied on citizen soldiers. Second-generation immigrants who were foreigners by *ius sanguinis* generally refused to be naturalized in order to escape military service. In his comprehensive study of German and French citizenship Rogers Brubaker has, however, argued against an 'instrumentalist explanation' which reduces different conceptions of citizenship between these two countries to different demographic and military interests. For Brubaker, the legacy of the French revolution's political concept of the nation was ultimately more important than purely military interests (Brubaker, 1992, pp. 14, 91–4).

23. A general exception is the case of children born out of wedlock who acquire their mother's citizenship.

24. Article 9 of the 1979 Convention on the Elimination of All Forms of Discrimination against Women explicitly grants women the same rights as men with respect to the citizenship of their children. France is exceptional among Western European states in adopting this rule very early. Since 1927 French mothers have transmitted their citizenship to children born in France and since 1945 also to children born abroad (de Groot, 1989, p. 85). *Ius sanguinis* from both parents was introduced in Germany in 1974, in Spain in 1982, in Italy and Austria in 1983, in the Netherlands, Belgium and Switzerland only in 1985 (pp. 44, 61, 118, 128, 148, 163, 183).

25. Document required by Nazi laws for the proof of Aryan descent.

26. Obtaining dual citizenship after birth can be the result of automatic acquisition of citizenship (e.g. on attaining one's majority or when marrying a citizen), or of naturalization without renouncing a previous citizenship (Hammar, 1990, pp. 106–14).

27. 'In Canada and Britain ... citizenship is transmitted unconditionally to the first generation born abroad, but only provisionally (in Canada) or upon the fulfillment of certain conditions of residence and registration (in Britain) to the second generation born abroad. In the United States the attribution of citizenship to even the first generation born abroad is contingent upon prior parental residence in the United States' (Brubaker, 1989c, p. 105). Belgian citizenship, too, is only attributed abroad if one parent has been born in Belgium. Belgium, Switzerland, the Netherlands and Sweden are among European countries which make the retaining of a citizenship attributed at birth abroad conditional upon later residence in the country (Çinar, 1994a, table 3).

28. For a strongly primordialist interpretation of ethnic identity see Isaacs (1975).
29. Habermas's discourse principle is a contemporary reformulation. It postulates that norms for action are valid if all those potentially affected could agree to them as participants in a rational discourse (Habermas, 1992, p. 138).
30. Citizenship acquisition by parents of minor children is sometimes automatically extended to the latter. This is, for example, a rule in French law. Before the reform of the *Code de la Nationalité* in 1993 parents could also apply for naturalization of their under-age children without changing their own citizenship. This possibility has been abolished now.
31. The gender difference in traditional rules for citizenship acquisition by intermarriage mirrors the Darwinist image of national communities as biological units of reproduction. In this view, a group gains in reproductive strength by conquering or admitting women from other groups while it is weakened when foreign men marry the group's female members.
32. The Decree Law on Greek Nationality, for example, allows ethnic Greeks who are stateless or of unknown citizenship to be naturalized even while living abroad (Article 5). Only Greek citizens by naturalization can be denaturalized when they leave Greece with the intention of not returning, while ethnic Greeks will retain their citizenship in this case (Article 19).

3. Foundational Consent

In the previous chapter I discussed two principles for the attribution of nominal citizenship: territorial residence and descent. The third principle according to which citizenship can be allocated is consent. Allocation based on consent is different from attribution, it presupposes agency and requires choice. In this perspective political communities are no longer seen as naturally given (because of the natural or divine authority of a sovereign or because of their common origin). If citizenship were thoroughly based on consent it ought to be understood as membership in a state conceived as a voluntary association. Everybody who is a citizen must have consented to be a member and the state as an association of citizens must have consented to each individual's membership. This is a very demanding rule. Whether it can be applied consistently to a liberal democracy will depend on the interpretation given to the concepts of consent and association. In this chapter I will examine the answers suggested by the three classical doctrines of social contract, elaborated by Thomas Hobbes, John Locke and Jean-Jacques Rousseau.

3.1. VARIETIES OF CONSENT

In order to simplify things I assume that the various interpretations of 'voluntary association' can be reduced to those of consent: a voluntary association is a group of individuals each of whom has in some way consented to be a member and accepted the rules which the association has given to itself. There are two relevant questions. What is to count as consent? At what occasion and by whom must consent be expressed?

The first question yields the following distinctions.

(1) Consent is *active* (express) when it can only be established by voluntary action, choice or verbal expression. It is *passive* (tacit) when it involves merely attributed interests, needs or opinions but no observable action or choice on the part of the consenting individual.

(2) Consent is *explicit* when it entails explicit agreement with a matter under dispute. It is *implicit* when it is derived from agreement referring to some other matter which is assumed to imply consent with the matter under dispute.

(3) Consent is *direct* when the person affected by a decision must have consented herself. It is *indirect* (delegated) when another person consents on the first person's behalf.

(4) Consent is defined *positively* when it requires agreement. It is defined *negatively* when it only requires the absence of disagreement.

Active, explicit, direct and positive consent are strong forms and their opposites are weak forms of consent.

Take as an illustration a patient who undergoes a difficult surgical treatment.[1] If the patient has been fully informed about the risks and has herself asked for the operation, her consent may be characterized as active, explicit, direct and positive. If she was brought to the hospital unconscious after an accident her consent can only be passive, i.e. attributed to her by the doctor: she would have consented had she been conscious. Now take the first case again, where the patient had consented to a specific surgical treatment, but suppose that it turns out during the operation that another organ has to be removed as well. The doctor may be required to stop the operation in order to get the patient's explicit consent. Alternatively, the surgeon may infer from the patient's general agreement to the operation that she has implicitly also consented to the removal of that other sick organ. Or, as a third option, the doctor might have to consult the patient's closest relatives and obtain their delegated consent. If consent is required in this situation it must be positive in any case. The mere absence of disagreement can only be taken as an indicator for consent when the person concerned is fully conscious and able to take a decision. It also follows from this that consent of minors or the severely mentally handicapped may be passive or indirect but it can never be defined negatively and only in rare cases as implicit. The person whose implicit consent is assumed must be ascribed the capacity to draw the inference herself.

The second question can be answered as follows: any form of consent involves mutual agreement about some decision, action, or opinion between independent actors. Associations are composed of several such actors and characterized by taking collective decisions about membership and internal rules. We can specify four elements of *associational consent*:

(1) *foundational consent*: consent between independent actors to form an association of which they will be members;

(2) *entry consent*: consent between an independent actor (or an independent group of actors) and the members of an existing association to admit the former as a new member (as new members);

(3) *exit consent*: consent between an individual member (or a subgroup of members) and the rest of the members about the renunciation or loss of membership by the former;

(4) *internal consent*: consent about collectively binding decisions among the members of the association including the decision to maintain the association.

When discussing the first three forms I will summarily refer to them as 'consent in membership' and distinguish them from internal consent which characterizes the democratic process of deliberation.[2] The analysis of the following chapters will follow this sequence of forms of consent. In this chapter I explore the ideas about foundational consent in classical social contract theories and look at their implications for the allocation of membership. I try to show how Thomas Hobbes consistently reduces all political consent to a foundational one, while Jean-Jacques Rousseau and John Locke tend to substitute internal consent and entry consent respectively for the requirement of foundational consent. Chapters 4 and 5 will examine more closely naturalization and expatriation and the forms of entry and exit consent involved in such individual changes of membership. Readers who are interested in conclusions more than in details can skip these two and turn immediately to chapter 6, which summarizes the different entry and exit decisions, explores the analogies with clubs, congregations, cities and companies of shareholders in order to contrast them with membership rules in liberal democracies and draws the conclusion that political membership in these polities is a question of will and consent only in the last instance, but in the first instance derived from the fact of social membership.

3.2. HOBBES – CONSENT IN SUBJECTION

Political rule can be legitimate because of an underlying weak consensus among those who rule and those who are ruled. This is the medieval idea of social contract. The sovereign is chosen out of an aristocratic caste which is naturally superior to other social classes and his position (although not he as a particular person) is embedded in a divine social order. As for those under his rule who are also considered to be children of God, the sovereign owes them protection while they owe him obedience. In this social contract both sides, rather than agreeing among themselves, agree with divine commands and natural laws expressing God's will. In contrast with the modern idea that contracts are concluded between independent and equal partners the premodern social contract aligns its participants (God, the sovereign, the people) in a vertical order.

The Hobbesian revolution in political thought has been to derive political legitimation from a very different sort of contract concluded between independent and rational individuals. This contract is foundational (there is no pre-existing natural or divine order from which the political order can be strictly derived); it is not only reciprocal (as is the exchange of protection against loyalty) but symmetric (what I transfer to you is the same as what you transfer to me); it is horizontal (all partners enjoy equal status) and concluded pairwise between all members. The last of these points means that the minimal formula for constituting a polity as a voluntary association (each individual must have consented in some way to being a member) is enriched with a second clause that all individuals must have in some way consented to the membership of each: '*as if every man should say to every man*, I authorize and give up my Right of Governing my selfe, to this Man, or to this Assembly of men, on this condition, that thou give up thy Right to him, and Authorize all his Actions in like manner' (Hobbes, 1973, XVII, p. 89, emphasis added).

Such perfect symmetry corresponds to a strong norm of equality both before and after the contract. There is natural basic equality 'in the faculties of body, and mind' from which 'ariseth equality of hope in the attaining of our Ends' (XIII, p. 63). The social contract among natural equals leads to a different form of basic equality which lies in equal subjection under the authority of a sovereign. The difference with medieval versions of social contract is that now human beings are not only equal as God's children but also equal as rational animals within a natural order which is no longer guided by divine decision. Each of the three classic modern versions of social contract starts with this idea of natural equality, and each concludes with a different idea of social equality. Hobbes's contract leads to equality of subjection, Locke's to equality of fundamental rights in civil society and Rousseau's to equality of political power.

Consensual membership is a powerful legitimation for collectively binding decisions. In interactions between individuals, consent is invoked in order to enforce contracts and more generally the keeping of promises. Individuals are said to be morally or legally bound to comply with obligations towards others, which they have voluntarily accepted in clear knowledge of the potential risks and consequences. However, the very nature of political decisions makes it impossible to apply this interactional model of consent consistently. A decision is collectively binding only if it is enforceable without the requirement of previous consent between each pair of individuals within the collective. Hobbes is clearly aware of this. His move is to relieve the enforcement of political decisions from any requirement of consent by deducing generalized legitimation of authority from a previous strictly *interindividual* consent in political membership. In the Hobbesian formula consent in membership is neither *derived* from consent in actual government nor *correlates* with it – the former effectively *substitutes* for the latter.

Let us now consider which allocation of membership would result from this type of contract in a universe of Hobbesian commonwealths. Some readers will doubt the salience of this question. For a realist view of politics, it might seem futile sophistry to imagine which international order of nominal citizenship would emerge if the principle of consent were not only applied to individual admissions of foreigners but also to the bulk of the population, who under present rules obtain their citizenship automatically at birth. However, theories of democracy have always based legitimacy of political rule on consent of those who are ruled. Theoretical thoroughness and consistency require that the question be asked whether those whose consent is necessary for the legitimation of political decisions within a polity have consented to be members of that polity in the first place.

A Hobbesian response would start from the observation that being a citizen of a political commonwealth is such a fundamental interest that it can be attributed to any rational human being. Just as the absence of state authority means a condition of war 'of every man against every man' (XIII, p. 64), individual statelessness puts persons back into that state of nature where they are exposed to violence without any other means of protection than their own weak forces. One may doubt whether universal fear in the state of nature will actually be sufficient to bring about an original contract. This is a prisoners' dilemma where each player has an incentive not to play co-operatively.[3] But once a Hobbesian foundational consent has been reached in all inhabited territories and sovereign states have already established their monopolies of legitimate force everywhere, there can be little doubt that individuals will only in exceptional cases prefer to remain stateless. They might have good reasons to choose between existing states. Yet in the Hobbesian paradigm this choice is strictly limited by the original social contract. Citizens have surrendered their natural liberty to a sovereign, and to choose another sovereign would be an explicit breach of the contract on their part. So a unilateral act of voluntary expatriation will not be tolerated.

Within this consistent frame of reasoning there is an obvious difficulty to explain how such an obligation of total loyalty could be transmitted from one generation to the next. A sovereign is not just instituted for the lifetime of a generation. Once the state of nature has been abandoned, political power is there to stay for an indefinite future. A periodical reopening of the original choice is not possible, since it would be against the clauses of the contract itself and would undermine the stability of sovereignty, which is the essential guarantee against falling back into the state of nature. It is important to remember that this holds also for representative democracy. There are regular elections of legislative assemblies and heads of government but no state is supposed to hold a periodic referendum on the continuation of its existence. The idea of popular sovereignty provides no answer to the question: how can those who are born under a sovereign's rule be assumed to have consented to be citizens of this particular state if they were never given the opportunity to choose another one?

Edmund Burke would have replied that individuals need not have chosen or consented because they are just transient parts of a permanent body politic that is meant to outlast mortal human beings (Burke, 1987, p. 100). For Hobbesians the only consistent answer seems to be that the social compact is not concluded at any particular Time One (Heller, 1987, pp. 248–56), but continually renewed at every moment when law-abiding citizens in their daily lives avail themselves of the protection given by the sovereign rather than choose the dangerous liberty of the natural state of war. Consent of this sort can at best be tacit and implicit and indicated only negatively by the absence of explicit dissent.

Consent is thus read into the motivation of actors who comply with laws. However, these laws are backed up by negative sanctions and compliance might be achieved by threat just as much as by voluntary consent. In a Hobbesian view there is no contradiction in this, because fear was already the driving motive for the original contract and now also motivates consent under civil government.[4] 'Feare, and Liberty are consistent' (Hobbes, 1973, XXI, p. 110). 'And generally all actions, which men doe in Common-wealths, for *feare* of the law, are actions, which the doer had liberty to omit' (XXI, p. 111, original emphasis). Hobbes's theory of foundational contract, which builds upon the strongest notion of explicit individual consent leads to the weakest possible interpretation of political consent in membership and government thereafter.

The allocation of citizenship (or rather subjecthood) which emerges from this view, is determined almost exclusively by effective state power rather than by voluntary individual choice. It will strictly correspond with the residence principle 'for the Soveraign of each Country hath Dominion over all that reside therein' (XX, p. 106). The validity of the social contract is limited by the state's territory. External citizenship status of foreigners and travellers that relates them to their country of origin is not derived from the social contract itself but from agreement among sovereign states. 'But he that is sent on a message, or hath leave to travell, is still Subject; but it is, by Contract between Soveraignes, not by vertue of the covenant of Subjection. For whosoever entreth into anothers dominion, is Subject to all the Laws thereof, unlesse he have a privilege by the amity of the Soveraigns or by speciall licence' (XXI, p. 117). By implication, emigration without permission must be strictly controlled. It is the only possibility for subjects to change their citizenship but this must be condemned as a breach of the promise of submission.

Hobbes does, however, allow for a termination of subjecthood in exile. 'If the Soveraign Banish his Subject; during the Banishment, he is not Subject' (ibid.). This is probably not regarded as an additional punishment for those expelled, but rather as their liberation from the obligation to obey the sovereign. His power does not reach beyond the borders. (Hobbes's conclusion would be different if the place of banishment were a colony.) By being banished from the commonwealth, the subject relapses into the state of nature with respect to the sovereign. But at the same time he becomes subject to the laws of the country where he lives. Statelessness in the sense of not being subjected to any sovereign would be possible only in a territory where there was no effective sovereign power. Thus in a Hobbesian universe of sovereign states there could be no voluntary but some involuntary expatriation, and yet virtually no statelessness. A change of affiliation would depend either on a lack of efficient control of states over emigration or on an agreement between both states involved. Multiple citizenship is excluded by the very nature of subjection to a single and unified authority 'for no man can obey two masters' (XX, p. 105).[5] A Hobbesian approach would thus support a complete, discrete and very stable order of nominal citizenship.

3.3. ROUSSEAU – CONSENT IN PARTICIPATION

The problem of intergenerational validity of the social contract does not arise in Rousseau's approach. The contract is renewed not only for each generation but at the beginning of each popular assembly (Rousseau, 1973, III.18, p. 273) and among citizens fully participating in public life, consent is active, explicit and direct. Rousseau thus identifies foundational with internal consent. Ernest Renan's famous definition of the nation as a daily plebiscite (Renan, 1882, p. 307) applies much better to a Rousseauian republic.

The republican solution shares with the Hobbesian one a justification for unrestrained state power over individual citizens. In both theories individuals are supposed to give up all their rights to the sovereign. The difference is that for republicans the sovereign is the ensemble of the very individuals who alienate all their rights and subject themselves to political rule. As the sovereign is unable to do injustice to itself, the people can not only change the form and composition of government at any time but can even revoke the social contract itself if they so please. Stability of political rule and protection against the relapse into tyranny or anarchy then depend entirely on the miraculous transformation of the will of all into a single general will. This puzzle is resolved by Rousseau at best at the level of philosophical speculation. As far as he considers it as a practical problem at all he resorts to political re-education, the preservation of morality through censorship and the promotion of loyalty through civil religion (Rousseau, 1973, IV.7–8, pp. 296–308). These features of Rousseau's theory have strongly discredited it among liberals ever since the Jacobin terror and Benjamin Constant's convincing critique (Constant, 1988). Liberal democracy expects legitimation from procedural rules that can be interpreted as operationalizing and transmitting popular consent rather than from reshaping the characters and preferences of individuals from above by coercive means.

Nonetheless, Rousseau's solution for the problem how political rule over a collective of individuals can be said to be legitimated by their consent provides some important insights that are absent in both liberal and 'realist' accounts along Hobbesian lines. While Hobbes starts with painting a dark picture of the nature of human self-interest and the resulting anarchy of stateless societies, Rousseau's overly idyllic view of early society before the emergence of states and private property is, nevertheless, based on a deeper understanding that solidaristic ties within self-contained communities rather than a war of all against all characterized this world. At least in the *Contrat Social* Rousseau's concern is not with either the dangers or the desirability of returning to that state of nature but rather with the predicaments inherent in modern politically organized society. The modern economy perpetually fuels the conflict of private interests and produces social inequalities and insatiable needs. All this subverts the search for the common good in the political sphere (Ignatieff, 1985, pp. 107–24). Charles de Montesquieu, David Hume, Adam Smith and Benjamin Constant all thought that the development of commerce and trade would have beneficial effects on both citizens' and governments' political attitudes. The pursuit of private business would moderate political passions and support for liberty would become safely grounded in economic interest. Rousseau held a different view. Passive citizens and tyrannical rule go hand in hand. The only solution lies in developing a political constitution within modern society which is able to counteract this degeneration by continuously activating citizens and constraining governmental exercise of power. Individuals become autonomous by obeying laws which they have given to themselves. The social contract enables them to become autonomous within a political collective.

For Rousseau, political integration can only be achieved by an institutional arrangement within society which promotes the pursuit of common interests and puts a premium on public virtues.[6] There are three possible solutions to this problem. The first lies in the separation of a political class of citizens from the rest of the population. The latter have to take care of the lower tasks of social and economic reproduction so that the former can become free to seek excellence and honour in public life. This is the Greek and Roman solution. The second answer is the separation of the individual into *homo oeconomicus* and political citizen and the attempt to create institutions which will educate individuals to subordinate the needs of the former to the virtues of the latter. This is Rousseau's approach. A third solution lies in the separation of societal spheres rather than of higher and lower strata of populations or of the self. In modern functionally differentiated societies individuals can be citizens in the political system, economic agents in markets and enterprises, and private members of families and circles of friends, without necessarily changing their basic identities when leaving one sphere and entering the other. A liberal democratic political system in such societies creates institutional guarantees for the articulation of a wide plurality of interests by all individuals rather than their selective suppression (either by suppressing a class of individuals or a class of fundamental interests). The priority of politics is no longer to be sought in generalized restrictions imposed on social actors and social activities, but in the capacity of the political system to enforce a rule of law throughout societal spheres. In the neoliberal interpretation this task is reduced to maintaining a framework for the spontaneous co-ordination of individual interests in the economy, in the associational life of civil society and in the private spheres of the family. In an egalitarian view the task of politics is extended to secure some basic equality of economic resources and of political power.

These are ideal-typic distinctions. As I will try to show, forms of exclusion that are explicit in the ancient republic resurface implicitly in the modern republican tradition associated with Rousseau. And even liberal democracy implies some separating of populations by assigning them political membership in different polities without their explicit consent. The essential difference between the three forms of separation which I have outlined is that the potential for inclusive definitions of membership extends with the transition from the first to the second and is maximized within the third.

Rousseau never considers explicitly criteria for political membership, but one can draw some inferences from occasional side-remarks and from the general thrust of the theory. The formula of the social contract contains a reaffirmation of individual membership in the republican polity: 'Each of us puts his person and all his power in common under the supreme direction of the general will, and, in our corporate capacity, *we receive each member as an indivisible part of the whole*' (Rousseau, 1973, I.6, p. 192, emphasis added). Individual dissent against a particular law does not deprive anyone of this status of membership nor does it invalidate the law as an expression of the general will. Consent to the implementation of majority decisions is implied in the contract. However, individuals remain free to oppose the contract itself and thus to refuse or renounce membership. 'If then there are opponents when the social compact is made, their opposition does not invalidate the contract, but merely prevents them from being included in it. They are foreigners among citizens. When the State is instituted, residence constitutes consent; to dwell within its territory is to submit to the sovereign' (IV.2, p. 277). In a footnote Rousseau adds that residence constitutes consent only in free states, 'for elsewhere family, goods, lack of a refuge, necessity, or violence may detain a man in a country against his will'. In another passage he refers without obvious disagreement to Grotius's opinion 'that each man can renounce his membership of his own State, and recover his natural liberty and his goods on leaving the country' (III.18, p. 273).

A Rousseauian allocation of membership by consent can be reconstructed in the following propositions. (1) Citizenship is a form of active political participation. (2) Those living in a state territory who dissent fundamentally with political rule by the people or those who simply wish to remain politically passive are nevertheless subjected to the laws decided by the sovereign and the decrees issues by his government. (3) Individuals are generally free to leave the country and can thereby escape subjecthood as well as renounce citizenship.

In conclusion, the requirement of active consent leads to a much less inclusive distribution of citizenship than does a Hobbesian interpretation of social contract. Apart from foreigners by origin there will also be 'foreigners' by internal dissent and 'foreigners' who have abandoned citizenship by being politically passive and pursuing exclusively their private interests.

This triple differentiation of citizenship for the fundamental dissenter, the politically passive and the foreigner is still inherent in contemporary republicanism. In his defence of this tradition, Adrian Oldfield emphasizes the first and the third distinction in a very outspoken manner: 'Citizenship is exclusive: it is not a person's humanity that one is responding to, it is the fact that he or she is a fellow citizen, or a stranger. In choosing an identity for ourselves we recognize both who our fellow citizens are, and those who are not members of our community, and thus who are potential enemies' (Oldfield, 1990, p. 8). 'Within civic republicanism, citizenship is an activity or a practice, and not simply a status, so that not to engage in the practice is, in important senses, not to be a citizen' (Oldfield, 1990, p. 5). Oldfield's distinction of status and practice obscures the issue. There is no way of conceiving of citizenship as a practice without a corresponding status. The pertinent question is rather: is citizenship a status enabling individuals to engage in public and political practice? Or is it a status bestowed only on those who are willing, or who deserve, to engage in these practices?[7]

In a more liberal vein, Michael Walzer has argued for recognizing the right to be passive and the right to dissent in the form of conscientious objection. How could those who were made citizens at birth and often had not even consented indirectly to their political membership by participating in a democratic vote be asked to risk their lives for a state? He dismisses the idea that politically alienated citizens could be exempted from the draft but would thereby forfeit their political rights. This would create two classes of citizenship, but in liberal democracy citizenship ought to be inclusive and equal (Walzer, 1970, pp. 99–119).[8]

In a world of Rousseauian republics, the territorial allocation of subjecthood which we have derived from Hobbes could be more or less reproduced with the important difference that both subjects and citizens are free to leave and to submit to a different sovereign. Citizenship would not be an enhancement of this basic condition of subjection with individual rights, but a status altogether different. Though potential citizenship may well be acquired at birth either by *ius sanguinis* or *ius soli*, actual citizenship is confined to the mature participant in political life. Choosing citizenship is not an act of subjection to a sovereign but an application for membership in a people which is itself the sovereign. While one may well submit to different masters, especially if the masters agree among each other to share in the subjection, the republican notion of sovereignty excludes any citizen from being a member of more than one sovereign people at a time. The global distribution of citizenship would thus be discrete but not complete. Overlaying the seamless patchwork of subjecthood it would, in Hannah Arendt's words, create spaces of freedom that resemble a pattern of islands in an ocean, or oases in a desert (Arendt, 1963, p. 279).

3.4. LOCKE – CONSENT IN ADMISSION

John Locke, who developed a more moderate liberal version of social contract and government by popular consent than either Hobbes or Rousseau, made the most radical argument for consent as the basic requirement for the allocation of political membership.

Locke uses the concept of the state of nature in five different ways. First, it characterizes the realm of unowned nature where men can seize property for themselves under the proviso that 'there is enough and as good left in common for others'[9] (Locke, 1956, V, §27, p. 15). Second, it refers to pre-state societies such as those of the American Indians (VII, §102, pp. 51-2).

Third, a state of nature in the sense of absence of higher authority reigns between sovereign states (II, §14, p. 9; XVI, §183, p. 93) and characterizes also, fourth, the position of 'every absolute prince in respect to those who are under his dominion' (VII, §90, p. 45). Fifth and finally, the state of nature is present in civil society as a condition of minors and foreigners who are subjected to a different authority than that of the reigning sovereign. It is this fifth meaning which is most relevant for understanding Locke's interpretation of consent. I will quote Locke's position at some length, first, because alongside Aristotle's it is the most elaborate theory of citizenship acquisition in classical political philosophy and second, because it is strikingly at odds with common political practice at Locke's time and until the present age.

The theory rests on the following basic propositions. (1) Full political membership is a status acquired for life by active, explicit, direct and positive individual consent. (2) Enjoyment of privileges and protection by the state implies passive consent with political rule and gives rise to temporary obligations corresponding to these rights.

'To those that say there were never any men in the state of nature,' Locke answers by affirming 'that all men are naturally in that state, and remain so, till by their own consents they make themselves members of some politic society' (II, §15, pp. 9-10). 'Men being ... by nature all free, equal, and independent, no one can be put out of this estate, and subjected to the political power of another, without his own consent' (VIII, §95, p. 49). The radical implication is that citizenship understood as membership in a civil society cannot be acquired at birth when the individual is unable to consent:[10] 'a child is born a subject of no country or government. He is under his father's tuition and authority till he comes to age of discretion, and then he is a freeman, at liberty what government he will put himself under, what body politic he will unite himself to' (VIII, §118, p. 61).

This formula contains Locke's solution for the problem of intergenerational validity of a social contract. As we have seen, Hobbes derives a long-term binding force of the original contract from the continuing rational fear of humans to fall back into a state of nature, while Rousseau suggests a perpetual renewal of the contract in political participation. For Locke the contract must be renewed for each generation and individual only once. 'Whatever engagements or promises any one has made for himself, he is under the obligation of them, but cannot by any compact whatsoever bind his children or posterity' (VIII, §116, p. 60). This impossibility of an intergenerational transfer of contractual obligations holds for both partners of the contract: the citizen and the state. In a plainly counterfactual statement, Locke asserts that governments 'claim no power over the son, because of that they had over the father; nor look on children as being their subjects by their father's being so' (ibid.).

Becoming a member of a civil society ruled by legitimate government is a decision for life taken separately by free individuals. It is similar in structure to a marriage contract: no one can be forced to enter such a contract, the choice of the contract partner is relatively unconstrained, and the decision is meant to be binding for as long as both partners are alive.[11]

The second essential element in Locke's theory of citizenship acquisition is the distinction between express and tacit consent. Tacit consent can be derived from residence and implies voluntary subjection to the laws of a sovereign:

[E]very man that hath any possessions, or enjoyment of any part of the dominion of any government, doth thereby give his tacit consent, and is as far forth obliged to obedience to the laws of that government during such enjoyment as any one under it; whether this his possession be of land to him and his heirs for ever, of a lodging only for a week; or whether it be barely travelling freely on the highway; and in effect it reaches as far as the very being of any one within the territories of that government (VIII, §119, p. 61). But submitting to the laws of any country, living quietly and enjoying privileges and protection under them, makes not a man a member of that society ... And thus we see, that foreigners by living all their lives under another government, and enjoying the privileges and protection of it, though they are bound even in conscience to submit to its administration as far forth as any denizen, yet do not thereby come to be subjects or members of that commonwealth. Nothing can make any man so, but his actually entering into it by positive engagement, and express promise and compact (VIII, §122, pp. 62–3).

The important point about Locke's concept of 'denizenship', which has been reformulated recently by Tomas Hammar (1990), is that it is not identical with mere subjection. It is a status derived from an implicit contract that involves basically similar rights and obligations to those of citizens. The contrast lies in the temporary and instrumental nature of this contract: 'obligation begins and ends with the enjoyment' (VIII, §121, p. 62). Foreign residents thus enjoy more liberty than citizens who are bound by their contract for life. Yet the price of this liberty is reduced security and representation of their interests within the state. While the actions of citizen-subjects are 'capable to be directed by antecedent, standing, positive laws ... what is to be done to foreigners ... must be left in great part to the prudence of those who have this power' (XII, p. 75).

In its allocational consequences for citizenship, Locke's approach broadly resembles Rousseau's. Both determine consent in citizenship as active and explicit. However, for Rousseau consent is defined positively with regard to legislation but merely negatively in the access to membership. Locke postulates the exactly opposite requirements. Rousseau operationalizes individual autonomy in the acquisition of citizenship as the possibility of dissent, but Locke insists that only positive voluntary commitment can establish membership.

One could assume that Locke's procedure of individual contracting by each and every citizen at the age of majority should lead to a larger number of native-born 'foreigners' among citizens who just do not apply for the citizenship of their country. However, Locke was certainly confident that rational perception of the benefits of citizenship would secure virtually complete inclusion of all male adult property owners, while Rousseau was probably aware that his demanding civic obligations would be felt as heavy burdens and as a potential deterrent from voluntary citizenship for individuals who pursue primarily their private interests.

Still, Locke's definition of citizenship by consent is explicitly exclusive[12] in two respects: first, it excludes those who are not free to enter a contract because they do not have the required maturity of reason, i.e. minors, as well as 'lunatics and idiots' (VI, §§52–76, pp. 27–39)[13] and second, as we have already seen, it excludes foreigners because they have no full and permanent interest in the commonwealth.

The consequence of Locke's strict requirement of consent is to exclude minors from even passive forms of citizenship. Locke was certainly an advocate of what might be called enlightened paternal government – the father's 'command over his children is but temporary, and reaches not their life or property' (VI, §65, p. 33) – but the power of the father in the family deprives the other family members (children and women) of their political membership. My point is not to criticize Locke because he did not endorse modern versions of children's rights, but rather that denying such rights could be inherent in a strong notion of citizenship by consent. Conversely, if we insist that in liberal democracies children, 'lunatics and idiots' must be recognized as citizens even if they cannot make use of all active rights of citizenship, this implies that the basic quality of membership is not derived from active and explicit consent but rather from attributed needs, interests and status, and from being subjected to the laws of a state.

A similar argument holds with respect to foreign 'denizens'. If citizenship depends on an act of free and voluntary consent, foreigners who enjoy the protection and privileges under enlightened government and who obey the laws of the commonwealth do not thereby become citizens. Moreover, even if they want to become citizens, the nature of the contract implies that they may be denied this possibility without any reason to complain. They are not injured in their status as free and equal human beings by being denied access to citizenship. One would have to add a Lockean proviso here that there ought to be 'enough and as good' other possibilities of acquiring membership left over for those who are not included in the commonwealth.[14] From this one can derive an obligation to naturalize stateless individuals and to admit foreigners fleeing from tyrannical regimes. Yet those who are already citizens of a free society but choose to live in another country have no right of access to citizenship on Locke's account.

This latter conclusion is of course still the contemporary wisdom. However, the point is that it follows consistently only from a premise which is no longer accepted (and in fact has never been accepted in Locke's radical formulation). The prerogatives of national citizens can be reconciled with the credo of natural equality and freedom of all human beings only if membership in states and civil societies is based on voluntary choices open to all. If membership is acquired without consent by most of the population, the argument breaks down and citizenship becomes a morally arbitrary matter of birth and descent. Those who still want to maintain the Lockean conception of natural rights and equality and his strong requirement of consent as a normative standard have to face the exclusionary consequences for the allocation of citizenship. The alternative is to accept that states distribute membership generally without individuals' consent and that active consent is only articulated in individual admissions of adults. The irony of the Lockean position when applied to these actual practices of citizenship allocation is that only naturalized aliens could be rightly regarded as free citizens, while the membership of natives would be devalued by its illegitimate origins.

Locke's theory effectively resolves many puzzles of political consent which arise in Hobbes's and Rousseau's accounts, by shifting the requirement of strong consent from foundation to individual entry. Before examining more closely the new problems which are raised by this move towards entry consent, I will briefly mention one more question for which this move seems to provide an answer.

A voluntary association comes into being and can be dissolved by its members' consent. The classic theorists were strongly concerned about the violent dissolution of commonwealths, civil societies or republics by war, civil war and conquest,[15] but none of them seem to have considered the possibility of a reversal of the original contract, i.e. consensual dissolution (see section 7.2). Each theory is carefully constructed in a way that excludes this option. For Hobbes, any agreement among citizens to dissolve a commonwealth while the sovereign is alive and in power would be an explicit breach of the original contract. For Rousseau sovereignty is inalienable and indivisible. While fusion might be an option available to the general will, separation can only express particular wills among the citizenry.

Both Hobbes's and Rousseau's solutions are difficult to accept. It is only within a Lockean framework that the question of voluntary dissolution can be circumvented without denigrating the basic idea of consent. In defending his thesis that 'all peaceful beginnings of government have been laid in the consent of the people' (VIII, §112, p. 58), Locke presents a narrative of the evolution of political power in which there is no original contract but a gradual shift from passive and implicit consent to more and more active and explicit forms (VIII, §§101–10, pp. 51–7). Consent becomes express only in a mature civil society when individuals take a decision about their citizenship. The state is already there and the decision to be agreed upon is only about the relation of the individual to the state, but neither about the creation nor about the dissolution of the state.

There is one historical moment when the Lockean theory of voluntary citizenship became actually relevant in a foundational situation. This was in the revolution in the British colonies of North America. 'Citizenship was created in the American Revolution as each inhabitant placed his consent in republican government, by that voluntary act approving its sovereignty and binding his allegiance to it' (Ueda, 1982, p. 152). 'Requiring the assent of the governed enabled the colonists to exchange subjecthood under the British king for citizenship in the American republic. Under the new state and federal governments, every man was theoretically free to choose to be citizen or alien' (p. 113). Yet even during this foundational moment the territorial principle prevailed in practice. 'As a practical expedient to legitimize consent, the Continental Congress in 1776 affirmed that simply residing in a state and receiving its legal protection constituted allegiance to the new political order' (ibid.).

Once the revolution was over, the attribution of citizenship became based on *ius soli* again as had been the determination of British subjecthood before. In the subsequent history of American citizenship, the territorial principle provided the justification for widening the range of inclusion, while the principles of descent and of consent were used to narrow it in different ways for immigrants as well as for native Americans. *Ius sanguinis* became important during the 19th century in racist exclusions from citizenship which first targeted freed slaves and later Chinese and other Asian immigrants: '...only the descendants of those who had made the compact to form the republic in 1787 and free white aliens were eligible for citizenship under federal law' (p. 122). The Lockean requirement of consent remained relevant for individual naturalizations and was affirmed in the ritual of the oath of allegiance. While the territorial principle thus overruled the test of consent for citizens by birth, the requirement of individual allegiance was also used as an ideological justification for excluding whole populations who would have had a natural right to citizenship according to *ius soli*. Judicial opinions in the early 19th century converged towards regarding 'each Indian tribal organization ... as a "nation" to whom Indians owed their primary allegiance; thus the courts designated Indians noncitizens because, although they were born in U.S. territory, their allegiance remained to the tribe' (p. 116). This peculiar exclusion of native Americans from citizenship was lifted by Congress only in 1924.

NOTES

1. This example is used by Elaine Scarry in a highly interesting discussion of the body as the locus of consent (Scarry, 1992).
2. In a critical review of Schuck and Smith (1985), Joseph Carens rightly emphasized the distinction between these two forms of consent. The point of his argument, which I fully endorse, is that neither discretionary denial of admission to citizenship nor denaturalization can be justified by a general democratic principle of consent. 'The principle that political authority must rest upon the consent of the governed is not the same as consent to membership. Similarly, the individual's right to leave (voluntary expatriation) is not the same as the community's right to exclude. The right to leave is linked conceptually and historically to the principle of government resting on the consent of the governed' (Carens, 1987b, p. 438).
3. As Robert Axelrod's experiments have demonstrated, rational players will in fact adopt conditionally co-operative strategies when the game is played repeatedly (Axelrod, 1984). See also Bill Jordan's interpretation of Axelrod's results that self-interest and interest in the common good can be reconciled in certain institutional settings (Jordan, 1989, chapter 3).
4. David Gauthier's Hobbesian theory of justice departs from Hobbes in this regard. In co-operation threat behaviour would be proscribed. Persons which are to gain from co-operation will not rationally choose maximally effective threat strategies in bargaining for the division of the benefits of co-operation. The initial bargaining position must therefore be non-coercive (Gauthier, 1986, pp.155–6, 199–200). Yet even if this were granted for the original contract, it would no longer hold for the relation between Leviathan and its subjects thereafter.
5   Bodin's position is more differentiated in this regard. In contrast with Hobbes, his notion of sovereignty still allows for many intermediary levels of authority. Bodin therefore concedes that an individual can be slave or vassal to more than one master, who in their turn are subordinated to a superior authority. However, he thinks it impossible that one single citizen could be the subject of several sovereign princes who recognize no higher authority unless these princes have reached an agreement among themselves (Bodin, 1981, I.6, pp. 173–4). Multiple citizenship is thus considered to be possible if such an agreement can be found.
6. For convincing reformulations of this problem within the context of contemporary welfare state democracies see, for example, Jordan (1989) and Offe and Preuß (1991).
7. Herman van Gunsteren goes even further in suggesting that 'citizenship is more than a status; it is an office' (van Gunsteren, 1988, p. 732). He sketches an attractive neorepublican vision of citizenship as competent dealing with plurality in a public-political sphere (van Gunsteren, 1992) which includes elements of the liberal and the communitarian traditions. Yet his approach, as that of other republican theorists, is insensitive to the inequality and exclusiveness of political status which may be derived from the ideas of citizenship as office, practice or virtue.
8   As a partial solution to the dilemma Walzer proposes to restrict conscription to those situations of war where the country itself is threatened with devastation. Conscription for the Vietnam war in the USA would have been illegitimate by this criterion, independently of whether military intervention was justified.
9. This famous Lockean proviso for property acquisition has been extensively discussed and reinterpreted in libertarian theories of justice. See Nozick (1974) and Gauthier (1986).
10. There is a striking parallel between Locke's argument and the religious doctrines of Baptists and some other Protestant churches which do not baptise minors. The difference is that the 'secular religion' of liberalism is thoroughly based on the notion of consent

whereas this idea cannot be easily reconciled with a belief in divine grace or predestination.

11. The right of popular rebellion which Locke cautiously endorses is not considered as a revocation of the social contract. As with Rousseau, the contract primarily constitutes civil society and only secondarily institutes a government. Legitimate rebellion is directed against miscarriages of governmental authority but not against society itself: '...the power that every individual gave the society, when he entered into it, can never revert to the individuals again as long as the society lasts, but will always remain in the community' (Locke, 1956, XIX, §243, p. 122).

12. As most other contract theorists, Locke also excludes women from citizenship without elaborating this. He only concedes that mothers have a share (not necessarily an equal one) in parental power. Hobbes presents a much more sophisticated argument for the exclusion of women. He starts with equal parental power of father and mother only to dismiss this later as impossible 'for no man can obey two masters'. In the state of nature dominion over the child lies with the mother because 'it cannot be known who is the Father, unless it be declared by the Mother'. However, in a commonwealth, parental authority can be attributed to either sex by civil law. In most commonwealths it is attributed to the father and women are subject to men 'because for the most part Common-wealths have been erected by the Fathers, not by the Mothers of families' (Hobbes, 1973, XX, p. 105).

13. 'The idea of the citizen as a free and independent person can also serve to justify the paternal regulation of significant sections of the population' (Hindess, 1993, pp. 32–3).

14. A similar proviso can be used to constrain the denial of immigration rights. See chapter 13 and Bauböck (1993d).

15. See Hobbes (1973, XXIX), Locke (1956, XIX), Rousseau (1973, III.10–11).

4. Consent in Entry

This chapter presents an analysis of rules for individual naturalization. Naturalization is a transition from one legal status to another one. Generally, such transitions can be structured in four different ways. They can be automatic, mandatory, discretionary or optional.[1] In naturalization, discretionary and optional forms are the most common ones. Apart from the structure of transition, the first section will also list different criteria used to define those who are eligible for naturalization. The second part focuses on the normative issues and argues that liberal democratic norms support optional admission and a minimal list of selection criteria. In the third section I examine hypothetically how changes of rules might influence the motivation and propensity of immigrants to apply for naturalization.

4.1. DISCRETIONARY AND OPTIONAL ADMISSION

In contrast with the foundational consent invoked by Hobbes and Rousseau, the contract about individual admission to membership is not horizontal, not symmetric and not concluded between all members of the association. I will consider the standard procedure of naturalization as a prototypic form of entry consent: the individual applies for membership and the state authorities (who in a democratic state will be empowered by internal consent of present members) grant it. Admission is consensual only if both sides are free to say no. The individual must have the liberty not to apply and the state need not grant admission to those who do apply. Where then are the asymmetry and inequality? They lie first in an imbalance of resources and interests between both partners of the contract and second in the sequencing of the agreement.

Inequality of initial positions of a state and an applicant for naturalization becomes obvious when we consider the substantially different impacts of a negative decision. A state, or any larger association for that matter, is rich in members and admitting a single individual will affect its interests only marginally. Even where multiple citizenship is possible, an individual cannot accumulate memberships in the same way as a state can accumulate members. More specifically and in contrast with other voluntary associations, if being a member of a state is of vital interest for an individual (as it presumably is in all social contract theories) the power of the state to say no makes the applicant more dependent on the state than her liberty not to apply could ever make her independent from the state. There may be, however, situations when this imbalance is overcome or even reversed. Aristotle's argument is obviously relevant here, that states sometimes badly need more citizens (or citizens of a certain kind such as wealthy and highly qualified immigrants, or ethnic relatives) and then tend to deviate from what he regards to be natural rules for the acquisition of citizenship (see section 2.3).

The second imbalance lies in the sequence of decisions and it is the more important one. The state has the power of the last word. Authorities are still free to say 'no' *after* the applicant has first made her move and said 'yes I will'. This is what makes decisions about naturalization *discretionary* rather than strictly *consensual*. It is not obvious that Locke had such a sequence in mind when he insisted that all citizens have to consent to their membership on reaching majority.[2] Imagine a reversal. Could not the state first declare that it thought this or that social category fit to become citizens? The individual would then still be free to accept or turn down this offer. This would make membership *optional* instead of discretionary. The state would give non-members a right to become members.[3]

Is such an admission procedure not incompatible with the characteristics of voluntary associations? It seems to undermine both foundational and internal consent. If the founders had to agree *simultaneously* about mutually granting each other's membership, how can latecomers be allowed to join without being constrained by the others' choices in a similar way? If all the associations' decisions depend on their present members' consent, how can outsiders constrain a collective decision about membership by claiming a right to be admitted? Finally, would a right to membership not blur the distinction between members and non-members, which is fundamental to any voluntary association?

Let me first consider the extreme case. As a radicalization of the Nozickian utopia (Nozick, 1974, chapter 10) one could imagine a world of voluntary associations with completely open boundaries of membership. Associations could take internally binding decisions for their present members but anybody who wished to join would be free to do so. As individuals have different needs and preferences, not everybody would like to join all associations nor would all associations produce the same kind of goods and benefits for their members. Such a pattern of associations would correspond to the spontaneous social order created by open and free markets in liberal economic theory. However, it would not allow for any associational solution to the problems of collective choice and of the distribution of public goods. Associations which, due to their members' efforts, were successful in producing benefits also desired by non-members, would immediately be overwhelmed by free-riders joining from outside. Furthermore, if a generalized right of exit corresponded to the right of entry, no association would be able to distribute burdens necessary for the production of some collective benefit to its members. People would enter to reap the benefits and leave to avoid the burdens.

Not many human activities and preferences could conceivably be organized within such a pattern of spontaneous association. Political decision-making and the usual benefits and burdens distributed by states to populations are certainly not among them. Associations of this kind could probably never be stable because any collective effort would be thwarted from the start. So a world of perfectly open associations would in the end be self-destroying. It could only be sustained if there were strong states which themselves would not resemble voluntary associations at all. Among the tasks that could be fulfilled only by non-consensual rule would be the enforcement of a general right to admission into any association in civil society. But by interfering in order to keep associations perfectly open, state authorities would effectively atomize and destroy civil society. In conclusion, I assume that some form of entry control is essential for stabilizing associations both within civil society and also at the level of democratic states if these ought to resemble voluntary associations.

There are two objections against turning this conclusion into an argument for discretionary admission to citizenship. First, liberal democratic polities deviate from the voluntary association model in essential aspects, or, to put it more precisely, they are a very specific kind of association (see section 6.2). While no association can be completely open, different kinds might be open in different degrees. Second, optional admission is not the same as uncontrolled entry. If the right to be admitted is not universal but granted to a particular group only or to those who meet certain criteria, the association still remains in control over admission by defining the group and the criteria. In actual naturalization laws and practices, discretionary and optional aspects of the procedure are mixed in different ways. Combinations of rules invariably produce a result somewhere between the extremes of perfect closure (no naturalization allowed) and perfect openness (all those who wish to become members must be granted admission).

A move towards more optional and less discretionary rules implies indeed a blurring of boundaries of membership but it does not eliminate them. As I have argued at the beginning of chapter 2, the benefits of substantial citizenship are rights distributed to members. Optional admission includes categories of non-members in the internal distribution of rights in a special way by giving them a *right to membership*. If this right is not a universal one so that everybody could freely choose any citizenship, it will create additional boundaries of inclusion and exclusion which are, however, wider than that of nominal citizenship.

In the inner circle there are those who are citizens by birth or by naturalization. Outside there are groups of potential members who enjoy an optional right to become full members. Beyond that second circle there is a third one for those who are allowed to apply for discretionary admission. A fourth group of potential members are those who are temporarily excluded from admission (e.g. because they have not been in the country long enough). The rest are excluded from citizenship negatively because they do not meet essential positive requirements (e.g. of being resident in the country). Cutting through this concentric structure of (potential) membership there are some segments of positively excluded groups who fulfil all the general requirements of their respective group, but are identified as undesirable by some specific criterion (e.g. by racial, ethnic or religious exclusion from naturalization).

Figure 2: Circles of membership created by rules of admission

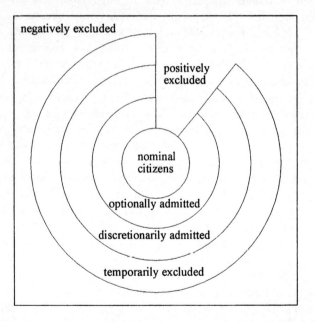

Ordinary naturalizations are rarely explicitly optional.[4] But administrative discretion in decisions on naturalizations is usually constrained. Those deciding do not flip a coin and they also cannot hold a referendum among the electorate whether a candidate should be admitted.

Constraints on discretion can be of different kinds. First, administrations are normally guided by certain rules of law and administrative practice and information about these should generally also be accessible to applicants. Therefore applicants are mostly selected in advance by standardized criteria and discretion is exercised only within the range of those criteria which cannot be easily standardized. Where criteria are completely standardized and known to all potential applicants, naturalization becomes optional for the eligible groups.[5] Second, discretion is constrained if reasons must be given for negative decisions in written notification.[6] Third, appeals may be possible to a higher administrative or judicial authority.

The discretionary character of a naturalization procedure is often emphasized by imposing substantial costs on applicants in terms of money as well as of time. Some countries, like Italy and Spain, do not require any fees for naturalization, others demand a symbolic sum or some rough equivalent for the costs of administration, while a third group raises fees to a level where they become an effective deterrent against application. In Germany fees depend on monthly income,[7] in Switzerland they differ strongly from one Canton to another (de Groot, 1989, p. 268). Discretionary naturalization is usually also time-consuming. In a few cases immigrants may be interested in naturalization only for short-term reasons, and will not apply if they know that the decision would take too long to achieve the desired benefit (for example to prevent the loss of a residence permit, or to be able to vote in a forthcoming election). The more important burdens, however, are those imposed on the applicant during the procedure of examining her request. Apart from the time spent in the office, immigrants frequently dislike the nature of the interviews which are experienced as interrogation. Sometimes they are unable to provide all the documents required. Naturalization in the United States of America, which is certainly much less cumbersome than in most Western European countries, has been aptly characterized by David North as a 'long grey welcome' (North, 1987). All these elements of discretionary procedures confirm the impression that naturalization is not the result of an immigrant's decision to join a political community, but a favour granted by a powerful authority. In optional forms of admission these barriers are either completely removed or substantially lower.

In the rest of this section I will discuss a list of naturalization criteria. I split them into two groups: on the one hand those which are used in order to facilitate naturalization, or to give it a more optional character, and on the other hand conditions which are imposed to emphasize discretion or to make naturalization less easily accessible.[8] We can easily distinguish both kinds of criteria when we imagine a standard model for ordinary naturalizations as a common core of all national procedures. This model would only specify a certain time of legal residence as the essential requirement, and would be broadly discretionary in the sense that it does not entitle an individual to obtain citizenship upon application after this period.[9]

Of course states differ not merely in their specific combinations of rules for facilitating or impeding naturalization but also in their residence requirements. Among Western immigration countries the general waiting period varies between two years in Australia and three years in Canada and New Zealand at the one end of the spectrum, and twelve years in Switzerland at the other extreme. In Western Europe, Ireland has the shortest residence requirement (four years). The most common period is now five years (in Belgium, Britain, Finland, France, Netherlands, Sweden and the USA). Residence requirements also differ considerably in length for different categories of foreigners within a single state. Two examples will illustrate the variety of reasons which can reduce or lengthen a residence requirement. In Austria ordinary naturalizations require a residence of ten years; facilitated admission (e.g. for political refugees, for minors of applicants and for spouses[10] of citizens or applicants) is possible after four years; after thirty years of continuous residence an immigrant acquires a legal claim to naturalization[11] (Austrian Nationality Act, Articles 10, 11a, 12, 16). In Spain, the residence requirement is one year for those born in the country or abroad by a parent of Spanish origins, two years for citizens of Spanish- or Portuguese-speaking countries and for Sephardic Jews, five years for Geneva Convention Refugees and ten years for other foreigners (Spanish Civil Code, Article 22).

The point of the following analysis is not to compare national naturalization regimes but to list a spectrum of criteria.[12] Notes on individual countries are therefore meant to illustrate a specific rule but not to give an overall judgement on this country's naturalization policy. I will consider only rules in contemporary Western liberal democracies. This narrow range for empirical references is partly due to a lack of information. However, it is also suggested by my general aim to develop a critique of the allocation of citizenship by using liberal democratic norms in order to assess the current practices of states claiming to be liberal democracies. I therefore do not only disregard a large number of countries but also some criteria which had been in force in Western states not so long ago, such as exclusion on racial grounds.[13]

In the following table the columns distinguish criteria into those facilitating or impeding naturalization, and the rows classify them according to their affinity to the three basic principles of citizenship allocation: territorial birth and residence, descent and family membership, and political consent. These affinities are not necessarily unique. Often, the same criterion can be interpreted in different ways. A criminal record can, for example, be seen as an indicator of social disintegration and therefore related to the conditions of ordinary residence in a state territory. But it may also be understood as a breach of the fundamental political obligation derived from tacit consent to respect the laws of the polity where one takes residence, and thus as proof that a person is not fit to become a loyal citizen in a democratic community which gives these laws to itself. The main idea is not to suggest a certain arrangement of the criteria but to show that, taken together, the three basic principles provide the underlying frame of justification for naturalization rules.

Table 2: Criteria for facilitated and impeded naturalization

		facilitated admission: shorter residence period and/or optional admission		impeded admission: criteria in addition to residence emphasizing discretion
territorial birth and residence	(1) (2)	birth in territory former citizenship or residence	(7) (8) (9)	social integration economic integration no public order threat
descent and family membership	(3) (4)	co-ethnic immigrants marriage and extension to family members	(10) (11)	proficiency in language cultural assimilation
political consent	(5) (6)	special services for the state political refugees	(12) (13)	political knowledge and loyalty renunciation of previous citizenship

(1) In many countries with *ius sanguinis* laws, birth in the territory is nevertheless a reason for facilitated or optional acquisition of citizenship. Article 44 of the French *Code de la Nationalité* was until recently a rare case of even automatic admission which combined *ius soli* and *ius domicili*. Children born of alien parents in France (who had not themselves been born in France) acquired French citizenship at the age of majority if they had lived in France for the last five years and unless they explicitly declined this offer. The new conservative government has now introduced a requirement of application which brings the French law in line with similar provisions in Belgium and Italy. Automatic citizenship attribution in the manner of the old law is still different from general birthright citizenship. Consent in the old law was defined negatively as the absence of explicit dissent and is now redefined as requiring a positive initiative on the part of the individual. Citizenship can be called optional in both cases because individuals can claim it as their right. Consent has been strengthened in the new law at the

expense of inclusiveness towards second-generation immigrants, which had been the overriding concern at the historical origin of the rule.

(2) Almost all states have some rule which gives preference in naturalization to former citizens. In the Belgian and French laws this is a weak option which excludes those who had gained their former citizenship by naturalization rather than by birth, and allows authorities to refuse an application. In Germany and Austria there are special legal claims of readmission for those who had lost their citizenship during the Nazi regime. The Netherlands and Switzerland provide only for facilitated naturalization of former citizens without giving them entitlements (de Groot, 1989, pp. 223–5, 232–3). The underlying reasons for these rules are not necessarily related to territorial membership in the society. Former citizens can also be readmitted because they had once been regarded as members of the political community or because they still belong to the same ethnic group. However, the territorial interpretation is the most plausible one. Someone who had never resided in the country of her citizenship and has voluntarily given up her status as an external member will hardly have strong ties to that country. Only where such persons had been arbitrarily deprived of their citizenship would there be good reasons for preferential readmission.

The territorial argument can be extended beyond the group of former nominal citizens. Belgium grants facilitated naturalization also to those who had been residents in the country during their childhood (de Groot, 1989, p. 230). In Germany the 1990 Aliens Act has introduced an option of return for second-generation foreigners who had spent their childhood in Germany. The same law included for the first time a 'regular claim to naturalization' (*Regelanspruch auf Einbürgerung*). Those living in Germany for 15 years and young foreigners who apply between their 16th and 23th birthdays, who have lived in Germany for eight years and have attended school for six years, will be generally granted naturalization. Since 1 July 1993 this 'regular naturalization' has been transformed into a legal claim of the applicant, i.e. into a kind of optional citizenship.

The combination of a right to reimmigration and optional naturalization will in some cases lead to citizenship admission based on former residence. A similar effect could be achieved in a much simpler manner by allowing for interruptions of the normal residence period required for naturalization. However, in most countries the whole period must have been spent in the country immediately before application. In Germany and Switzerland this is required only for five years (out of the ten and twelve demanded in these states), in the Netherlands two years before application are sufficient for those who have lived in the country for a total of ten years (de Groot, 1989, p. 240).

(3) While, until the recent cautious changes described above, Germany has been extremely restrictive in naturalizing its guest workers,[14] it has simultaneously given the strongest possible option to those who are considered to be ethnic Germans; they obtain citizenship automatically when immigrating to Germany. Citizens of the former GDR were in a peculiar position; even while they lived in that state they were legally considered to be German citizens of the same kind as West German ones. In section 2.3 I have already mentioned the Israeli Law of Return which has similar provisions for Jews of any geographic or ethnic origin. Facilitated naturalization after only two years of residence for citizens of Latin American countries in Spain can also be quoted as an example for preferential treatment of co-ethnics.

(4) Until well into the 20th century, citizenship rights were considered to be a male privilege. The citizenship of wives followed regularly that of their husbands. A married woman generally could not acquire a membership different from her husband's by option or by naturalization. A female alien received citizenship automatically by marriage and she lost it similarly by marrying a foreigner. In the USA automatic acquisition was abandoned in 1922 and automatic loss in 1931 (Ueda, 1982, p. 135). Both rules were prohibited in the 1957 New York Convention concerning the nationality of wives (de Groot, 1989, p. 32, 309). Thereafter, the system of unitary citizenship of the family eroded gradually in Western Europe, too. When finally, equal treatment of genders was established much later during the 1970s and 1980s, it generally had the effect of making access to naturalization by marriage more difficult for women rather than easier for men. Today this method of citizenship acquisition is no longer automatic in any OECD country. Only Belgium, France, Italy, Portugal and Turkey make it available by declaration, while Austria in this case grants a legal claim to regular naturalization. All other states require an application for discretionary naturalization.

However, in the USA and in most Western European countries, marriage to a citizen is still seen as a reason for optional or facilitated citizenship.[15] Many also reduce residence and other requirements for spouses who apply to be naturalized simultaneously with their partners. Thus gender discrimination has given way to what could be called the discrimination of singles. Nevertheless, there is certainly reason to assume that persons sharing a household might have an essential interest in sharing the same citizenship and that this adds to their claims as individual members of the receiving society. Easier access to naturalization can facilitate family reunification and prevent involuntary separation if an alien spouse loses residence entitlements. Granting facilitated admission does of course not mean that applicants should be pressed to naturalize their whole family.[16] If general naturalization became more optional than it is now, the only privilege for spouses would be a reduction of residence requirements. Currently, there is a counter-tendency in Western European legislations prompted by the aim to prevent the acquisition of citizenship by marriages of convenience.[17] France and Belgium have recently lengthened waiting periods from six months to one and three years respectively.

Minors used to have the same position in nationality law as women. In *ius sanguinis* their citizenship followed that of the father. Only if they were born out of wedlock did they acquire the mother's citizenship. When the father acquired a new citizenship that of his children changed automatically. The later modification that citizenship can be transmitted by both parents has increased the scope of choice with regard to the children's affiliation. However, it is still basically the parents' choice, not the child's. Only a few laws require the assent of a minor for a change of citizenship[18] or even allow such a child to apply for naturalization. Legitimation of an 'illegitimate' child by the father, or adoption, are further ways of acquiring a new citizenship during childhood.

(5) If naturalization is understood as a privilege granted by the state rather than as a right exercised by the applicant, it seems an obvious idea to take into account special merits of individuals and special interests of the state. Discretionary procedures therefore frequently allow for a shortening of residence requirements when the applicant has performed a valuable service for the state or can be expected to do so in future. Many states take this possibility into account by allowing for exceptions in favour of an applicant with regard to the standard criteria of naturalization. Some, like France and Austria,[19] specify the requirement of exceptional achievements. In Greece voluntary service in the army is also a path towards citizenship. A similar provision allowed many European emigrants and refugees to be naturalized in the United States during World War II.[20]

(6) Article 34 of the Geneva Refugee Convention is a rare example of an international convention containing provisions about naturalization in member states. It obliges states of asylum to facilitate the integration and naturalization of refugees and to reduce the costs of the procedure as far as possible. This is also exceptional because entitlements to integration and naturalization here seem to be derived from specific needs of a group of immigrants rather than from special bonds of territory, descent and voluntary membership. In states which require the renunciation of a previous citizenship in naturalization, refugees are generally exempted from this provision. It would be absurd to ask them to obtain permission for voluntary expatriation from their persecutors and to give the state of origin an opportunity for denying its victims a change of citizenship.

Facilitated naturalization for refugees can also intend to show the receiving state's liberal democratic character. This was a major motive for accommodating emigrants from the Soviet Bloc during the Cold War period, and the absence of a strong international camp ideologically opposed to the West helps to explain present reluctance to host the more recent flows of refugees. For similar reasons refugees who are the victims of wars, civil wars or famines have not been given the same consideration as those who are individually persecuted for their political beliefs and actions. What distinguishes refugees of all sorts from other kinds of migrants is that the former have been deprived of the basic elements of substantive citizenship, i.e. of protection of their fundamental rights by their own state. In this sense, the provision that receiving states should not only provide a temporary shelter but also a new citizenship, derives from a deeper understanding of the problem. By accepting refugees as new citizens states of asylum also emphasize the Hobbesian image of the polity as a voluntary association of those who seek protection from violence.[20]

The need for a new citizenship conflicts with a different priority in refugee policies, which is to encourage repatriation whenever possible. The United Nations' High Commissioner for Refugees (UNHCR) understandably sees this as one of its main tasks because receiving states are willing to take in more refugees when they can be assured that many will not stay for long. Article 1C(5) of the Geneva Convention as well as national laws also provide for a loss of asylum status when the situation in the state of origin changes so that the refugee no longer has a well-founded fear of being persecuted upon return.[21] Rather than restricting access to refugee status and to citizenship for those deemed to be only temporary refugees, receiving states should keep both options open and let people, who can be assumed to have a strong interest in returning anyway, make their own decisions whether to apply for citizenship.

(7) Procedures for ordinary naturalization can be biased in favour of, or against, admissions. The former is the case when criteria in addition to residence are few, precise, easy to meet and when an applicant meeting them can be certain to be admitted. The German law on citizenship of 1913 and the naturalization guidelines of 1977 are among the clearest examples of the opposite tendency. Here discretion is biased against admission. The general principle is that awarding German citizenship can be considered only when there is a public interest in naturalization.[22] Personal wishes and economic interests of an applicant cannot be regarded as decisive since resident foreigners enjoy far-reaching rights and liberties anyway (guideline 2.2).

The most plausible interpretation of the criterion of social integration is simply legal residence. Somebody who has lived for a long time in a society and has been legally permitted to reside, is integrated in that sense of the word which must be regarded as the only relevant one for decisions about legal status. Yet if it is left unspecified, the criterion of social integration can give authorities the broadest scope for discretionary decisions or for the implementation of administrative guidelines beyond and outside the letter of the law. In Germany this criterion is defined as 'integration into the German ways of life' and comes in addition to cultural and linguistic assimilation and requirements of political loyalty. Article 14 of the Swiss citizenship law defines the individual suitability of an applicant in very similar terms. In contrast with this retrospective integration requirement, the Belgian law demands from the applicant the 'will to integrate' (de Groot, 1989, p. 251).

Even the simple criterion of residence itself leaves considerable scope for diverging interpretations when it is seen as a proxy for social integration. One variation which has already been mentioned under (2) above results from the possibility of interruptions within a given residence requirement, another one from the definition of *legal* residence. Virtually all states demand that an applicant for naturalization must have a valid residence permit or must not have received a deportation order at the time of application. Some states, however, extend this condition explicitly to the whole period of residence while others make it at least theoretically possible to include periods of irregular stay. Many national laws take an in-between position and demand that an applicant ought not to have been expelled at any time in the past. In others this condition is implicitly covered by the requirement of a clear record. In the USA, Australia and in Britain, residence is projected into the future as well (as is integration in Belgium). An undertaking to reside in the country after naturalization is required in these states.

(8) Apart from gender and racist discrimination, property qualifications have been the most important exclusionary characteristic in the history of democratic citizenship. The latter still persist in some countries' rules for naturalization. In Germany and Austria applicants must have sufficient means of existence; in Switzerland this criterion is strongly applied at the level of provincial administrations (de Groot, 1989, p. 263). Most other Western citizenship laws do not state this explicitly. However, independent income is frequently a necessary condition for legal residence anyway so that a separate test in naturalization is rather redundant.

There seem to be two different rationales behind this criterion. One is to save on expenses for social welfare entitlements which are tied to nominal citizenship. This is obviously less relevant in contemporary Western welfare states where social rights are primarily derived from residence and employment. However, in a number of these states immigrants may lose their residence entitlements even after living in the country for many years if they become dependent on public assistance. Excluding them from naturalization thus keeps open the option for the receiving state to export unemployment and poverty. The second reason is an ideological one related to the exclusion of welfare recipients from active citizenship, which was common in 19th century democracies. The idea is that only citizens with independent means of subsistence can be trusted to form an independent opinion in political matters. While this rule can no longer be applied to native citizens a majority of whom have become dependent in essential ways on public arrangements for social security, the same old arguments are still brought forward with regard to immigrants.

(9) The most common criteria of social integration is good character. Where it is defined positively (such as in Britain) it creates a large scope for administrative discretion. The corresponding negative formulations are absence of a criminal record, no convictions, no public order offences, not having been expelled before, etc. They constrain discretion by shifting the burden of proof for rejection towards the authorities. However, in some laws a threat to public order must not necessarily be documented by past criminal offences and convictions. Unspecified state interests or an evaluation of the applicant's past life by administrative bodies can result in rejection, too.

(10) Proficiency in the dominant language of the country is the most frequent cultural requirement.[23] It can be related to the nation seen as a homogeneous linguistic community, but could also be considered as a social integration indicator. The test whether the first or the second aspect dominates lies in the general policy of linguistic training and education for immigrants. Where only few or costly courses are offered, the linguistic naturalization criterion serves to maintain the citizenship boundary between language groups. Where immigrants are genuinely encouraged to learn the local language without being deprived of their own one, the same criterion can be intended as both an incentive and a test for social integration.

Knowledge of a language can of course be tested in very different ways. In the USA the 1952 Immigration and Naturalization Act 'significantly raised the qualifications for citizenship: an applicant not only has to be able to speak and understand English, but he must be able to read and write "simple words and phrases"' (Ueda, 1982, pp. 46–7). The German guidelines require proficiency in oral and written German to that extent which can be expected from persons of the applicant's social position.

(11) Some nationality laws are explicit in requiring not only social integration and linguistic education but also cultural assimilation in a wider sense. In addition to integration into the German ways of life the German guidelines stipulate a voluntary and permanent affiliation (*Hinwendung*) with Germany, which can be understood to refer to the nation in a political

as well as a cultural sense. Similarly, Article 14 of the Swiss law asks authorities to test whether an applicant is familiar with the Swiss ways of life, customs and habits. In France assimilation is primarily documented by knowledge of French, but the decree regulating the application of the law mentions customs and habits, too (de Groot, 1989, p. 91).

(12) Political integration criteria most explicitly link consent in admission to an internally consensual construction of the political community itself. An applicant has to know and to respect those rules by which the polity democratically governs itself. As positive criteria, knowledge of the constitution and history of the country are frequently applied. Section 313 of the US Immigration and Naturalization Act provides an example of a negative regulation by excluding communists and all those who advocate a violent overthrow of the government. Austria has a peculiar provision that an applicant must not entertain relations with a foreign state which would damage the interests or reputation of the republic if naturalization were granted (Article 10 (1) Z.8).

The oath of allegiance which often closes a naturalization procedure cannot be regarded as a test of political integration. It rather serves as an initiation ritual for the new member of the community. This oath is oriented towards the future rather than towards the past. It does not document whether the applicant has successfully integrated into the political community but implies a promise to be a loyal citizen. Because of its ritualized form the promise may of course be faked. The kind of commitment which it is meant to express cannot be tested either during or after naturalization. Only when conditions are such that voluntary commitment can emerge spontaneously among immigrants and can become the major motive for naturalization will this ritual not be an empty one (see section 4.3 below).

(13) The requirement to renounce a previous citizenship has been traditionally among the most important and also most common naturalization criteria. A number of Western European states have liberalized their citizenship laws in this respect recently (Çinar, 1994b). For first-generation labour migrants who have significant interests and rights in their states of origins, this rule works as a very efficient deterrent that keeps naturalization rates generally low. It also confirms an essential aspect of the self-image of the political community that citizenship should be unique and exclusive of other affiliations of the same kind. This demand can be derived from both nationalist and republican traditions. Membership in a nation is always construed as exclusive in this manner. For cultural and primordialist nationalism one single national membership is ascribed at birth. Political nationalism in the French tradition can allow more easily for voluntary

changes of affiliation but will interpret the wish to retain a former nationality as an indicator of insufficient assimilation and commitment.

Republican hostility towards multiple citizenship is rooted in the idea of sovereignty, not in that of voluntary association. In the civil society model of voluntary association, memberships in different associations are generally not mutually incompatible (see section 6.2). Neither foundational nor internal consent imply exclusivity of membership. Sovereignty, however, seems to require just this. States cannot be called sovereign if foreign powers occupy part of their territories and can enact and enforce laws therein. In a similar manner sovereignty has been associated with distinctive ranges of jurisdiction over mutually exclusive sets of persons. This view becomes untenable once it has been understood that the territorial and the personal aspect of sovereignty already conflict with each other once there are foreign residents in a state. The scandal of dual citizenship for traditional republicans lies not in sovereignty *tout court* but in the identification of the people with the sovereign. The quintessential right of citizenship is that of political participation in the process of collective self-determination of the *demos*. Dual citizens are not only subject to two different sovereigns but they are themselves integral parts of two sovereigns. The image of Siamese twins comes to one's mind.

In a purely procedural view of democracy, states conceived as voluntary associations might have the *right* to decide that their membership is incompatible with that of all other or of certain other states but there is no imperative *necessity* for adopting such a rule. Representative forms of democracy, in which citizens do not literally rule themselves, considerably reduce the plausibility of the objection that one and the same person cannot be a member of two different sovereign peoples. If a democracy is, furthermore, committed to liberal principles the norm of inclusiveness in the allocation of citizenship will provide the strongest argument against renunciation requirements.

Other political traditions and considerations may lead to tolerating dual citizenship only within certain limits. There are three ways of modifying dual citizenship which are again related to the basic principles of descent, territory and consent respectively. First, multiple membership may only be allowed with certain states which share a common history, language and culture. Spain and Portugal have accepted and sometimes even encouraged dual citizenship for people from their former Latin American colonies.[24] Second, the non-residential citizenship may be regarded as dormant, i.e. completely inactive. Again, dual citizenship between Spain and Latin American states provides an example for this model. Where the territorial element of sovereignty is more emphasized than national membership, dormant dual citizenship must seem an attractive solution which will help to avoid conflicting claims of states towards individuals. The problem is that not all rights which connect individuals to states become irrelevant when they live outside the territory.[25] Third, dual citizenship may be granted as a temporary and transitional status only. After some time citizens are expected to choose one country, i.e. declare where their subjective preferences or stronger ties lie. In Italy, from 1983 up to the new citizenship law of February 1992, dual citizens had to opt for one of their affiliations within one year after reaching their majority (de Groot, 1989, p. 124). In most other cases dual citizenship is made transitional only after acquiring a new citizenship by naturalization. This can be done by both sending and receiving states. After a certain time, sending states can denaturalize their citizens who have been naturalized abroad and similarly, receiving states can make naturalization conditional upon the renunciation of a previous citizenship after a few years. However, citizenship is not an item you can first borrow for testing before finally purchasing it. Whatever the conditions of acquisition are they cannot be followed by harsher conditions for retention. Such rules imply that dual citizenship has only been tolerated as a temporary but irregular status. Making dual citizenship transitional in this way is clearly derived from the idea that, ultimately, the political commitment of membership must be expressed in unique loyalty.

4.2. EVALUATION OF ADMISSION CRITERIA

Our brief and incomplete overview over the variety of rules in admission should have demonstrated sufficiently that there is a broad range of feasible policies emphasizing discretion or option and that both principles express different conceptions of consent. A standard model of discretionary admission in naturalizations cannot be deduced from the basic principle of consensual membership in voluntary associations. Instead, it has to be argued on normative grounds why certain admission criteria are necessary or legitimate and why certain groups ought to be preferentially admitted or generally excluded. When there is a large population of potential citizens in the country, rules of naturalization will often be a better indicator for the self-image and the ideological traditions prevailing in a state than official pronouncements. Legal rules and administrative practices confirm liberal, republican or nationalist principles by defining who is entitled to membership, who can be considered as a candidate and who must remain outside.

As shown above, the most common forms of optional citizenship today are those for co-ethnic immigrants, for children born in the territory of alien parents, for readmissions of former citizens and for alien spouses of citizens. Some liberal democratic authors have recently argued for also extending optional citizenship more generally to long-term resident immigrants. Michael Walzer, who defends rather restrictive norms for the admission of immigrants, at the same time insists that 'the processes of self-determination through which a democratic state shapes its internal life, must be open, and equally open, to all those men and women who live within its territory, work in the local economy, and are subject to local law. Hence, second admissions (naturalization) depend on first admissions (immigration) and are subject only to certain constraints of time and qualification, never to the ultimate constraint of closure' (Walzer, 1983, pp. 60–1). Joseph Carens thoroughly examines different naturalization criteria and arrives at the following conclusion: 'Naturalization laws should therefore make citizenship available to all long-term residents requiring only the passage of time and the meeting of modest, inexpensive formalities.' Referring to Rogers Brubaker's distinction between discretionary and as-of-right models Carens argues that 'only the as-of-right model is morally permissible' (Carens, 1989, p. 46).[26]

But have not guest workers and many other immigrants voluntarily agreed to conditions which provided only for temporary residence and envisaged eventual remigration? How can a receiving state be morally obliged to offer them citizenship if this was never included among the conditions under which they had been admitted as immigrants?

A first answer could be that not all terms of contract can be accepted as morally binding because of mutual consent alone, if alternative options were severely constrained for one of the partners and if the effects of the contract seriously violate individual autonomy. Thus, voluntary submission into slavery is generally regarded as impermissible.[27] One might dismiss the binding force of consensual conditions of entry on the grounds that some of these conditions imply renouncing fundamental rights. However, not all restrictions imposed by entry clauses are inherently morally wrong. If somebody agrees to be let into a country on condition that she leaves it again within a specified time, this need not be an illegitimate requirement in many cases (unless the person is a refugee and the situation causing her flight persists). Even renouncing one's right to political participation by agreeing to be excluded from voting rights during a limited period of residence can hardly be regarded as consenting to an immoral demand.

Both Walzer and Carens also attack this second line of defence for the validity of restrictive entry clauses. 'After a while, the terms of admission become irrelevant' (Carens, 1989, p. 44). But why should consent in conditions of entry lose its binding force as time passes? Walzer hints at a substantial distinction: 'this kind of consent, given at a single moment in time, while it is sufficient to legitimize market transactions, is not sufficient for democratic politics' (Walzer, 1983, p. 58). Commitments incurred from voluntary market contracts at a single moment can be binding for a long span of time without becoming thereby irrelevant. Political consent in democratic rule is qualitatively different because it concerns 'the ability to make decisions over periods of time, to change the rules' (ibid.).

I would interpret this argument in the following way: the time horizons of democratic politics allow for exclusion of those who merely come as visitors. They do not share the relevant collective experiences of the past, do not take part in ongoing processes of public opinion formation in the present and will not be able to make credible commitments for the future. Being in a territory means being subject to the laws of a sovereign but not necessarily *at the same time* being entitled to participate in the exercise of sovereignty. There is a temporal disjuncture between the single moment of entering a country and the process of becoming a resident member of a society.

However, long-term resident immigrants gradually turn from mere subjects of the state into members of society. In an inclusive liberal democracy they become thereby entitled to all the rights of political membership. Nobody can remain indefinitely excluded from liberties and rights of participation in collective self-determination when entering a community which defines membership as sharing in these rights. The norm of inclusiveness which specifically characterizes liberal democracies means that one enters the political community *de facto* by becoming a resident. Entry into a territory is not sufficient and formal acceptance of membership by the state through naturalization is not necessary for the basic qualification of membership. In liberal democratic polities civil society is independent from the state with regard to its criteria of membership, and at the same time represented in the state with regard to the processes of political deliberation without excluding any social group. If representation is tied to nominal membership, then acquisition of nominal membership must be optional rather than discretionary. The only question open for debate is after what period people are no longer visitors but not whether they ever acquire a right to full membership.

But why stop then with optional citizenship, rather than guaranteeing total inclusion by attributing citizenship to long-term residents in the same manner as citizenship by birth? Citizenship is a status of basic equality in a political community. Should not the ways of acquisition be equal for all as well? If the essential quality of democratic citizenship is that it expresses a consensual form of membership it ought to be consensual for all and not just for immigrants. If, however, the value of citizenship is in the bundle of rights which are attached to the nominal status and if citizenship acquisition cannot be consensual for all, why should it then be consensual for anybody? The latter view might thus lead to the conclusion that naturalization ought to be automatic or even mandatory rather than optional. When including all its adult members in a status of equal citizenship is of overriding importance for a political community this sounds like a good reason not to ask long-term immigrants whether they would like to become members but to make them so without their consent.

Liberals will object to this latter view that it is always better to have more choices rather than less. I still have not given sufficient reasons why there cannot be a universal liberty of choosing one's citizenship. Although some of the paradoxes inherent in this Lockean idea have been already mentioned in the previous chapter, the argument is yet to be completed. I will argue now why conditions of entry into citizenship are unequal for immigrants and natives, and will discuss the parallel question why conditions of exit are unequal for resident citizens and emigrants in the following chapter.

If choosing one's citizenship were a basic liberty it ought to be equal for all. If it is impossible to universalize this liberty it cannot be considered as a basic one. From this latter view it does not follow that no one should enjoy it. I want to suggest that there are two reasons for letting immigrants choose whether to become citizens of their host countries. First, this liberty is of substantially different value for immigrants and for natives. Second, the choice is a meaningful one for immigrants in a way that it is not for natives. Under favourable conditions it expresses commitment to the political community beyond the instrumental value of citizenship rights.

At first glance this looks like defending an unjustifiable privilege. When liberty is defined negatively as the absence of restraints on choice it is exactly the same for everybody who enjoys it. Yet its worth will be different depending on the conditions under which choice is exercised and on its consequences for the individuals' life plans. Following Rawls one can define the worth of liberty to persons as proportional to their capacity to advance their ends within a framework of equal liberties (Rawls, 1971, p. 204). In liberal egalitarian theory this fact does not justify an unequal distribution of liberties, but secondary norms for redistribution in order to give people in different social positions equal opportunities, resources or capabilities.[28] The problem we are discussing presently cannot be solved by redistribution. In order to compensate for the diminished worth of the liberties and rights of citizenship for immigrants, they ought to be given an additional liberty to choose their citizenship.[29]

Let me illustrate this by examining the worth of political liberties.[30] For native citizens, the freedoms of speech, assembly and association mean a chance to influence public opinion in civil society and to convince other citizens of their political proposals for the future of the state and society where they live. Foreign residents nowadays mostly enjoy the same liberties

which had been long denied to them. However, their corresponding
activities still have a different impact and so the same liberty is of different
worth. They can choose to orient their political action towards their
countries of origin. Assuming that this is not restricted by the receiving state
for reasons of good foreign relations, exile politics still faces the difficulty
of achieving an impact from outside the society towards which their
proposals are directed. Alternatively, immigrants can choose to get involved
in the politics of their host state (assuming again that they are allowed to do
so). Yet here the fact that they have not lived in this society all their lives
and their status as foreign citizens who are not, or not fully, represented as a
part of the electorate, will severely restrain their political impact. When
immigrants are denied access to naturalization this will perpetuate the latter
handicap; when they are pushed into a citizenship they do not want, this
will hamper their orientation towards societies of origin. Allowing them to
choose between different nominal citizenships does not fully compensate
for their political marginalization but this liberty enables them to maximize
the political impact of whatever orientation they choose for themselves.
Similar arguments can be made for other fundamental liberties such as
secure residence in a host state and the right to return to one's state of
citizenship.

Some readers might object that by choosing a country of immigration
and by staying there voluntarily, immigrants have already implicitly opted
for membership in the receiving society and this justifies mandatory or
automatic procedures of naturalization for them. However, many
immigrants have not chosen their state of residence and most have not
chosen it because of its political constitution. Native fundamental dissenters
might also claim that they have not chosen their country of whose
constitution they do not approve. Could they not with similar reasons insist
on a right to choose a different citizenship? I will attempt to show in the
following chapter that their demands are sufficiently met when there are
democratic instruments for changing the constitution and when they are free
to change their citizenship after leaving their country. Where these
fundamental choices are open to them they will find little additional worth
in a more extensive liberty of actively choosing or renouncing the
citizenship of their country. Immigrants, however, have a citizenship to lose
which they might have good reasons to retain and the citizenship of their
country of residence may be of little value to their own goals in life.

The argument for mandatory or automatic citizenship for immigrants[31]
thus consists of two parts both of which should be rejected: adopting the
nominal citizenship of their host state is neither naturally implied in the
social circumstances of long-term residence nor is it implied in previous
conscious choices which can be attributed to them. The first implication is

denied by showing that, in contrast with native citizens, migrants have a wider framework of social ties of membership and may refer to different states as the focus of their interests. The second implication can be rejected by demonstrating that the ties of full social membership of long-term immigrants and their attendant claims to substantial citizenship rights do not always depend on their voluntary choices. Therefore, a naturalization decision need not be implied in such choices either.

Yet the argument is still a rather weak one as long as naturalization is only considered as an access to equal rights. Many of the objections against automatic or mandatory naturalization lose their force when multiple citizenship becomes a rule. Would not this guarantee full inclusion of immigrants in the society of residence while not depriving them of their ties to a society of origin? Certainly they should be given the choice to opt out of their previous citizenship if they wish to do so. But why should they be allowed to remain aliens forever in a society that highly values equal citizenship for all its residents? Here a second reason comes in: the acquisition of citizenship is not only of different value for immigrants and natives, but has a different meaning for them, too.

Seen from another angle the liberty to choose naturalization involves a duty, too. This duty is to make a conscious and public choice about one's membership in a political community. Such choice is not only influenced by the balance of legal rights and obligations but also by the immigrants' levels of commitment towards both the states of origin and of residence. Native citizens are never asked to make such a choice. If immigrants were naturalized automatically they would not have to declare their commitment either. If naturalization were mandatory for them, the primary motive ascribed to them would be to avoid negative sanctions (such as losing their right of residence) rather than voluntary commitment.

Why should immigrants then have to show their commitment? The answer could be found in a theory of political socialization in liberal democracies. Any such state has to educate its future citizens to be committed to democratic norms, and it has to create a system of institutional incentives for adult citizens so that respecting these norms becomes both rational and reasonable for them. Commitment to liberal democracy is, however, not the same as commitment to a particular liberal democratic state. In such a state politics is restrained but not completely determined by these norms at the level of constitutional, legislative or administrative decision-making, and any such state will have its particular traditions and institutions. Native citizens who have learned to respect basic norms will also learn to be committed to the more specific institutions not so much by their education as by continuously participating in public life.

This is an experience which is not available to immigrants in the same way. Voluntary and optional naturalization thus indeed expresses a specific kind of 'political resocialization'.[32] It would be misleading to think of naturalization as a test of education in liberal democracy. Even immigrants who come from authoritarian and totalitarian states cannot be submitted to re-education in this sense. The capacity to be a citizen of a liberal democracy must in principle be ascribed to any person who has not given strong evidence of the contrary in speech or deeds. A summary discrimination of groups of origin in this respect would be in plain contradiction with liberal norms. During World War II German political refugees in Western Europe and Japanese detainees in the USA experienced this kind of suspicion and discrimination. Today it is articulated in only slightly more subtle forms against immigrants from countries where Islam is the dominant religion. What is expressed in voluntary and optional naturalization is not more and not less than an individual decision to become a citizen of this particular democratic state but not a decision to convert to democracy. In order to avoid misunderstandings, some further peculiarities of this process of political resocialization ought to be spelled out.

First, this is primarily an act of self-education. The receiving state is not in the position of a teacher, the immigrant is no student and the citizenship document is no examination certificate. In voluntary naturalization the immigrant states implicitly that she has acquainted herself sufficiently with the political and legal system of the country to decide responsibly about her future membership. This is why immigrants can enjoy a claim or option to naturalization without being tested for their individual qualification.

Second, the contents of the curriculum are not written down in a syllabus. Immigrants do not have to take courses in constitutional law, political system, geography and history of the country.[33] Such knowledge may be useful but is external to the process of self-education. Catching up with the native citizens' political socialization is for migrants a result of their participation in civil society and public political life.

Third, this path of integration can be blocked by two major obstacles: barriers of social structure and of communication. Ethnic segregation and distinctive languages of immigrants can transform into such obstacles but need not always do so. The immigrant enclave in a receiving society can also serve as a pool of resources for the newcomer which allow her a smoother process of integration. And keeping a native language alive can help to maintain a feeling of self-esteem that is often essential in an unknown and potentially hostile social environment. Segregation and linguistic plurality turn into obstacles for social and political integration when boundaries become impermeable, when immigrants become trapped in their communities because they are locked out from social positions outside and when they do not learn the language of the receiving society because they do not feel any need to communicate with its members. Politics cannot always do much about deeply entrenched divisions cutting civil society into different segments. But politics can certainly make things worse. Sanctioning immigrants who are seen as unwilling to integrate is always a counterproductive strategy in the context of liberal states. Attempts to break the horizontal segmentation of society by forceful desegregation and assimilation will rarely achieve their aim, and will reinforce vertical hierarchies in which groups of immigrants are kept at the bottom. The only strategy that will work is one of increasing opportunities and creating incentives for mobility and for learning the language of the receiving country.

Fourth, naturalization must be seen as an open choice among fair alternatives. The result of becoming acquainted with the political and legal system of the immigration state can as well be a decision against naturalization. What does it mean to say that these alternatives must be offered at their fair value? It implies, for example, that naturalization should not be made more difficult by high fees diminishing its net value below that of the substantial citizenship which can be achieved afterwards. It also implies that options are no longer fairly balanced when a negative decision is charged with the threat of sanctions such as a potential loss of one's residence permit.

Fifth, a decision against naturalization need not be argued. Those who do not apply cannot be understood as implicitly rejecting the political system of their host country. Their reasons may as well lie in strong ties to their countries of origin and intentions to return there, even if these plans are never carried out. Optional citizenship becomes available upon application. This means that application documents a kind of public commitment while reasons for non-application remain private. Automatic or mandatory citizenship would reverse this by exposing the reasons against naturalization to public attention and scrutiny. Discretionary naturalization may lead to turning the reasons for applying into private ones. Where the final result depends on the judgement of public administrators rather than of applicants, the latter will often try to conceal their preferences from others. Naturalization then becomes reduced to an attempt to improve one's legal position and disconnected from any form of public commitment.[34]

Sixth, a naturalization decision takes a certain time, during which experience with this state and its institutions can be accumulated. In a perspective of optional citizenship the time of residence acquires a specific meaning. It is not just an indicator for the factual consolidation of social membership from which citizenship ought to follow automatically, but rather a period needed for integration into a political and legal system. It is also not a test period during which the state examines the immigrant's worthiness to become a full citizen, but rather an opportunity for the immigrant to carry out her own tests which also take some time before a sound decision can be made. The duty implied in this is that the immigrant ought to have tested the receiving state sufficiently before reaching a conclusion.

Seventh, training for citizenship by acquiring practical experience with the political and legal system presupposes the granting of citizenship rights already before naturalization. In order to understand this essential conclusion, compare a liberal democratic state with a hierarchical one and with an egalitarian, but exclusive democracy. In a hierarchical system of estates immigrants can integrate without much difficulty. Membership in the political system is mediated through membership in estates. As all the rest of the population immigrants will be equally subject to the supreme authority and as all the other groups they will be assigned a specific bundle of obligations and rights. Integration does not presuppose that these bundles are of equal weight or content. In the egalitarian but exclusive democracy of the classical Athenian *polis,* the immigrant *metics* were neither slaves nor citizens. Some could be naturalized sometimes. Yet they certainly did not enjoy a right to become citizens. Their status outside the *polis* but within the city was never seen as a challenge to the internal legitimacy of the democratic system. Liberal democracy differs normatively from both models. It combines the drive for inclusion of the former with the demand for equality of rights among citizens of the latter. Political integration in such a system does not just require rights for all those subject to political rule but essentially *equal* rights. Practicing for this kind of citizenship is impossible when there is an entrenched cleavage between first- and second-class status. This does not imply that *all* rights have to be equal. But the common legitimation of different rights for immigrants and nominal citizens in exclusionary democracy must be reversed. Instead of starting with a self-evident distinction between citizens and aliens and then extending some rights of citizenship to aliens, exceptions from equality have to be argued for and the only reasons which can be accepted for inequality will be those that refer to requirements for maintaining liberal citizenship itself.[35]

I contend that these considerations sufficiently justify making the decision to acquire a new citizenship an unconstrained option offered by the state and an active choice for long-term resident immigrants rather than an automatic, discretionary or mandatory transition. However, an optional procedure of naturalization does not yet fully preclude restrictive or inegalitarian rules for the admission of immigrants to nominal citizenship. First, it need not guarantee voluntary access for all permanent residents.

Even if a state grants entitlements to naturalization it can still reduce the eligible population by adding further admission criteria. Second, once they have been admitted must naturalized citizens also be accepted as full and equal members of the polity? Optional procedures do not match well with individual tests for fitness and with discrimination against the newly admitted members. They require fairly objective criteria of eligibility such as residence or birth in the territory. The normative argument for making naturalization optional rather than discretionary can be completed by dismissing a number of common criteria as irrelevant or illiberal. The second question is easier to answer and I will take it up first. In liberal democracies membership must be equal independently of the mode of acquisition. This has not been generally recognized until recently and the full implications of this principle remain to be drawn. Conceiving of entry into citizenship as an option strengthens the position of those newly admitted within the association and thus helps to support their claim for equal status.

Distinctions between old and new members can be of different sorts: they are temporary or for life, they concern either all immigrants or only certain categories, they involve different kinds of rights and they can be formally expressed by different procedures of admission. Let me give some examples for each of these aspects. Although this is a rather marginal form of discrimination, the best-known example for a lifelong discrimination of all immigrant citizens is the US American law which excludes a naturalized person from becoming president.[36] In Sweden, Cabinet ministers had to be native born until 1973; since then the requirement is only that immigrants must have been naturalized for at least ten years.[37] France introduced during the 1930s a number of '*incapacitations*' for naturalized citizens, which denied them access to certain professions and political rights (Arendt, 1967, n. 40, p. 285). The last vestiges of this policy were only eliminated under the first Mitterrand government. Until 1973 the newly naturalized had to wait five years before being allowed to vote and until 1983 they were not eligible as candidates in political elections for ten years after naturalization. In Belgium a similar distinction was highlighted by two formulas of admission. Only citizenship acquired by '*grande naturalisation*' implied full active and passive voting rights and access to certain public offices (such as judges or juries) while citizens by '*naturalisation ordinaire*' remained excluded (de Groot, 1989, p. 49). There was a minimum waiting period of five years between the two stages of naturalization. This distinction and the legal status of Belgian by birth as different from Belgian by naturalization was finally abolished in 1993. British citizenship remains today the one example among Western liberal democracies where members are split into different categories according to their origins. However, unlike the American, French and Belgian cases in Britain this distinction does not concern political participation but immigration rights.[38]

How should we assess such differentiations of citizenship status by origin? A general associational norm of equality is clearly violated by an entrenched distinction between members by birth and members by later admission. But many associations assign a special status to new members which is regarded as a period of candidacy for full membership. Just as with the test criteria for admission discussed above, it is not the model of association as such which makes this problematic, but the specific properties of liberal citizenship which appear to be incompatible with even a temporary status of second class. In the distribution of citizenship, equality is a very strong norm; any form of explicit inequality in basic individual rights seems to spoil some essential quality of this kind of membership. This norm does not only rule out inequality of political status between old and new members but can even serve as a lever to combat social inequalities as well. Frequently, citizens by naturalization are still socially discriminated because of their origins, culture, language, or skin colour. Such inequality cannot be simply abolished by law, but liberal democratic citizenship provides a strong legitimation for special forms of protection against, or compensation for, group discrimination which impairs the equal standing of individuals in the public sphere (see chapter 12).

Let us now consider whether liberal democratic states are free or even ought to select among resident immigrants those who are seen as fit for citizenship because of their individual characteristics. For the sake of the argument we can assume that there are entirely standardized tests which entitle anyone who passes them to naturalization. While this would make citizenship certainly less than optional, it would not make the decision entirely discretionary either. As shown in the previous section these tests may involve cognitive abilities (knowledge of the language, the constitution, history and geography of the country) but can also concern individual social status (sufficient income, standard housing, absence of a criminal record).

One common objection against using such criteria for selective naturalization is that many native citizens would not pass these tests and still would not be expelled if they were seen to fail.[39] Thus criteria for admission are more demanding than for the continuation of membership, and people are treated differently in entry and in exit. But it is not obvious according to which norm admission ought to be symmetric with expulsion. The most elementary rule of formal justice is that like cases should be treated in a like manner but certainly voluntary entry and involuntary exit are not comparable situations, neither from the point of view of the individuals concerned nor from that of an association. A second and substantial norm of justice that (just) promises ought to be kept will reinforce the moral asymmetry. An association which has pledged to protect its members ought not to deprive them of this protection without serious and well-defined reasons. Non-members might be able to base their claims to be admitted on special needs or on contributions they have already made but they can only in rare cases refer to a clear promise by the state.

The asymmetry between admission and expulsion is irrelevant as an argument of normative critique. Much the same can be said for the idea that nothing should be required from applicants which cannot also be fulfilled by present members. Different standards for applicants and for present members would be certainly fair as long as all members once in their lives had to submit to the same kind of entry examination. The salient point of critique is rather that native citizens receive their membership at birth and without having ever to pass the tests required from immigrants. I have tried to explain above why admission for natives cannot be made voluntary and why immigrants should not be attributed citizenship without asking for their consent. Yet this does not imply a justification for prohibitive admission criteria. The fact that some are privileged in their access to citizenship by inheriting it is a strong argument against making access difficult for those who want to acquire it. This conclusion is not shared by political theorists who maintain that in order to become self-determining a polity must be clearly delimited and rather exclusive in its membership.

In the republican tradition residence is certainly not enough to substantiate a claim for membership in a political community. The community is perceived as sharing fundamental political values and judgements rather than merely coresidence. Immigrants may under certain conditions become entitled to be admitted, but the community reaffirms its own identity by demanding a proof of integration along those cognitive and emotional dimensions which are constitutive for its own cohesion. Responding to Walzer, Herman van Gunsteren has suggested a list of three basic requirements necessary in a neorepublican understanding of citizenship: a) general citizen competence defined as capability of dialogic performance; b) competence to act in this particular community, operationalized as knowledge of the language and respect of the laws; c) access to an *oikos*, i.e. a reasonably secure access to means of existence in order not to be forced to sell oneself or one's judgement (van Gunsteren, 1988, p. 736).[40] These conditions should not be interpreted too rigorously: 'All one may ask for is clear intentional and behavioral indications that the prospective citizen will "grow into" these requirements in due time' (p. 737). Van Gunsteren takes a view that 'the naturalization decision is partly constrained [for authorities, which means optional for the applicant] partly judgmental and discretionary' (p. 738). I will discuss the three conditions for admission in reverse order.

There are two different ways of assessing such proposals for naturalization criteria. One is whether selecting persons who meet them will reassert and strengthen some positive feature of the receiving community. The second one is to ask whether excluding those who fail to meet them would be acceptable. In my view van Gunsteren's list meets the first but largely fails the second test when liberal democratic norms guide the assessment.

This is most obvious for the requirement of independent livelihood. It was essential for the ancient Greek and Roman notions of citizenship and was still invoked in the 19th century exclusion of women and propertyless classes from voting rights.[41] Social citizenship in the 20th century welfare state has reinterpreted rather than abandoned the requirement of some basic material means for social security. It is still fundamentally true that without an *oikos*, an independent private sphere of social reproduction, individuals become dependent and unable to act autonomously in the public realm. The inmates of total institutions such as prisons, psychiatric hospitals and even many homes for the elderly might receive provision for their basic needs for food and accommodation. But they lack means of existence and a home which is exclusively theirs and this largely or completely disables them as active citizens.

The neoconservative critique of the welfare state has pointed out that the system of benefit distribution as a whole tends to foster dependence, and to discourage autonomous activity and self-reliance also among the broader population. Is the welfare state itself a gigantic total institution keeping the general population in dependence? Maybe it is, but what are the alternatives? Being fully exposed to all the risks of labour markets certainly does not make individuals more independent, but merely means that a very large number will be *de facto* excluded from citizenship. In capitalist market economies, including the majority of the population in a political community of citizens is only possible when there is a strong element of social citizenship rights which enables those without higher education, high income or inherited wealth to build and maintain their own *oikos*.

How should a state which adopts a comprehensive system of social protection for its own members treat applicants for admission who are also in need of such protection? One line of argument would insist that internal rules for members can be different from those for new admissions and that admitting more poor will make the community poorer as a whole and less able to take care of its least fortunate members. The opposing view would point out that by locking the poor out of citizenship they are still not locked out of society. Sending back those who have lost their independent income has always been the intention of guest-worker policies. But this has become more and more unacceptable in democratic welfare states.[42] Social rights have even been gradually extended for long-term residents independently of their nominal citizenship. Providing for social security on a more or less equal basis for citizens and resident aliens alike, but excluding the latter from naturalization if they receive welfare benefits, is inconsistent. Although this is one of the most frequently required naturalization criteria it is difficult not to see it as a remnant of the old class conception of citizenship.

A similar test of the consequences of exclusion can be applied to the other criteria suggested by van Gunsteren. Certainly common knowledge of a national language (or at least one *lingua franca* in pluri-lingual states) is indispensable for participation in a public sphere where anonymous citizens have to communicate with each other. Immigrants who do not speak the local language would indeed experience exclusion from full citizenship even if they were formally granted all rights. Yet a language test at the time of first immigration would lead to a very narrow selection in most cases and after immigration only school children can be exposed to compulsory learning of a national language. So a linguistic naturalization criterion seems the only way that adult immigrants can be tested to see whether they really meet this basic requirement for active citizenship.

I have objected above that incentives and opportunities will work better in this respect than selective naturalization. When acquiring the citizenship of a host country is of overriding importance for an immigrant this will also be an incentive for learning the language and a test will be readily accepted. When, however, naturalization is no longer an inevitable step in the settlement process of each immigrant, this criterion will rather deter a larger number from applying for full naturalization than prompt them to improve their linguistic skills. So exclusion from naturalization will not diminish the number of members of society who are linguistically disabled in their participation but may even increase it. Offering immigrants language training independently of their interest for naturalization is a much more promising way to reduce this deficit than requiring a language test for naturalization.

The criterion of respect for the law of the country is generally applied in naturalization by excluding applicants with a criminal record. The rationale for this is stronger than for linguistic assimilation. While states may organize multilingual societies, their very existence depends on a unified system of laws[43] which are generally respected. They defend this system against individuals who break the law and against any self-appointed authority which would attempt to establish its own laws for some groups of society or in part of the territory outside a constitutional framework of federalism. With regard to criminal activities, territorial sovereignty gives states generally the right to punish foreign immigrants just as they punish their own citizens. Alien citizens are, however, often subjected to the 'double penalty' of being first punished and then deported. This practice turns exclusion from naturalization into a dubious and inconsistent rule. When naturalization applicants have broken the law in ways that were not severe enough to justify their deportation, and when they have already been punished and have completed their sentence, on which grounds could they then be denied access to citizenship? The exclusion from naturalization could be seen as a way of reaffirming the general value of law-abidingness only if it were no longer merely a legal precaution for maintaining the deportation power of the police. The case for excluding applicants with a criminal record would thus be much stronger if deportations were strictly limited to those foreign criminals who cannot be regarded as resident members of society (e.g. those who have come as tourists or members of international gangs). Foreign criminals who can no longer be expelled because they enjoy unconditional rights of residence and who have not yet served their sentence may well be denied naturalization. But the criterion of residence must eventually override that of a clear record. Even convicted murderers should not be denied nominal citizenship when they have been born in the country but have been turned into aliens by *ius sanguinis*. The same goes for those who have spent most of their lives in the country. As prison inmates are deprived of active citizenship anyhow their exclusion from naturalization would be hardly more than a symbolic gesture. The question becomes a relevant one only after a criminal has served a sentence. Life exclusion from nominal citizenship cannot be justified as an ongoing punishment. And social reintegration will be severely hampered by the double handicap of a criminal record and alien status.

Respect for the law is often also seen as a criterion for naturalization in a different sense referring to collective and cultural characteristics of immigrants rather than to their individual social integration: immigrants from countries with fundamentally different legal systems are sometimes seen as unfit to become citizens not because they are criminals but because they are perceived as an ethnic or religious minority which challenges the validity of the established laws. There are indeed areas where migration leads to problems of incompatibility between national laws. Conflicting family laws with regard to divorce and custody for children are a well-known example. However, these conflicts concern primarily the status of resident aliens and will not be resolved by restricting naturalization. On the contrary, naturalization can be seen as alleviating problems because it confirms that the law of the receiving state takes priority for the individual concerned. Compared with the status of foreign residents whose bonds of nominal citizenship are only to the sending state, even dual citizenship makes it easier for receiving states to insist on this primacy of their own law.

Often, however, the problem of incompatible systems of laws is interpreted as one of cultural assimilation. Conflicting family laws are then seen as an expression of deep-seated cultural and religious difference and immigrants are assumed to have been socialized so that they are unable to conform to the rules underlying the law of the receiving state. While laws of Western states now no longer exclude entire national, religious or 'racial' groups from access to citizenship, such reasons are prominent in public debate and undoubtedly also shape the ways in which administrations use their discretion and interpret general assimilation requirements. A unified system of laws in liberal democratic states must allow for a variety of different cultural or religious affiliations. Pluralism in societies open for immigration will often be ridden with conflicts, and these will also involve the interpretation of laws and demands for specific collective rights. A naturalization requirement that *de facto* excludes some of these cultural or religious groups would only deepen these cleavages within society by denying some recognition and representation within the political system. In liberal democracy the limits of pluralism can only be defined in public debate and deliberation among equal citizens, but never by excluding a part of the population from citizenship.[44]

From this it follows straightforwardly how van Gunsteren's first criterion of general citizen competence, defined as capability of dialogic performance, should be interpreted. A liberal view must attribute to anybody a basic capacity to be a citizen of a democratic state regardless of ascriptive group memberships. This criterion cannot be used to select among resident immigrants those who are considered worthy of becoming citizens without denying the most fundamental universalistic norms underlying liberal democracy. Of course, citizens are not equally active or competent in their judgements. But in contrast with civic republicanism liberal democracy does not require unreasonably high levels of competence in this regard.[45] As I have argued in section 3.3, those who raise these stakes might end up with 'denaturalizing' the incompetent and the inactive.

Immigrants can certainly not be excluded because such incompetence is attributed to their origins.[46] Yet their particular interests may well reduce their level of interest, activity and involvement in the public and political sphere of the host country. This will be especially true for the most mobile groups of migrants who come primarily for economic reasons and are inclined to return as soon as possible. Where foreign residents have been granted local voting rights,[47] their turnout rates have been generally lower than among the citizen population and have decreased over time.[48] From the fact of reduced political interest one can neither derive diminished competence nor a normative conclusion that participation rights ought to be reduced for this group as well. On the contrary, as I have argued above, immigrants ought to be given as many opportunities for participation as possible in order to enable them to educate themselves as citizens without pressing this choice upon them.

My discussion of naturalization procedures and criteria has supported two broad normative guidelines. First, procedures ought to establish optional citizenship for long-term resident immigrants rather than automatic, mandatory, or discretionary naturalization. Once this is accepted as a general principle there will still be some scope for the other procedures. Citizenship can be made automatic for a second or third generation of immigrant origin born or raised in the country, it can be made mandatory for stateless permanent residents and it can be granted discretionarily before the threshold for optional citizenship has been reached.

Second, admission criteria in optional naturalization should generally not go beyond a reasonably short period of residence. Asking whether such and such practice and virtue, knowledge and competence would positively enhance citizenship, would express the idealized self-image of a free political community and should be shared as widely as possible, are legitimate questions for political deliberation and decision-making *within* a framework of common citizenship. When admission criteria are at stake the relevant question is a different one: what sort of community would result from excluding those from naturalization who are seen to fail by any of these criteria?

In conclusion, liberal democracy does not require total identity between nominal citizens and the resident population. (If it did, naturalization could no longer be a choice for immigrants.) Nor does it demand that all nominal citizens participate equally in public political life. But it does require a political community with genuinely open access to nominal citizenship as well as to the exercise of citizenship rights for all members of society.

4.3. UTILITY AND COMMITMENT IN NATURALIZATION

A normative assessment of naturalization rules is different from the sociological and psychological question of how these rules shape the attitudes and choices of immigrants. Some empirical research has been done in this field.[49] However, problems of validity are substantial, especially when naturalization rates calculated from statistical data of the foreign resident populations and yearly naturalizations are used as objective indicators. A proper indicator for a group's propensity of naturalization would have to divide yearly applications for citizenship by the number of persons entitled to naturalization. As far as the numerator is concerned the problem is that the number of applicants is strongly influenced by the probability of success. If costs are high and if the decision is discretionary, many among those who are eligible and interested will not apply. On the other hand, automatic naturalizations can also not be taken as an indicator of a group's desire to acquire citizenship. Only from strictly optional procedures can one infer that the number of applications reflects a distribution of individual preferences within the group. With regard to the denominator the first problem is that the total size of the group of foreign citizens depends on the rules for attribution of citizenship at birth. *Ius sanguinis* inflates the number of foreigners within the same group of origin while *ius soli* and double *ius soli* reduce this number. Groups who are citizens by birth in *ius soli* states will usually have a higher propensity of naturalization where they are born as foreigners which will tend to increase the overall rate there without any difference in naturalization preferences.[50] Comparison of groups of the same ethnic background across receiving countries presupposes therefore either identical rules for attribution or some method of standardization. A second problem in the denominator is to define the eligible population.[51] Again, discretionary criteria make this virtually impossible. For example, if one takes as a basic reference group all those who have been resident for at least the number of years required for naturalization, all other additional conditions are ignored and thus the number of those who would be naturalized if they applied is systematically overestimated.

Instead of reconstructing naturalization motives from observed behaviour, i.e. actual applications, one may also predict future behaviour by studying underlying motives. Immigrants have been asked in surveys about their intentions to become naturalized. Methodological problems are similarly severe with this kind of data. They go beyond the usual difficulties faced by opinion polls which try to predict future behaviour, for example that of voters in a forthcoming election. The difference is that voters know that elections are coming and that they will be enfranchised. Therefore the assumption that they do have preferences which they can be asked about is not altogether unrealistic. With naturalizations many immigrants do not know whether they are eligible and, if they are, they might still never have considered whether it would be worth applying. Naturalization decisions may be triggered by unforeseeable events concerning the immigrants' families or occupational position or the political and economic situation in the countries of origin and immigration.

All these methodological questions are not relevant for our discussion here. When pleading for optional naturalization it is, however, important to know whether this corresponds to the needs and interests of those to whom it is offered. A model of naturalization motives will be useful independently of how well it predicts the actual number of naturalizations.[52]

The propensity of immigrants to apply for naturalization is often taken as a major indicator of an immigrant group's will to integrate. Low naturalization rates seem to indicate a lack of commitment towards the host society. These assessments rest on two problematic assumptions: first, immigration is imagined as a one-way street which leads towards definite settlement and abandoning social and political ties to societies of origin, and second, naturalization is imagined as if it were a free option for anybody living in the country.

While the first assumption ignores the social and economic forces which increase transnational mobility in the modern world[53] and can only marginally be influenced politically, the second assumption ignores the effect of rules which have been adopted within receiving states and can be changed by political decision. I will focus here on the impact of rules rather than of patterns of social mobility. Quite obviously, restrictive rules of admission have the effect of selecting a smaller number of successful applicants among a larger population who would like to be naturalized. How this selection is achieved has been discussed in the first section of this chapter. Now I want to show how the rules also shape the immigrants' preferences with regard to naturalization.

In a rational choice approach, the motives of immigrants who consider whether to apply for naturalization can be seen as those of pure utility maximizers. A rational immigrant would first compare the bundles of rights and obligations tied to citizen status in the country of immigration and to her present legal position as a resident alien. If naturalization requires renouncing her previous citizenship she will also consider rights and obligations she enjoys as an emigrant citizen with regard to her country of origin. She would then assess the specific utility of each bundle for her present social position and future plans in life and calculate whether naturalization would improve her position. If it does, she will consider the reduction of gains by transaction costs such as fees or waiting time imposed by the administration. Finally, where the decision is discretionary she will estimate the probability of actually obtaining the new citizenship after applying for it.

In an earlier paper (Bauböck, 1992b) I argued that in addition to these rational interests a realistic model also has to take into account that choices of membership are influenced by identities and affiliations. The way in which immigrants feel they are members of their societies of origin, of the receiving society, and of families, neighbourhoods and ethnic groups in both societies will determine whether they consider an option to be naturalized as attractive. This is an expressive kind of rationality in contrast with an instrumental one (Habermas, 1981, vol. 1). My suggestion was that individuals strive towards harmonization of what they perceive as their interests and their identities. When they conflict identities may block the pursuit of interests. When interests are strong enough to prevail in the decision in spite of opposing identities, individuals might come to adapt their identities *ex post* to the decision they made. It is important to emphasize that rational interests of immigrants do not always favour naturalization and that their identities do not always block it. Furthermore, rules of naturalization are not only relevant to interests in the way outlined above, but may also shape identities by marking boundaries between groups.

For the present discussion I want to apply this approach to one specific aspect of identity only – commitment towards the receiving state – and suggest how this attitude might be influenced by different conditions for naturalization. In the previous section I have argued that under ideal conditions a naturalization decision ought to express voluntary commitment. In order to make such normative ideas also politically relevant, one has to demonstrate that conditions can be created under which persons will be motivated to act in accordance with this norm. This is where sociological and psychological theory and research is needed. I want to show now that a sufficiently comprehensive model of immigrants' motivation to apply for naturalization could support my previous assumptions that liberal democracy creates the best conditions for strengthening the commitment motive.

Empirical evidence for backing up the following three hypotheses is still rather thin. It can be provided only by comparing the results of single-country studies with in-depth interviews of immigrants about their attitudes towards naturalization. We therefore know much more about the influence of different backgrounds of the citizenship of their home countries on the immigrants' propensity to be naturalized than about the effect of different naturalization rules in receiving countries. The shape of functions in my graphical presentation of the hypotheses in figures 3 to 6 on the following pages is not based on any empirical findings but on mere conjecture.

(1) The more naturalization is turned into an option, the stronger both motives of utility as well as of commitment will support choosing this option.

(2) The less naturalization deprives immigrants of substantial rights in their countries of origin the stronger will be both the utility and commitment motives for naturalization.

(3) The more secure the legal position of resident aliens is and the more it approaches that of citizens, the weaker the motive of utility and the stronger the motive of commitment will become.

In order to show how both motives combine in shaping a naturalization decision, suppose that they were embodied in two different persons: U is an individual utility maximizer who only decides by weighing rights and obligations implied in her present status with those after naturalization and discounts the result with the costs and probabilities of obtaining the new citizenship. The other immigrant is C, a communitarian who thinks of membership in a community as a part of her identity. Yet she does not see her present memberships as fixed for life. She chooses a new membership when she feels committed towards the cause or the people of this community and when she sees it as a positive contribution towards what she would like to be, i.e. to her desired identity. I certainly do not want to claim that C's attitude could not also be conceptualized as utility maximizing. C might act just as rationally as U in realizing her preferences for being a member of a community towards which she feels committed. It may be possible to reduce the difference between U and C to how they argue their preferences. I only assert that this will lead to different choices when both are confronted with specific conditions for naturalization.

(1) According to the first hypothesis, both U and C would become more attracted towards naturalization when it becomes less restrictive and more optional. However, their reasons are different and so the strength of the motive may be different as well. For the utility maximizer of individual rights the propensity to apply for naturalization is zero when she knows that she is in a category excluded from access to citizenship. Whether procedures are discretionary or optional matters only as far as it influences the probability of success and the costs of the transaction. It does not affect the basic comparison of rights before and after the change. Therefore U's naturalization propensity increases steadily but only slightly with such a change of rules.

The commitment-oriented immigrant C will reason differently. Being excluded from citizenship is in itself a condition which devalues this form of membership. When asked, C will not answer that she would very much like to be naturalized but unfortunately is not eligible, but will rather insist that she could not imagine herself as a citizen of this country anyway. Unlike the fox in Aesop's fable, C does not *change* her preferences by pretending that the grapes she cannot reach are sour.[54] When C is excluded by ascriptive markers she does not form a preference for membership in the first place. Commitment may only begin to develop when exclusion is merely temporary so that C can imagine herself as a future member. Discretionary procedures are seen by C not only as something which might reduce the probability of admission but also as a manifestation of exclusionary power which reduces her inclination to become committed. If she can be rejected in spite of her subjective efforts and of her meeting the required objective criteria it may be less attractive for her to be naturalized.

With other kinds of associations C might react quite differently. It is well known that difficult admission tests or painful initiation rituals increase the loyalty of members who have successfully passed them. Where the obstacles of entry increase the value of membership this may also increase the wish to become a member and lead to anticipated commitment. This effect can be observed in two contrasting situations: first, where admission procedures create an artificial value for a membership in which everybody will be included anyway and second, where tough selection among applicants serves to confirm the elite status of members. Initiation of adolescents to manhood or womanhood exemplifies the former situation and exams for admission to private universities illustrate the latter. In naturalizations both effects are rather unlikely. On the one hand, the transition is not predetermined so that everybody will be included, but it depends on individual choices. Newcomers do not have to be told that they acquire a new membership by subjecting them to harsh treatment because they have decided themselves that they want it. On the other hand, being a citizen means joining a big majority rather than an elite. Although the status may be very valuable this value lies in the equality of rights it spreads throughout society. It is not a *relative* value whereby the happy few distinguish themselves from the mass of people. Tough admission tests enhance an inequality of acquisition between native citizens and newcomers which is at odds with the egalitarian nature of the status itself. One can thus expect that their deterrent effect will be generally stronger than the special attraction of joining a club which is so selective. For political refugees it may be sometimes very desirable to become a citizen of a liberal democracy so that obstacles of admission will not influence their intentions negatively. However, such obstacles will hardly ever have a positive impact on the desire.

C's propensity to consider naturalization will increase when admission becomes optional. In contrast with either discretionary or automatic rules, optional ones demonstrate to her that she is given a choice and respected as a bearer of rights not only after naturalization but already in the process of admission. The right to become a citizen enhances the value of citizenship above that implied in the rights of citizenship. It reinforces the image of the political community as an association of a particular kind with a strong emphasis on entitlements of its individual members towards the association itself.

In the following figure the different responsiveness of the utility oriented and the commitment oriented person to a change in rules is illustrated by the lower propensity of the latter to become naturalized when procedures are strictly discretionary, and the stronger increase of her inclination to apply for citizenship when they become optional.

Figure 3: *The impact of exclusionary, discretionary and optional rules on* *naturalization propensity*

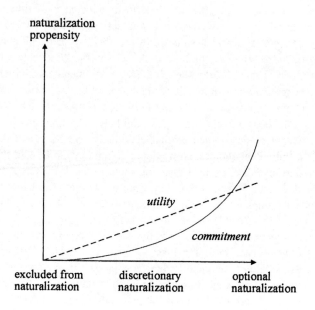

(2) For the utility maximizer of rights, her citizenship of origin may have considerable value. Abandoning it can mean a loss of property ownership, of rights to inherit, of the right to return and of all other citizen rights after returning. Obligatory renunciation of an existing citizenship will therefore often be a decisive obstacle for naturalization. The immediate added value of rights in the country of present residence is often substantially smaller than the dramatic reduction of future opportunities resulting from expatriation. Transitory dual citizenship which has to be given up at a certain age or after a certain time will not change this much. People are usually not dual citizens because they cannot make up their minds but because they have already made up their minds not to give up a citizenship which they might still need. Dormant dual citizenship will increase the value of naturalization in these cases. It implies that only the present gains from possessing a second citizenship are lost, while future ones can be

activated at any time. Dual citizens might be denied the right to vote in the state where they are not residents but they retain the right to return there and to regain all their rights as citizens. Unrestricted dual citizenship will add some further benefits but not too many. These considerations determine the shape of the curve for U's propensity to naturalize in figure 4. It will be different where immigrants perceive their citizenship of origin as a burden rather than as a benefit as may be the case with refugees from stable authoritarian regimes. In this case the renunciation requirement will not diminish the propensity to become naturalized.

Commitment-sensitive immigrants will again react in a slightly different way to these restrictions and incentives. On the one hand, the obligation to give up their present citizenship when becoming full members of their present state of residence can be a decisive obstacle for those who are strongly attached to their countries of origin, and who perceive nominal citizenship as a symbol of this attachment independently from the importance of rights involved in it. On the other hand, the development of commitment towards the state of residence will not depend so strongly on whether dual citizenship is allowed. Where this commitment grows because immigrants feel accepted in this society and by this state it may lead to a conscious decision to stay among those who had always intended to return.[55] Given generally favourable conditions for the development of commitment the denial of dual citizenship will not deter immigrants completely from naturalization. They will have to make a difficult decision between two mutually exclusive affiliations, but the perspective of becoming a citizen in the country of immigration will have some positive weight. In figure 4 I have assumed that generally C's propensity to naturalization under a strict regime of singular citizenship is higher than zero and probably even higher than U's, whose perspective of maximizing individual rights should make her very reluctant to give up those which she already possesses. When rules change towards a more liberal regime of allowing dual citizenship this propensity will increase at a lesser pace than U's. A commitment-sensitive person is not so keen on accumulating memberships as U is on accumulating rights. However, the option of retaining or renouncing her previous membership as she herself thinks fit, should again have a positive impact on her response to the offer of naturalization. It signals that she will be welcome and fully accepted in her new membership as the person she is without having to deny her immigrant background. The option of dual citizenship can be understood as a reassertion that naturalization will not imply enforced assimilation. Voluntary commitment can better develop where individuals do not have to hide where they come from. I have therefore assumed that there is a steady but slow increase in C's propensity to apply for naturalization as rules for dual citizenship become more liberal.

Figure 4   *The impact of obligatory renunciation of a previous citizenship on naturalization propensity*

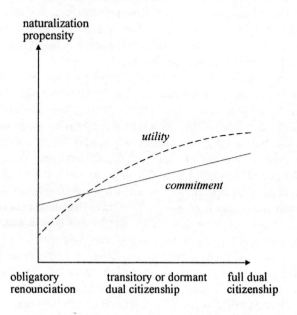

(3) It is the third hypothesis where the difference between the two naturalization motives becomes obvious. For the utility-oriented immigrant the decisive reason to become naturalized is that this improves her legal security and rights in the country of residence. If she can retain her previous citizenship this means that the value of internal citizenship must only be higher than that of 'denizenship'. This will usually be the case and therefore dual citizenship provides a strong instrumental reason for naturalization. If, however, the former citizenship has to be renounced, the single value of the new citizenship must exceed that of a combination of residential and emigrant rights. Once we add transaction costs to this it becomes clear that U will only be inclined to apply if her citizenship of origin, or her residential rights, or both are of very little value for her. As we focus here on the rules of naturalization in receiving countries we take the value of the original citizenship as given. So the naturalization propensity will rise with the extent of legal discrimination of resident aliens and drop towards zero when rights of settled immigrants and citizens become more or less the

same, or when the additional rights conferred by naturalization are of little interest for the immigrants.

There is empirical evidence for this. In a recent study in Austria we found that a further tightening of the already quite tough laws on residence in 1993 led to an increasing interest in naturalization among groups of labour immigrants from Turkey and former Yugoslavia, who saw this as their only chance to secure residence in the future (Riegler, 1994). While rates of naturalization have increased, especially among Turkish citizens, in recent years, they have declined dramatically for German citizens. There are several explanations for the latter phenomenon but one factor seems to be that as members of the European Economic Area Germans already have enjoyed free access to employment in Austria since January 1994, and will become even more privileged in comparison with other aliens when Austria joins the European Union in 1995. Unless dual citizenship is permitted, most European Union citizens living in other EU member states will no longer have instrumental reasons to become naturalized there. Peter Schuck argues that in the USA a steady expansion of the equal protection and due process principles 'have not only minimized the alien's incentive to naturalize; they have also altered the social significance of citizenship' (Schuck, 1989, p. 52).[56]

Non-instrumental expressive rationality may lead to an altogether different attitude. Where immigrants feel that the receiving state actively discriminates against them or does not protect them against social discrimination they will hardly develop commitment towards it. Instead, they will reassert or even reinvent their particular ethnic identities which in turn may block the naturalization option, especially if the national ideology of the receiving society, too, construes its citizenship as an expression of ethno-national identity. The level of commitment will not be zero as long as they have voluntarily immigrated, but whether this first decision leads to a second one in favour of naturalization strongly depends on how they perceive their situation as members of society who are excluded from the polity. When the rights of resident aliens are raised towards those of full citizens this will strengthen commitment and might in itself contribute to the decision to join the political community as a full member. Again, there is some empirical evidence for such an attitude among immigrants. In Australia, where citizenship can already be obtained after two years but does not imply much legal advantage, the naturalization propensity is still quite high, especially among non-European immigrants and among youths who have grown up in Australia. Evans interprets these results as a gradual growth of commitment. 'The decision to become an Australian citizen should be seen as a ritual, public affirmation of that commitment' (Evans, 1988, S. 246). 'In states like Canada, Sweden, and the United States, where

naturalization is easily available, many aliens seek citizenship even though
the status of permanent residence is relatively secure. Only if citizenship is
offered on reasonable terms will we know that those who do not pursue it
do so of their own accord' (Carens, 1989, p. 48).

Figure 5   The impact of alien discrimination on naturalization propensity

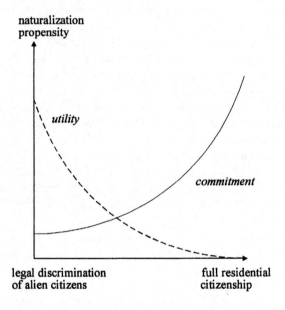

Of course the separation of utility from commitment and of instrumental
from expressive rationality is only an analytic one. Most immigrants will be
sensitive to both kinds of motives. Thus commitment-oriented immigrants
who have long refused to consider changing their citizenship because they
did not feel accepted among the native population or because they had firm
attachments to their home countries, may still want to be naturalized when
this has become necessary in order to make their residence or employment
more secure. If we do not consider potential interaction effects between
utility and commitment we might get a rough idea about the combined
motivational impact by adding the two graphs in each of the above
diagrams. In figure 5 this would lead to a u-shaped curve which could
explain this attitude of higher naturalization propensity at the extreme ends
of the spectrum of conditions. In figures 3 and 4 the shape of C + U would
follow that of C and U respectively, with a steeper increase as we move
towards more liberal rules.

Just as the motives of C and U are not mutually exclusive ones, so the conditions for naturalization specified along the horizontal axes of the figures can be combined as well. Empirically as well as conceptually there is an obvious correlation between the three sets of conditions. Extensive exclusion from naturalization mostly goes hand in hand with a denial of dual citizenship, and with widespread legal discrimination and a lack of policies against social discrimination of immigrants. What I have identified as liberal democratic principles of admission is at the opposite end of the spectrum: optional citizenship which can be chosen under conditions of roughly equal rights for resident aliens and with no obligatory loss of the sending country's citizenship. We can condense the three figures into a single one (figure 6) without too much loss of information.

Figure 6: The overall impact of restrictive and liberal rules on naturalization propensity

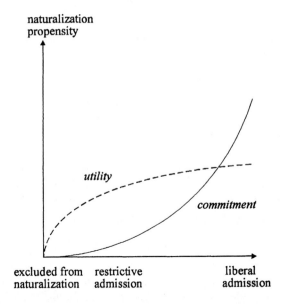

For U the positive effects of alien discrimination and the negative effects of losing rights in the sending country will more or less cancel each other out. So the overall function of her naturalization propensity will be rather similar to that in figure 3, i.e. a slight increase due to the reduction of transaction costs in optional citizenship. At the point of total exclusion we cannot add the three graphs because the utility of applying will still be zero. But it will jump to a relatively high level of propensity as soon as there is a chance of being admitted because of the strong incentive to escape alien discrimination under an illiberal regime by naturalization. Combining the three graphs for C leads to a very different function which first remains at a low level but increases quickly as we move closer to the liberal admission regime because all three rules characterizing this regime have a positive effect on the emergence of voluntary commitment.

This is how we can make plausible the conjecture that liberal rules of admission will contribute to the emergence of spontaneous commitment which in turn will increase the number of applications for membership. The underlying hypothesis is that commitment increases parallel with choice. In our analysis, freedom of choice has been broken down into three fundamental dimensions: first, the extent to which a result is determined by the option an actor has chosen herself – applied to citizenship this means optional admission instead of discretionary procedures or exclusion; second, an extended range of options among which to choose – the possibility of combining several citizenships increases that range; third, offering alternative options at their fair value[57] – which means no discrimination of resident aliens that presses them into naturalization.

I have not tried to give a complete list of all relevant naturalization motives. As I said in the beginning of this section, the instrumental benefits depend strongly on the stability of residence, and other kinds of commitment towards one's family, neighbourhood or ethnic group also have an impact on the decision. They could be taken into account in an extended analysis. I will just give one example how utility and commitment may determine naturalization decisions within families in quite different ways. In our study among immigrants in Vienna we found that in some families a collective decision had been taken that only one adult member would become naturalized while the others would retain their citizenship (Riegler, 1994). This is a strategy of optimizing rights under adverse circumstances which prohibit dual citizenship. At the same time it is also a decision inspired by a sense of commitment towards the family. The alien members of the family would profit indirectly from naturalization by gaining a more secure status of residence and being exempted from restrictions with regard to free choice of employment. At the same time the family as a whole kept open the perspective of return. (Renaturalization for the one adult who had become an Austrian would not be a problem in most cases.) Other families had decided that either none or all of them would be naturalized. In this case family commitment turns naturalization into a decision about a collective national identity and this blocks the strategy of optimizing rights. In a third group, the decision to apply for naturalization had been taken individually by a single member (often an adult child) in opposition to the others. Family commitment here did not influence the naturalization propensity, or possibly the decision was even influenced by negative commitment, i.e. a wish to distance oneself from the family. We might now consider the impact different rules of extending naturalization to family members will have upon these various motives.

I will not develop this further here. The point of the analysis is only to show that normative considerations about liberal rules of admission are not at odds with individual motivations and would thus not lead to perverse effects. Liberal policies of admission to citizenship have a dual target. One is to make the distribution of substantial rights of citizenship as inclusive as possible within society, the second one is to provide incentives for citizens to develop some voluntary commitment towards the common good of this society. Increasing the rate of naturalization among immigrants is not itself a target but not more than a possible side-effect of pursuing these two.

It is also important to emphasize that the second target does not involve a moral assessment of individual motives. Individuals do not act immorally when they want to be naturalized because it is advantageous for them or when they refuse to do so as long as they do not gain any additional rights. In contrast with republicanism, liberalism concentrates its normative critique on the institutions and decisions of states and governments rather than criticizing the motivational background of individual actors. An orientation to maximize individual rights is not only a perfectly legitimate one within a liberal framework, but one which itself contributes positively towards developing this framework. The problem is that it is not sufficient to sustain it. A well-ordered liberal democracy needs committed citizens. The answer to the puzzle how this can be achieved is that liberal states have to create institutional arrangements within which commitment is not opposed to interests in individual rights but can develop beyond a purely instrumental rationality. Even figure 5, where instrumental and expressive rationality appear to be at odds, illustrates just this. While it is not rational for the utility maximizer to apply for naturalization when she does not gain any rights that offset her transaction costs, it is also not irrational in the sense that she would have to sacrifice some of her rights. This is the basic precondition for a spontaneous development of that form of commitment which is necessary to consolidate liberal democracy. Under favourable conditions the individual decision to apply for naturalization may be motivated by commitment. But this need neither be regarded as the only legitimate motive for naturalization nor will all immigrants who participate actively in the public and political life of a receiving state have to document their commitment by becoming naturalized.

NOTES

1. I have first used and explained this typology of transitions in Bauböck (1991).
2. As Joseph Carens points out, Locke 'says nothing ... about whether the community must consent to the individual before the individual can claim membership' (Carens, 1987b, p. 416). For Locke, consent in admission seems to be optional rather than discretionary. This view was apparently not restricted to citizenship acquisition by natives on reaching their majority but extended also to the naturalization of immigrants. That is confirmed by a short essay on naturalization written in 1693, in which Locke advocates an extremely liberal immigration policy from an economic point of view and argues that easy access to naturalization is a corollary of this policy (Locke, 1987).
3. Joseph Carens and Rogers Brubaker have coined slightly different labels for the same distinction between discretionary admission and optional citizenship. Brubaker distinguishes discretionary and 'as-of-right systems' of naturalization (Brubaker, 1989b, pp. 108–9) while Carens speaks about individual versus mutual consent in admission to citizenship (Carens, 1987a). Yet admission to citizenship always involves two agents, an individual and a state, and consent reached between them can never be unilateral. Even optional admission to citizenship implies mutual consent. The individual takes the final decision but in its laws the state must have consented first that individuals of this kind or in those circumstances will be admitted. The difference between option and discretion lies in the sequence of consent, not in individual or mutual determination of decisions and outcomes.
4. The Canadian Citizenship Act is an exception. It includes ordinary naturalization in a chapter under the title 'The Right to Citizenship'. The Act specifies that the Minister *shall* grant citizenship to any person who meets the requirements whereas the Minister *may, in his discretion*, waive on compassionate grounds some of these requirements in favour of the applicant (Canadian Citizenship Act, Article 5). In contrast with this, the US Immigration and Naturalization Act formulates that no applicant shall be naturalized who does not fulfil the requirements, and the Australian Act says that naturalization may be granted to applicants. In spite of these different legal formulas, naturalization may be said to be rather close to the optional model in all three countries because of the highly standardized administrative procedures (Brubaker, 1989b, p. 110).
5. I use the term 'optional' in a more general sense so that it includes two different forms of naturalization. The stronger kind of option is acquisition by declaration of the applicant without an extensive list of individual criteria. A weak option exists where the list of criteria is sufficiently standardized and where the applicant is legally entitled to acquire citizenship, and authorities are obliged to grant it, if she meets all the requirements.
6. The Greek law maintains discretion in its most extreme form by explicitly stating that a negative decision does not need any justification (Article 6(4) of the Decree Law on Greek Nationality).
7. Fees used to be comparatively high but have been recently lowered as part of a deal between the government coalition and the SPD in exchange for the latter's consent to a revision of the German Basic Law's provision for political asylum.
8. My normative discussion in section 4.2 covers only criteria making naturalization more difficult. Those making it easier would partly become redundant if citizenship were made strongly optional. Some among these criteria would, however, retain their justification even then. I regard preferential access for those born and raised in the country, for those married to citizens or to applicants for naturalization, and for refugees as a recognition of special entitlements or needs rather than as an unwarranted privilege.
9. In most countries, ordinary naturalization furthermore presupposes that the applicant has reached her majority. However, everywhere naturalizations of adults can also be extended to minors and there are some exceptions where minors can apply themselves. In a few countries they have to consent to their parents' choice to change their citizenship when they have reached a certain age (e.g. in Austria 14 years) (see de Groot, 1989, pp. 237–9). Although age requirements may in practice have an impact on facilitating or impeding naturalization this is generally not their intention. They result from considerations which have little to do with the selection of applicants according to their bonds to the receiving country and their individual fitness to become citizens. Minors are not regarded as unfit to become nominal citizens but only as not yet fit to make a conscious and responsible choice

of their political membership. I will therefore not include age thresholds in the list of criteria to be discussed.

10. Spouses of citizens or of applicants for naturalization who have been married for one year must have been resident for four years. If they have been married for two years the residence requirement is reduced to three years. After five years of marriage no residence is required which means that spouses can then also obtain naturalization abroad (Articles 11a and 16).

11. This is a rare example of optional admission based on pure *ius domicili* without any element of *ius soli*. Birth in the territory is totally irrelevant for naturalization in Austria.

12. Apart from de Groot's (1989) extensive survey, useful comparative summaries of naturalization regimes and requirements can be found in Brubaker (1989c), de Rham (1990) and Hailbronner (1992). Brubaker's sample includes Canada, USA, Britain, France, Germany and Sweden while de Rham's contains only Western European states but adds the Netherlands, Belgium and Switzerland to the list. Hailbronner's survey covering 15 states is the most extensive one and also includes some sending countries.

13. This refers to totalitarian and authoritarian regimes in Western Europe, as well as to democracies like the United States where Asian immigrants and aboriginal Americans remained excluded from citizenship even after the 14th amendment to the constitution had established a common and uniform federal citizenship.

14. In 1988 46,783 persons newly acquired German citizenship, only 35.6% of whom were discretionary naturalizations of foreigners, almost all the rest being automatic naturalizations of ethnic German immigrants. In 1991 the overall number rose to 141,630 citizenship acquisitions. Although the number of ordinary naturalizations of foreigners increased in absolute numbers it declined in relative terms to 19.3%. The naturalization rate of non-German foreigners in 1991 was 0.5% of the resident foreign population. This is the lowest number among Western European immigration states (source: Statistisches Bundesamt Wiesbaden).

15. Canada is exceptional in disconnecting marital status from citizenship not only in automatic acquisition and loss but also in facilitated admission. The law of 1977 does not at all take into account marriage with a citizen.

16. In Austria naturalization is regularly extended to dependants and some administrative authorities even refuse to grant it unless the whole family agrees to become naturalized.

17. The Austrian supreme court has recently decided that a marriage may be annulled if its primary purpose was naturalization, whereas it is valid if the aim was to obtain an exemption permit (*Befreiungsschein*) which exempts alien spouses of Austrian citizens from restrictions of access to employment. Some governments, especially in France and in the Netherlands, have been strongly concerned that foreigners with irregular status may obtain a residence permit by marrying a citizen.

18. See note 9 above.

19. Austria is probably among those countries which lay the strongest emphasis on merit and state interest in naturalizations. Article 10 (4) allows citizenship to be given to foreigners without any residence requirement if this is in the republic's interest because of their exceptional achievements, especially in the fields of science, economics, arts and sports. An internationally unique provision says that foreign university professors have to become Austrian citizens when obtaining a chair. (This is a remnant of an older rule for the whole civil service.) Renunciation of a previous citizenship is strictly required in Austrian law, but not in these cases.

20. This century's record numbers of naturalizations were reached in the period from 1941 to 1950 with a yearly average of 194,000 applications (Ueda, 1982, p. 151).

21. In their book on global refugee movements and politics Zolberg, Suhrke and Aguayo (1989) have given a broader definition of refugee movements as 'escape from violence'.

22. In Austria there have recently been some cases where refugees who came from Czechoslovakia or Hungary more than 20 years ago lost their residence permits because of political reform in these countries.

23. Such public interest in naturalization is generally assumed for alien spouses of German citizens and now since the reform of the alien law in 1990, also for those young or long-term resident foreigners who enjoy a 'regular claim' to be admitted to citizenship.

24. Even in countries where this does not figure explicitly in the law, it will frequently be a decisive element of a general test of integration or assimilation.

25.   See Article 11(3) of the Spanish constitution of 1978 according to which Spanish citizens
      can be naturalized in countries with which Spain has a special link (*vinculación
      particular*) without losing their Spanish citizenship, even if those countries do not have a
      reciprocal rule for their emigrants living in Spain.
26.   Van den Bedem points out a further disadvantage. 'For a single country ... that wants to
      create a system in which plural nationality is accepted ... the creation of a system of
      dormant nationality is not possible' (van den Bedem, 1994). In contrast with full dual
      citizenship, dormant citizenship presupposes a framework of bilateral or multilateral
      agreements between states that mutually renounce their claims to represent their citizens
      abroad. At the same time this is a step beyond the mere toleration of a second citizenship
      which is the prevailing attitude in most countries where multiple citizenship has been
      permitted to proliferate. Full dual citizenship would imply mutual recognition of the
      second citizenship by both states involved, and this could well go beyond the half solution
      of dormant dual citizenship. On the one hand, it would reduce conflicting multiple
      obligations following the model established by the 1963 Strasbourg convention for dual
      military obligations (see section 5.1) and, on the other hand, it would broaden
      opportunities for the exercise of citizen rights towards both states involved. Of course this
      presupposes stable and friendly relations between states. The less demanding rule of
      toleration will therefore generally facilitate the acquisition of dual citizenship in a world of
      conflicting state interests and diverging legal systems.
27.   In the same volume, Kay Hailbronner defends the opposite view on the realist grounds that
      citizenship policy is a political, not a moral issue and 'every nation, on the basis of its own
      history, tradition, and contemporary situation, has to decide what citizenship policy would
      best accord with its own interests' (Hailbronner, 1989, p. 75). Nonetheless, Hailbronner
      does give a general recommendation that the acquisition of citizenship should not be seen
      as a means of integration but 'should be more appropriately seen as the result and
      consecration of a successful process of integration and assimilation' (Hailbronner, 1989, p.
      79). Hailbronner has taken a much more liberal view in a recent report on dual
      citizenship, where abandoning a strict requirement to renounce one's established
      citizenship is explicitly seen as an instrument to give permanently resident foreigners the
      opportunity to full integration (Hailbronner, 1992, p. 11).
28.   Robert Nozick's belief that a free system will allow an individual to sell herself into
      slavery is exceptional in this regard (Nozick, 1974, p. 331).
29.   Rawls suggests that 'the basic structure is to be arranged to maximize the worth to the
      least advantaged of the complete scheme of equal liberty shared by all' (Rawls, 1971, p.
      205). This serves as an argumentative bridge between the first principle of justice which
      demands a fully adequate system of equal liberties and the difference principle which
      requires social inequalities to be arranged in favour of the least advantaged.
30.   I will later argue that a free choice between alternative options is not enough
      compensation to satisfy the norm of equal rights. Immigrants ought to be given a chance to
      combine their old with a new citizenship, and the baseline from which they assess these
      options ought to include a maximum of rights of citizenship for resident aliens.
31.   In his recent book on Political Liberalism, Rawls pays much attention to the problem of
      how the fair value of political liberties can be maintained (Rawls, 1993a, pp. 356–68).
32.   Throughout this discussion I assume that naturalization implies a positive balance between
      rights and obligations of citizenship for immigrants with regard to their legal status in
      receiving societies. Where naturalization is perceived to increase obligations more than
      rights and where the benefit for the receiving society outweighs that for the immigrant,
      states will be obviously much more inclined to adopt mandatory or automatic rules. Both
      the arguments from equity and from utility were strongly present in the French debate
      during the second half of the 19th century when automatic naturalization at the age of
      majority was introduced for all those born on French territory. 'En France même, la
      naturalisation obligatoire apparaît aujourd'hui comme une necessité politique et
      économique. Ce n'est pas seulement une mésure équitable, destinée à rétablir l'égalité des
      charges et des profits entre tous ceux qui habitent en France: c'est encore le meilleur et le
      seul moyen auquel nous puissions recourir pour remédier au ralentissement regrettable de
      notre population. Puisque nous n'avons pas assez d'enfant, adoptons les enfants des
      autres' (Arthur Mangin, 1885, quoted from Wihtol de Wenden, 1994, pp. 4–5). 'In France
      herself, obligatory naturalization appears today as a political and economic necessity. It is
      not only an equitable measure destined to re-establish the equality of burdens and benefits

between all those who live in France; it is also the best and the only means on which we can fall back in order to remedy the regrettable diminution of our population. Since we do not have enough children, let us adopt the children of the others' (my translation).

33. On the political resocialization of immigrants see Hammar (1990, pp. 148–50).

34. After the big immigration wave at the turn of the last century teaching citizenship became a gigantic programme of adult education in the USA, with courses not only in English but also in civics and a final 'certificate of graduation'. It was aimed at immigrants from Southern and Eastern Europe who were seen to be less fit for citizenship because of their cultural and political backgrounds and because of their primarily economic motivation for emigration. Simultaneous disabilities for aliens, especially with regard to economic liberties, ensured that even poor and overworked immigrants attended these classes in large numbers (Ueda, 1982, pp. 137–41).

35. In a survey among immigrants in Vienna we found telling empirical evidence for this conjecture. A characteristic answer by a naturalized immigrant from former Yugoslavia was: 'I don't know whether or not other of my Yugoslav friends are naturalized, too, because some may have naturalized but do not want to say it. You do not enter so deeply into one's private affairs' (Riegler, 1994).

36. Bruce Ackerman uses a similar argument in pleading for a *prima facie* right to immigration in liberal states which I will examine critically in section 13.1 (Ackerman, 1980, pp. 88–95).

37. At the Constitutional Convention of 1787 'some delegates, including Madison, suggested a plan by which applicants would receive incremental rights as, step by step, they fulfilled the basic requirements of citizenship. They also debated limiting the vote and membership in Congress to the native-born. In the end, however, the convention agreed that the only disadvantage to be placed upon naturalized citizens would be ineligibility for the presidency of the United States' (Ueda, 1982, p. 115).

38. Personal communication by Tomas Hammar.

39 Instead of first defining citizens and then granting them all civic rights, including that of immigration, the definition of British nationality in the Act of 1981 followed the previous categorization of people according to their immigration rights. There are five different groups: British Citizens, British Dependent Territories' Citizens, British Overseas Citizens, British Subjects as defined in Part IV of the Act and British Protected Persons. A sixth category of British Nationals (Overseas) was created later for some people in Hong Kong. The last three of these six groups lack immigration rights. On the other hand, voting rights are not tied to British nationality even for national general elections. Citizens of member states of the Commonwealth and Irish citizens are fully enfranchised whereas British Protected persons (who hold British passports) are not (Dummett and Nicol, 1990, chapter 13, Dummett, 1994).

40. Herman van Gunsteren reports that in Dutch parliamentary debates the objection was raised against special admission requirements 'that they violate equality because they demand more from newcomers than is expected from quite a number of native citizens' (van Gunsteren, 1988, p. 737). Van Gunsteren thinks that this argument is mistaken on two counts: because it suggests a moral symmetry between admission and expulsion and because 'what is at issue in the first place is precisely whether newcomers will acquire the right to equal treatment with Dutch citizens' (p. 737). I disagree with the second point only. In a liberal democracy the right to equal treatment reaches far beyond the boundaries of nominal citizenship. Would we call a democracy liberal where foreigners were not entitled to equal treatment in court? When there is a general presumption for equality of treatment among residents, we need some justification for using different standards for the acquisition of nominal citizenship by natives and immigrants. In my view maintaining automatic procedures for the former and optional ones for the latter can be justified whereas restraining the option by adding a long list of additional criteria cannot.

41. Joseph Carens briefly discusses a partially overlapping list of modest requirements: competence in the dominant language, no serious criminal offences, an overt expression of commitment to the regime. While he thinks these must be ruled out for children born and raised in the county, they have somewhat more justification for those who come as adults. However, 'it is hard to see why these considerations should be a barrier to citizenship for those who have already been granted permanent residence status' (Carens, 1989, p. 47).

42. John Stuart Mill who was an ardent defender of the inclusion of women, at the same time thought it self-evident 'that representation should be co-extensive with taxation, not

stopping short of it, but also not going beyond it' (Mill, 1972, 'On Representative Government', pp. 304–5). In order 'to reconcile this ... with universality' he suggested 'that taxation, in a visible shape should descend to the poorest class' (p. 305). The receipt of public assistance to the poor (parish relief in Mill's time) should, however, 'be a peremptory disqualification for the franchise. He who cannot by his labour suffice for his own support has no claim to the privilege of helping himself to the money of others' (ibid.).

43.   Saying that policies of enforcing remigration for economic reasons have become unacceptable does not mean that they have become impossible. In most states of Western Europe, such programmes are a major electoral issue for antiliberal and antidemocratic parties and are quite often also adopted by mainstream conservatives and social democrats in their chase for votes from the right wing. Nor do I want to suggest that earlier guest-worker policies denying immigrants residence and citizenship rights have ever been compatible with liberal democratic principles. What is different now is that such policies aim at reversing a long trend of social as well as of legal integration which has gradually unfolded over the last decades. The implications of this are much more obvious than they had been when the first guest workers were recruited in the 1950s and 1960s.

44.   Britain is exceptional in having two different legal and judicial systems, the Scottish and the English one, but one common legislature.

45.   Jürgen Habermas distinguishes two stages of assimilation of immigrants: consent with constitutional principles and acculturation to cultural forms of life. In liberal democracies the former, but not the latter, may be required from immigrants as a condition for naturalization (Habermas, 1993, p. 183). Liberal constitutions go beyond universal moral principles and human rights and articulate particular historic traditions and ethical projects (which will themselves change with a changing composition of the citizenry due to immigration and naturalization) (pp. 164–71). Consent to such a constitution implies therefore a process of political socialization independently of one's cultural origins and of whether one has been raised under a liberal democratic or an authoritarian regime, in a secularized or a strongly religious society. However, as I have tried to show above, this kind of socialization should not be understood as a just requirement imposed by the receiving community, but as a process of self-education which presupposes liberal conditions of admission.

46.   Citizenship as competence is a central theme of Herman van Gunsteren's essay (1992).

47.   Nevertheless, such arguments have of course been used extensively throughout the modern history of naturalization and were especially prominent in the nativist movements of US American history. 'The unfamiliarity of some new immigrants with democratic government, their acquaintance with monarchical regimes and authoritarian religions, and their ignorance of English cast doubts in the minds of nativists as to their readiness for citizenship rights' (Ueda, 1982, p. 153).

48.   Local voting rights have become disconnected from nominal citizenship in Sweden, Norway, Denmark, Finland, the Netherlands, Eire, and in the Swiss Cantons Neuchâtel and Jura. In other countries such as the UK or Spain they have been extended to certain groups of foreign citizens only.

49.   Tomas Hammar explains this trend with a list of factors including social and demographic composition, percentage of new arrivals, plans to return, social isolation, cultural and linguistic barriers, lack of specific immigrant issues in electoral programmes, etc. (Hammar, 1990, pp. 142–7).

50.   See Friedrich-Ebert-Stiftung (1986), Evans (1988), Portes and Curtis (1988), Pachon (1988), Hammar (1990, chapter 6), Van den Bedem (1994), Bauböck et al. (1994). A general overview of the literature is given by DeSipio (1988).

51.   A simple example can demonstrate this. Suppose that the naturalization propensity of foreigners of a certain origin is the same in all countries of residence and only depends on whether they have been born abroad or in that country. In the former case it is 5%, in the latter it is 10%. Suppose further that in a *ius sanguinis* state A, two-thirds of all foreigners have been born abroad. The overall naturalization rate of the group there will be 6.7%. In *ius soli* state B, those born in the country are no longer counted as foreigners and therefore the rate among the same group is reduced to 5%.

52.   For an attempt to correct ordinary naturalization rates in Germany in this way see Fleischer (1987).

53. Empirical support for such a model can best be obtained from qualitative interviews among three groups of immigrants: those who have been naturalized, those who have applied but not yet obtained citizenship and those who are eligible but have not applied so far. This was the design of the recent small-scale survey among immigrants in Vienna mentioned in n. 34 above (Riegler, 1994). Some of the conjectures in the following discussion seem to be supported by the results of this study.

54. Naturalization rates will decline quite naturally where migration becomes a process of going back and forth and where the option of return is kept open even when settlement takes place. This is not an altogether new phenomenon. Contrary to widespread beliefs, even European migration to the USA after the turn of the century was frequently unstable and oscillating and led to concerns about naturalization: 'The post-1900 remigration was probably a new phenomenon for the United States. ... Remigration discomfitted Americans for several reasons. The lack of commitment to the United States that it signalled was an affront to the American beliefs that the decision to immigrate should involve political motivation even more than economic and that those who came should turn their backs on their homelands, at least to some degree. Low rates of naturalization among groups inclined to remigration reinforced the negative image of them' (Archdeacon, 1992, p. 538).

55. For an exploration of the sour grapes paradox in rational choice theory see Elster (1984).

56. Frequently immigrants take such a decision not motivated by commitment but because of a deterioration of return perspectives in the sending country or because they sacrifice their own plans for the sake of their children's future in the receiving state.

57. Schuck thinks that automatic citizenship for all born in the territory even from illegal immigrants and easy access to citizenship from a starting-point of roughly equal rights does not only diminish the instrumental utility of naturalization but also devalues the status of citizenship in its political, cultural, spiritual and emotional dimensions (Schuck, 1989, pp. 60–61).

58. This does not imply that the options of denizenship and naturalization must be made equally attractive in order to make the choice between them free. The 'fair value' of denizenship will have to be determined by independent considerations of which rights and duties ought to be attached to this status because they are normatively derived from residence and employment. Once normative agreement has been achieved on the proper distribution of rights it would be unfair to withhold some of these rights (to which they are morally entitled) from resident aliens just in order to increase their incentive for naturalization. I have to thank Thomas Faist for asking me to clarify this point.

5. Consent in Exit

As in the previous chapter, I will discuss in this one first the most common rules regulating legal transitions between the status of alien and citizen, only that now the transition is in the opposite direction and concerns the ways in which citizens can lose their membership. In political theory the right of voluntary expatriation has often been seen as an indicator for internal political consent. Section 5.2 addresses this question and completes the argument of the previous chapter by showing that the allocation of liberal citizenship cannot be made fully consensual either in acquisition or in exit.

5.1. RULES OF EXPATRIATION AND DENATURALIZATION

Admission of new members into a political community of citizenship is usually supposed to be voluntary even when it is automatic or when it assumes a certain mandatory character because there is social pressure on immigrants to apply. A new citizenship is not forced upon people against their explicit will. This is different with exit which can be voluntary as well as involuntary. Denaturalization is mostly compulsory rather than merely mandatory, i.e. the individual is not just under an obligation to renounce her citizenship but it is simply taken away by the authorities. A second difference is that the standard procedure of entry is *discretionary* admission, whereas the standard form of voluntary expatriation is *optional* exit. In the latter case the sequencing of the interaction is that the state first lays down certain criteria under which individuals can renounce their citizenship and the individual is then free to decide whether to do this or not. So the rule of decision is clearly biased against the state.

There are regulations which deviate from the standard in this transition, too. In some cases, exit is made discretionary so that the citizen first has to get individual permission to abandon her membership and state authorities decide ultimately whether to grant it or not. Democratic citizenship is, however, incompatible with generalized forms of compulsory, mandatory or discretionary exits. These are characteristic for an authoritarian form of subjecthood. When Hobbes discusses emigration he lists only categories whose exit is compulsory, mandatory or discretionary: they are those banished, those sent on a message and those who have been given leave to travel (Hobbes, 1973, XXI, p. 117). I will consider in this chapter primarily regulations of exit in states that can be broadly characterized as parliamentary democracies.

Not all of these states allow voluntary expatriation. France and Spain do not have any general provisions for renunciation but many exceptions listed in the law make expatriation possible in quite a number of cases (de Groot, 1989, pp. 93, 189). Greece and Turkey are among those countries where expatriation is discretionary and requires special permission by the home ministry or the council of ministers respectively. For Greek emigrants it seems to be particularly difficult to obtain this permission. States which do allow for expatriation often try to deter their citizens from leaving by raising high fees. A notorious example has been some of the Yugoslav republics and now successor states, which already collect such fees for issuing a document stating that an emigrant has applied to renounce her citizenship. When the receiving country does not allow dual citizenship and also demands substantial fees for naturalization, the monetary costs imposed from both sides can add up to a barrier preventing a change of citizenship among persons who would be otherwise perfectly eligible. Other states of emigration have taken different steps to discourage expatriation which seem to be equally effective but fully compatible with a principle of optional expatriation. They allow facilitated renaturalization of former citizens even when these have just obtained another citizenship. Thus the renunciation requirements of some states have been circumvented either tacitly or even within the framework of existing legal provisions.[1]

Figure 7: Coercion and choice in exit from citizenship

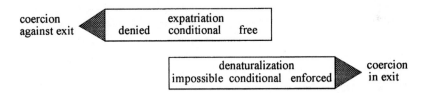

Individual freedom in exit is not just the right to renounce one's citizenship but also the right to retain it. Mass denaturalizations and arbitrary rules for depriving individuals of their citizenship have been a widespread practice in the 20th century (Arendt, 1967, n. 20, p. 277 and n. 25, p. 279). Today, this is no longer regarded as within the legitimate power of democratic regimes. Yet full protection against involuntary deprivation of citizenship is still quite rare.[2] Figure 7 shows how coercion pulls into two opposite directions. We can imagine the area of freedom as a central range in a spectrum of rules which is delimited by the denial of voluntary renunciation at the one end and by enforced denaturalization at the other end.

The extent of restriction of free choice in conditional exit can be measured along two different dimensions: one is the nature and scope of general criteria for denying expatriation or enforcing denaturalization; the second one is the amount of state control over individual decisions. Free choice is unduly restrained when criteria are unreasonable or difficult to meet or when state authorities have the power to deny expatriation or enforce denaturalization arbitrarily or within a broad margin of discretion. Individual exit freedom is maximized where expatriation is an option for every citizen under minimal and reasonable conditions and where denaturalization can only be enforced in rare and well-specified cases.

In the rest of this section I will discuss a (probably incomplete) list of eight criteria which are relevant for both kinds of transition from nominal citizen to alien status. Some of them are positive conditions for permitting expatriation, as well as for enforcing denaturalization. Others are negative and lead to a denial of voluntary exit. Three of the criteria in the list are only used in rules for one kind of exit but are not relevant for the other. In one instance signs are reversed and the criterion can justify prohibiting expatriation but can also be a positive reason for denaturalization. All this is illustrated by the plus, minus and zero signs in table 3. A further important distinction which cannot be captured in the table is whether a condition is a necessary one, a sufficient one, or both necessary and sufficient. In this respect rules vary between different legal traditions and normative approaches and have to be discussed in more detail.

Table 3:   Criteria for expatriation and denaturalization

	expatriation	denaturalization
(1) permanent residence abroad	+	+
(2) naturalization abroad	+	+
(3) acquiring a foreign citizenship in the country	+	+
(4) holding public office in another state	+	+
(5) serving in a foreign army	0	+
(6) obligations of military service	–	0
(7) criminal record	–	+
(8) faulty naturalization	0	+

Underlying this list of criteria there are two main reasons which are used to justify restricting voluntary exit or enforcing involuntary exit. The first one involves social ties and political links to another state, the second one loyalty and obligations towards the state deciding about exit rights. According to the first reason, an individual may have *de facto* become the member of another society or also formally the citizen of another state. This may be seen as a reason for granting expatriation as well as for automatic denaturalization. So this reason operates as a positive one for both kinds of restrictions. It is present in (1), (2), (3) and (4) of the above list. Social ties to a foreign state will become strongest when a person takes permanent residence there (1) and the most obvious indicator for political links is adoption of a foreign citizenship (2). Yet individuals may also orient socially towards another state because they are or have become members of a family which has strong ties to this state. Marriage with a foreign citizen has been a frequent reason for internal expatriation as well as denaturalization (3). Until not so long ago exit rules in most countries used to be gendered in this respect in the same manner as the corresponding entry rules discussed in chapters 2 and 4; they applied only to women.[3] Holding a public office is a strong indicator that not only the individual orients towards another state but that she is also accepted by this state (4).

A breach of loyalty will mostly operate as a positive reason only for denaturalization. Serving in a foreign army is taken as an obvious indicator of disloyalty by many states (5). The enforcement of obligations can, however, also act as a reason against allowing expatriation, as in the case of young men who have not yet completed their military service (6) or of criminals against whom legal procedures are pending (7). In some states there are special provisions for the denaturalization of naturalized citizens which do not apply to native ones (8). Frequently, though not always, this is used as a sanction against those who have not lived up to their obligations as new citizens. Loyalty and obligations are however, also at stake in most interpretations of the criteria (2) to (4). Where emigration rights are denied, even the mere fact of living abroad without a change of citizenship (1) may count as a severe disloyalty.

I will first discuss the most obvious case of persons who live permanently abroad and become naturalized there. Individuals who have in this way shifted both their social and their political membership to another country will be often disinterested in being counted as citizens in the registers of their state of origin. Others may even actively attempt to cut all ties that bind them to a state which they no longer perceive as theirs. In a liberal view it does not matter how well-considered their motives are and whether they want to distance themselves politically from the regime or socially and culturally from the society where they have come from. They should generally have the right to formalize their alienation if they so wish. Others may with similar good reasons want to retain their citizenship in emigration because they intend to return, because they remain deeply involved with developments there even when living permanently abroad, or because they see it as a symbol of their ethnic identity in the country of immigration. It appears that this does not present any difficulty for liberal theory which favours individual freedom of choice, wherever this does not collide with a similar freedom for others and does not jeopardize general conditions for social order.

This freedom is, however, frequently restricted from both sides of the spectrum: by making the option of expatriation conditional upon the acquisition of a foreign citizenship, upon emigration, or upon both, and by denaturalizing those who fulfil these conditions also if they do not wish it. Let me consider in turn the situation of those who are naturalized abroad, who acquire a foreign citizenship in the country, and those who emigrate without changing their citizenship. What justification is there for both kinds of restrictions?

A liberal case for restricting expatriation abroad can be made only when either the emigrant or the receiving state refuse naturalization there. If the obligation to avoid generating statelessness is as strong as I have argued earlier, expatriation may be denied unless a person already possesses another citizenship or will acquire it simultaneously. However, there are two different ways to avoid statelessness. One is a denial of exit, the other one is an obligation of admission. In a liberal perspective both are obviously not equivalent. The latter has to be reinforced in order to make the former dispensable: statelessness should be avoided by guaranteeing individuals access to a new citizenship rather then by refusing them the right to leave an old one. Take the example of refugees from an authoritarian state. Although becoming a stateless refugee in orbit is certainly no solution for their problems, it might be preferable for them compared with the threat of being returned to their persecutors because of their original citizenship (Arendt, 1967, p. 286).[4] The most important rule for avoiding statelessness is that each country should be primarily responsible for naturalizing those of its residents who have either formally lost their nominal citizenship or *de facto* lost the protection of their state of origin.[5] Sending states' responsibility for their citizens abroad need not go as far as protecting them against the dangers of voluntary statelessness by denying expatriation. Where the problem is the receiving state's refusal to naturalize, pressure should be on that government to allow for a change of citizenship rather than on the emigrant not to expatriate. However, expatriation may be made conditional upon acquiring another citizenship without paternalistic motives when a person chooses statelessness as a way of avoiding obligations towards both the state of origin and the receiving state.

Is acquiring another citizenship abroad also a sufficient reason for denaturalization? Quite a number of European countries have such provisions in their laws (de Groot, 1989, pp. 282–3). This can be explained by a general policy of avoiding dual citizenship. However, such policies need not be symmetric for denaturalization abroad and for new admissions in the country. Generally speaking state policies in this regard are determined by nationally specific combinations of three different motives: making citizenship of the country a unique and exclusive relation, increasing the number of citizens in the country, and retaining a maximum number of emigrants as citizens living abroad. Symmetry is required only when the first motive overrides the others, or when the second and third reasons are equally important. Most states assign, however, very different weight to them and are therefore hardly concerned about formal symmetry. Nations with a history of emigration have mostly tried to maintain their emigrants' citizenship. This is one factor explaining why some European states allow their emigrants who become naturalized abroad to keep their former citizenship while at the same time forbidding immigrants in their territories to retain theirs.[6] Where citizenship rules are strongly determined by specific state interests that result from a particular concept of nationhood or position in the international system, it would be naive to expect states to show an abstract concern for symmetry in how their nationality laws apply abroad and in the country.

Would a liberal democratic approach require symmetry in this case and would it justify denaturalization when a second citizenship is acquired abroad? If, as I have argued in chapter 4, naturalization in the country should be made easy by tolerating dual citizenship there will hardly be a special concern about avoiding it among citizens living abroad. However, a quite different argument can be made in favour of some restriction: it cannot be desirable policy for a liberal democracy to retain forever those as nominal citizens who have no social or political ties whatsoever to the country. Doing this would lead to an increasing disjuncture between nominal citizenship and active membership in a political community. The chain of endless ascriptive transmission of citizenship in emigration by *ius sanguinis* should therefore be broken at least in the third generation (de Groot, 1989, p. 292). A second generation could be offered the citizenship of their parents' country of origin as an option because they might need it when they are involved in family plans for return or pendulum migration. Some countries have a rule that children born abroad of citizen parents will lose their citizenship automatically at a certain age after reaching their majority unless they take up residence in the country whose citizenship they had inherited.[7] As far as the first generation of emigrants is concerned denaturalization is certainly not required, but it might well be made automatic. Emigrants who show no interest in retaining their citizenship could be denaturalized. The acquisition of a new citizenship abroad is no indicator for such disinterest, but a prolonged period of residence in the country after naturalization with no visits to the country of origin may *prima facie* be interpreted as disinterest. The simplest indicator is probably when a person no longer takes the effort to renew her passport (de Groot, 1989, p. 294). As a precaution against possible hardship and unforeseen consequences such emigrants ought to be notified before a decision is taken, they should have a right to protest and should be given an option of easy renaturalization later on.

From what has been said so far it follows clearly that emigration in itself without a corresponding change of citizenship is no sufficient reason for denaturalization. The length of residence abroad can only become a relevant criterion in combination with the acquisition, or the possession since birth, of a foreign citizenship. This seems to be commonly respected in national laws of liberal democracies. Although it is not a sufficient condition, emigration is certainly a necessary one for denaturalization. Are there any circumstances under which a state should be allowed to denaturalize some of its citizens while they continue to live in the territory? This raises the question whether political links of an ethnic or national minority to a foreign power can also become a relevant reason for depriving them of their citizenship. That possibility has not been included in my list because it does not concern individual exit from a stable group of citizens but a radical transformation and redefinition of the core group itself.[8] Yet it is the extreme cases of collective denaturalization of native populations which best illustrate the dangers inherent in the power of nation-states to define their own rules of exit.

Let us first think of cases where a colonial power has established a formally independent government and invaded a country by a large number of settlers. When the native majority manages to seize power again, would it be entitled to denaturalize these settlers? That sort of question can hardly be answered by postulating abstract rules. However, in most cases it seems to be just that kind of historical injustice which cannot be reversed without creating new injustice of a similar kind. Where colonialists have been a small bureaucratic, economic and military elite isolated from the wider society, or have been in the country only for a short time, denaturalization might be nothing but an instrument for enforcing their emigration. In Northern Ireland, Southern Africa or Israel the situation is very different and no democratic programme would contain a proposal of denaturalizing the descendants of the settlers.[9]

One might think of the Soviet successor states outside Russia as borderline cases (see also sections 2.3 and 7.3). The Baltic states certainly had good reasons for not giving automatic citizenship to members of the Soviet armed forces stationed in the territory. The old ethnic Russian minorities were included in the new citizenships anyway. The problematic aspect of the policy was temporary denaturalization in Estonia and Latvia for those who had come mainly as industrial workers after 1945 and who form local majorities in some parts of these countries. The driving motive was not to push out these populations but rather to disenfranchise them during the initial phase of political reconstruction. In contrast with Lithuania,[10] where the inclusive allocation of citizenship followed the idea that a new state had been founded, Estonia and later also Latvia[11] adopted a restored-state model which implied automatic citizenship only for citizens of the pre-war states and their descendants (Brubaker, 1992, p. 282). Teaching formerly dominant minorities a lesson that they will have to accept the political institutions of the nation-state and to learn its national language[12] is an understandable desire. Yet suspending their membership must be seen as a deeply problematic move, not only because this strongly violates the liberal principle of inclusive citizenship but even on consequentialist grounds, as it risks permanent political alienation among the minority and the strengthening of forces hostile to the new state.[13]

In other situations, enforced denaturalization of populations living permanently in the country has been a prelude to civil war, mass expulsion or extermination. I have already mentioned the case of Jews in Nazi Germany and Vichy France. The escalation of the break-up of Yugoslavia into war and civil war can hardly be explained without understanding the power of threats to withdraw from minority populations the protection of full citizenship, especially when the credibility of such threats is enhanced by living memories of mass killings committed by one or both sides in the past.[14] The tragic events illustrate a Hobbesian core of citizenship. When a group of the population becomes convinced that its state is no longer capable or no longer willing to defend it against organized violence and aggression, self-defence and counter-aggression will be the answer wherever the group has the military means for this. In this sense the threat of collective denaturalization was a major mobilizing factor. 'Ethnic cleansing' then became the way in which the threat was actually carried out. On the one hand, minorities were formally denaturalized in order to be expelled, and on the other hand, they were driven out of their home territories in order to deprive them of any claim to citizenship there.[15]

I have argued that, generally speaking, emigration is a necessary but not sufficient condition for denaturalization. Is this also true for expatriation? Again, the second part of the answer has already been given above: the desire to avoid statelessness and to prevent citizens from fleeing their obligations can justify restrictions in some cases, but as a general policy those who have left for good should be granted expatriation. The more difficult question is whether expatriation should only be permitted after emigration. Henry Sidgwick thought of this as an indisputable principle: 'We may lay down, then, that expatriation is to be free, and renunciation of citizenship – with certain restrictions to prevent the evasion of special or temporary obligations – but on condition of leaving the country. So far as I know, it has never been even proposed that individual members of a State should be allowed to renounce citizenship while remaining within its territorial limits' (Sidgwick, 1897, p. 231). Today we can no longer state this requirement in such a categorical manner. I will discuss in the following section a contemporary contractarian proposal to generally allow expatriation also for persons who live in their country of citizenship. I do not think that this is either a feasible or desirable policy as long as the reasons for such internal expatriation are purely subjective ones. Certainly, political links to a state can also become very weak for those living there. They may be either totally disinterested in political membership or they may be actively opposed to the constitution and the regime. Nevertheless, expatriation can legitimately be made conditional upon prior emigration.

Exceptions are frequently made from this rule where the political links or social ties of the expatriating person to another country are of an objective sort. This is the case when they are already dual citizens or when they marry a foreign citizen or are adopted by a foreigner. In many of these instances one may still think it problematic that a citizen can turn into an alien while staying in the country. States with a strongly territorial definition of citizenship, such as the USA, generally deny expatriation also to those who marry a foreigner unless they leave the country.[16] In a framework of citizenship by descent, as it prevails in continental Europe, family membership can override the criterion of residence in such cases. This is certainly not a question involving fundamental liberal democratic principles. But there may be pragmatic reasons for some exceptions to the rule that emigration is a necessary condition for expatriation. Some states allow dual citizenship for a limited period only and the dual citizen should be free to decide in this case which citizenship she prefers to give up (de Groot, 1989, p. 289). If the dual citizen or person married to a foreigner intends to settle in this other state, it might be perfectly reasonable to renounce the citizenship of the state where she presently lives in order to facilitate migration and integration abroad. Here again paternalistic reasons to protect persons against the consequences of their own imprudent decisions become largely irrelevant when optional renaturalization is offered.[17]

Acquisition of a foreign citizenship while living in the country, which is mostly the result of marrying a foreign citizen, is also a reason for automatic denaturalization in some states. Yet this is not a common rule even where there is a general policy of avoiding dual citizenship. As mentioned earlier, rules are frequently asymmetric in this respect. Germany, for example, permits the acquisition of dual citizenship for its own citizens as long as these live in the country.[18] Austria is today among the few states in Europe which still denaturalize their own citizens residing in the country.[19] Exceptions are made only when retaining the Austrian citizenship is in the interest of the state. At the same time, Austrian policy is quite inconsistent because it does permit dual citizenship acquired by *ius sanguinis* from mixed parentage. Denaturalization of spouses of foreigners is one of the most obvious cases where the attempt to make citizenship a unique and exclusive form of membership leads to consequences which are unacceptable in a liberal view of membership. This is not because denaturalization should be used only as a sanction against severe acts of disloyalty. As the case of national minorities has shown, such an accusation can be a dangerous tool in the hands of authoritarian power. Denaturalization need not be a sanction. For those who live and become naturalized abroad it can be a simple consequence of a loosening of social ties. What makes denaturalization of those who acquire a new citizenship by marrying a foreigner fundamentally wrong, is the assumption that the social ties of residence will no longer be relevant for their political status.

Serving voluntarily in a foreign army or holding public office for a foreign state are irrelevant for expatriation but had been probably the most important criteria for denaturalization in past centuries. They were the clearest indicators that a person had turned into a citizen of another state as long as nominal citizenship was not yet registered thoroughly by state bureaucracies and before international passports became the common means of identifying foreigners. As an indicator of a *de facto* change of citizenship this criterion has become largely redundant today.[20] Yet these acts can also be seen as a breach of loyalty which goes beyond that of adopting a foreign citizenship. States which allow for the acquisition of a second citizenship abroad could thus be motivated to retain a provision for denaturalization for such cases. This is not without plausibility. However, there are relevant objections against generalizing these rules and broadening their scope of application.

First, the boundaries between public administration and public office are not always clear and the former can cover many occupations which are in no way sensitive to the interests of other states. Second, such a rule would exempt important occupations from free access to occupation and employment in the European Union (de Groot, 1989, pp. 299-300).

Constitutional barriers for the exercise of public office by other Union citizens háve already been removed in member states. Third, for some kinds of public office it might be especially important to appoint foreigners or let them run as candidates. Take as an example special branches of public administration whose task is to fight discrimination of immigrants or to promote their integration. Even in the sensitive area of security services it might be advisable to recruit foreign residents for the local police force of immigrant districts.[21] Finally, if the receiving state accepts foreign citizens for a certain public office why should the sending state denaturalize them unless the nature of the office particularly affects its national interest?

Do these arguments also apply to dual citizens? They are certainly in a different position. On the one hand, denaturalization would not threaten to make them stateless. And one could argue that by exercising a public office in one state they have in fact chosen one of their two memberships. On the other hand, if they choose to be dual citizens and therefore cannot exercise public office in either state they will be deprived of some important citizen rights, such as the right to be elected for parliament. Dual citizenship would thus become a degraded and passive form of citizenship no longer compatible with the republican idea of being ruled and participating in rule.

Rather than understanding the exercise of public office as an indication for specific and exclusive loyalty towards one state which is incompatible with being a citizen of another state, a liberal solution ought to define relevant state interests as narrowly and concretely as possible. One should determine the most sensitive areas where holding the citizenship of another state is unacceptable because conflicts of loyalty are unavoidable. For important public offices outside this narrow area one might adopt another restriction which prohibits the *simultaneous* holding of another public office in, or for, a foreign state. Foreign or dual citizens could thus be officials in one state while also being ordinary members in another one,[22] but they could not accumulate offices in both states. This simple rule would appease fears that in exercising their office they could represent the interest of another state rather than of the local population.[23]

Dual obligations for military service have been one of the main obstacles for dual citizenship. Articles 5 and 6 of the 1963 Strasbourg Convention developed a solution for this problem based on four simple rules: (1) a plural citizen shall have to fulfil military obligations only in one of the states in which he is a citizen, (2) dual citizens will be drafted in the state of their habitual residence, (3) nevertheless, until the age of 19, individuals have a right to choose to serve in the army of one of these states, (4) each state will accept that dual citizens who have already served in the army of another contracting state are no longer liable to be drafted. This model can only work if serving in a foreign army will not be regarded as a reason for denaturalization. Furthermore, most governments will be quite inclined to allow their citizens to serve in a foreign army if this is the army of a close ally.[24] So, just as with public office, the threat of denaturalization for serving in a foreign army should be properly limited to situations of emergency or war or where national security and interest are otherwise plausibly affected.

While military service for another state is a traditional reason for denaturalizations military obligations towards one's own state may be counted as obstacles for expatriation. Rules and practices are different in this respect. Some deny the possibility of expatriation for male emigrant citizens who would be liable to be drafted if they lived in the country, others make it discretionary by requiring special permission, still others allow their citizens living abroad to buy themselves out of this obligation.[25] Similar obstacles for expatriation exist for military staff or even more generally for civil servants. The idea is that such persons are especially obliged towards their state because they have not yet fulfilled their duty to serve in the army, because in their occupation they have acquired knowledge which is sensitive for national security, or because as civil servants they have entered a special commitment of lifelong loyalty. The provisions of the Strasbourg Convention just mentioned provide an alternative solution also for these cases. Military purposes would quite naturally override concerns about membership rights if we lived in a Hobbesian international system where 'Kings and Persons of Soveraigne authority, because of their Independency, are in continuall jealousies, and in the state and posture of Gladiators; having their weapons pointing, and their eyes fixed on one another; that is their Forts, Garrisons, and guns upon the Frontiers of their Kingdoms, and continuall Spyes upon their neighbours; which is a posture of War' (Hobbes, 1973, XIII, p. 65). However, if governments want to avoid this build-up of threats between their states they ought to conclude contracts which give priority to membership rights over military concerns. Conscription was the dominant state interest that led to a gradual formalization of nominal citizenship since the early 19th century. Yet liberal principles today support de Groot's assertion that 'legal constructions of citizenship are improper solutions for problems of conscription' (de Groot, 1989, p. 289, my translation).

Criminal activities of citizens may affect their membership status in two opposite ways. They can in certain instances be deprived of their citizenship as a special form of punishment. Or they may be denied expatriation because state authorities want to put them on trial or in prison. Denaturalization as a consequence of criminal conviction can only be understood as a relic form of banishment which has become obsolete in all liberal democratic states. Even the most severe crimes are today no longer punished by expulsion. This obsoleteness may not be altogether due to humanitarian progress in penal codes. Banishment is also ineffective as a sanction or deterrent when there are many other countries to go to where one can live quite comfortably. For political refugees, exile may be just as hard a fate in modernity as it was in antiquity. But this is no longer true for criminals, who quite often inhabit a truly international world. In liberal democracies today denaturalization is generally no longer used as a sanction against criminals living in the state of their native citizenship. Some countries apply such a rule only against those who have acquired citizenship by naturalization, while a few others maintain it also for native citizens who commit acts abroad that severely damage national interest or prestige (de Groot, 1989, pp. 295–8, p. 301). Austria and Greece are among those countries which also deny expatriation to criminals.[26] I have argued that changing international relations have helped to disentangle membership rights from the issue of military service. The same can be said for the persecution of criminals. Neither a foreign residence nor a change of citizenship puts a person automatically or completely outside the effective reach of criminal justice. States ought to agree among each other on who is responsible for persecuting a crime and mostly this will be the state in whose territory it has been committed. Treaties of extradition will facilitate the enforcement of such rules.

This brings us to the final criterion of the list in table 3. In section 4.1 I have shown that distinctions between the legal status of native and naturalized citizens have been largely abolished in liberal democracies. This is more true with regard to the positive rights of citizenship than with regard to exit. In many countries the fundamental right not to be deprived of one's citizenship against one's will is secure only for native citizens but not for naturalized ones. Denaturalization of the former may be either a consequence of a breach of loyalty and obligations or of reversing a decision about naturalization which was based on false premises. Apart from committing a crime, some states also punish naturalized citizens in this way for supporting the enemy during a war or for other acts that severely damage national interests. A naturalization decision may be regarded as invalid either because of the applicant's fault or because of objective circumstances which were not known at the time of the decision. Citizens may thus be denaturalized for making false statements or providing false documents during the application. But they may also lose their citizenship in cases where they had been perfectly sincere. This can, for example, happen when citizenship had been acquired automatically by marrying a native whose own citizenship had been falsely registered.[27] Austria is now one of the few remaining countries in Western Europe which also denaturalize those who have not renounced another citizenship within a certain period of time in spite of an obligation to do so.[28]

Normative criticism of these rules from a liberal point of view can be quite straightforward. First, if naturalization is access to full citizenship rather than to a second-class status, the conditions for exit ought to be the same for all citizens as well, no matter how they acquired their membership. Second, a legal decision which was based on false premises may certainly be revised. However, this should never be to the detriment of a beneficiary of the decision who had not consciously manipulated presuppositions of this decision in her favour. Third, even in cases where there had been such manipulation there ought to be a statute of limitation. Depriving somebody of her citizenship is a grave intrusion into a basic human right, whereas not granting naturalization in a discretionary procedure is in most cases not. Entry and exit rules are morally asymmetric in this respect. Reversing a decision on naturalization can therefore never be justified by simply stating that the applicant would not have obtained citizenship in the first place had all the facts of the case been known.

In conclusion, let me consider more generally the logic connecting citizenship obligations with exit rules. There are views of citizenship which emphasize obligations of individuals towards the state and maintain that the enjoyment of rights by all depends upon everybody's contribution to the political community. These approaches will consistently require rather extensive restrictions on expatriation and will support similarly extensive provisions for denaturalization.

Non-compliance with obligations incurred from the social contract or from previous enjoyment of benefits, and free-riding on others' contributions to the common welfare can be individually rational behaviour which is destructive for the political community. Some obligations may be easily enforced as long as the individual lives in the territory. Exit becomes then the only way to avoid the obligation and denial of exit may be necessary in order to enforce it. Where citizenship is understood as involving ascriptive and never-ending obligations, voluntary expatriation will at best be a favour granted discretionarily by the sovereign but never a right. Where obligations are more limited in scope and time, citizens who want to quit membership must first prove that they have done everything required of them (completed their military service, paid their taxes, fully paid any fine or served any prison sentence) and will be denied exit as long as they have not returned what they owe to the state. Expatriation will therefore be transformed from a liberty into a strongly conditional right.

Other obligations may be difficult to enforce also in the state territory. It then becomes imperative to deter free-riders who try to enjoy all the benefits of citizenship while refusing to contribute towards their communal production. In this case the threat of compulsory exit, i.e. banishment or denaturalization, will be an effective deterrent or also a punishment for those who have severely failed in meeting their obligations. It might, for example, be used against army deserters (unless they receive harsher punishment anyway) or against corrupt public administrators. Apart from the specific obligations of soldiers or those who hold a public office, the most important obligation of citizenship, which is also the most difficult one to enforce, is that of loyalty towards one's state. In this perspective denaturalization turns into a proper sanction for disloyalty.

The opposing view that freedom of exit ought to be extended and protected against restrictions on expatriation as well as against enforced denaturalizations rests on a very different idea of membership. Here substantial citizenship is first of all conceived as a bundle of fundamental rights. Rather than seeing rights as contingent benefits which arise from first accepting fairly unspecified obligations, it is obligations which are necessary and justified only as far as they contribute to the provision and sustainability of citizenship rights (see chapter 12). In rights-based citizenship, benefits will usually exceed burdens for the big majority of citizens. Voluntary compliance with obligations can be reasonably expected and there is certainly no general justification for denying exit in order to enforce them. The 'right to have rights' (Arendt, 1967, p. 296) is the cornerstone of citizenship.[29] In a world of nation-states it translates into a right to nominal membership (see section 2.1). This right is at the same time a liberty, namely the liberty to quit membership and to choose a different one. The right to membership has a value which is independent from that of the other more specific rights and obligations of citizenship. So in each case where individuals have not met their obligations their right to membership must be counted as a strong, and in most cases overriding, argument against denaturalization as well as against denying expatriation.

Restrictions may still be justified in both cases where they are necessary to maintain the basic structure of citizenship itself. In a world of nation-states this structure has a strong territorial reference (see chapter 1), although it reaches beyond state borders in many aspects. Rights of citizenship can become largely obsolete where people have lost all their social and political ties to a state by living permanently outside its territory and have acquired the membership of another state where they have taken residence. This consideration justifies restricting the extension of citizenship by *ius sanguinis* beyond second-generation emigrants, and it may also justify denaturalizing a first generation as long as this is not enforced against their will. That is a possible but not strictly necessary restriction. With the exceptions discussed above, prohibiting voluntary expatriation by citizens living permanently in the country of their citizenship is not merely a possible rule, but a necessary one in order to maintain an inclusive distribution of citizenship rights in a country. Whether this restriction of liberty contradicts the requirements of internal consent will be discussed in the following section. In both cases the denial of expatriation and the enactment of denaturalization largely lose their character as sanctions, and turn instead into restrictions which preserve the general preconditions for close relations between citizens and their state. In this view, sanctions against non-compliance with necessary obligations and against free-riding have to be enforced within the relation of citizenship but not by manipulating membership itself.

5.2. CONSENSUAL MEMBERSHIP AND FREE EXIT

My account of foundational consent in chapter 3 has suggested that under contemporary conditions all three classic strategies for deriving citizenship from every member's consent are doomed to failure. A Hobbesian narrative about foundational consent is no longer acceptable for liberal democracy. Its basic fault is not that it refers to some mythical origin of states or that it gives a distorted account of social life before the emergence of states. The problem is that the contract generates state sovereignty but not rights of citizenship. Rousseau was himself quite sceptical about the possibility of realizing his republican vision of collective self-determination and actualization of internal consent under the conditions of modernity. Furthermore, as with Hobbes, his theory is neither sufficiently democratic nor liberal enough to provide a normative model. Locke's premises have been certainly more acceptable to liberal theorists. However, his substitution of consent in admissions for foundational consent seems to be just as inapplicable to contemporary politics as those of Hobbes or Rousseau. Yet this conclusion might be premature. Could one not derive consensual membership from exit rather than from entry?

In examining the different rules of expatriation and denaturalization which can be found in existing legislation of liberal democracies, I have already stated and defended what I see as a liberal democratic perspective on exit rights. In the second part of this chapter I will discuss whether rights of exit also serve the purpose of defining and legitimating political membership and rule as consensual. Before turning to this idea it should be emphasized, however, that freedom in exit has not been supported by many political regimes of the past nor by many of the most influential political theories. Only a specifically liberal version of consensual membership will provide a solid foundation for exit rights.

Those strands of political thought which insist that citizenship is an innate characteristic of an ascriptive group or that it is attributed by the state rather than chosen by the individual are consistent in denying such choice not only in entry but also in exit. For ethnic nationalism voluntary expatriation is a perversity. Citizenship is derived from membership in a nation conceived as an ethnic community of descent. Nobody can choose her descent and so nobody can choose citizenship either. An ethnic nation might assimilate foreigners or admit them as members when they marry native citizens. Even then it is not these individuals who have chosen their new citizenship but rather the nation which has chosen them. Similarly a state may decide to expel some disloyal member but no individual born as a citizen may renounce membership. What could be granted without inconsistency is discretionary expatriation for those who are naturalized citizens. However, as we have seen in discussing national legislations, today even states which hold on to the principle of descent in the transmission of citizenship and strongly restrict new admissions, such as Germany, Austria and Switzerland, do allow for voluntary expatriation when the individual lives permanently abroad and has adopted another citizenship.

Apart from ethnic nationalism, expatriation can also be denied by postulating a permanent obligation towards a sovereign. The conservative doctrine of perpetual allegiance which preceded the early modern notions of social contract in 17th century England is the classic example.[30] Here it is not an innate characteristic of the individual but the political circumstances of her birth which lead to inalienable citizenship. In the divine law conception, God has entrusted the sovereign to rule over all born in the territory; in the natural law perspective introduced into the debate by Sir Edward Coke, perpetual allegiance is derived from the fact that the sovereign has provided protection to the child during infancy. Just as one owes a lifelong gratitude to one's parents the same obligation is due to the sovereign for similar reasons (Schuck and Smith, 1985, pp. 12–20). While the ethno-nationalist view leads to the conclusion that expatriation is either impossible or perverse, the idea of perpetual allegiance makes it possible but an act of sin which gives the sovereign a right to punish the perpetrator.

Does social contract theory lend better support to free expatriation? If individual consent is the basis for admission into, as well as for the legitimacy of political rule inside, the polity, then any individual who dissents should presumably be allowed to leave the community. When a person is forced to remain a member of an association against her will how can she be said to consent to its collectively binding decisions? But, as we have already seen in chapter 3, this is not the view taken by classic contract doctrines. For Hobbes, individuals give up all their rights when they turn voluntarily into subjects, including the right to renounce their allegiance to the sovereign. In Locke's view the contract must be concluded by each and every individual but only once in a lifetime, and it remains binding for the rest of this life. Rousseau's framework of participatory citizenship seems to permit the relatively widest leeway for voluntary exit but only at the cost of more powers for the community to deny admission and also to expel undesirable members.

The principle that citizenship is a matter of individual choice both in access and in exit is a distinctively liberal one, and it emerged only towards the end of the 18th century. As mostly happens with ideas that later become regarded as universally valid this one, too, was born out of a specific historical constellation of political forces and interests: in their fight for independence, a right to emigration as well as expatriation from Britain became of vital importance for the North American colonies.[31]

Nevertheless, an affirmative position on exit rights can already be found in a classic text of Greek political philosophy. Plato's dialogue 'Crito' records Socrates' refusal to escape from prison and his argument for accepting the death sentence although he regards it as unjust. Socrates imagines the laws of Athens speaking to him:

> [B]y the very fact of granting our permission we openly proclaim this principle, that any Athenian, on attaining to manhood and seeing for himself the political organization of the state and us its laws, is permitted, if he is not satisfied with us, to take his property and go away wherever he likes ... On the other hand, if any one of you stands his ground when he can see how we administer justice and the rest of our public organization, we hold that by so doing he has in fact undertaken to do anything that we tell him. And we maintain that anyone who disobeys is guilty of doing wrong on three separate counts: first because we are his parents, and secondly because we are his guardians, and thirdly because, after promising obedience, he is neither obeying us nor persuading us to change our decision if we are at fault in any way (Plato, 1961, 51d,e, pp. 36–7).

Like an eloquent lawyer in her address to the jury, the personified laws give different and not necessarily mutually compatible reasons, which all support the same conclusion that fleeing the execution of a sentence means destroying the laws and the constitution of the city. The first reason is close to the idea of perpetual allegiance to a sovereign political community modelled on obligation to parental authority: the laws have been Socrates' parents and guardians. The second reason involves a social contract idea of consent: escape would mean a 'breaking of covenants and undertakings made with us, although you made them under no compulsion or misunderstanding, and were not compelled to decide in a limited time' (52e, p. 38). Once the underlying idea of political community is accepted, these two arguments do indeed allow for far-reaching restrictions of exit rights and a moral obligation of individuals to comply with these restrictions even when they are against their fundamental interests. But there is little reason to accept this image of community as relevant for a modern liberal state. Two other reasons given by the laws are more interesting. The third one lies in the argument that Socrates is obliged to stay and accept his sentence because he has enjoyed the right to voice his dissatisfaction and even opportunities to change the laws. The fourth reason, finally, contains an outright paradox: the laws had given Socrates the liberty to leave without restrictive conditions or prohibitively high costs. (He would have been allowed to take his property with him.) The fact that he had not used this liberty of legal exit in the past now counts as a reason for dismissing the opportunity of clandestine exit offered by Crito.

Socrates' justification for his obligation towards the laws of Athens combines, in Albert Hirschman's terminology, voice with exit (Hirschman, 1970). In the language of Rousseau and Kant, the argument from voice can be formulated as an obligation to obey a law which we have freely given to ourselves. Even under the conditions of direct democracy in Athens this does of course not mean that all citizens must have individually consented to each law. But it does mean that each citizen can be assumed to have consented to a law which he did not attempt to change in spite of all the opportunities for proposing alternatives. In representative democracy these sources of consent and obligation have largely vanished. We can still argue with Habermas that the normative validity of laws rests on the possibility that those concerned by them could have consented in a rational dialogue (Habermas, 1992), but this obligation can certainly not count as a reason to obey even an unjust application of a just law. Such a strong obligation could only arise from actual participatory consent. In a direct citizens' democracy it might indeed be impossible to assert one's individual rights against a judgment issued according to the rules and with majority support without thereby undermining the constitution itself. But a representative liberal democracy would certainly not be destroyed if citizens who are convinced that their punishment is unjust tried to resist with all possible non-violent means, including that of flight. Any modern version of citizenship must start from Locke's idea that political obligation ends where governments or judges no longer protect the citizen. 'If the raison d'être of the state is the provision of protection, no state which actively menaces its own subjects can have a sound claim to their dutiful obedience' (Dunn, 1991, p. 33). This is certainly sufficient reason to dismiss the whole argument in Crito when applied to an unjust decision by the judiciary. Far from destroying the foundations of liberty, individual resistance or collective civil disobedience must be seen as necessary to restore them in such instances.

However, consent is also involved in justifying political obligation to obey laws which do not contradict basic rights of liberal citizenship. So it might still be important to consider the salience of Socrates' reasons for the legitimation of political rule in contemporary democracies. John Dunn argues that political obligation in a liberal state with a highly individualistic culture can no longer be derived exclusively from gratitude (towards the laws as parents and guardians) or from fairness (of the basic constitutional arrangements). 'Only the eminently individualistic criterion of consent retains comfortable force'. This force is, however, greatly reduced by the 'severely limited presence of anything that could readily be mistaken for consent in the practical political life of modern societies' (p. 46).

Undoubtedly representative democracy makes internal consent in government to a large degree passive, implicit and delegated. But consent expressed in this form of government is still more than only hypothetical. The rules of delegation give citizens active power to change the governing personnel. And passive consent is not merely attributed but has to be confirmed by opportunities of active dissent. This is where exit rights come into play. Only where citizens enjoy fairly unconditional rights of emigration can one assume that they stay in the country by their own consent. That is hardly more than a simple tautology. However, the inference has often been far-reaching: those who do not leave although they could do so are thereby seen as consenting not only to stay but also to being ruled in the way they are. And conversely, systems of government have been justified as resting on the consent of those who are ruled where emigration and expatriation have been more or less free.

In his essay 'Of the Original Contract' David Hume attacked this line of argument. He maintained that political obligation derives neither from promise and contract nor from tacit consent, but from the social utility of submitting to authority which itself arises from superior force. Hume totally dismissed the idea that tacit consent could be deduced from exit rights with three arguments.

First, there is no real choice of exit for most people, either because they themselves think that this would violate their duty of allegiance or because they do not possess the necessary knowledge and means for emigrating: 'Should it be said that, by living under the dominion of a prince which one might leave, every individual has given a tacit consent to his authority and promised obedience, it may be answered that such an implied consent can only have place where a man imagines that the matter depends on his choice.' Yet no such choice exists where he thinks – 'as all mankind do who are born under established governments' – that he owes allegiance to a sovereign or government by his birth or where not knowing a foreign language and living 'from day to day by the small wages he acquires' makes emigration impossible even if it were permitted (all quotes from Hume, 1953, p. 51).

Second, Hume denies that sovereigns are in any way obliged to grant their subjects rights of emigration and expatriation: 'And did a prince observe that many of his subjects were seized with the frenzy of migrating to foreign countries he would doubtless, with great reason and justice, restrain them in order to prevent the depopulation of his own kingdom. Would he forfeit the allegiance of all his subjects by so wise and reasonable a law?' (ibid.). Hume also maintains that an emigrant who has voluntarily submitted himself to another sovereign can be denied expatriation by his state of origin: 'his native prince still asserts a claim of allegiance to him' (p. 52).

The third of Hume's arguments is that tacit consent is expressed in voluntary immigration rather than in merely not emigrating. 'The truest tacit consent of this kind that is ever observed is when a foreigner settles in any country and is beforehand acquainted with the prince and government and laws to which he must submit; yet is his allegiance, though more voluntary, much less expected or depended on than that of a natural-born subject' (ibid.). Here, Hume unwittingly echoes John Locke, for whom the rights of aliens were indeed based in tacit consent whereas those of citizenship required active consent (see section 3.4).

Hume mocks at Socrates' refusal to escape from prison because he had tacitly promised to obey the laws: 'Thus he builds a *Tory* consequence of passive obedience on a *Whig* foundation of the original contract' (p. 61, original emphasis). If we reject Hume's Tory position that exit rights are a mere chimera and can be denied without injustice, could we then build a Whig consequence from a Whig foundation, i.e. reassert the positive contribution of the liberty of emigration and expatriation to a liberal democratic idea of consensual government?[32]

Under such government people presumably know that they are neither morally nor politically bound to stay in, and to remain loyal citizens of, the state of their birth. In addition to guaranteeing political conditions for exit, liberal democratic states tend to promote also the social conditions for making it a realistic choice. The obstacles mentioned by Hume will be partly removed by the teaching of foreign languages and by social welfare policies. (Besides, in industrial capitalism low income turns from a barrier for emigration into a major incentive.) Hume's justification for exit restrictions has become obviously unacceptable outside authoritarian and totalitarian states. The building of the Berlin wall in 1961 in order to stop the 'frenzy of emigrating' which had seized East Germans at that time can hardly be considered a 'wise and reasonable' policy. And liberal sending states no longer assert strong claims to the allegiance of their emigrants. Exit rights are by now so firmly anchored in the canon of democratic liberalism that they have been elevated beyond citizenship to the level of universal human rights, which ought also to be respected by non-liberal regimes.

As far as immigration is concerned there is as little reason for assuming that voluntary entries always involve a strong form of consent with the regime of the receiving state as there is for supposing that all emigrants are political dissidents. It is naturalization rather than immigration which under ideal conditions expresses political consent – not with a government and not even necessarily with a constitution but with being a member of this particular political community and with sharing its future destiny. This consent is not tacit but explicit. Liberal democracies do grant immigrants far-reaching rights of citizenship before naturalization and they do oblige them to respect the laws of the country. However, neither the rights nor the obligations of immigrants are derived from consent expressed in their choosing this particular state for immigration. Immigrants who have been brought into the country without choosing it (e.g. stranded refugees) or who have chosen it without alternative options to go elsewhere (e.g. close family members of earlier immigrants) will enjoy the same rights and be submitted to the same obligations. Not the circumstances of their entry but their residence turns them into members of the society and makes them eligible for inclusion in citizenship. Implicit mutual agreement between immigrants and receiving states is relevant in distinguishing legal forms of immigration from illegal ones.[33] However, only the right of residence itself depends on this element of tacit consent while other rights of immigrants derive from the fact of their residence.

From rejecting Hume's arguments it neither follows that exit rights must be granted unconditionally nor that their guarantee is already sufficient proof for consent in government. I suggest that the following three relations between exit and consent are characteristic for liberal democracy. First, exit and consent in government are disconnected. Leaving a country or renouncing one's citizenship voluntarily need not be due to political dissent with its form of government. Therefore, staying where one could leave does not imply political consent either. Conversely, those who are politically dissatisfied cannot be expected to leave the country because this would imply severing their social and cultural ties in addition to their political ones. Therefore, those who stay do not thereby document their acceptance of political authority.[34] Second, exit and consent in membership are connected. The right to voluntary expatriation is the necessary condition for making attributed membership free and consensual as far as this is possible. Native citizens would be unfree as members if they could not renounce their citizenship with the consent of the state that had attributed it to them at their birth. Third, exit from membership is generally conditional upon exit from the territory. A universal right of expatriation in the country would be incompatible with maintaining an inclusive form of citizenship which is the foundation for consent in government in representative democracies.

While the first and second statement appear to me sufficiently evident, the third one still needs further explanation. In section 3.4 I dismissed Locke's proposal that the acquisition of citizenship ought to be always consensual and therefore must be made a free choice at the age of majority. In section 4.2 I suggested that choosing a new citizenship ought to be an option for immigrants because this choice is more essential for them than for native citizens. Now, I want to complete this line of argument by showing why a right to renunciation of membership without prior emigration would be a contradictory element within liberal citizenship.

Whether the idea of tacit consent is a mere ideological device of justification for an imposed decision or a plausible account of its validity, depends to a large degree on the opportunities of choice offered to those who are said to have consented tacitly to one of the options by not choosing a different one. If citizens first have to emigrate before being allowed to renounce their membership their choice is certainly severely restrained by this prior requirement. It seems, therefore, an attractive proposal to strengthen tacit consent in membership by reformulating Locke's theory for exit rather than for entry into citizenship. The problem arising from Locke's assertion that minors cannot be citizens would thus be circumvented. On reaching their majority all citizens should be given an opportunity to renounce their membership formally without having to leave if they choose to do so.

Peter Schuck and Rogers Smith have developed and defended this idea. They assert the Lockean principle that 'political membership can result only from free individual choices' (Schuck and Smith, 1985, p. 4). The following legislative changes should make US citizenship more consensual. First, native-born children of undocumented aliens should no longer be attributed citizenship ascriptively by *ius soli*. Second, all American citizens should be given a meaningful opportunity to expatriate themselves at the age of majority. Third, all children of American citizens born abroad who have not been attributed citizenship by *ius sanguinis* anyway should be given an option of naturalization. I will discuss here their second proposal only, which departs much more fundamentally from current international standards than the other two.[35] It is an attempt to turn the allocation of nominal citizenship into a result of mutual consent about membership between each individual and the community.

In a radical understanding, mutual consent might mean that not only must both partners have explicitly consented to an agreement, but that the agreement will also be binding only as long as there is mutual consent among all involved. The inference would be that states could arbitrarily denaturalize citizens and that nobody would have an independent right to become a citizen. Schuck and Smith are aware of these implications. If 'consent must be mutual, expressed by the existing community as well as by the individual ... a society could freely denationalize citizens against their will, reducing their security and status, perhaps even leaving them stateless' (p. 37). 'The tension between government by consent and full protection for inalienable rights, visible in liberal theory almost from its inception, is dramatically evident if a democratic government denies all obligations to those who are compelled to turn to it but who are not admitted to be its citizens' (ibid.). The authors are also aware of the converse problems resulting if a large number of individuals living in a state refused to become its citizens or renounced their citizenship (p. 38). Their own proposal attempts to avoid both implications without abandoning the idea of mutual consent as a foundation for membership. Nonetheless, as I will try to show, voluntary internal expatriation would have perverse effects of blurring, rather than highlighting, distinctions between citizens and non-citizens and of devaluating substantial citizenship. The former effect could be regarded as desirable for a liberal policy but the latter must lead to rejecting the idea.

A first point to be noted about Schuck and Smith's suggested procedure for voluntary expatriation is that it only expresses *tacit* consent: 'Failure to expatriate oneself formally and intentionally when provided the opportunity to do so should be taken as tacit consent to citizenship, just as it is today. That consent could be made all the more plausible by permitting those who did choose to renounce American citizenship to remain in the country as permanent resident aliens with all the attendant rights and duties of that status, if they so desired' (Schuck and Smith, 1985, p. 123). Locke, however, maintained that tacit consent was merely sufficient to ground the rights and obligations of aliens. Only positive and explicit consent, expressed in voluntary application for membership, can plausibly substitute for foundational and internal consent in a contractarian theory. Once the positive consent requirement for citizenship is transformed into a negative one, the essential distinction between citizens and aliens has already become blurred. Tacit consent to be ruled derived from the mere fact of residence is what citizens and resident foreigners share in common. Rather than reasserting the value of nominal citizenship for natives this seems to provide a good argument for equalizing citizenship rights and obligations for both groups. Certainly, a formal procedure where every citizen was asked on attaining her majority whether she wanted to expatriate herself, would have a symbolic effect of revaluating citizenship. However, I fail to understand in which way it would also legitimize distinctions of legal status between citizens and resident aliens.

A second point concerns the consequences of expatriation for those who choose it. As mentioned in chapter 2, Michael Walzer has argued in favour of voluntary expatriation for conscientious dissenters. Schuck and Smith are rather concerned about the possibility that this might be a reason for many to renounce American citizenship. So they propose to restrict this right if its exercise would be contrary to the interests of national defence (p. 125). On the other hand, they argue that under present American law resident aliens may also be drafted, so that male voluntary expatriates staying in the country 'would still be obliged to perform all the most burdensome duties of American citizens' (p. 124). The irony of this latter point is that extending the obligations of military service to foreign residents further undermines whatever difference persists in substantial citizenship between these and nominal citizens and should therefore be rejected from the point of view of authors who wish to draw a clearer line.

An option of voluntary expatriation cannot be made costless. If the costs were so high that no rational individual would ever choose it the option would become meaningless. Schuck and Smith are aware of the risks implied in statelessness. Although they see this as a problematic choice, they nevertheless defend the right to choose statelessness as grounded in individual autonomy. Given a sufficient level of protection and constitutional guarantees of rights granted to foreign residents, people might safely opt out of their citizenship (p. 124). While this seems a plausible argument, there is again a perverse consequence. Outside her state of regular residence a stateless individual would enjoy much less protection, and most other states would not let in stateless persons who cannot even claim refugee status because they have chosen this fate for themselves. So the price to be paid for voluntary internal expatriation would be abandoning one's options of travelling abroad or emigrating. This would render the situation of a voluntary expatriate substantially worse than that of legally resident foreigners who generally have the right to travel abroad, and to be readmitted into their country of nominal citizenship as well as into their country of residence.

Expatriates could become like foreign residents in the country only if they were also guaranteed an option to become naturalized in another state while staying where they are. This will be impossible for two reasons: first, the state of expatriation is unable to give such a guarantee for other sovereign states and second, it will probably want to restrain this option for reasons of national security. (Imagine that during the Vietnam war American citizens would have first expatriated in order to avoid the draft and then would have adopted North Vietnamese citizenship while staying as residents in the United States.)

As a final paradox of asserting consensual citizenship by extending an option of expatriation, consider the consequences for the value of citizenship if individuals could not only expatriate but could also choose the citizenship of a state in which they do not live. Citizenship would then indeed be actively chosen and consent would be positive. But once acquired, the status of a nominal citizen would be largely void of any substantial meaning. How could such persons possibly participate in the political life of the state whose citizenship they have chosen? All their important rights and obligations would remain tied to residence. If choosing a different citizenship is not just a purely symbolic gesture, they will have lost some of these rights (such as the right to vote) and some of their obligations (such as military service) while not gaining anything of comparable importance for their status as members of a political community. So the overall effect of such a rule would be a general devaluation of the substantial aspects tied to nominal citizenship.

Discussing proposals such as voluntary internal expatriation at such length might seem an exercise in mere sophistry without any practical relevance. However, the conclusion seems to me of considerable importance for liberal political theory. There appears to be no acceptable way in which citizenship allocation for the general population can be made more consensual and based on voluntary choice, beyond the options of acquiring a second citizenship while staying in the country or expatriating after leaving the country. If one tried to make citizenship consistently more optional one would thereby also make it more exclusive and less substantial in its value.

The same conclusion can of course also be derived from a realist point of view which starts from state interests. 'These core obligations of citizenship [of loyalty and service] are too important to the state to permit individuals to opt out of them at will. ... Despite the concern of liberal political theory to found political obligation on the voluntary consent of individuals, the state is not and cannot be a voluntary association. For the great majority of persons, citizenship cannot help but be an imposed, ascribed status' (Brubaker, 1989c, p. 102). For normative theory in the liberal tradition it will be difficult to accept that vital state interests are sufficient legitimation for denying autonomous individuals a voluntary choice of membership. My argument is that these choices are not only limited by state power but also by the demand for consent in government and for substantial rights of citizenship. It is impossible to maximize consent simultaneously in both dimensions. The freedom of choice in membership cannot be consistently universalized for all without thereby devaluing what is chosen. This is a challenge theories of political legitimation by consent should not easily ignore, because it is raised on their home territory.

NOTES

1. Germany and Turkey provide a good illustration. Under German law, retaining a former citizenship in naturalization is made very difficult (although some exceptions have been introduced in 1993). Yet a German citizen residing in Germany cannot be expatriated for obtaining another citizenship. Turkey has always been eager not to reduce the size of its largest emigrant community, in which attempt it was strongly assisted by the tough German rules for naturalization. However, when realizing that a second and third generation abroad would strongly opt for German citizenship if this became easier to do, Turkey adapted its policies by allowing for dual nationality and offering easy renaturalization. Although Turkey has not signed the Strasbourg Convention on dual nationality and dual military obligations, dual citizens who have served in the German army are now no longer liable to be drafted in Turkey as well.

2. Spain is one of these rare cases. However, the law distinguishes in this respect between Spanish citizens by birth and those by naturalization. Only the former cannot be denaturalized under any circumstance (see Article 11 of the Constitution and Article 25 of the Civil Code).

3. In Switzerland, until 1990, only the woman lost her Swiss citizenship by marrying a foreigner if she possessed or obtained her husband's citizenship, unless she declared her intention to retain her Swiss citizenship. Residence in or outside the country was irrelevant.

4. The rule of *non-refoulement* as specified in Article 33 of the Geneva Refugee Convention is meant to prevent such extradition. Without revoking it formally, recent reforms of national asylum laws in a number of European states have undermined this guarantee for refugees. One of the consequences is that asylum seekers today again resort to voluntary statelessness by throwing away passports and personal documents in order to prevent deportation to their countries of origin. Some receiving states have reacted to this by regarding the applications of undocumented asylum seekers as 'manifestly unfounded'. See for example the Austrian Asylum Act of 1991.

5. One might well go further and argue that liberal democratic states should provide the protection of their citizenship for those whose nominal citizenship serves to keep them hostage while they are being deprived of all their rights. This would amount to a principle of no longer recognizing a nominal citizenship as a binding legal relation between individual and state when it does not protect the most basic human rights. It would under certain conditions entitle and enable liberal states to follow the practice of Raoul Wallenberg, mentioned in chapter 2, who attributed Swedish citizenship to Hungarian Jews in Budapest in order to bring them out of hell. Of course, this cannot be understood as a general obligation to intervene from outside in any state that persecutes its minorities. What it could mean is that once a liberal democratic state has become involved, it bears an obligation towards the refugees and displaced persons there that extends beyond providing shelter only for those who have reached its home territory by their own efforts.

6. Switzerland was a good example for such double standard, until the law was changed in 1991 to allow also for dual citizenship for naturalized immigrants. Until 1993 the Netherlands had a policy of compulsory denaturalization if an emigrant adopted another citizenship. A policy change towards toleration of dual citizenship for immigrants took place in 1993 which will re-establish symmetry under the new liberal rules. According to the amendment under discussion in December 1993, an emigrant can prove her alliance to the Netherlands by renewing her passport every five years. Both immigrants and emigrants are expected to renounce their older citizenship when the objective ties upon which it was grounded have been loosened, but they are not compelled to do so (Van den Bedem, 1994).

7. The Swedish citizenship law takes into account most relevant considerations. According to Article 8, a Swedish citizen born abroad who has never taken residence in Sweden and has also not stayed in the country under circumstances which indicate an attachment to Sweden, loses her Swedish citizenship on her 22nd birthday. Authorities can, however, grant permission for her to retain it upon application.

8. I will discuss changes in collective membership in chapter 7.

9. Michael Walzer asserts that 'non-recognition of citizenship is not a reason for expulsion' in new states confronted with 'alien groups which have been admitted under the auspices of the old imperial regime' (Walzer, 1983, p. 42). This raises the additional question of

which reasons could justify not recognizing these groups' citizenship once their expulsion is regarded as illegitimate.

10 In Lithuania, persons who had been neither citizens of the pre-war republic, nor were descendants of such citizens, nor had been born in the territory and permanently resident therein, were given two years within which they could freely declare their citizenship (Brubaker, 1992, p. 280).

11. In June 1994 the Latvian Parliament adopted the most restrictive citizenship law of all Soviet successor states which would make 500.000 ethnic Russians stateless until the year 2000. At the moment of writing, it seems likely that this law will still be modified due to strong objections raised, among others, by the Latvian President, the Russian Government, and the Council of Europe.

12. Both Estonia and Latvia require knowledge of their respective languages for naturalization.

13. The situation in the Central Asian republics appears to be very different. Here, keeping the Russian population in the country is a major concern. Russians occupy key positions in the economy and a mass exodus which is already under way in some of the states could lead to a breakdown. The new governments have therefore offered citizenship to ethnic Russians. In Kazakhstan, for example, all inhabitants who do not apply for a different citizenship before 1 March 1995 will become Kazakh citizens automatically. Still, Kazakhstan and Uzbekistan want to emphasize their independence by refusing to grant dual citizenship, a demand which has been raised by Moscow and has already been granted by Kirghizia, Turkmenia and Tadzhikistan (Austrian Press Agency, 25 January 1994). The irony of the dilemma is that by closing the door to future entry in Russia, the demand for unique citizenship might prompt a larger emigration now, whereas dual citizenship would induce more Russians to stay by enabling them to leave at any time in the future.

14. The importance of the latter point in explaining the escalation of violence in ethnic and national conflicts was stressed by Rogers Brubaker in a discussion during a lecture in Vienna in October 1993.

15. The new Croatian nationality law gives citizenship only to ethnic Croats and to those born in Croatia. All others have to apply. Authorities do not have to give any reason for rejecting an application. Those deprived of citizenship also lose many of their social rights and quite a number have been forced into emigration (*Wiener Zeitung*, 3 February 1994). This appears to be considerably harsher than the Baltic laws. Of course, Croatia was a victim of Serb military aggression on a scale different from the few incidents in the Baltic involving former Soviet security forces. However, the exclusion of many Serbs from citizenship after the war must be felt by the Serb minority as a confirmation that their fear of being deprived of their rights as a minority in the new state was indeed justified.

16. According to section 351 of the US Immigration and Nationality Act 'no national of the United States can expatriate himself, or be expatriated, under this Act while within the United States' Section 349 provides exceptions for voluntary expatriation during a war with the Attorney General's confirmation that the renunciation is not contrary to the interests of national defence, and for denaturalization for acts of treason, conspiracy and similar crimes against the state.

17. There is a purely hypothetical scenario which would justify further restricting a choice of internal expatriation even for these special categories. Suppose that, as a strategy of undermining A's regime, state B would generously offer its citizenship to any citizen of A who travels to B. If A is a liberal state which grants dual citizenship this will have little effect. However, if A also has a rule permitting all dual citizens to expatriate themselves in the country this might open a back door for the dissatisfied and those who want to avoid obligations. If this became a real threat it could be easily countered by denying internal expatriation to those dual citizens who have acquired the citizenship of a foreign country by voluntary naturalization after birth.

18. See note 1 above.

19 The new Czech republic, whose government was anxious to make separation from Slovakia as clear-cut as possible, adopted the same policy, while Slovakia does allow its nationals to hold a second (Czech) citizenship. This has recently led to an interesting case. As a sign of protest against partition Petr Uhl, a former Czech dissident and signatory of Charta 77, acquired Slovak citizenship while continuing to live in Prague. He was subsequently deprived of his Czech citizenship and thus turned into a foreign citizen in his native homeland (*Der Standard*, 18 November 1993, p. 4).

20. In de Groot's comparative study of nine European citizenship laws, only four have retained this criterion for denaturalization. These are France, Italy, Austria and Spain (de Groot, 1989, p. 298).

21. This is particularly important where most immigrants are not naturalized. Some German cities have recently started to recruit foreigners for the police for this reason.

22. For a neorepublican view such as van Gunsteren's (1992), which understands citizenship itself as an office rather than as membership based on equal rights, this solution would probably be unacceptable.

23. This is a purely hypothetical possibility anyway. While there are already a number of dual citizens among delegates in European parliaments without causing political concern, 'dual representation in the sense that one person is a member of more than one state's parliament is practically and politically impossible. The electoral procedures and the requirement that a candidate have done years of political work before nomination, are effective restraints' (Hammar, 1990, p. 119).

24. Denaturalization for this reason is therefore frequently discretionary rather than mandatory. In the USA, a citizen will not be denaturalized for serving in a foreign army when he has obtained written permission from the Secretaries of State and of Defense (section 349 of the Immigration and Nationality Act).

25. Austria is an example of the first kind of rule, Germany of the second (de Groot, 1989, pp. 288–9) and Turkey of the third. If male Turkish citizens who are resident and employed abroad and are liable to be drafted pay a sum of DM 10,000 they have to serve only one month in the Turkish army.

26. In Austria, expatriation may be denied if an Austrian citizen has resided abroad for no longer than five years and if there are legal procedures pending which might lead to a prison sentence of more than six months (Article 37 of the Austrian Nationality Act). In Greece, an expatriation permission may not be granted if the applicant is liable to be drafted for military service or is persecuted because of crimes or misdemeanours (Article 14 of the Decree on Nationality).

27. Some Austrian examples were recently published in the magazine *Wiener* (December 1993).

28. Generally, applicants must first prove that they have been released from their previous citizenship before they obtain the Austrian one. In many cases, however, authorities of the country of origin take a long time to issue such a statement. An applicant may then be naturalized under the condition that she will be denaturalized again unless she attempts by all means available to be released from her previous citizenship within two years. If she has, however, held a second citizenship for six years without being denaturalized she may keep her Austrian citizenship. A similar rule exists in Luxembourg which is now, together with Austria, the Western European country with the strictest prohibition of dual citizenship.

29. '[T]he core of the very meaning of basic rights entails the "right" to assert rights on the part of the citizenry. This "right" is of course neither a particular positive right nor a negative liberty, but rather a *political* principle involving a new and active relation on the part of citizens to a public sphere that is itself located within civil society' (Cohen and Arato, 1992, p. 396).

30. The best-known representatives of this view were James I (The True Law of Free Monarchies, 1589), Sir Edward Coke, who developed a comprehensive theory of subjecthood in what became know as Calvin's Case (1608), and Robert Filmer (Patriarcha, 1680).

31. Voluntary expatriation was an especially acute issue during the Napoleonic wars when British officers searched American ships for British subjects and attempted to press American seamen into military service for the Crown.

32. For a general discussion of the right to leave one's country and one's citizenship see Whelan (1981) and Dowty (1987).

33. Although it has to be said that often illegal immigration and employment is tacitly tolerated by authorities who are reluctant to enforce sanctions against employers.

34. The second aspect of this disconnection is very clearly argued by Rawls: '[T]he government's authority cannot be evaded except by leaving the territory over which it governs, and not always then ... normally leaving one's country is a grave step: it involves leaving the society and culture in which we have been raised. ... The government's authority cannot, then, be freely accepted in the sense that the bonds of society and culture,

of history and social place of origin, begin so early in life and are normally so strong that the right of emigration (suitably qualified) does not suffice to make accepting its authority free, politically speaking, in the way that liberty of conscience suffices to make accepting ecclesiastical authority free, politically speaking' (Rawls, 1993a, p. 222).

35. For a comprehensive critique of the other aspects see the review by Joseph Carens quoted already in notes 2 and 3 of chapter 4 (Carens, 1987b).

6. Membership Decisions and Associations

This chapter is a summary and draws conclusions from the preceding ones. The first section analyses the structure of decisions about changes in membership. The second part explores analogies with various types of associations which could help to understand better the specific nature of membership in a liberal democratic state. In the third part I argue that citizenship in such a polity follows from the fact of social membership, but is still different from it in giving more scope to individual will and associational consent.

6.1. ENTRY AND EXIT DECISIONS

In chapters 4 and 5 I pointed out that entries and exits with regard to nominal citizenship can be distinguished by the degree to which the decision is shaped by the individual or by the state. Rules for discretionary, automatic or optional admission and for compulsory, discretionary or optional exit have been discussed extensively there. I will now present a more systematic overview of what I think is a complete list of decisions leading to a change of membership or blocking such a change. This analysis is not specific for states and could be applied to other organizations as well.

Table 4 shows decisions about membership[1] as the outcome of an interaction between an individual (in some cases also a group) on the one hand and a collective (mostly certain institutions or authorities within the collective) on the other hand. The idea is that identical outcomes have to be sharply distinguished with respect to the ways in which they have been reached. In a view which pays respect to autonomous agency, it is the choices of actors and their impact on the result which have to guide our assessment of inclusion or exclusion. All choices recorded in the table refer to changes in a membership relation between an individual and a collective or organization. Each of the two actors has three possible ways of acting: affirming a change (yes), opposing it (no) or remaining passive and not revealing her preferences (silent). The table lists only those choices with regard to a (potential) change of membership which are relevant for a certain decision structure and distinguish it from others. A decision structure (or mode of decision) is a characteristic combination of choices by the individual and the collective with an outcome. Generally only two different choices made by one of the actors are involved in characterizing each decision structure.

Table 4: Decisions about changes in membership

	entry decision	exit decision	exit/entry choices of individuals	collectives	outcome entry/exit
(1)	abduction or	expulsion or	no	yes	yes
	mandatory entry	mandatory exit	silent	yes	yes
(2)	invasion, devious entry,	escape,	yes	no	yes
	compulsory admission	compulsory release	yes	silent	yes
(3)	excluded	confinement	yes	no	no
	admission		silent	no	no
(4)	ascriptive	ascriptive	silent	yes	yes
	membership	non-membership			
(5)	automatic	automatic	silent	yes	yes
	admission	exit	no	yes	no
(6)	optional	optional	yes	yes	yes
	admission	exit	silent	yes	no
(7)	discretionary	discretionary	yes	yes	yes
	admission	exit	yes	no	no

(1) In abductions or mandatory entry, inclusion of the individual is achieved against active or passive resistance. The individual may oppose or may remain silent, the outcome is nevertheless inclusion. If the person pressed into entry agreed, this would not be relevant. The decision is characterized by the absence of consent and the dominance of the collective. This dominance may manifest itself in the actual use or the threat of force. Alternatively, the inclusion may be pushed through by establishing it as a social norm and making non-compliance costly for the individual. Abduction is characterized by the former, mandatory forms of entry by the latter way of reaching the outcome. The same decision structure applied to exit characterizes expulsions and mandatory exits. With regard to decisions about citizenship, entries are rarely forceful but quite often assume a certain mandatory character. Conquest leads to forceful inclusion in which the relation of individuals to states is one of subjection rather than of entitlements. Citizenship may be regarded as forced upon people against their will where colonial rule leads to the inclusion of a territory into that of the colonial power. Thus, before independence Algerians were regarded as French citizens. We might regard ordinary naturalizations as mandatory when there is strong social pressure to apply or when foreign immigrants are kept in a very insecure position and become naturalized just in order to

protect themselves against legal discrimination or expulsion. Denaturalization is expulsion from citizenship. This loss of membership is usually compulsory rather than mandatory because in withdrawing an individual's legal status state authorities do not depend on her compliance. However, when denaturalization is conditional, administrations sometimes cannot verify whether individuals are liable to be expelled from citizenship. Denaturalization then becomes mandatory. This is, for example, the case when dual citizenship is excluded but authorities have no way of controlling whether naturalized immigrants have retained or regained their previous citizenship.

(2) Invasion and escape are those forms of inclusion and exclusion where individuals or groups force their will upon the collective or organization. The outcome is the same as in (1), i.e. a change of the previous relation, but now the roles of the individual and the collective in reaching this outcome have been switched. Entry characterized by this decision structure can be reached in three ways: by the open use or threat of force which totally paralyses the decision-making power of the collective (invasion), by forcing the collective to take a positive decision about admission (compulsory admission) or by circumventing entry controls of the collective and sneaking into membership (devious entry). Citizenship can never be acquired directly by invasion because forceful entry of this kind destroys the preconditions for equal membership among peers. Invaders, however, can assume political membership in the community they have conquered where this is a strictly hierarchical one. Thus, Mongol invaders became Chinese emperors. Much the same is true for compulsory admissions. One might imagine cases where a weak democratic state is forced by a powerful neighbour to admit immigrants from there as citizens against the will of the community. Sneaking into citizenship is a form of entry which will be relevant only where conditions for admission are restrictive but at the same time difficult to control. Escape is a mode of exit which implies that there has been a previous situation of confinement in which power was totally concentrated in the collective. By escaping, the individual breaks this structure, regains autonomy and thus asserts her power over the collective. Parallel with the three ways of non-consensual entry just discussed, this form of exit can be achieved by forcing one's way out of a collective or organization without involving its decision, by forcing it to release the individual, or by sneaking out without its knowledge and permission. If individuals try to escape from their citizenship this implies that they are denied renunciation and this is generally an indicator of authoritarian rule. Escape presupposes emigration. Individuals may try to escape the *obligations* of citizenship while living in the country, but they have no way of getting rid of their formal status unless the state agrees to

release them. Once in exile, emigrants may quite easily sneak out of their former membership without the state of origin knowing it or being able to prevent it. The real test of whether they have indeed escaped not only from territorial sovereignty but also from oppressive citizenship comes only when the emigrant travels back to the state of origin with the passport and diplomatic protection of her new state.

(3) In excluded admission and confinement the roles are again the same as in (1) but now the choices and outcomes are the opposite ones. Excluded admission is not just defined by rejecting applicants. This can be as well the result of a discretionary decision. What characterizes this form of entry denial is that the applicant is excluded already *a priori*, independently of her attempt to acquire membership. Individuals are also defined as excluded when they are silent. It might seem strange that in table 4 this form of exclusion is related to entry and that confinement, which is a form of inclusion, is related to exit. However, the table lists choices with regard to *changes* of membership. Therefore, confinement is a decision about exit, namely its forceful denial by a collective or by its institutions. The relevant choices of the individual which correspond to the 'no' statement of the collective are 'yes' or 'silent'. They express dissent or non-consent. The possibility that the individual might also choose to stay confined is irrelevant. Excluded admission is of course an important feature in many naturalization rules. As discussed in chapter 4, exclusions can be summary when they concern ascriptive categories of persons, they can be conditional when they depend on individual acts or achievements or when they are only temporary. Similar forms exist for confinement in citizenship, i.e. for a denial of voluntary expatriation. I have argued in chapter 5 that what is formally speaking confinement in membership for those living in the country cannot be regarded as oppressive where emigration is permitted and where there are reasonable opportunities to go abroad.

(4) Ascriptive membership represents a special case in so far as there is no interaction in reaching the decision. The individual is excluded as an actor in any regard. She is not given a chance to consent or dissent and is not even present as someone against whose opposition an outcome is enforced. In ascriptive entry and exit it is taken for granted that membership or non-membership is decided by the collective only. Generally speaking, any principle of ascription which does not give membership to all humanity at the same time also ascribes non-membership. However, the emphasis on ascriptive non-membership differs strongly when a bounded concept of society instead of a global one is used as a reference point. Societies can be bounded in different ways. In chapter 1, I have suggested that for the purpose of studying citizenship, societies should be understood as collectives and institutional ensembles roughly delimited by the scope of

territorial sovereignty. Non-citizenship is a relevant form of exclusion for those who could otherwise claim some kind of membership in societies so defined. In this view *ius sanguinis* perpetuates non-membership over generations while strict *ius soli* ascribes non-membership to first-generation immigrants only. An ascriptive principle of residence *(ius domicili)* would lead to only temporary non-membership. It would turn non-members living in the territory into members after a certain time without asking for their consent or dissent. If societies were instead understood as national communities of descent independent from actually existing state boundaries, *ius sanguinis* would allow for the most perfect inclusion. In this perspective strict *ius soli* would lead to the most extensive exclusion by ascription as it withholds citizenship from all members of the nation born abroad, while *ius domicili* would compensate this deficit at least for those who immigrate into the national territory.

(5) Ascriptive entries or exit might also be called automatic as they operate in a mechanical way. They do not require choices or actions on the part of the individual and the collective establishes rules which require no further case-by-case decisions. However, not all decisions that can be called automatic are of this kind. Entry and exit is automatic but still non-ascriptive when individual consent is not required but when dissent can block the transition. The individual is given an option of opposing a change intended by the collective. Remaining silent is, however, taken for tacit consent and the change will come into effect in this case. In chapter 4, I analysed the old French rule of citizenship acquisition on coming of age for children born in France of foreign parents as a case of automatic entry. Denaturalization for emigrants (who have acquired another citizenship) when they no longer renew their passports would be a rule of automatic exit.

(6) Optional admission and exit require active consent in order to become effective. Furthermore, it is the individual whose decision triggers the change. Her status quo of membership continues as long as she does not declare her intention to enter or to leave. Yet this should not be mistaken for a concentration of all decision-making power with the individual. Optional admission and exit differ from what I have called invasion and escape, in that the individual cannot enforce a change against the collective's dissent. An option for the individual depends on a prior positive decision by the collective that the category to which the individual belongs is eligible for a change. If the collective chooses the 'no' option instead, this leads to excluded admission and confinement. In order to determine the inclusionary or exclusionary effects of optional transitions one must therefore always relate them to the corresponding forms of denied admission and exit. I have argued in chapters 3 and 4 that in a liberal perspective release from

citizenship as well as new admissions to citizenship after birth should be generally optional. This is rarely contested for exit but is still highly controversial for entries. Once this norm is accepted the important question is to fix the conditions for both transitions, which means at the same time determining who will remain excluded from admission or who will be denied exit. I have proposed a residence criterion as the main indicator for social membership. Generally, optional expatriation should be granted to citizens who permanently reside abroad and optional naturalization to foreigners who have become permanent residents in the country.

(7) Discretionary admission and exit rules combine features of (3) and (6), only that now the collective takes its final decision after that of the individual applicant. While this sequencing of the interaction clearly shifts power from the individual to the collective, it would be a mistake to think that the latter completely controls the allocation of membership simply because its 'yes' or 'no' choice always corresponds with the outcome. Those individuals who do not apply remain outside this control and have the power to prevent changes of the status quo. Most discretionary rules for a change of citizenship also prevent an arbitrary use of power towards those who have applied. This can be achieved by constraining discretion *a priori*, in its exercise, or *a posteriori*. The first constraint operates by specifying the categories of persons eligible and not eligible, the second by laying down in the law publicly known criteria for the decision by authorities, and the third constraint becomes effective when judicial appeals can be filed against negative decisions. Where discretion is completely constrained it is transformed into option. The final decision by the authorities may then be reduced to a formal approval. Voluntary expatriation used to be discretionary in many liberal democracies until not so long ago. The standard procedure for naturalization is still discretionary to a substantial degree.

The most general definition of power which can be used for evaluating the structural imbalances in decisions about membership is the extent to which an actor is able to determine the outcome by her own choices. There are three different ways in which this power can manifest itself. The first is by determining an outcome against the explicit opposition of the other actor, the second by determining it in the absence of such articulated opposition and the third lies in sequencing, i.e. in being able to determine the result by one's own choice after the other actor has already committed herself to one option. With regard to consent in membership we can group the modes of entry and exit into the non-consensual ones (1), (2) and (3) which are characterized by the first kind of power; the consensual ones (5), (6) and (7) where the second and third manifestations of power are relevant;

and the ascriptive ones (4) where there is no interaction and therefore, strictly speaking, also no power involved.

In the first three decision structures the individual and the collective are opponents and all power is concentrated on one side. (It has to be kept in mind that 'power' here is used only to describe the impact of choices on outcomes with regard to inclusion or exclusion.) Abduction/expulsion, invasion/escape and exclusion/confinement represent the total absence of consent in the enforcement of decisions about entry and exit. By simply ignoring the other actor's choices and enforcing a decision, the opponent is denied any voice. In the extreme cases physical force is involved in enforcement. It is no coincidence that the paradigmatic examples also refer to entry and exit as a physical movement of bodies in space. Individuals or groups may be pushed out of, or into, a territory, they may force their way out of, or into, a territory, and they may be kept out from, or confined in, a territory. In Hobbes's view 'Liberty, or Freedome, signifieth (properly) the absence of Opposition; (by Opposition, I mean externall Impediments of motion;) and may be applyed no lesse to Irrationall, and Inanimate creatures than to Rationall' (Hobbes, 1973, XXI, p. 110). Power relations backed up by physical means of coercion determine the extent of this liberty where the external obstacles to unimpeded movement of human bodies in space are other human beings and physical obstacles and instruments used by them.

Abduction and invasion are generally insufficient for the acquisition of membership where membership is a symbolic status in a collective rather than mere physical presence in a territory associated with the collective. Slaves brought into the country by force will remain excluded from social membership and invaders will rather establish a new regime than become members of an existing one. Similarly, expulsion or escape from the territory are often not enough to dissolve all bonds of membership. Exiled dissidents and refugees are regarded as temporary guests by receiving countries. They often engage in homeland policies and sometimes can even achieve a substantial impact on developments there. Only the denial of exit and entry by keeping individuals out of a territory where they have not lived before or preventing their emigration there is generally an efficient way of also denying them a desired change of social membership.

A symbolic status of membership such as citizenship rests on general recognition rather than on the physical location of bodies in space. Recognition need not be derived from consensus, but force cannot bring about recognition in the same way as it can kill or maim or drag away a body. Non-consensual recognition of membership requires compliance by the side whose position is overruled. This can be achieved by the threat of sanctions or by eliminating all alternative options. Abduction/expulsion is thus transformed into mandatory entry or exit and invasion/escape into compulsory admission or release. In a similar way, admission to a territory can be excluded and confinement can by enforced by physical barriers and the use of physical force against those who try to come in or to break out. Alternatively, admission can be denied by imposing sanctions on those who enter, which are severe enough to deter them effectively, and confinement results also from preventing escape by raising the 'costs of freedom' so that no one can afford them. When prison gates are open but out there is a desert, those who do not leave have not thereby consented tacitly to their ongoing confinement.

In automatic, optional and discretionary decisions the power of determining the outcome is shared to some extent between the actors. Whereas in non-consensual modes outcomes are always the same independently of the interaction by which they are reached, the requirement of consensus implies that the result can be a positive or a negative one within each single mode of decision . In these cases, power imbalances lie in the chances to determine the outcome in the absence of explicit opposition of the other actor and in the sequencing of choices. It is these three decisions about entry and exit which can be called consensual models of membership allocation. Outcomes are achieved by recognizing the other actor as capable of making choices which can be expressed in speech acts.

However, only discretionary decision requires an actual performance of speech acts by both actors in positive as well as in negative decisions. This is therefore the one mode of decision which is most thoroughly based on a strong notion of mutual consent. For this reason it has often been defended as the most adequate one for deciding about membership in a self-determining political community. However, this form of consent is at the same time asymmetric in favour of the collective. In optional admission or exit the consent criterion is only slightly weakened and biased in favour of the individual who gains a right to membership or to non-membership. Decisions about a change of membership still require active consent among both actors. A negative decision simply means a non-decision, i.e. retaining the status quo. The individual can choose to keep her present status in a passive way by not responding to the suggestion of the collective that she should join or leave. The fundamental change compared with discretionary decision lies in the sequence of choices. It is far from obvious that the strong notion of consent implied in discretionary admissions ought to prevail in a liberal democratic conception of citizenship. My discussion in the previous chapters has led to the conclusion that such a conception of citizenship cannot rely on one single way of deciding about membership. Ascriptive rules are involved as well as consensual ones, and even the non-consensual forms of excluded admission and confinement are legitimately applied in certain cases. Nonetheless, we can roughly summarize the liberal approach by stating that optional admission and exit are the dominant rules for individual changes of membership. Non-optional decisions restrict individual liberty with regard to a fundamental right to membership. They can only be justified where it can be shown that broadening the scope for individual choice of nominal citizenship would jeopardize its very substance.

6.2. CLUB, CONGREGATION, CITY AND COMPANY[2]

In the preceding section I have left the nature of the collective or organization unspecified. I will now show how particular social collectives, which I call associations, can be characterized by the rules of membership with which they operate. In my definition an association is a social collective in which membership is in some way consensual, either in entry or in exit or in both. For the purpose of this discussion I leave out foundational consent. Only associations which do not exist for more than one generation can claim that their membership is consensual because of the way in which they were founded, although they allow neither for consensual entry nor exit. States are transgenerational institutions. If they pretend to be associations, a narrative about a consensual act of foundation is never enough to substantiate this claim. This can only be achieved by showing that there is also some form of consent about membership among present and future generations.

Even the most democratic and liberal states cannot be regarded as voluntary associations of their citizens. However, in liberal democracies the polity is imagined as a voluntary association in discourses about the legitimacy of the exercise of political power. The normative legitimation of laws and political decisions is achieved by arguing that citizens could have agreed to them as reasonable participants in a rational discourse (see Habermas, 1992, chapter 3). Conceiving of membership in the polity as voluntary is a necessary (although not sufficient) presupposition for this legitimation of democratic rule.

Rather than computing all feasible sets of rules and constructing corresponding models of associations, I will choose a less formal approach than in the first part of this chapter. The numbers of different kinds of associations and the variations of membership rules are potentially unlimited and I cannot pretend to give a complete overview anyway. So I discuss some relevant analogies instead. These are clubs, religious congregations, cities, and companies of shareholders. Using such analogies in order to explain what sort of membership rules democratic citizenship implies is not a new idea. Michael Walzer has done this before by comparing states with clubs, neighbourhoods and families (Walzer, 1983, chapter 2). The first two of his analogies are also included in my own list, while 'family' remains excluded because it illustrates one kind of ascriptive rules of membership, rather than the associational features of a liberal state. The point of my exercise is not just to introduce two more models of association which are left out in his discussion. It is also different in the way I want to use these analogies. While Walzer explores what democracies have in common with clubs, neighbourhoods and families in their rules of membership, I want to show why they are essentially different from other models of association in just this aspect. I use five test criteria for the rules of membership which are characteristic for a type of association. Which position do the rules of admission assign to those who want to become members? Is simultaneous membership in other associations of the same kind tolerated? What is the attitude of the association towards voluntary exits of their members? Is the association entitled to expel members and, if it is, under which conditions? Finally, what is the position of non-members with regard to the association and how exclusive are the rights of membership? As usual I will first summarize the result in a table and then discuss each model of association in some detail.

Table 5: Models of association and rules of membership

	(1) club	(2) congregation	(3) city	(4) company	(5) liberal democracy
(a) rule of admission	discretion	confession	residence	payment	conditional option
(b) multiple membership	non-competitive	no	restricted	unrestricted	conditional option
(c) voluntary exit	unrestricted	restricted	unrestricted	unrestricted	conditional option
(d) expulsion	yes	yes	no	no	no
(e) rights for non-members	no	universal moral commands	gradual membership	no	residential and human rights

(1) Clubs

a) Entry into a club requires an application for admission. The assembly of present members or the executive committee speaking in their name decide whether to grant it. In a positive decision agreement is mutual but sequential in the way already discussed. If it is negative the applicant usually has no opportunity of appeal. Among all models of association the distinction between members and non-members appears to be most clear-cut for clubs.

b) This cannot be said for the distinction between different clubs themselves. Clubs may well overlap with regard to their membership. Competition among organizations of the same kind is not a defining element for clubs. A football association is in natural competition with other football associations in the same league, but it need not compete with those in a different league and it will never compete with a chess club. A sauna club does not compete with any other clubs. Plural membership is therefore generally only prohibited between strongly competing clubs. In their leisure activities individuals may exercise many different sports and can be members of many different associations.

c) Clubs usually do not attach strings on voluntary renunciation of membership. Individuals who want to leave cannot be forced to stay and will rarely be expected to justify their decision to other members. Members may resent it when others quit but exit will not be regarded as immoral.

d) Clubs assume a right to expel members. Members do not have a right to their membership which fundamentally restricts the decision-making power of the association. The association is free to adopt general criteria for a loss of membership in its statutes. This may provide some protection against arbitrary decisions. Furthermore, in contrast with new applicants for membership, present members can protest against their expulsion by claiming violation of the club's statutes. Appeals may be filed against expulsion but not against non-admission.

e) Clubs are exclusive with regard to the rights of members. The quintessential right of club members is participation in collective decision-making. Clubs are associations whose self-determination requires a strict boundary of membership. This is not to say that clubs never refer to the needs and rights of outsiders as intrinsically valuable for their own activities. Many clubs organize charities or sell goods and services to non-members who are respected as bearers of customers' and clients' rights. Fighting for the rights of non-members can even be the collective target of a club. However, individuals from a group whose rights are promoted by a club will still be excluded from all the internal rights of members unless they are themselves members.

(2) Congregations

a) In selecting new members for admission many religious congregations are like ethnic groups. Children of members will automatically become members themselves. In ethnic religions membership is acquired ascriptively by descent; in others it is confirmed in a ceremony by the parents on behalf of the child. However, most religions also allow for the new admission of adults whose parents have not been members and in some all adults have to be baptized in order to become full members. What is generally required from applicants is to demonstrate their belief in the doctrine and to confess the new faith. This principle for new admissions is different from discretion. Those who confess and undergo all the rites of passage acquire a claim to membership. It would be morally wrong to deny true believers who have observed all religious demands access to the congregation just because present members do not want to take in any more. Proselytic religions even see it as a major duty of their members to go out and convert others. In their vision the congregation should ultimately include all humankind.

b) Pagan beliefs often allowed for simultaneous multiple membership. Civic religions in the ancient Alexandrian and Roman empires were thoroughly syncretic, too. Monotheistic, scriptural and proselytic religions have radically abolished such pluralism. Worshipping foreign gods or taking part in the religious ceremonies of another group is the clearest sign of infidelity towards the true God of the respective congregation. Even where religious wars have been tamed into peaceful coexistence congregations still do not tolerate multiple memberships of single persons and most have great difficulties in accepting different affiliations within families.

c) Voluntary renunciation of membership is not possible in all congregations. Even where it is tolerated it will never be regarded as a morally neutral choice. Overt sanctions against renegades have been dropped or have become ineffective only where congregations have turned into associations among other associations in a secularized civil society. This depends on the separation between church and state (an achievement of modernity which is far from being completed even in many liberal democracies). Where exit is no longer persecuted it may still lead to social stigma. In any case those who leave the congregation will be regarded by believers as liable to divine sanction of some sort (by forfeiting, losing temporarily, or weakening their state of grace and their hope for salvation).

d) Congregations usually have rules for excommunication. The most common reason for this sanction is not sinning against religious commands in one's private life but public professions of disagreement with the fundamental articles of faith. In contrast with clubs, expulsions need not always be justified to present members. Often priests have divine power to admit as well as to expel.

e) The great scriptural religions have postulated universalistic moral principles which guide actions not only towards members but also towards strangers and infidels. Foreigners, apart from being included as beneficiaries of general moral commands, also enjoy a particular right to hospitality and protection. Non-believers can be regarded not only as enemies but also as potential converts and thus as persons who could acquire a claim to membership. Members will enjoy specific privileges in most religions and they always have to fulfil specific obligations. But the collective target of transforming whole societies or even all humankind, instead of organizing a limited sphere of life for a small group of members as clubs do, makes rights for non-members a characteristic feature of this type of association.

(3) Cities[3]

a) The modern nation-state with a liberal constitution creates a space for free internal migration. Walled towns and cities turn into open settlements. Native dwellers, citizens from other parts of the country and foreigners who legally reside in the state have the same right to enter cities and to settle there. There is a selection among newcomers when accommodation and employment opportunities are scarce in relation to the attractiveness of a city for influx. But this selection is achieved by open markets rather than by political decision and control. If we understand the city not merely as a constructed physical environment but also as a local community, membership cannot be achieved by mere physical presence but only by continuous residence. Membership in this community is more or less an automatic consequence of a consolidation of social relations over time. In contrast with clubs and congregations, the acquisition of membership does not require a conscious decision taken at a certain point in time. For those coming from outside, choosing a residence or job in the city may be regarded as such a decision. However, membership is a side-effect of such choices but usually not their immediate purpose. In modern nation-states cities are also local political communities with their own administration and elements of self-government. In some federal states larger cities even form separate provinces. Urban citizenship thus has its political component admission to which mostly only requires a permanent residence and registration with the police or local authorities.

b) As urban membership depends on the location and duration of one's residence, multiple membership in different local communities is quite constrained. Only a few people simultaneously have several residences in different cities. Even these might have to declare one of them as their regular one. Local voting rights and social recognition as a member of the community will often be enjoyed only there.

c) In contrast with nation-states, modern cities are generally open for immigration. *A fortiori* they are also open for emigration. Voluntary renunciation of local community membership does not take more than changing one's place of residence. Mostly those who leave do not even have to notify the authorities. There is neither legal sanction nor moral pressure constraining exit from cities.

d) In liberal nation-states expelling individual residents from a city would not only be difficult to justify as a form of punishment. Because of general free internal movement it would also be ineffective unless coupled with confinement to a place of banishment. In another sense, however, the automatic loss of membership and communal rights by moving elsewhere may also be regarded as an involuntary form of exit.

e) When compared with the clear-cut distinctions in clubs and congregations, the boundaries of membership in local communities are notoriously blurred. Social recognition and formal political membership need not coincide. Periods of time which distinguish visitors, temporary and permanent residents need not be identical for the different benefits of membership. Non-members in one respect can thus be granted full membership rights in others. Generally, the claims to equal recognition and treatment are weaker for those who have not been here for long. This can result in a hierarchy of positions according to the time of arrival, where people's claims are graded across several generations. The descendants of the old native group will then enjoy greater privileges compared with those from more recent waves of immigration. In some political aspects, such as voting rights, local membership depends upon citizenship at the state level. However, in a number of Western European states, local voting rights have also been granted to foreigners.[4] This shows that within present democratic constitutions local definitions of membership can become much more open than national ones.[5]

(4) Companies

a) Clubs and congregations may collect membership fees, but paying these is not sufficient for becoming a member. Individuals join a company of shareholders by buying shares. No other criteria are necessary for selection among those interested to join. However, present members and the company's board may exercise some control over admissions by limiting or stopping the issuing of new shares. The motive for joining as well as for admission is individual maximization of profits.

b) Owning shares of several companies is not only legitimate but will even be seen as a rational strategy for risk diversification. Certain shareholders may invest all their money in one company because they want to gain control over its policy, but they rarely do this for sentimental reasons of loyalty. Where companies competing for market shares are interconnected because their shareholders are multiple owners, this may lead to conflicting interests but it can also facilitate solutions. One of these solutions is a merger of companies. Multiple membership is thus not only compatible with stable boundaries of separate associations but the stability of these boundaries is no longer even a primary goal of the association shared by its members. What members share with each other are common private interests that dominate the association and may quite naturally lead to radical changes of its boundaries by fission or fusion.

c) Any shareholder can sell some or all of her shares at any time and thereby leave the company.

d) Companies cannot expel members who have rightfully acquired their shares, as easily as clubs and churches. Exclusion would mean confiscation of property and here civil laws clearly override the power of the association to decide about membership. A different solution which avoids this consequence is to compensate a member whose actions have severely harmed the company's interests by paying them off for their loss of shares.

e) For companies of shareholders, rights of non-members are only relevant as external constraints. They neither support such rights in their activities nor extend specific benefits of membership to non-members. However, they may promote a wider diversification of ownership by issuing shares with a lower denomination. Not only are non-members excluded but rights of membership are also internally unequal. Votes at the shareholders' meeting are weighed by the number of shares held by each owner.

(5) Liberal democracy

a) I have argued for making entry into citizenship an option for all individuals who have resided in the territory for a minimum period. This admission procedure differs from all the other four models of association. However, in current practices of naturalization we can easily find traits of each of these. The standard procedure for ordinary naturalization in most countries is still to a substantial degree discretionary, so that states appear to act like clubs in this area.

There are also elements of confession which are expressed in criteria such as support for the values of the constitution, or an oath of allegiance in the initiation ceremony when the applicant is formally received as a new member of the community. The model of congregation is especially relevant for some versions of republican thought. The French revolution granted citizenship to foreigners who confessed loyalty to its ideals. During the Cold War, Western democracies had a similar policy of preferential admission to the territory and to citizenship for refugees from communist regimes. These are, however, exceptions rather than the rule. Access to citizenship is not open for all those who are adherents of a democratic faith. And, conversely, those who apply for naturalization are not scrutinized to find out about their political beliefs.[6]

Length of residence is the most important criterion for naturalization. In this aspect membership in the city seems to provide the closest model for citizenship. However, *ius domicili* is never used as an ascriptive principle leading to automatic attribution of membership in a state. Residence is a precondition for optional acquisition but the individual has to take a conscious decision whether she formally wants to become a citizen. Membership in a city requires no such choice and membership in a state does not require this choice from every native citizen. However, as I have argued in section 4.2, those who join during their adult life should be given the right to choose and can also be expected to document their commitment in choosing.

Naturalization fees are high in some countries and they can be an efficient deterrent. As payments for admission these are different from periodic membership contributions raised by clubs. In contrast with the purchase of company shares, these entrance fees also are not investments where financial returns are expected. A related difference is that after having paid admission fees the new citizens are equal with all others, whereas members in the company have unequal power in relation to the value of their shares. Citizenship would be like membership in a company if there were a free market for votes and citizenship rights. This would of course contradict the fundamental democratic principle of 'one person one vote'.[7] However, consider a different system with equal votes where one would have to pay a substantial sum for entering one's name in the electoral register. This is essentially how naturalization fees work and why they should be abolished or kept at a minimum.

The shareholders' company is a more relevant analogy when the costs and benefits of acquiring citizenship are not reduced to purely monetary ones. The attitude of the 'utility maximizer', introduced in section 4.3, is that of a person conceiving of rights of citizenship as if they were shares. I have tried to show that liberal democratic rules of admission do not prohibit such attitudes but create incentives for different and not purely instrumental ones.

We can not only draw the analogy between immigrants and potential buyers of shares but also between states and companies. Some states regulate immigration rather similarly to the issuing of shares by fixing yearly contingents. Others operate more like clubs which select individuals who qualify for entry. Both approaches can of course be combined. In limiting and selecting immigrants, states pursue the goal of maximizing collective utilities for their population or for certain powerful groups of citizens. Such concerns are reflected in priority for immigrants who bring in investment capital, who are highly qualified or who fill vacant jobs. However, it has to be said that not all commonly used criteria for admission can be understood in this perspective. Family reunification and admission of refugees follow a different logic (although not necessarily one of pure altruism). And admission criteria for citizenship are generally less influenced by considerations of collective utility than those for immigration. In their naturalization policies democratic states rarely behave like companies.

b) Dual citizenship can be denied for three different reasons associated with the models of club, congregation and city respectively. The first reason is derived from seeing states as organizations competing for the scarce resource of power in the international system. Just as clubs have to make sure that members do not support a rival association, states will prohibit dual citizenship either generally if they see all other states as potential rivals or only for those states with whom relations are not friendly. The second idea is that states can only be self-determining associations when citizens voluntarily assume responsibilities and obligations and develop a strong sense of loyalty. A servant may serve two masters but no citizen can simultaneously share in the self-determination of two autonomous political communities (see section 4.1). Republican citizenship requires patriotism rather than nationalism but both cannot tolerate multiple allegiances. Thirdly, dual citizenship will also be seen as problematic if rights and obligations are strictly tied to territorial sovereignty. In this view all residents of a state ought to be, or to become, citizens, but according to the same principle emigrants who have abandoned their residence should no longer be accepted as citizens. Voting rights for those who do not live in the country would be a problematic achievement because they give people a say in deciding about laws which will not affect them. Only dual citizens' fundamental right of freely entering each country whose citizenship they possess would be fully compatible with such a strictly territorial view of citizenship. This leads naturally to the proposal to tolerate dual citizenship but to regard the non-residential citizenship as dormant, i.e. completely inactive. As I have already objected in section 4.1 individuals may have relevant ties and claims to rights towards states also when living outside the territory. This distinguishes membership in a polity from residential membership in a city.

If states became companies trading in citizenship rights there would be no problem of accumulating membership titles like some aristocrats did with titles of nobility. Individuals would act rationally in collecting the most valuable citizenships they can afford. This development might even lead to qualitative changes with regard to the boundaries of states. Citizens with multiple voting rights might bring about democratic majority decisions about mergers between the states in whose membership they had invested. This is not an altogether detestable fantasy. However, it would devalue completely what citizenship is all about: making political rule in territorially bounded states democratic by giving equal liberties and rights to those who are subjected to this rule and who have a stake in the common good of this society. The liberal reason for tolerating multiple citizenship is contained in this. Some people who have a stake are not permanent residents in the state. Some rights of citizenship are also relevant when one does not live in the territory. In mobile societies citizenship must therefore become transnational to some extent, but should not be completely disconnected from residence and social membership. Not everybody should be offered an opportunity to become a multiple citizen. A selection according to these criteria of residence and social ties will be achieved when only second-generation immigrants receive dual citizenship automatically by combining *ius soli* with *ius sanguinis*, and when naturalization depends on residence or marriage without requiring renunciation of a previous citizenship.

c) Three out of the four models of association support a liberal stance on voluntary exit. Nevertheless, the exception illustrated by religious congregations is a significant one. In contrast with a widespread view, optional exit is not an indispensable test criterion for the voluntary nature of an association. Let me illustrate this with the specific example of monasteries. In some of these the denial of exit rights is, or used to be, a defining feature of the association. However, membership can be regarded as voluntary because of admission procedures. In modern secular states most of those who join a religious order are assumed to do this of their own free will. If the order has a rule that does not allow leaving it and if the individual is of full age and accepts this consequence, one may still speak of voluntary membership even though exit is prohibited. In a liberal state individuals who later change their minds and want to leave a monastery will find laws and judges that defend their right of exit. However, the liberal view is generally that associations which do not permit optional exit need not necessarily be outlawed as long as individuals fully agree with this rule when joining. This means that as an *internal* rule, exit denial within associations seems to be acceptable to liberalism as long as there is a possibility of *external* enforcement of optional exit.[8] In the case of sovereign states there is no such external enforcement: the universal human right of expatriation can only be guaranteed by corresponding national legislation.

While liberal democracy obviously supports this right it does this in a way which is different from companies, cities and clubs. In all these associations necessary conditions for exit are just the inverse of necessary criteria for membership and in this sense they are unrestricted. By selling her shares and by moving away, a person simply reverses the action which had implied membership in a company or had led to membership in a city. Similarly, exit from a club means formally declaring that one no longer wants to be a member and/or stopping all participation and contributions that distinguish members from outsiders. Liberal citizenship, however, has a two-stage rule for expatriation with a necessary condition that in itself does not yet imply non-membership. One must first emigrate (or acquire otherwise strong social ties to another society) before one is free to renounce citizenship. Exit from citizenship is therefore a conditional option rather than an unrestricted one. In contrast with membership in a city, emigration is not yet an act of voluntary renunciation of citizenship. One does not acquire citizenship by simply living in the country without applying for it and one does not lose citizenship by simply living abroad without renouncing it. Residence is relevant as a necessary criterion for naturalization and for expatriation, but it is neither a necessary one nor a sufficient one for being a citizen.

d) Freedom of exit consists of both the right to leave and protection against expulsion. Only two of the four models of voluntary association pass this test. While religious congregations ought to be rejected as models for a liberal state because of their demand for perpetual allegiance, clubs should be equally rejected because they allow for a unilateral cancellation of membership by the association. Clubs may be seen as the prototype of voluntary association: first, because explicit and mutual consent is required in admission, and second, because membership is not just a side effect of a social fact (as in the city) or of the pursuit of strictly individual interest (as in the company) but is valued as an end in itself. Yet this strong consensual notion of membership restricts individual opportunities of entry as well as liberties of exit. Both transitions are biased in favour of the association.

States behave like clubs where collective sovereignty and self-determination are overemphasized at the expense of individual liberties and rights. In a liberal democracy, denaturalization will practically never be used as a sanction for individual disloyalty or non-compliance with obligations. Denaturalization may, however, be the formal ratification of a factual termination of membership for emigrants who have acquired another citizenship and have lived abroad for a long time. This is the same difference as between expelling a member from a club because she has publicly attacked its targets or cancelling her from the list of members when she has not turned up at meetings and has not paid contributions for a long time. In the latter case most clubs will first notify the non-active member of their intention to terminate her membership. States should do this as well.

e) Both clubs and companies distinguish sharply between members and non-members. Needs and entitlements of outsiders may become targets of activity for the former while they can only be external constraints for the latter. Congregations are ambivalent towards non-members: their attitude wavers between seeing them as children of God or as enemies of the true faith. In the model of the city the wider distribution of benefits is due to a blurring of boundaries of membership.

Liberal democratic citizenship is different in combining apparently contradictory requirements. Like the city it extends most rights of members to everybody living permanently in the territory. Furthermore, citizenship builds on a foundation of human rights which are due to any non-member, independently of her residence or nominal citizenship. It shares this notion of universal membership reaching beyond the associational one with some religious doctrines. There is nevertheless a clear distinction between members and non-members not unlike that of a club. What club members share beyond their specific duties and rights is the name of the club. By joining they obtain that name as an attribute which they may – but need not – use to characterize themselves. Most people acquire their nominal citizenship like their family name: at birth and without any choice. A few acquire it like their first name: by their parents' choice. The others, however, acquire it like the name of an association which they have joined voluntarily and by conscious decision. Even if all the substantial benefits of citizenship were extended to non-members, nominal membership would still mark a difference as long as it is allocated by birthplace, descent and choice rather than ascribed to anybody who happens to be in the territory.

The shareholding company is unacceptable as an analogy for liberal democracy, not only because of its total exclusion of non-members but also because of its internal allocation of rights among members. Rights are unequal and fully alienable in this model. In the city, too, rights may be graded, although to a lesser extent and without becoming the object of market transactions. The simultaneously inclusive and egalitarian drive of liberal citizenship has two important consequences. First, nominal citizens are completely equal in substantial rights. No citizen has a claim to privileges because of her descent. And the very next day after naturalization immigrants can vote or stand as candidates in elections just as native citizens can. The second consequence is that even rights for foreign residents cannot be arbitrarily graded or reduced but, as far as they are granted, have to be granted equally. While the first norm has become more and more accepted in contemporary Western democracies, the latter one is almost as frequently ignored as it is respected. The recent extension of certain political rights to European Union citizens without also giving them to third-country residents is in obvious contradiction to this norm. However, the uneasy justifications by governments and the outspoken opposition to this hardening of distinctions between foreign citizens of different origins, articulated especially within the European Parliament, show that the norm is reaffirmed even in the breach.

6.3. SOCIAL AND POLITICAL MEMBERSHIP

In his reply to Schuck and Smith's proposal for making American citizenship more consensual, Joseph Carens pointed out that 'The key difference between ascription and consent lies in the question of whether membership ought to be regarded, in the first instance, as a question of fact or a question of will (whether the will of the individual or of the community)' (Carens 1987b, pp. 425–6). Let me briefly recapitulate how the approach I have chosen would answer this question.

The first point to clarify is: which kind of membership? Membership in a territorially bounded society is a question of fact much more than of will. We cannot choose the place where we are born and raised when we are young. Our membership in a wider society results from being immersed into a culture and a dense network of social interactions. This is one reason why society is not an association:[9] 'Thus, we are not seen as joining society at the age of reason, as we might join an association, but as being born into society where we will lead a complete life' (Rawls, 1993a, p. 41). As we grow older the scope of choice with regard to membership in different institutions, organizations and associations becomes wider – although it often remains quite narrow for many people. A civil society differentiated from both the state and the face-to-face communities of private and intimate life-worlds is the locus of social membership in modernity.[10] Associational freedom in this sphere and the choice of particular memberships which it offers, is essential for the very idea that we can become members of a society rather than merely of families, villages or ethnic groups. This membership is first only an attributed one. By participating in civil society people subsequently confirm their membership in their daily actions and choices. However, they generally do not choose the society of which they want to be members.

I have argued above with regard to membership in the city that it may be a side-effect of other choices but is rarely itself a primary object of choice. The image of the city as a social configuration is that of a spatially concentrated civil society. Membership in society can be conceived of in similar terms as that of the city. It is a result of participation in a wide and dense network of interaction and communication between anonymous individuals who accept each other as free agents.

Some migrants may exercise a certain choice with regard to the country where they go. In this respect their social membership is also a question of will. Others will have virtually no choice because they travel along with their parents, because they go where their family has gone before, or simply because they 'choose' the only country accessible to them. Will is implied in social membership for migrants only in so far as there is a range of options and adequate opportunities to choose among these. Yet does the choice of a destination really involve that of social membership as well? Migrants are not members of society the day after their arrival. But after some years they will have to be regarded as members even if they themselves have always planned to return to their country of origin. Membership is acquired gradually and mainly as a function of the length of residence. Again, this presupposes an open civil society which is not deeply divided by class or ethnic cleavages. If a society is strongly segregated along cultural boundaries immigrants will indeed have to make a choice whether they want to become members by assimilating, and institutions of the receiving society will control this admission by defining the criteria of successful assimilation (see Bauböck, 1993b, 1994d).

Maybe the idea of an open civil society where membership is acquired gradually and automatically seems to some readers a rather idealistic abstraction from a pervasive reality of segregation in modern society. One could still insist that modern societies are incomparably more mobile than any premodern ones have ever been. Yet that is not my point here. I should make it clear that I am not referring to a strictly sociological concept of civil society. Civil society emerges as an answer to the question: what are the characteristics of the most comprehensive social unit liberal democracy refers to? In this sense, the open civil society is a political projection as much as a tangible social reality. However, it is not a utopian projection directed towards a distant future, but a guideline for present efforts to transform given social structures so that all members can perceive each other both as equal citizens in the polity and as free agents in civil society. I have argued in the first chapter that the plurality of territorially organized states creates a territorial image of societies as seen from the political sphere. The idea that liberal democracies produce an image of their social reference unit as an open civil society is both a specification of the earlier hypothesis for a particular kind of political regime and a shift from an analytical concept of society towards a normative view.

What the idea means with regard to immigrants is that they *ought to be seen* as members of society after some period of residence, no matter whether they themselves have made a conscious choice about this, or whether institutions of the receiving society have so decided. Even if they live at the social margins and if they do not participate in the majority culture, they still have to be regarded as members of this society because not doing so would jeopardize the social foundations of liberal democracy. Seeing them as members in this normative approach does not mean closing the eyes to the social facts of their non-membership. Rather it leads to challenging their social exclusion by granting them all rights which they need in order to become fully participating members of civil society.

In contrast with social membership, political membership in democracy is a question of will more than of fact. Although the vast majority of people acquire their nominal citizenship at birth and never change it during their adult lives, this attribution is different from that of social membership. It is achieved at a single point in time by an administrative decision regulated by law. The law cannot decide whether someone is a member of society, but it can decide about membership in the polity. If there were just one natural rule by which individuals acquire citizenship at birth the legal decision would be just a formal ratification of social membership. But as there are two different rules (*ius soli* and *ius sanguinis*) the decision about which one to adopt for the attribution of citizenship is a thoroughly political one that can be the object of internal deliberation and consent among members of a democratic polity. When individuals change their citizenship by naturalization or expatriation this is again a decision at one single point in time. If the transition is optional or discretionary, consent is much stronger than in automatic attribution. Both the individual and the polity explicitly agree about this change. This form of controlling the boundaries of membership confirms the idea that the polity itself is a kind of voluntary association based on consent in its internal mode of decision-making.

Certainly, it is not free and unconstrained will and not necessarily a strong form of consent which characterizes a liberal representative democracy. The number of options among which citizens can choose – different parties, candidates or programmes – is always a limited one and ordinary citizens have very little influence on the issues they might be asked to decide in referenda. However, their consent cannot be assumed unless they do have a real choice. Moreover, democratic consent is not only expressed in decision-making (where it is only weak) but also in discourses of deliberation and legitimation which precede or follow it. But the aggregation of individual preferences in order to determine collective decisions (or the delegates who are to take these decisions) is still the essential core of democracy. Without this core, subjection to laws and orders given by political authority would be just an imposed form of membership, an external constraint on the interactions of individuals in society.

A democratic polity is never entirely identical with a society. If there were full inclusion of all social groups in citizenship and little migration, people might become unaware of a difference which no longer manifests itself in different categories of persons. But a democratic procedure of decision-making creates its own kind of membership, which identifies individuals as potential voters and not just as participants in social interactions. The feature which visibly distinguishes political from social membership is that the former can be quantified by comparing the weight given to individual votes in the determination of a collective decision. In a liberal democracy all weights are equal, at least at the level of general elections and referenda. Modern societies may be egalitarian or hierarchical to a different extent in different spheres, but outside the political one there is no general and basic equality of status involved in being a member of a such a society.

Yet while membership in the polity is different from that in society the range of choice is also severely constrained with regard to the former and both forms of membership can be intimately linked to each other on normative grounds. Choice involved in being a member of the political community is never like that between alternative parties or candidates. The difference lies not in the reduced number of options. The point is that even if an option of political membership is available that deviates from one's social membership (which can be determined by one's past as well as by one's present residence) it will either be a costly or an irrelevant. More generally, a stable territorial membership is a precondition for democracy because only then will all citizens also be affected by the decisions they and their delegates take. The opportunities of choosing a citizenship which does not correspond either to one's past or present residence will therefore be restricted, and this does not violate basic needs or legitimate interests. All those constraints turn membership even in the most democratic polity into a question of fact for most people most of the time.

Overemphasizing the aspect of consent in political membership would sever the polity from the civil society in which it is embedded. This is what republican views of politics try to achieve. Hannah Arendt's critique of 'the rise of the social' in modern society and her image of the political sphere as the only one where freedom can be realized, has been the most eloquent expression of that idea in our century (Arendt, 1958). The difference between the liberal and the republican vision of democracy can be highlighted by focusing on the allocation of membership. Consent is the ultimate basis for membership in both approaches. But the republican one tries to demarcate the boundary between society and polity by denying that membership in the former gives individuals a claim to be also accepted as full members in the latter. In this view the internal constitution of the polity requires specific rules for membership. The realm of society is that of work and labour, of the material necessities of life and of group interests tied to them. The political realm is where all members are connected to each other by common obligations and where individual men and women are judged according to their merits in promoting the common good and their excellence in civic virtues. The quality of politics in a society will depend not only upon the quality of its political institutions but also upon the quality of the members of whom it is composed. There are two ways how the quality of membership can be raised or protected from deteriorating. One is by emphasizing education for citizenship, the second one is by selecting the citizen. This vision of the polity therefore lends itself easily to exclusive definitions of membership. Those who are individually less virtuous can be denied admission or can be expelled. And groups whose members are assumed to be unable of forming an independent judgement on political matters because of their dependent position in society, or because they have not been well educated, can be legitimately excluded from the polity. This view is not a purely republican one. It was still prevalent among 19th century liberals such as John Stuart Mill.[11] But it is no longer acceptable for contemporary liberal democracy.

Today such polities are bound by their own norms to establish rules for the allocation of citizenship which make it inclusive with regard to society. Education for citizenship certainly remains an important task but those who are to be educated are already members from the start. Similarly, democracy needs broad participation, and those who are politically active do not only document their will with regard to the issues on the political agenda but also their will to be members of this particular polity. But liberal democracy normally does not require strong commitment and full participation from each citizen. People who do not go to the polls will not be excluded from citizenship. Their rights to membership are completely independent from a general obligation to share in the political life of the community. Liberal neutrality between a plurality of conceptions of the human good implies the liberty for citizens to lead a non-political life without being denied citizenship. It is only in naturalization and voluntary expatriation that membership becomes explicitly a question of will. As I have argued in section 4.3, commitment will be strongly impaired under non-ideal conditions even in these decisions. And yet the fact that in a liberal democratic state naturalization and expatriation require a conscious choice on the part of the individual, rather than being an automatic consequence of residence, clearly expresses specific associational features of the polity.[12] It indicates that ultimately a will to membership is attributed to all members of the polity even if they are never called to manifest it in a decision. Together with the basic equality of status among members, this is the second feature that distinguished citizenship from social membership.

In contrast with a society, a polity is thus in important aspects an association where membership expresses will and consent. But liberal democracies normatively constrain their own choices with regard to the selection of members, by postulating that social membership should be fully represented in the polity. This norm of inclusiveness does not collapse society and polity into one single entity. The distinction between both remains visible in the modes of transmission and acquisition of membership. We can answer the question posed at the beginning of this section by saying that membership in a liberal democratic polity is in the first instance a question of fact, but in the last instance one of will and consent.

NOTES

1. I concede that the idea of 'membership' is rather strained in those decisions which violate the interests and choices of individuals. The essential notion here is that of inclusion/exclusion which can be also applied to such decisions.
2. The ideas of this section were first developed in a paper for a conference on 'Discrimination, Racism and Citizenship in Great Britain and Germany', organized by Czarina Wilpert and Zig Layton-Henry in November 1993 in Berlin.
3. For a more extensive comparison of national and urban citizenship see Bauböck (1993a).
4. see n. 47 in chapter 4.
5. In some countries, constitutions clearly do not allow the extension of the local suffrage to non-citizens. However, in the European Union, these constitutions already had to be amended in order to give active and passive voting rights to citizens of other EU member states. Since then pretending that there are fundamental constitutional obstacles for giving the same rights to third-country aliens must be regarded as sheer hypocrisy.
6. Liberalism tolerates and even promotes a plurality of such beliefs. Mutually incompatible but reasonable philosophical or religious doctrines can support a liberal democratic order from their own divergent points of view (Rawls, 1993a).
7. One should remember that a 19th century liberal like John Stuart Mill still advocated restricting the franchise to taxpayers and a meritocratic system of plural votes for the better educated citizens (Mill, 1972, 'On Representative Government', chapter 8).
8. Even liberal states do not always guarantee optional exit from their own organizations. Secret services are a good example. Just as in the case of monasteries, secret service agents are sometimes recruited in a less than consensual procedure. But others obviously join out of their own free will either for the thrill of the job, for money or for their careers. Those who join will generally not be allowed to leave because they are bearers of worldly (rather than divine) secrets. Loyalty is essential and it is expressed in renouncing the exit option. In this case there is no external enforcement of exit rights. The only exit option available is non-consensual: fleeing to another country and asking for protection from the enemy.
9. The second reason given by Rawls is that a society 'has no final ends and aims in the way that persons or associations do' (Rawls, 1993a, p. 41). In this way Rawls rejects traditional social contract doctrines and their libertarian revivals, but he also distances himself from the communitarian approach: 'While a well-ordered democratic society is not an association, it is not a community either, if we mean by a community a society governed by a shared comprehensive religious, philosophical, or moral doctrine. ... To think of democracy as a community (so defined) ... mistakes the kind of unity a constitutional regime is capable of without violating the most basic democratic principles' (p. 42).
10. For a comprehensive discussion of the concept of civil society in political theory see Cohen and Arato (1992).
11. See n. 7 above.
12. Rawls does not distinguish between a well-ordered society and a liberal democratic polity and he adopts a closed model in which individuals are assumed to live a complete life within one particular society. The specific associational features of the polity become much more obvious once we drop this assumption and apply liberal norms to the regulation of immigration and naturalization (see chapter 13).

7. Collective Membership and Self-determination

I have suggested liberal rules of entry and exit with regard to nominal citizenship and pointed out that a political community which supports these rules is a very specific kind of association. Democratic decision-making in any association presupposes clearly defined boundaries of membership for the collective as a whole. A liberal polity is necessarily democratic although not all forms of democracy are also necessarily liberal (in the sense of protecting individual rights against collective decisions in addition to granting rights of participation in decision-making). In this chapter I will discuss whether democracy imposes constraints on the collective definition of membership in a polity. Is that definition arbitrary, or must it necessarily include all the residents who are subjected to democratic rule and who are able to participate in it? This is the question of the first section. The second part explores paradoxes of territorial self-determination. Can democracies settle disputes about their external territorial borders by means of a consistently democratic aggregation of votes? While this must be denied I argue in the concluding section that once territorial borders are accepted as given, democracy and liberalism can reinforce each other in a dynamic of inclusion of social groups which were traditionally excluded from nominal citizenship or from active political participation.

7.1. IS DEMOCRACY NECESSARILY INCLUSIVE?

Quite obviously, my argument for optional naturalization and expatriation favours narrowing the scope for democratic decision-making on this issue by widening the area of individual rights. In international law sovereign states may be regarded as free in adopting their own specific laws of citizenship. However, the allocation of citizenship touches upon human rights as well as upon more specifically liberal norms concerning the relation between individuals and states. This is no morally neutral terrain where policies are to be determined by considerations of state interests, expediency or collective utility. It is of course widely accepted today that democracy is only a viable and morally defensible form of government when it is constrained by individual and minority rights entrenched in constitutions.

Jon Elster has recently pointed out that 'these limits and constraints can ultimately have no other normative foundation than a simple majority decision' (Elster, 1993, p. 179). The use of the term normative is rather unfortunate in this context. Only classical utilitarians will wholeheartedly agree that majority preferences are the proper normative benchmark for all political decisions. But Elster seems to be right that any constraint, whatever its normative foundation, will only become effective as a binding legal rule in a democratic regime if it can ultimately be derived from simple majority consent. 'The fundamental logic of constitution making remains that of a simple majority deciding that a simple majority may not be the best way to decide some issues' (p. 180).

The allocation of citizenship is a genuinely constitutional question because it affects not only fundamental principles of liberalism but also of democracy. A regime that does not pretend to give people a say in the way they are ruled does not require a clear-cut definition of membership. Democracy, however, depends on settling this question. The puzzle which underlies the enquiry in this section is whether this can be done in a thoroughly democratic way.

I will start with a minimalist notion of democracy which relates only to the procedure of aggregating individual preferences to collectively binding decisions by equal votes on alternative options. A general referendum is the purest direct democratic procedure. In representative democracy most issues are not decided by referenda but by votes among delegates. Enfranchised citizens choose between competing candidates or parties rather than deciding themselves on the issues. For the following discussion I assume nevertheless a referendum model of democracy, because the puzzle arises with regard to a specific issue and not in selecting decision-makers. In order to give some empirical plausibility to the problem of whether issues of collective membership can be consistently decided by majority voting, one could think of a democratic constitution which requires that a fundamental change of the constitution must be supported by a majority in a referendum.[1] Basically the problem remains the same if we imagine a constitutional assembly of delegates who have to settle a dispute about collective membership of their respective constituencies by majority vote among themselves. The idea of using the referendum model is to find out, first, whether the procedural core of democracy as a method of reaching collectively binding decisions necessarily fails to settle contested questions of membership. If it does, a basic allocation of membership has to be taken as given. Democratic majorities may *approve* of this limit to majoritarian decision-making but they cannot *decide* upon it in all situations where it is contested. Collective membership would therefore have to be regarded as an exception to Elster's rule.

Can a democratic polity decide democratically on who is to be a member of this very same polity? Logic seems to require that settling questions of membership must precede any democratic deliberation. Votes cannot be counted when there is uncertainty about who the enfranchised voters are. The idea that this latter decision should also be decided by a majority leads into a circular argument. Majoritarian decision-making will fail to produce unique results when applied to this issue without presupposing some fundamental constraints which themselves cannot be put to the test of the vote.

Before generalizing this conclusion too hastily, we have to be aware that we are now dealing with a kind of consent very different from that discussed in chapters 4 to 6. Consent in individual membership is articulated in the dualistic interaction between an individual and a collective that is itself seen as a single actor, whereas democratic consent is articulated in aggregating a large number of individual choices into a collective decision involving the collective formed by these very same individuals. As long as the membership decision is about single cases no difficulty will arise. The kind of entry and exit decisions concerning individuals which we have analysed so far can be taken in a perfectly democratic manner without circularity or contradiction. A given collective may decide by democratic vote, either directly whether a certain individual should be admitted as a new member, or it can adopt a procedure which will regulate entries without requiring an aggregation of preferences in each case. Exits can be regulated in the same way. In larger political communities, decisions will always be about rules rather than about individual cases, and it is obvious that only present members can vote in any decision about such rules. Before leaving or being expelled the future emigrant will have an equal vote with regard to the general rules regulating exit. We can also imagine a small face-to-face community which collectively decides in each individual case of admission to, or loss of, membership. Here it seems again quite natural that the vote of the individual concerned cannot be counted in entry but ought to be counted in exit. If the individual were not allowed to vote on her own exit this would imply that she had already been excluded before the vote was taken, which in turn implies that there must be a general rule that decides the case without requiring a vote in each single case.

All the constraints on rules of acquisition and loss of individual citizenship which I have proposed in the previous chapters are not required by democratic procedure in the minimal sense defined above but by liberal norms. They are not derived from preconditions for a sustainable democratic aggregation of preferences within a political community but from certain assumptions about the nature of modern societies, about the relation between individuals and the state in such societies and about the normative priority of equal liberties and protection for individuals over the assertion of state interests. Each of these constraints could be put to the test of democratic voting, and if they were rejected the result would be legitimate in terms of democracy although no longer in terms of liberal values. These constraints are of the sort Elster refers to: ultimately they do need majority support in order to become law in a liberal democracy. But as individual rights they ought to be protected against frequent exposure to a change of preferences among majorities. The best way to do this is to entrench them in constitutions which cannot themselves be changed by simple majorities and which are made effective by judicial review of ordinary legislation.

Individual transitions with regard to membership do not present a problem for democratic decision-making because the collective and its boundaries are accepted as given. Rather than questioning the shape of these boundaries the regulation of individual transitions in fact confirms them and makes them visible. I suggest that three different states of boundaries of membership should be distinguished. In state one they are completely fixed and impermeable; in state two individual transitions are regulated in a way that unambiguously distinguishes collectives from each other; in state three the boundaries themselves become contested and no longer delimit collectives in a clear manner.

For the first type of boundary, suppose membership in a political community were determined by some entirely objective and unchangeable fact such as place of birth. Immediately after birth each person would be marked by a fake-proof tattoo indicating her membership in the state where she was born.[2] Persons belonging to different communities could interact freely outside the political sphere, but the question of changing their membership would never arise. Boundaries towards other groups would become completely irrelevant to the internal structure of political communities. An anthropologist visiting this society would probably find that they did not even seem to notice these boundaries and simply could not understand her question why they excluded members of the other communities from their internal deliberations. It is only when boundaries of membership can be crossed both ways by individual entry and exit that they become a well-defined and important element of the structure of a community.[3] In this second state boundary definitions and rules for individual transition characterize different kinds of association (as I have tried to show in the previous chapter).

The third state is an entirely different situation. It means that boundaries have not only become permeable but also indeterminate or unstable.

Indeterminacy need not be a problem if the collective is of a kind that does not require a clear distinction between members and non-members. Instability is a problem when this distinction is essential. Membership in modern societies is of the former kind in most regards. In a public sphere of communication and in market transactions the identification of individuals as members of collectives is less relevant than in any premodern society. In the spheres of labour, leisure and family life, membership of particular groups and organizations will be more important than that in the wider society. Membership in associations with some kind of internal democratic self-determination is always of the latter kind. It must be well-defined and relatively stable over time both for the aggregation of individual choices and for the implementation of decisions which are binding for members only.

Democratic polities are a peculiar kind of association different from a club. They establish a monopoly of power within a territory and they organize populations as collectives which are continuous over generations. I have argued that intergenerational stability of membership in political communities can only be achieved if citizenship is attributed according to the principles of territorial birth or residence and of descent or ethnic membership. But in democracy, consent is the ultimate criterion of legitimation. *Ius sanguinis* and *ius soli* do not *per se* establish membership in the political community. These rules are not given by some immutable law of nature or history but can be tested by asking whether a majority would agree to them. Furthermore, democratic constitutions can make a choice between both principles or mix them in different ways. At the most basic level, membership in democracy is not grounded in descent or birth in the territory, but in consent, although not in the individual consent of the person to whom citizenship is attributed but in the democratic consent of citizen-voters and their delegates about the proper rules of attribution. So far there is no consistency in claiming that democracies can democratically decide their own rules for attribution, entry and exit.

Yet this presupposes that the territory and the population with regard to which *ius soli* and *ius sanguinis* transmit citizenship to the following generation are themselves stable. What happens when the external boundaries of a polity in terms of its territory or of the social groups included in citizenship become a contested issue? Can democracies also decide in a consistently democratic manner how to settle such boundary disputes?

Let me start by considering two ways to solve the puzzle which are rather similar to Alexander's solution for untying the Gordian knot. The first one is that any arbitrarily determined boundary of membership has to be regarded as democratic as long as the polity which it delineates is internally a democratic one. This does not answer the question. Obviously it is impossible to define non-arbitrary procedures for deciding conflicts about arbitrarily constructed boundaries. Moreover, the voluntaristic solution fails to realize that territorial rule fundamentally distinguishes membership in a democratic polity from that in other kinds of voluntary associations. The second solution defines inclusive membership as an essential feature of democracy. This presupposes some further definition of a social collective which must be fully included in the political one. In this view social boundaries are given objectively and democracy normatively requires corresponding political ones. Boundary disputes would have to be resolved by establishing the facts of the case rather than by aggregating relatively unconstrained individual choices. These two approaches can be found in writings of the theorists of democracy, Joseph Schumpeter and Robert Dahl.

Joseph Schumpeter became famous in political science for his devastating attack on the classical concept of democracy as rule by the people. As an alternative definition he suggested that democracy is an arrangement in which rule over the people is acquired by a competitive struggle for the people's votes (see section 1.1). In the same book which developed this elitist notion of democracy, Schumpeter also defended the apparently contrasting idea that the body of citizens itself could decide upon who its members are. He answered affirmatively to his own question: 'Must we not leave it to every *populus* to define himself?' (Schumpeter, 1950, p. 245). Schumpeter arrived at this conclusion because he tried to separate democracy as a method of decision-making from liberal norms which outlaw distinctions of citizenship according to class, religion, gender, or 'race'. Any body politic which takes collectively binding decisions according to a democratic method can be called a democracy, no matter how inclusive or exclusive it is with regard to the population living in the territory. The Athenian *polis* can be regarded as an *illiberal* regime because of its exclusion of slaves, women and *metics*, but not as *undemocratic*. However, Schumpeter did not even try to show how a democratic *populus* can define itself in a democratic way when questions of collective membership become contested issues within or across polities.

Robert Dahl strongly objects to Schumpeter's view and argues that he conflated two different propositions, namely that 'System X is democratic in relation to its own demos' and that 'System Y is democratic in relation to everyone subject to its rules' (Dahl, 1989, p. 122). Dahl proposes a principle of inclusion according to which 'The demos should include all adults subject to the binding collective decisions of the association' (p. 120). In his final formulation of this same principle, Dahl appears to introduce the same conflation which he criticizes in Schumpeter: 'The demos must include all adult members of the association except transients and persons proved to be mentally defective' (Dahl, 1989, p. 129). This hardly clarifies the issue. The condition of subjection (in the first formulation) does not make an individual a member of an association (in the second formulation). A political association ruling a state can subject many more people to its collective decisions than those who are regarded as members of the association. When we combine both statements, Dahl seems to be saying that the *demos* must include as a member of the association every adult subjected to its rule who is neither mentally defective nor a transient.

This is a much more attractive idea than Schumpeter's barren formula of the democratic method. Yet it raises a number of questions. A first one is whether premodern democracies would fail or pass. The combined criterion of association and subjection is still not sufficient to dismiss Schumpeter's claim that the Athenian *polis* can be regarded as democratic in spite of not including the large majority of the population. On the one hand, women, slaves and free foreigners in ancient democracies clearly were not considered as members of the *demos* as a political association. On the other hand, they were also not subject to its *collective* decisions. Women and slaves were subject to private decisions within the *oikos* rather than to collective ones in the *polis*. Free foreigners (*metics*) were in a different position regulated by public laws but there existed simply no territorially inclusive notion of society which would have encompassed any of these three excluded groups. In this sense the laws were really given by male adult property-owning citizens to themselves rather than to a larger society which they subjected to their rule. While Periclean Athens can be regarded as a democracy in this sense, dictatorship by a collegial elite in a modern society can not. Stalinism would have been clearly undemocratic according to Dahl's principle of inclusion even if the Communist Party had been internally democratic in its decision-making (Dahl, 1989, p. 121). Dahl fails to see this difference.

Schumpeter's approach, on the other hand, which reduces democracy to a method 'incapable of being an end in itself' (Schumpeter, 1950, p. 242), leaves too much scope for indeterminacy. Certainly, groups of people have been excluded from internally democratic regimes because of their sex, religion, lack of property or education, or other criteria which have become unacceptable only in modern liberal democracy. But this does not mean that any bunch of people could declare themselves to be a democratic polity as long as they agree on majority voting among themselves. Clubs can be formed in this way, but polities can not. All the exclusions quoted by Schumpeter as proof that democracy is historically indeterminate with regard to its *populus* share one element in common: they are not generated by collective decision, but exist in society prior to, and independently of, the democratic process. Only a club can define its membership in a completely tautological manner by stating that non-members are all those who have not been admitted as members.[4] Polities always relate to a wider society which they see as their reference population that ought to be included. Territorial rule creates the external limits of this society while caste or class, gender, religion, age, property and education have been used in different ways to define a society in the original sense of the word *societas* (association) within the wider territorial population. Before modernity, the idea of society was thus linked much more closely to the political realm. Membership in society meant essentially being a free citizen subject to the territorial sovereign rather than subject to the private and domestic power of another free citizen. Yet in contrast with non-hereditary aristocracy the citizenry was never defined arbitrarily as all those who had been granted that status. Wherever it existed as a relevant status, citizenship always rested on the *social* identification of some group among the population which was assumed to be qualified for it.

A second question is about those exclusions which Dahl regards as justified. What is the status of those who are justly excluded from the *demos* because they are too young, mentally defective or transients? Dahl uses a narrow concept of the *demos* as those citizens who are entitled to participate in political decision-making at the state level. Yet are other members of society wholly excluded from liberal democracy? Is their relation to the state only that they are subject to collective decisions reached with the consent of enfranchised citizens? Can they not also be regarded as citizens by virtue of possessing other rights than the suffrage which make them members of the polity?

Dahl admits that 'the definition of adults and transients is a potential source of ambiguity' (Dahl, 1989, p. 129). But the ambiguity is not only about the age and the period of residence that qualify for inclusion in the *demos*. It concerns the very nature of the boundaries between *demos*, citizenry and society. In liberal democracy the young ones are not only under paternal authority as they are in Locke's theory. They are already nominal citizens by birth and they enjoy a substantial bundle of citizenship rights before they acquire the right to vote. Their citizenship may be passive and latent in many respects but it is more than merely virtual. Foreigners who are regarded as only transient members of society are not fully excluded from the citizenry either. They even enjoy a number of active rights denied to minor citizens such as the right to conclude contracts and also political liberties like those of free speech, assembly and association. So their citizenship is less passive but at the same time still partial when compared with that of adult citizens.

A third question concerning the principle of inclusion as formulated by Dahl is that it appears to make membership in the *demos* entirely dependent upon membership in society, and thus to eliminate altogether choice and consent as criteria for determining membership, i.e. those very aspects that allow the *demos* to be seen as an association. While partial inclusion is what minors and foreigners share in common, there is one important difference between them in all liberal democracies which is completely missing in Dahl's discussion. Minors automatically become full members of the *demos* at the age of majority while foreigners have to make a decision about this. Dahl's principle of inclusion would suggest that all foreigners who are no longer transient members of a society ought to be automatically included in the *demos* or else the political system cannot claim to be democratic. Neither optional nor discretionary naturalization would be acceptable. Dahl's formula leaves open whether *only* those who are subject to its binding collective decisions can be regarded as members of the *demos*. If this were so, emigrants who are not merely transiently staying abroad would automatically lose their citizenship. If it were not, emigrants could choose to retain their previous citizenship but they would be compelled to acquire the one of their country of residence.

A first conclusion from these considerations is that the principle of inclusion presupposes a concept of society as given prior to the *demos* but at the same time externally bounded by the territorial sovereignty of a state. If the *demos* were truly an association of all those who voluntarily adhere to it as members it would lack any external reference population with regard to which it could become inclusive. Second, inclusion as understood by Dahl presupposes not only the abolition of specific discriminations of class, gender, race, religion, property and education but a modern concept of society as a territorial population rather than as a *societas* of free citizens. Third, in liberal democracy criteria of inclusion are different for nominal citizens, for members of society entitled to basic rights of citizenship, and for the enfranchised electorate. If we maintain with Dahl and against Schumpeter that democracy implies a principle of inclusiveness, this must be broken down into a more complex set of rules than Dahl's definition allows for.

7.2. FOUNDATION, SEPARATION AND FUSION

Asserting that all democratic polities must have a standard of inclusion and that liberal democracy in this respect basically refers to the territorial population, still does not answer the question how disputes about the boundaries of territorial populations could be settled. The problem of circularity in democratic deliberation about the allocation of collective membership is most acute in the foundational situation; it re-emerges in separation and fusion and in decisions whether to extend the franchise within the population. Referenda have been held to decide territorial disputes and to redraw state borders. But borders have never been drawn for the first time by democratic decision. In order to find out whether this is just an unfortunate fact of human history or a necessary constraint on democracy we have to turn to science fiction examples. We will gradually move closer to the real world by accepting those conditions of membership as intrinsic constraints which cannot be consistently determined by democratic procedures.

As a thought experiment imagine a foundational situation where a very large number of men and women settle on a foreign planet. They are completely free to design their own political system for that planet.[5] Impressed by the arguments which I briefly summed up in chapter 1, a large majority of the first general assembly after landing decides to have an international system of separate territorial states rather than a single one. The next proposal to decide is whether to have a bipolar system or rather one with a larger number of small states. Let us assume that a majority is convinced that a system of two states of roughly equal size would offer the best chances to create a permanent equilibrium which would help to avoid war and at the same time stimulate the perfection of government by peaceful competition. Pointing to the disastrous experience on planet Earth with a system generating a multiplicity of small nation-states they strongly reject the idea of reintroducing it in their new world. The bipolarists win the vote, but by a narrow margin only. Now a group of stubborn smallstaters comes forward and announces that they had already agreed to make their own separate state during the space journey. They had formed an association, each of whose members had individually consented to be a citizen of this future small state. So their decision had been reached by unanimous vote amongst their own group whereas the marginal majority of the general assembly was much less representative of the collective will of the total population. Against this a speaker of the bipolarists argues that in a vote about whether to have this particular state or not the majority of the assembly would by far outnumber the small group. The smallstaters remain unimpressed. Their intellectual leader points out that the proposal to have a single government for the planet had already been dismissed by a large majority. So the general assembly could no longer act as if it represented a future democratic state within which majority decisions are collectively binding. Any further majority would now have to be relative to the population of one of the future states of the planet. They had already decided to form their own state in a perfectly democratic manner, fulfilling Rousseau's requirement of unanimity in the original social contract without violating the rights of anybody who did not wish to be a member of this state. Furthermore, by claiming a small territory only they had also respected the Lockean proviso 'to leave enough and as good in common for others' to form their own states. He accuses the bipolarist majority of planning to include forcefully a large number of people in their states who were unwilling to be members, and of not leaving any empty space on the planet where they could go and found their own polity. He finishes his speech by announcing that the smallstaters would immediately secede if they were incorporated in a larger state. The bipolarists remain convinced that democracy requires that the greater overall number ought to prevail but they are aware that by deciding against a single state they had already abandoned that institutional arrangement which would have allowed them to enforce such majority decisions. Furthermore, they realize that the price they would have to pay in order to bring about their utopia would be just the nightmare of war they had wanted to avoid.

The story shows that there is indeed no strictly democratic solution for the problem of how to found a plurality of democratic states *ex nihilo*. We might find comfort in the consideration that this problem never arises on planet Earth. What is different here is that all people live already in a given territory and that, apart from small numbers of stateless persons, everybody is at any point in time a member of a state with a fixed territory. However, the fact of territorial residence alone is not enough to solve the problem. Suppose that the settlers on the foreign planet had first each peacefully occupied a plot of land (with the conspirational group of smallstaters making sure that their joint territories were geographically contiguous). Or, alternatively, imagine that two terrible weapons had been used in a global war on earth, one destroying all records of political maps and the other one causing a collective amnesia so that nobody remembers any more of which state she had been a citizen before the war nor what the shape of territorial borders had been. There is no democratic way of deciding how to draw a new political map in these situations. Imagine that each adult individual were given a geographic map to draw the political borders of her future preferred state in which her plot of land will be included. A computer would then digitalize and aggregate all these political maps and calculate the shape of those borders which produce the smallest average deviation from all individual borders. However, for this statistical operation one would first have to tell the computer at least the number of states into which the territory can be split. So we are back to the initial problem. Moreover, there are important objections against accepting the results of such a purely statistical operation as an expression of majority opinion. If voters were asked whether they agreed with the result after the computer had calculated its optimal political map, a majority may say no without inconsistency or change in their preferences.

Radically democratic nationalists, who are a rare species in real political life, might propose a substitute procedure for the one just dismissed as both unfeasible and undemocratic. Their concern is to give all individuals the broadest possible opportunity to live in a state in which their national group forms a majority (without having to migrate). Instead of letting people choose their preferred state territory they would choose their preferred national group instead. The underlying assumption is that individuals generally prefer to live in a state which is homogeneously populated by members of their national group. Presumably, there is only a limited set of such groups among which individuals may choose their affiliation, so any territorial division will produce at least relative majorities for certain groups. We would now again start with a purely geographical map. Individual national affiliations would be registered in a census within an area encompassing all disputed territories. The task is to search for that subdivision of the total territory which will create the most stable majorities. If there were no further constraints, the optimum achieved by this method would be a complete segregation so that all territories comprise only homogeneous populations. Where several groups are scattered over a larger territory such a solution would lead to mini-states for the small groups and to geographically discontiguous state territories for the larger ones.

However, the point of national self-determination is not just to create homogeneous populations but also to create sovereign states. When constraints of size and contiguity are introduced in order to achieve sustainable territorial sovereignty, the solution which provides the most stable majorities could be defined as that division of the territory which maximizes the average distance over all the subunits between the percentage of the largest group and the second largest one within each subunit. That would of course produce strongly dissatisfied minorities who will be worse off in this kind of solution compared to any other division of the territory, because their size and thus their power to negotiate minority rights is minimized. Much the same result can be achieved by first calculating borders without constraints of size and contiguity and allowing then for negotiated swaps of territories between the national groups. We know quite well from history, what happens when people and territories are turned into objects of exchange between states. The target of creating stable majorities in viable states has been invoked to justify the 'ethnic cleansing' of populations, i.e. mass expulsion or even genocide.

A second problem is that taking national affiliation as an indicator for preferences concerning territorial borders of states severely restrains democratic choices. A census is no method for reaching democratic decisions. An individual may well consider herself a member of national group A but still prefer to live in a state where group B forms a majority. Maybe such a state would be economically more prosperous than one formed only by group A in its own territory and the person is optimistic that group A will enjoy substantial minority rights in this state. Drawing state borders so as to optimize national majorities means effectively denying individuals the most important choice: to decide collectively between *alternative* state affiliations of their territory.

The conclusion is obvious: neither stable territorial settlement nor stable national affiliations help to overcome the democratic dilemma settlers would face on a foreign planet. Democratic self-determination cannot start from scratch. It is impossible to conceive of state borders as the result of democratically aggregated unconstrained individual choices. Only wars and authoritarian political rule can create completely new territorial borders which do not take into account existing ones.

But certainly a democratic principle of national self-determination could serve to *correct* existing divisions of territories between states? Let us examine in a next step how this could be achieved by separation and fusion, which is what we can call secession and annexation when they are the result of democratic deliberation involving both parts rather than being declared unilaterally. I assume a situation where the problem is simplified because borders of regions are both given and uncontested. The contested issue is whether a certain region will form an independent state, or join another state. Suppose there had been a referendum on the separation of Czechoslovakia. Which procedures would have satisfied requirements of democracy? Separate majorities in both parts of the country, an overall majority, or a majority in only that part which wanted to separate? If there are only yes-votes and no-votes in two regions of a state, A and B, we can write the three propositions in formal notation as:

(1) y only if $(y_a > n_a)$ and $(y_b > n_b)$
(2) y only if $(y_a + y_b) > (n_a + n_b)$
(3) y only if $(y_a > n_a)$ or $(y_b > n_b)$

Proposition (1) implies (2) and (2) implies (3). (1) establishes the highest threshold for separation, (2) is somewhat less demanding and (3) is a minimal requirement which effectively declares a right to secession rather than separation.

Looking at the internal constitution of a federation of states might help to find out which of these proposals is the more democratic one. Such constitutions typically combine all three rules: there will be issues which have to be supported by majorities in a majority of states;[6] others require a simple majority among all citizens of the federation and still others can be decided by a majority at the level of a single state. The first rule will apply where the co-operation between state administrations is required for implementing a decision in the whole federation. The second rule is relevant for all issues under the responsibility of the federal government and the third one for those which primarily concern the local population of a single state. Most constitutions presuppose a given state territory and do not provide for separation or fusion.[7]

A proposal for separation is practically always regarded as a challenge to the constitution, which therefore can no longer serve as a common frame of reference for deciding which rule is adequate. In contrast with fusion, separation also requires working out of at least one new constitution. Rather than accepting the old constitution as still relevant, political leaders which advocate secession will therefore orient towards working out a new constitution for their desired independent state.

A proper solution in this situation would be a 'deconstitutional assembly' with the task of defining the rules according to which a decision about separation can be achieved in a peaceful and democratic manner, just as in a foundational constitutional assembly delegates in a deconstitutional one cannot be constrained in their decision by an already existing set of rules. In their deliberation they would have to consider which solution would satisfy norms of democratic decision-making but also take into account the particular historical circumstances of the country and the actual line-up of forces. In terms of practical politics this solution is of course illusory. Where there is a strong will to separate in one part of the country, it will be impossible to agree on the convening and the composition of such an assembly in the first place. Agreement in constitutional assemblies is possible because each constituent part expects to gain from a future common state, and thus has an incentive to accept the authority of the majority of the assembly as long as its decisions do not reduce these gains to zero. In a deconstitutional assembly there is at least one faction which expects to gain from dissolution of the state, and has no incentive to accept majority decisions taken within the existing framework which would reduce these gains. Only the threat of force could enforce compliance but this would contradict the purpose of the assembly of reaching voluntary agreement about a democratic procedure. For similar reasons we can also not hope to fix in the established constitution the rules for calling such an assembly and for choosing its delegates. Let us assume nevertheless that all these obstacles could be overcome, and that delegates would be perfectly enlightened liberal democrats who will always prefer that rule which they can consistently wish to be universally applied.

I do not think that any set of sufficiently general procedural rules for democratic decision-making provides an answer as to which of the rules is more democratic. Some delegates might argue that rules (1) and (3) have to be rejected on two separate grounds: first for biasing the result in favour of one of the two alternatives to be decided in the referendum and second for giving unequal weights to individual votes depending on the size of the regions. Suppose that all separatists are concentrated in region B which has only a quarter of the total population. A single vote above 12.5% of the total electorate would then be sufficient to enforce separation, whereas opponents would need seven times as many votes in order to prevent it. If for the purpose of the referendum the territory were subdivided into two equal parts with all separatists still on one side of the line, any vote above 25% would be sufficient for them to achieve their political target.[8] Exactly the same effects would work in favour of unionists under rule (1). So rule (2) could be seen as the only defensible one because it is procedurally impartial between alternative options and because it gives equal weight to all votes.

The argument is, however, flawed. In any strongly territorialized form of democracy there is a structural bias in favour of certain options. The British system of first-past-the-post elections gives no weight to votes for minority candidates in the constituency. There is a trade-off between proportional representation of voters' preferences at the national level and regional representation of voters in the constituencies by a local Member of Parliament. A second trade-off is between voters' influence on the composition of parliament (which is maximized in proportional representation) and on that of government (which is stronger in simple majority voting in constituencies because government will usually be formed by one of the two largest parties). While virtues and vices of both systems can be discussed at length, none of them violates any obvious requirements of democracy.

The second objection concerning the unequal size of populations which augments the inequality of votes seems more serious. In any territorial form of democracy, results will strongly depend on the subdivision of the territory into electoral constituencies. The general democratic norm of equality of votes requires that in a voting system like the British one constituencies must be of roughly equal size. Yet this rule cannot be applied to federal constitutions. The justification for aggregating votes within regional subdivisions in federalism is essentially different from that of territorial constituencies for a national parliament. The former implies that the state is seen in some respects as an association of territorial associations of citizens where regional boundaries are already given by historical circumstances. The claim of equal votes for the different territorial subunits when matters of federal interest are decided is just as strong as that of equal votes for citizens within the subunits in regional concerns and across all subunits in national elections.

Theoretically, a federal constitution need not necessarily lead to less cohesion than a strongly centralized one. Rule (1) equalizes aggregate votes between the federal units just as rule (3) but the former rule allows these units to block each others' votes and to reduce thus the autonomy of the separate parts of the state. Rule (1) will rarely be used for internal decision-making in a federal democracy but just as (3) it does not violate any procedural norm of democracy, and different parts of a state which strongly depend on each other might well agree to adopt it as a precaution against short-sighted particularistic interests which could provoke a break-up.

Being unable to decide in favour of one rule by considering what democratic procedures require, delegates in the deconstitutional assembly then turn to liberal norms and values in order to assess the consequences if each rule were applied universally. As a universal rule (1) would more or less freeze the status quo; (2) would generally allow only for the break-up of states into parts of roughly equal size; and (3) might lead to an chain-reaction in which ever smaller states are formed.

Some liberals may feel intuitively that when an issue as important as separation is at stake, the greatest danger is that of oppressive majorities abusing their power to overrule the wish of minorities to self-determination of their own membership. As each of the three rules can claim to be democratic they will consider which one achieves the best protection for minorities. If the minority wants to separate, rules (1) and (2) effectively block its right to do so unless they can muster the support of a majority in the state as a whole or even in that part which opposes separation. In most cases this is a threshold so high that it turns the principle of self-determination into an absurdity. Yet no rule for majority decision, not even (3), consistently protects minorities. It gives minorities a right to secession but it does not protect them against partition which they do not want. There are not many historical examples of states abandoning voluntarily a part of their territory against the wish of the majority living there and without external enforcement by a third power. However, the Czech/Slovak case comes quite close. At the time of separation, majority opinion in the Czech lands seemed to have been in favour of separation while smaller and economically weaker Slovakia would have preferred to stay in a confederation. Few liberal democrats would have regarded partition as legitimate had a referendum been held with an overall majority supporting, but a Slovak majority opposing, separation. In this case rule (1) seems the appropriate one. Combining both situations into a single rule would in fact mean that it is always the minority and the minority only which decides about partition. In this case the exit of subunits would become optional in the same way as it is for individual citizens in a liberal democracy. This might be regarded as a reasonable constraint on majoritarian democracy. A constitutional majority may well adopt it in order to bind its own hands against future abuse of its own power towards the weaker parts, and to reassure them that they will benefit from the federation.

However, other liberals may argue that rules of exit for the constituent units can be different for the state seen as an association of individual citizens and for the same state seen as an association of (regional, ethnic or national) associations. Whereas the exit of citizens must be optional and under their own control, this is not similarly evident for the exit of subunits. Moreover, they will reject the supposition that such a strong right of secession is generally beneficial for minorities. Not all arguments against optional secession are simply those of self-interested majorities. Minority rights are a means of balancing and tempering the power of majorities in democracy. But their ultimate liberal justification is the protection of rights of individuals who are discriminated against or disadvantaged in the wider society because of their minority origins or affiliations (Kymlicka, 1989). Where the thresholds for separation and state formation become too low, it is just the protection of individual rights of minority members which might suffer most. Majorities will have strong incentives not to respect these rights both before and after separation: before they will be cautious in reinforcing the sense of collective identity among potential separatists by giving them too much recognition; after separation they will treat remaining minority members in their territory as natural supporters of a foreign state and tell them to emigrate there if they are dissatisfied. Among the minorities, it is usually an intellectual elite which gains most from separation. A sovereign state offers them resources for building their own political, economic and cultural institutions. At the same time, partition destroys some of the established infrastructure and communicative networks and reduces benefits for the larger population which result from open markets and universal citizenship rights in larger state territories. Furthermore, minority rights will be even more difficult to enforce in new nation-states which have just been formed by partition than in the states from which they have broken away. A process of self-determination which results in separation, is nearly always accompanied by outbreaks of hostility against minorities whose very existence seems to tarnish the legitimacy of a newly founded state (Arendt, 1967, pp. 267–77).

In contrast with the impossibility of settling disputes about how to draw completely new territorial borders by democratic deliberation, the possibility that separation between already existing units can be legitimated by democratic self-determination must be granted. However, neither procedural requirements of democracy nor liberal norms for individual and minority rights provide a general rule about how such a decision ought to be taken.

Fusion poses fewer problems. Here it is obvious that the rule which must be applied to distinguish fusion from annexation is (1). Fusion is legitimized by democratic decision only when there are separate majorities in both parts which join to form a single state. However, consider the following case: There are two states A and B and three national groups G_A, G_B and G_C. G_C is the largest of the three. G_A and G_B live only in their respective nation-states where they form a majority of the population, while G_C is split between both states and is the national minority in each of them. Suppose that voter preferences are completely determined by national affiliations. Are the claims of G_C to national self-determination weaker just because it is geographically less concentrated? Is unification between states really only legitimate in cases where the groups advocating it are already majorities in the separate territories? The answer is probably yes because unification could be immediately challenged and reversed by regional majorities claiming their right to self-determination according to the strongest possible criterion (1). But what the case illustrates is that, once more, the majority principle on its own is not sufficient to determine unique territorial solutions.

The argument that a correction of borders by fusion or separation may satisfy democratic requirements of majority approval, but might at the same time worsen the situation of those minorities which are newly produced by a change, or still remain minorities after it has been carried out, deserves some further consideration. The democratic paradox involved in this is that minorities may well be a part of numerical majorities and nevertheless be unable to exercise their right of territorial self-determination. The example I have mentioned above is just one among three possible cases which can be labelled as those of exclave, diaspora and dispersed minorities.[9]

Local majorities might be denied the option of joining another state when they live in a regional exclave unconnected with the 'homeland' of their national group. The only choices open to them, according to the principle of democratic self-determination, are to form their own state or to submit to a national majority within a larger territory. This restriction could be lifted by allowing for geographic discontiguity of states. There have been historical examples for this. Some states have overseas provinces. Landlocked countries may be connected with a sea port by a corridor. Ethnic exclaves like Armenian Nagorny-Karabakh in Azerbaijan present the most intractable problems. If a part of a state lies within the territory of another state, this obviously creates obstacles for the effective exercise of territorial sovereignty by state administrations, as well as for the exercise of basic rights of citizenship such as free movement within the *whole* of the national territory. In this situation it also becomes almost impossible to distinguish between defensive acts of protecting a state's citizens in its own

territory and military aggression against a foreign territory. Probably the
only stable solution for national exclaves is to provide for a shared exercise
of sovereignty by both states involved.

I call diaspora minorities those which have a nation-state they can refer
to, but which do not form a majority in any territory outside this nation-
state.[10] These minorities can still ask a state to protect their minority rights
by international treaties and they can exercise their right of self-
determination in a very restricted and indirect way by emigrating into this
'homeland'. Other minorities are completely dispersed among national
majorities and cannot enjoy even such residual benefits of national self-
determination. The rules of democracy seem to imply that they will be
collectively excluded from exercising their right to self-determination, even
if each single individual member perceives the group as a separate nation
and supports its political sovereignty. As I have shown above, this
conclusion holds even for a dispersed minority which cannot form a
majority in any regional subdivision of existing states, but which would
become a national majority if separate states were unified.

So far we have discussed difficulties with establishing territorial borders
between states by majority decision. A second kind of problem arises when
we consider conflicting claims of collectives to a given state territory that
refer to past events. A group which has been turned into a national minority
by illegitimate means such as mass expulsions or territorial annexations,
may argue that procedures of democratic self-determination can only
become legitimate after historic injustice has been rectified. However,
rectification must obviously be limited in time. If all claims to territories,
which are based on some violation of this rule in the past, were dismissed,
we would end up with the paradoxical result that many territories cannot be
claimed by any group in spite of their being inhabited at present by a strong
national majority. Conversely, if all claims raised by any group which had
been a majority in the territory at some time in the past were legitimate,
most territories could be claimed simultaneously by different groups.
Furthermore, reinstatement is impossible when the group which had been
expelled has been greatly diminished in size because of killings, natural
deaths, geographic dispersal or assimilation. Can a former majority still
claim to become hegemonic in its state or region of origin if it could no
longer form a new majority, even when all its members who were willing to
come back were invited to do so?

The conclusion is that not all historical injustice can be rectified. Once
this is conceded, disputes over boundaries of territories will be transformed
into disputes over thresholds in historical time. There seems to be no
obvious general criterion for settling the latter ones. Should all claims of an
expelled group to their territory end after one generation? The children of

those who committed the crimes cannot be made responsible, but neither can the children of those who were expelled be told that they have to suffer the consequences of crimes committed against their parents. This is an issue truly 'beyond justice' (Heller, 1987).

As soon as we drop the assumptions of stable resident populations with unique national affiliations things get even more complicated. I will just list a few questions in order to show the difficulty of giving any general answers to dilemmas of self-determination. Territorial mobility may reverse numerical relations between groups without any use of force or other illegitimate means. Mexican immigrants in Southern regions of the USA today certainly do not intend to reunite with Mexico these territories which had been Mexican until the mid 19th century. But would they be entitled to demand this where they now have become a majority?[11] Can the French Canadians of Québec legitimately give strong priority to immigrants who speak French[12] and require that all immigrant children are sent to French schools in order to stabilize their provincial majority and keep alive the option of separation (Richmond, 1988, Carens, 1994)? One might object that international migration is subject to control by receiving states anyway. But an upsetting of regional numerical balances can of course also be achieved by internal migration. People may not only change their territorial location but also their national affiliations. I have already pointed out above that even stable affiliations need not imply the wish to live in a territory where this group is hegemonic and therefore voting on that issue cannot be replaced by a census on ethnic and national identities. But historic claims to a territory can only be raised by groups which have preserved a certain identity of this sort (see section 2.3). Any theory that does not 'racialize' national identity must also allow for the possibility of voluntary changes in this regard. Deciding national disputes by democratic referenda would make no sense anyway if identities were an objective rather than a subjective phenomenon, if they were inherited at birth and immutable during adult life. Can a group claim autonomy rights in a territory where it used to be a majority but was turned into a minority because of widespread intermarriages and voluntary assimilation?

7.3. EXTENSION OF CITIZENSHIP WITHIN THE POPULATION

Similar paradoxes of self-determination in the collective allocation of citizenship as those discussed above can arise when a new state is founded or an old state is restored after a long period of annexation. In such situations, the question of borders has already been decided, not by democratic means but usually by military strength and political relations of forces. In the best cases, superior force has been gained by mobilizing popular support for powerful historical claims to a certain territory. Rogers Brubaker's analysis of citizenship struggles in the Soviet successor states nicely captures the circular paradox resulting from applying democratic procedures to resolving questions of membership in such a foundational situation: 'If questions of citizenship ... must be decided by a newly elected Sejm (legislative assembly) or by popular referendum, then who should have the right to elect the Sejm or to vote in a referendum?' This question 'brings out the problems involved in trying to settle the contested question of citizenship through a procedure (electing a parliament or voting in a referendum) that itself presupposes citizenship' (Brubaker, 1992, p. 283). Yet I will try to show that, in contrast with the examples discussed above, this kind of paradox allows us to use democracy at least as a yardstick for evaluating alternative solutions.

In order to illustrate how this may be done let me compare this Baltic puzzle with a similar question that could also come up in any stable nation-state with well-established rules determining citizenship. Suppose a referendum is to be held about lowering the voting age from 21 to 18. Should the age group between 18 and 21 be allowed to vote in this referendum? On the one hand, if they are not, the 'natural constituency' for one of the two options is excluded and the result may therefore be regarded as not binding by these young people. On the other hand, if they are included there is really nothing to vote about any more because the question has been decided in advance. They have been turned into enfranchised citizens by allowing them to vote. It would be clearly undemocratic to include the young people as citizens only for a single vote and to exclude them again as a result of the vote. The conclusion from this example is paradoxical twice over: the principle of inclusion would be violated by including in a referendum about their voting rights those who have not enjoyed voting rights so far. Yet if a majority in the referendum upholds further exclusion this may be legitimately criticized as undemocratic, and need not be regarded as a binding decision by those excluded.

Two more general insights can be derived from the example. The first one concerns the prohibition of collective exclusion of minorities from the citizenry. This negative form of the liberal principle of inclusion is much stronger than the positive one. The point which is of interest for our discussion here is whether collective exclusion would also violate the conditions for stability of democracy over time. If a majority could decide to exclude minorities from membership, the *demos* might become ever smaller and smaller by successive democratic votes. After a series of such exclusions the remaining members may well be a tiny minority of the original *demos*, a result which would never have been supported by a majority in the beginning. Certainly, any association can take a democratic decision to dissolve. But allowing collective exclusion would mean that a democratic association can vote itself out of existence against the wish of its majority.

The second insight is that although a majority of the present *demos* may decide democratically not to extend the suffrage or citizenship to a hitherto excluded group, the alternative decision to include them may be called a more democratic one. How can this be argued if we try again to abstain from smuggling in liberal notions about inclusive representation of all individuals who are members of a modern society? The shrinking of the *demos* against the wish of its majority can be seen as a threat to democracy in its own terms. It shows that sustainable democracy has to establish a list of taboos upon which voting cannot be allowed independently from any liberal notion of individual rights. From this it does not yet follow that a continuous expansion of the *demos* by including ever more groups is *per se* more democratic than keeping its membership stable.

The argument has to take one step backwards from decision-making towards agenda setting. There must be a selection mechanism for those issues which are put to a vote. Democracy cannot work if every single citizen of a state could force a vote on each issue she is interested in. Once the proposal for including the 18–21 age group has been raised in public debates, and once it has been decided to hold a referendum on it, this presupposes that a substantial group must be in favour. Second, democracy can also not work where there is no free public debate before an issue is decided. Even though the 'natural constituency' will not be allowed to vote about its own inclusion, it would be impossible to shut them out from public debates preceding the decision without thereby constraining also the deliberative freedom of the enfranchised population. This freedom must include the right to hear the arguments of the excluded group and the right of the proponents of inclusion to present these arguments to the opponents. In putting the question on the agenda, the excluded group is thus already included in the sense of becoming accepted as *potential* citizens or members of the *demos*. A decision in favour of inclusion is more democratic than one which excludes those who have already been partially included in the deliberative process. Furthermore, the vote itself also marks a turning-point with regard to the legitimacy of exclusion. Before the issue has been raised at all, exclusion cannot be called illegitimate. After the campaign and a negative vote, the excluded group will have become very aware of its exclusion. At the same time, because they could not participate in the vote, the group is not bound to accept even a large majority decision which perpetuates its exclusion. They will be entirely justified in calling the decision an illegitimate one after the vote.

Certainly this purely democratic argument for inclusion remains much weaker and much more indeterminate than the liberal one. As long as we stick only to the implications of sustainable democratic decision-making we have no way of deciding in advance which groups ought to be included in the *demos*. There was simply no way in ancient Athens to argue that democracy required the inclusion of women or slaves. But once labourers, former slaves and women had raised their voices in modern liberal democracies demanding inclusion, it became obvious that class, racist and gender exclusion would have been undemocratic even if confirmed by majority vote. However, the argument whether a particular group is unjustly excluded or indeed unfit for citizenship or for the suffrage cannot be resolved by appealing to procedural rules of democracy. For this we need a theory of citizenship that links social to political membership.

Using the discussion about the voting age to assess the Baltic case, we can safely assume that a decision for a citizenship law which implies long-time exclusion of Russian postwar immigrants is in itself undemocratic. Whether or not these minorities ought to have been enfranchised already for the first elections and referenda before a new citizenship law had been adopted, is a different question. It depends entirely on whether the new state accepts continuity of its citizenry with the citizenry of the Soviet republic or insists on a symbolic restoration of the previous independent state. In the former view, disenfranchising the new Russian minorities would be just that kind of collective exclusion which must be ruled out in order to make democracy sustainable over time. This also implies that in a referendum there cannot be a question whether Russian minorities who take part in the vote should be excluded from citizenship afterwards when the new law comes into force. In the latter view, Russian immigrant minorities had been never citizens in that state which is now about to be rebuilt. So they cannot be given the vote in the first elections or referenda, just as young people below voting age cannot participate in a general vote on their own inclusion. However, as I have tried to show, even in this case a decision to exclude them from citizenship can be criticized as undemocratic independently from whether they had taken part in it. In order to make this critique irrelevant it would be necessary to show that Russians can be rightly regarded as unfit for citizenship, because they are not an ordinary resident minority but invaders of an occupying foreign power who still remain loyal to that power and disloyal towards the new state. This argument cannot be resolved by appealing to either democratic or liberal principles but only by assessing the historical and contemporary facts of the case.

The main results of my analysis in this chapter are the following. Territorial boundaries of political membership cannot be consistently created and tested by democratic methods. Generally they have to be taken as a contingent outcome of historical processes. Democracy can neither step out of history nor reverse it towards an earlier stage. Corrections and changes of existing borders can be submitted to votes, but the method of aggregating votes into decisions can be contested with no obvious solution provided by democratic as well as by liberal criteria. Full and equal citizenship for all members of a society within given territorial borders is a specifically liberal norm which cannot be derived from procedural requirements of democracy. Although exclusion in democracy can never be as arbitrary as in other kinds of associations, a system of rule which excludes large parts of a territory's population can be democratic on its own terms. But when a dynamic of social inclusion has developed, liberalism and democracy will reinforce each other in a virtuous circle: contestation by excluded groups can refer to liberal norms of equal human rights and the full representation of society in political decision-making. This helps to bring the issue on the agenda of democratic deliberation which is then pushed towards more inclusion by its own norms. Once a group has been legally recognized as entitled to citizenship, the democratic bar on collective exclusion will help to entrench this as a quasi-constitutional right. This will in turn feed back into the public perception of membership in society so that other forms of exclusion can be seen as illegitimate which had before been accepted as self-evident.

This perspective should not be mistaken for an optimistic description of historic evolution in Western societies. It is nothing more than an analysis of how the *norms* of liberalism and democracy may reinforce each other in extending citizenship. Of course, these developments may be reversed, and indeed have been reversed at different times in history. The dynamic interplay of norms does not permit forecasting, but it provides us with a yardstick for assessing achievements or backlashes in political systems which claim to be liberal democratic. When groups of former citizens are legally excluded this is a sure indicator that liberal democracy has already been abandoned, no matter whether this decision was taken according to formally democratic procedures. When groups have acquired membership in society but remain persistently excluded from citizenship, this is a sign that liberal democracy is in jeopardy because it lags behind social development.

The question underlying the enquiry of this book is of how transnational migration affects perceptions of social membership, and what it would mean to make citizenship inclusive in transnationally mobile societies. Let me at this point briefly anticipate the line of argument which will be developed more fully in the concluding chapters of the second part.

Only a strictly cosmopolitan approach that ignores the territorial boundaries of politics could set an ultimate standard of inclusion towards which liberal democracy aims: equal citizenship for all mankind in a world state. Once we reject this as a fantasy, there are neither final targets nor fixed limits for a dynamic of inclusion. There will always be a plurality of territorial states as the given frame within which democratic politics can develop. But with increasing mobility between these states, the territorial boundaries of societies which serve as the frame of reference for the norm of inclusion become more and more fluid. Making citizenship more inclusive in transnationally mobile societies is not only about reducing residence qualifications for naturalization, just as enhancing the citizenship status of minors is not only a question of lowering the voting age but concerns also the rights they will enjoy before they are enfranchised. Optional admission, which means giving non-members a right to membership, is an outreaching form of inclusion. The same can be said about general toleration of dual citizenship. Residential citizenship rights for foreigners and external citizenship rights for non-residents are two further ways how benefits of membership can be extended beyond national and territorial boundaries of politics respectively.

Migration rights have been an expansive element of liberal citizenship, and have been decisive for the recognition of immigrants' social membership and of their claims to political membership. Migrants will only be seen as potential citizens when migration itself has become a right linked to citizenship. In the contemporary world migration rights are fundamentally asymmetric. The universal right of free emigration is supplemented only by some particular group rights of immigration. Global free movement is not on the agenda. However, in contrast with the utopia of a single world state, this is a vision which is neither impossible to realize nor undesirable if it could be realized. We can study today how free migration and settlement within a small number of wealthy states in Western Europe links up with rudimentary forms of a supranational citizenship. But we can hardly imagine yet how a human right of free movement would change liberal democratic notions of membership in territorial political communities.

NOTES

1.   This is, for example, a rule in the Austrian constitution.
2.   Natural phenotypic differences between human groups which are used as markers of membership, such as skin colour, never distinguish individuals in this way without

borderline cases. This is why racism is so obsessed with defining clear-cut boundaries that cannot be found within the species itself. The only distinction which is both dichotomous and visible is the sexual one. Even this difference is of course culturally transformed so that it may be emphasized but also relativized or even individually crossed (see section 11.1).

3. Fredrik Barth (1969) has analysed ethnic boundaries in this way.

4. Even for clubs, liberal democracy sets constraints on collective exclusion from admission. Private associations which provide some kind of service to the general public are not allowed to deny admission on 'racial' or gender grounds.

5. The idea is similar to that of an 'all-inclusive original position with representatives of all the individual persons in the world' who ought to settle 'the question of whether there are to be separate societies' (Rawls, 1993b, p. 65). In Rawls's discussion the representatives would, however, also have to decide on the principles of justice that ought to govern the relations between states. He finally dismisses the device of an all-inclusive original position because, by representing individuals as free and equal persons, it seems to be biased in favour of liberal principles for relations between societies (p. 66). My example is much less ambitious. It takes principles of democracy as given and only points out that in a global assembly of individuals or of their representatives these principles do not sufficiently determine procedures for reaching collectively binding decisions on the question of whether to have separate states.

6. In representative federal democracies there is usually a second chamber or house of parliament, where delegates from the regional subunits or states have the power to introduce legislation themselves or to block legislation introduced by the other parliamentary body that emerges from an aggregation of votes at the federal level.

7. There are exceptions such as the constitution of the Soviet Union, which contained a right of secession, and the Basic Law of the Federal Republic of Germany, which envisaged unification with Eastern Germany as a state target. However, neither adopted a clear procedural rule of democratic decision about a change of the state territory.

8 J.S. Mill noted the same effect in a system of two parliamentary chambers: 'assuming both the Houses to be representative, and equal in their numbers, a number slightly exceeding a fourth of the entire representation may prevent the passing of a Bill; while, if there is but one House, a Bill is secure of passing if it has a bare majority' (Mill, 1972, 'On Representative Government', p. 352). Mill did not think that this was a practical problem because two chambers elected on the basis of the same suffrage will hardly disagree on any issue to that extent. This is of course different in a referendum on separation.

9. Minority affiliations as well as their ties to an external 'homeland' are considered as given here only for the sake of simplifying the analysis at this stage. Analysing the cases of Russian minorities in Soviet successor states and of Hungarians in Romania and Slovakia, Rogers Brubaker has pointed out that national minorities in nationalizing states, and external national homelands to which these minorities refer, form a dynamic field of relations. While the escalation of nationalist mobilization is predictable in such constellations, outcomes in terms of the strength of affiliations and the degree of violence in particular conflicts are rather contingent (Brubaker, 1993).

10. Of course the classic diaspora minority of Jews did not have such a state until 1948 but they referred to a territory as their common origin and Zionism redefined this as the territory of a future Jewish state. In these respects Jews differ from the dispersed minority of European Roma and Sinti, whose origins are traced to India but who do not see this as their 'homeland' in either religious or political terms.

11. For a discussion of US responsibility towards Mexican immigration see Lichtenberg (1983).

12. In fact, Québec's policy is quite liberal in this respect. Immigrants are ranked according to a point system. They receive up to 15 points for knowledge of French whereas English counts for not more than 2 points. (In the rest of Canada, both languages count equally.) Immigrants who do not speak any French still have a reasonable chance of being admitted. From 1969 to 1989 the percentage of immigrants with French as a first or second language was around 30% of all new admissions (Ministère, 1990, p. 28).

PART II

Rights

8. Entitlements and Liberties

The first part of this book has dealt with citizenship as membership. In the second part I will be concerned with the substantial rights of citizenship. Equality of membership and inclusiveness of rights are the two basic norms of democratic and liberal citizenship. Democracy implies an equal status of membership in a polity, and liberalism demands that every person subjected to political power ought to enjoy liberties and rights which secure her autonomy in relation to that power. These norms mutually reinforce each other but they can also come into conflict. The dynamic of citizenship results from the cross-application of norms so that membership becomes more inclusive by extending rights, and rights become instrumental for securing equal membership.

In the first part of the book I suggested that membership in the polity ought to be made more inclusive by giving every permanent resident a right to the acquisition of nominal citizenship. Such inclusion will, however, increase to some extent the inequality of status by reflecting different social positions and choices of individuals. Native citizens and naturalized immigrants are in equal positions of membership but they have made different kinds of choices to get there. Native citizens have been attributed citizenship at birth without their consent and their choice is limited to expatriation after emigration, whereas naturalized immigrants had to take a decision themselves whether to acquire full membership. Dual citizens have decided to retain a second membership, while other permanent resident foreigners are *de facto* members in most regards who have declined the offer of naturalization. The point is that these inequalities of membership have to be accepted in a liberal conception which acknowledges that native citizens, emigrants and immigrants face different options of membership, and respects their individual choices. Inclusion would become oppressive if membership were perfectly equalized, i.e. if naturalization became automatic or mandatory for all permanent residents and if it implied the loss of their previous affiliation. Inclusion is therefore achieved by equalizing the substantial rights of citizenship and extending them to the resident population as a whole independently of nominal membership.

In the second part I make a parallel argument about the rights of citizenship. If these rights are to be inclusive and comprehensive they cannot be perfectly equal. Just as natives, residents and migrants are in different social positions which become relevant for their political membership, so men and women, children and adults, ethnic minorities and national majorities, workers and employers, are in different social positions which become relevant for their rights. But nevertheless, rights of citizenship are not special privileges of social groups. While the norm of inclusion pushes towards extending the distribution of rights beyond membership, the norm of substantial equality of individual membership in the polity is the basic reference point for determining the rights of citizens.

Membership is not given prior to rights and rights do not exist independently from membership. This view differs from both theories of natural membership and of natural rights. The former maintain that individual membership is given simply by the circumstances of birth, be it those of descent or of territory, while the latter claim liberties and rights which individuals are said to enjoy independently and outside of any social or political membership. Natural membership theories are incompatible with regarding naturalization and expatriation as individual options. A natural rights perspective separates universal human rights from those of citizenship, and does not relate the former to membership in polities where only they can be claimed and enforced.

'Citizenship is a status bestowed on those who are full members of a community. All who possess the status are equal with respect to the rights and duties with which the status is endowed. There is no universal principle that determines what those rights and duties shall be' (Marshall, 1965, p. 92). Instead of discussing a list of citizenship rights in a normative or historical perspective, I want to examine in which way they contribute to achieve this equality of status. My argument is with approaches that defend narrow or strongly biased conceptions of rights. This chapter suggests that citizenship contains not only legal but also moral rights, not only active but also passive entitlements and not only negative but also positive liberties. Chapter 9 argues that although citizenship rights relate to membership in polities they are not special rights but general ones. This makes it possible to see human rights as a universalized form of citizenship. Chapter 10 dismisses a property rights approach which could justify extensive inequality of citizenship. If rights were considered as a commodity, i.e. as scarce and alienable goods, such inequality would emerge from free transactions. In chapter 11, I suggest that collective rights can be an element of equal individual citizenship. Chapter 12 proposes that liberal citizenship is based on rights rather than on obligations, and largely disconnects the former from the latter. The underlying question in all these chapters is in which way rights must be differentiated and must take into account social inequalities and differences in order to contribute to the idea of equal membership in a democratic polity.

The final chapter does not present a summary but addresses the greatest challenge raised by a transnational conception of citizenship. Apart from rights for resident foreigners, optional naturalization and universally valid human rights, must such a conception also endorse a global freedom of movement of people between states? My conclusion might seem ambivalent. The right of free migration should be asserted as a long-term target while I also maintain that a comprehensive form of equal membership at the level of separate polities can justify restrictions in the present world. The idea of transnational citizenship does not resolve all the acute migration policy dilemmas. But it allows the contradiction to be overcome at least at the level of normative argument, by showing how the long-term goal ought to constrain immigration control and leads to extending special immigration rights.

8.1. LEGAL AND MORAL RIGHTS

Let me start with a preliminary definition of what is implied in speaking about rights: a right is a resource provided by social institutions which protects and legitimates the existence, the needs and interests, or the actions of the bearer of the right. The emphasis on institutions is meant to refute the idea that rights can be 'natural' in the sense of being attributes of individuals in a state of nature. Any right depends on being recognized by other human beings. Even animal rights only make sense as rights institutionalized within society in order to protect the existence or needs of non-human beings. Rights also do not emerge from occasional interactions. Only in a shared institutional framework will promises or contracts between individuals generate rights and obligations.

Yet this institutional frame is not necessarily a legal one only. Rights are claimed and defended in social discourses, and legal rights generally refer to some kind of norms which are not themselves generated in the legislative process itself. Legal positivism has sharply separated rights from morality. The classical argument for this separation was stated by Jeremy Bentham: 'In proportion to the want of happiness resulting from the want of rights, a reason exists for wishing that there were such things as rights. But reasons for wishing that there were such things as rights, are not rights; a reason for wishing that a certain right were established, is not that right – want is not supply – hunger is not bread' (Bentham, 1987, p. 53). True enough, but a right to bread is not bread either. And the cry for bread is not the same as hunger. What we can call a right is not the lack of a resource but a claim to this resource articulated according to generalizable norms. Such claims may be addressed to legislative and judicial bodies in order to achieve an institutionalization of the right. However, even if we understand factual rights to be enforceable ones, it would be wrong to deny the factuality of rights outside positive laws.[1] Rights which are generally recognized in a certain culture can also be enforced by direct social pressure without the interference of legal institutions.

All rights depend on social recognition, but rights do not exist only when they can be enforced. While the former premise is directed against natural rights philosophy, the latter rejects the philosophical claims of utilitarianism and legal positivism.[2] We can distinguish various kinds of rights by combining the aspects of normative charge and institutional enforcement.

(1) Moral rights which are neither formulated as positive law nor generally accepted but which can be derived from basic normative principles supported by the constitutional order or by general moral convictions.

(2) Socially recognized rights which are not formulated as positive laws but are generally accepted as valid: e.g. special rights created by promise outside legally enforceable contracts. In the same category are norms which require legal institutionalization but have not (yet) been formulated as legal texts.[3]

(3) Unenforceable legal rights: e.g. rights formulated only as principles or targets and lacking judicial or administrative enforceability, such as a constitutional prohibition of discrimination on racial or sexual grounds without laws that define what counts as evidence and without specification of sanctions and enforcement agencies.

(4) Rights which are both socially recognized and legally enforceable. In a liberal democratic state, citizenship rights must be generally in this category because the democratic procedures of representation and division of power are meant to generate legislation that conforms broadly to socially accepted norms, and enforcement of these rights is what justifies the state monopoly of violence in such a state.

(5) Rights which are legally enforceable and which establish rules that are not derived from normative principles. The legitimacy of these rights is only secured procedurally, i.e. derived from the way in which the rules have been decided by authorized persons or bodies, and from the expediency or necessity of having binding rules. Traffic rules generate rights of this sort.[4]

(6) Legal and enforceable rights which refer to socially contested norms (e.g. the right to abortion and the right to life of the foetus) or which violate socially recognized norms.

Rights of citizenship can be articulated at the levels of moral norms, of contested or generally recognized social norms, and of institutionalized legal norms. What is specific about citizenship rights is that their background justification always lies in a strong norm of equality, and that they always aim at legal institutionalization. Equality of citizenship refers, on the one hand, to the citizens' relation towards governments which are obliged to treat them with equal concern and respect (Dworkin, 1977, p. 180) or *as equals* – which is different from saying that they should treat all citizens equally (p. 273). On the other hand, citizens are also equal among themselves as members of a democratic polity. Both notions of equality imply the necessity of translating rights of citizenship into positive law. In democratic polities the rules for governmental action towards citizens as well as for the citizens' ultimate popular control over legislation are formulated in the code of law. Informal cultural and social norms can become relevant for rights and obligations of citizenship only when they can be translated into the language of the law. I have suggested in earlier chapters that the democratic norm of equality combines with a liberal norm of inclusiveness, so that the definition of who has to be counted as a citizen entitled to equal status and treatment becomes itself a major normative issue of citizenship.

Liberal political philosophy has explained in different ways the moral foundations of this norm of equality. It can be derived from a principle of neutrality (Ackerman, 1980, chapter 1) or impartiality (Barry, 1989, chapter X), from the Kantian idea of autonomy which informs the theories of Rawls (1971, 1993a) and Habermas (1992), but also from a communitarian point of view that limits itself to exploring the shared meanings of citizenship in contemporary liberal democracies (Walzer, 1983). I do not want to enter this never-ending controversy. Essential for my argument is only the acknowledgement that such norms do exist at a level of social recognition, which makes it possible to challenge persistent forms of inequality and exclusion in the moral as well as in the legal and political sense.

Unlike theories of natural human rights which try to derive a catalogue of rights from assumptions about human nature, citizenship is thus a concept pointing to a certain distribution of rights among their holders rather than to a specific content of these rights. Nevertheless, we can identify an essential or minimal content. An equal right to eat caviar would not be considered. The obvious candidates are equal basic liberties and protection by the law, equal rights of political participation, and some baseline of social equality maintained by public education and social welfare rights.[5] The list of citizenship rights is open ended and varies with particular political traditions, social structures and cultural understandings, but all entries in this list can be understood as applications, extensions, supportive or corollary rights of these three basic elements.

8.2. ACTIVE AND PASSIVE RIGHTS – THE CONCEPT OF ENTITLEMENT

How do rights of citizenship refer to human agency? I will consider two aspects of this question: (1) What is implied in attributing rights to the non-human world? (2) Are citizenship rights passive because they emphasize entitlements rather than active involvement in society and politics?

(1) One further aspect of my initial definition of rights which might seem peculiar is that it refers to actions, needs and interests, but also to the existence of the bearer of the right. The idea is to avoid a narrowly activist conception of rights. Before attempting to determine the passive or active character of citizenship rights, one should first think about whether any kind of rights can ever be completely passive and protect no more than the very existence of the bearer.

The notion of rights clearly changes when we ascribe them to the non-human world. Rights of animals can still be derived from an idea about what they have in common with human beings. There is a double meaning involved in saying that we have something in common with higher species of animals. First, we think that they have similar sensual experiences and some of our cognitive capacities. Utilitarians such as Jeremy Bentham, or Peter Singer in our time, have grounded the rights of animals upon their capacity to feel pain. If one defines as the essential moral task the reduction of the overall amount of pain experienced in the world, it is quite obvious that higher species of animal life should be included in the 'felicific calculus'. Second, we can ascribe rights to animals not because of their experiences but because of our own ones which we share with them. Thus the rights of domestic animals to receive food and to be treated well have been more safely grounded in most cultures than those of wildlife (rather independently of the animals' evolutionary relatedness to humans). With higher species we may even ground their rights in their communicative capabilities (Habermas, 1991, pp. 223–4). Domesticated animals can develop a repertoire of communication that they share with their 'masters' which refers not only to individual needs, such as that for food, but also to a broad range of feelings, including those of attachment between the human and the animal.

Animals can be attributed needs, but how about plants or inanimate nature? Does it make any sense to speak about 'rights' of trees to the preservation of their species or of a specific ecological formation such as the Antarctic not to be used for human settlement? Some radical ecologists have even suggested that rights should be attributed to Gaia, the planet Earth conceived as a single organic being (Lovelock, 1979, quoted in Dobson, 1990). I doubt whether these ideas can be made philosophically consistent and meaningful. However, at a political level, the problem seems to me less intractable. Speaking about rights of nature involves two assertions. The first one is that a human society ought to impose certain prohibitions of interference and obligations for some positive action on its own members, which prohibitions and obligations are assumed to protect or benefit the targets of the inhibited or commanded actions. The second assertion is that the targets of these human actions should be protected because of their moral worth: 'A right ascribes a particular status or worth to the rights-bearer. In their protective capacity for certain human (or group) attributes rights signal the special importance of the entity endowed with those attributes. Hence rights are more than the reflection of duties towards passive individuals' (Freeden, 1991, p. 8). The entities which are ascribed such special importance and worth need not be human beings, only the ascription itself is necessarily a human activity and, moreover, a social one. Once a society of human beings takes a political decision that certain kinds of interference with elements of their natural environment shall be outlawed and others shall be required, they thereby create prohibitions and obligations which are correlates of a right. These correlates do not yet strictly imply 'rights of nature'. A prohibition to swim in a lake may be either due to a desire to protect the water flora or to dangerous currents and thus to a desire to protect human beings. The former prohibition might be conceived as creating a right of the protected object but not the latter.

Moral worth is attributed to the entity if it cannot be entirely reduced to a means for human purposes. Consider the contrast between animals and objects of art. The amount of protection given to a Vermeer painting or the amount of resources devoted to the conservation of Venice may be much greater than that used for the preservation of some rare species. But talking about the rights of paintings or buildings is moral nonsense because, no matter how much we value them as human creations, they receive their worth only from the purpose of satisfying human needs and desires. Saying that animals and even inanimate nature can enjoy rights implies that they are different in this respect. Whether or not a target of human action in nature can be properly called a 'bearer of rights', i.e. a subject, is a matter for philosophical speculation without any obvious implications for the institutionalization of such rights in political communities, whereas the appeal to their moral worth is politically important in claiming rights for targets that are of no immediate instrumental value to human beings. Different philosophical views could converge on this point. However, arguing for such rights as a moral constraint on human action has some anthropocentric implications.[6] Rights of animals and plants can only be institutionalized within human societies. They imply rules by which men and women bind themselves in their actions towards nature and the safest foundation for such rights are broadly shared moral convictions of a society. There is no such thing as rights in natural evolution. Even the utilitarian principle to minimize pain cannot be perceived in interaction between different species in nature. It is not because humans are themselves an animal species and thus integral parts of their natural environment that they are able to attribute rights to nature, but because they distinguish themselves as social, cultural and political beings from this environment. We may appeal to our biological commonalties with higher animal life in arguing for animal rights, but the very idea that we are able to respect something that is a right confirms our difference from them.

For a discussion of citizenship, the important point is that the notion of a right does not necessarily imply that its bearer must be seen as an agent fully capable of communicating those of her own needs and interests which are to be protected by the right. In extreme situations or cases a person holding a right may be completely passive. The purpose of the right may then be no more than a specification of prohibitions of harmful interference and of obligations to provide certain benefits, i.e. of actions by other human beings towards the bearer of the right – although the reason for formulating this as a *right* always goes beyond this purpose. While the beneficiary of a right need not even be human, the providers must always be more than simply human beings: they must be ascribed full capacities of cognition and action.

What is specifically required for citizenship are not capabilities of communication and participation but collective decisions about inclusion. These decisions oblige institutions as well as other members of society to refrain from certain kinds of interference and to provide certain kinds of assistance. Minors, severely handicapped or mentally disabled people can be citizens even if they are unable to express their needs and interests in the public realm. Social contract theories have always tended to reserve citizenship status for those who are able to claim their rights themselves. In his contemporary version, Bruce Ackerman asserts: 'A liberal state *is* nothing more than a collection of individuals who can participate in a dialogue in which all aspects of their power position may be justified in a certain way; to participate in such a dialogue of justification, actors must be intelligible to one another; to be intelligible, one's utterances must be translatable into the language comprehensible to other would-be-participants' (Ackerman, 1980, p. 72, original emphasis). Thus, as Ackerman argues, the rights of stones, of animals, of extraterrestials, of minors, of solipsists or idiots are either non-existent, or at least 'on a more uncertain footing than those of full members of the liberal community' (p. 79).

But from the fact that rights can only be safely institutionalized in a liberal democratic community of free and fully active human members, it does not follow that rights which such a community grants to less capable members will always be uncertain. Citizenship rights do not emerge from a dialogue between the claimant and potential provider (as they do in Ackerman's model), but from a wider 'polylogue' of political deliberation among the active citizens and their representatives. The beneficiaries of the right must not necessarily participate themselves in this deliberation – although whenever possible they certainly ought to be included. One might object that rights for non-participants can only rely on paternalistic reasons and will therefore depend on the goodwill of the exclusive group of power-holders. Yet this need not be the case. Consider the rights of minors. As long as they are seen as non-citizens who are entirely under parental power until attaining their majority, their rights depend indeed upon benevolent paternalism. If, however, children obtain rights as citizens which also give them certain claims towards their parents, these rights are ultimately constraints which fully active citizens impose on each other's actions. By specifying parents' obligations and by accepting responsibility for the provision of rights which parents fail to respect, state authorities act not only on behalf of the children, but also on behalf of all other citizen-parents who agree with these rules that also bind their own actions.

Regarding children as future citizens will help to strengthen respect for their citizenship, much as the consideration that frail elderly people once have actively contributed to the society which now provides them assistance, serves as a reason for not depriving them of their rights. However, citizenship status is not even strictly conditional upon being a fully active participant in civil society at some point in time during the course of a complete life. Persons mentally disabled from birth can nevertheless be citizens in a liberal democracy. Citizenship does draw a line, but it is not that between active and passive beneficiaries of rights. The line includes all those who can be regarded as members of a community which is capable of self-determination *as a collective*. This does not require that each single individual must be an active participant or must be able to become such a participant. In a society with an animistic religion, one could possibly have citizenship for animals and plants. In modern societies the basic prerequisite for citizenship is being human but not more than that. The *image* of the citizen is always that of a person capable of participating in collective deliberation. But this image does not provide us with a test criterion for exclusion. We cannot imagine animals sitting in parliament even during a debate on animal rights. But we can *imagine* children or the mentally disabled speaking rationally about their needs and interests when we deliberate about their rights. In contrast with their rights, those granted to animals express a difference that is more than inequality. It is the difference between forms of life which we might value, respect or even love and those with which we can share a social community.[7]

The norms of equality and inclusion apply only for human rights and rights of citizenship.[8] They refer to universal sociability among human beings from which animals or plants are necessarily excluded. Attributing *equal* rights to *all* animals, the chimpanzee as well as the mosquito, would strike us as absurd. This is not because non-human nature is so differentiated and varied that we could not find common denominators for equality. The reason is that as an animal species, human beings can only survive in their natural environment by treating different kinds of life unequally. The attribution of rights can neither alter this basic fact nor is it in contradiction with it. Not all rights are necessarily equal ones or those of equals. In the human world, too, many kinds of rights are meant to manifest inequality of status. The rights attached to membership in feudal estates mirrored an image of human society split into a hierarchy of 'species'.

The notion of passive rights of citizenship is not only relevant for those who are incapable of active participation. Citizenship is also passive in many regards for fully enfranchised adults. Elaine Scarry has even suggested that the very notion of political consent does not imply activity but can be derived from the model of the unconscious body receiving surgical treatment (Scarry, 1992). Tacit consent in being ruled is the normal condition of citizenship in representative democracy. I have argued in the first part of this book that consent cannot be inferred from mere residence when there is an option of emigration. It needs more than that. But a combination of free exit, of passively receiving substantial benefits of citizenship in the country and of being offered *opportunities* of active participation in political decision-making might be sufficient to assume such consent.

Characterizing certain citizenship rights as passive does not imply that no activity is necessary in upholding them, only that it is not the beneficiary who must be active. Passive rights of citizenship may be either entitlements or negative liberties. Entitlements are strongly institutionalized positive rights to the provision of some benefit. The activity implied by them is that the immediate provider has to do or to give something rather than merely forebear from intervening. Negative liberties have been traditionally conceived as rights to non-interference with somebody's choices or actions. However, what matters for institutional enforcement is to prohibit infringement and not so much whether this will actually allow the beneficiary to choose or act. As shown above, such prohibition may even create a kind of right for beneficiaries who are naturally incapable of claiming this right. In this case, the activity which upholds the right is that of the institution guaranteeing it. Both negative rights and entitlements may be considered as enabling and activating by giving beneficiaries first the necessary freedom and second the necessary resources to act. But none of these kinds of rights strictly requires action in order to be enjoyed. This is different from the third category of citizenship rights which are those of participation, or, in a broader sense, positive liberties.

(2) Both defenders and critics of contemporary liberal citizenship have emphasized that its rights have more and more assumed the character of entitlements. Distinguishing entitlements from other kinds of rights emphasizes two important connotations. First, the term entitlement often stresses the distributive aspects of justice; it is about rights to receive a benefit in transactions. The holders of the right are therefore seen to be passive in contrast with the active mode of participating (Ignatieff, 1990, p. 27). Second, entitlements are strongly institutionalized rights (Plant, 1990, p. 57); they imply that the provider can be held accountable and that the right can only be abrogated in clearly delimited circumstances (Held, 1990, p. 21). Strong institutionalization of distributive entitlements could be more extensively defined as follows: there is a general set of rules applied to all cases which is not only internally laid down by the distributing institution but can be publicly known; these rules are interpreted as giving the applicants or potential recipients claims over that share of the good which the distributive rule would allot them; and there is some external institution which can intervene in order to correct distributions that have violated the rule.

While the development of the modern welfare state has obviously strengthened the entitlement character of social rights in the first respect, this is not so obvious with regard to the second one. 'The entitled were never empowered because empowerment would have infringed the prerogatives of the managers of the welfare state' (Ignatieff, 1990, p. 31). The neoliberal attack against welfare entitlements was directed against both aspects. It attacked the unaccountability of giant welfare bureaucracies and it contrasted the self-reliant and economically independent citizen with the passive and dependent recipient of state assistance. A liberal egalitarian view can often agree with the first kind of critique, the consequences of which would in fact strengthen the entitlement character of social rights. However, it ought to reject the second one that directs resentment against specific groups which are said to profit from redistribution while others are net contributors.

There are limits to the transformation of rights into entitlements. One such limit lies in scarce resources, the other one in distributive principles which cannot be fully translated into entitlements. In the first case equal entitlements may appear as suboptimal and in the second case as unjust. We could call pure entitlements those rights that are not subjected to either limitation. In this section I will examine whether conflicting distributive principles sometimes can override entitlements of citizenship.[9] David Miller's distinction between needs, deserts and rights as three different principles for distributive justice can serve as a useful starting-point (Miller, 1976, pp. 24–31). How do these relate to each other? Miller points out that deserts and needs *necessarily* conflict with each other, while rights and deserts, and rights and needs, are *contingently* in conflict (pp. 27–8), i.e. both deserts and needs can be translated into rights.

Needs are quite elusive as criteria for distributive justice because they are ultimately as singular as individuals themselves.[10] However, rules of distribution can refer to socially attributed and standardized needs and thus transform them into entitlements. If we say that a sick person has a right to medical care we refer to what we see as an urgent need. In a welfare state, hospitals and doctors are not only under a moral obligation to provide treatment, but there are insurance schemes and public funds which make it possible to do this under neither purely market-oriented nor purely altruistic arrangements. With services in kind like medical care there will always be a tension between standardized arrangements for the provision of assistance and individual needs. If she gets monetary benefits instead, the recipient is free to make her own choices among market goods and services. Yet there are needs for which money cannot buy the means of satisfying them. And there are needy people who are unable to buy themselves what they would need. So services in kind cannot be altogether replaced by monetary benefits without disregarding some essential needs.[11] Desert or merit is different because it is always based on the recognition of actions by others. But recognition of desert (e.g. when selecting a candidate for promotion) can be either a matter of discretionary judgement or it can be standardized according to rules. In the latter case, desert becomes transformed into an entitlement, too.

This is still a slightly inaccurate statement. Needs and deserts themselves are not transformed into entitlements, but entitlements are rather attached to need or desert. In most cases it is not at all difficult to recognize whether entitlements are based on need, on desert, or on neither. A student who has passed a test may be entitled to be admitted to an institution of higher education, but this entitlement is attached to an achievement. A person who qualifies for social assistance may also be entitled to receive it because she has passed a test. But this test defines what is regarded as a social need.

Pure entitlements are different in that they do not refer to any background justification of desert or need in such an obvious way. On the other hand, some reference of this sort can be found in almost any reconstruction of the origins of entitlements, even in those of property rights. Robert Nozick's theory of entitlements maintains that distributions are just if they result from just acquisitions and a series of just transactions (Nozick, 1974, chapter 7). Nozick's concern is with defending entitlements emerging from free transactions against redistribution in the name of need. Yet Locke's theory of just acquisitions still emphasized a justification for property rights in terms of both desert and needs. Locke maintained that property originates from mixing one's labour with natural resources and thus can be deserved. Simultaneously, he formulated the proviso, quoted in section 3.4, which takes into account the needs of others as a moral constraint on acquisitions.

Civil and political rights of citizenship have generally become pure entitlements broadly disconnected from needs and desert. Republican thinkers might want to keep alive the relation between political rights and merit, but that is incompatible with the generalization of these rights in modern liberal democracy. Merit does play a significant role in access to higher education or public office. Here, equal rights of citizenship guarantee that there is no arbitrary or collective exclusion in admission to these positions (for example on grounds of gender or 'race'), and they will also entail some kind of equalization of opportunities for disadvantaged groups. But citizenship cannot guarantee an equal distribution of these positions independently from individual merit. With regard to the citizens' status of membership, however, all deserve to be treated as equals. Desert is a distributive principle that translates equal conditions or opportunities into unequal outcomes and arranges recipients in a hierarchy of ranks. Citizenship is both equal in its substance and makes for equal status among members. Its allocation is thus fundamentally opposed to a principle of desert.

Social rights of citizenship are different from civil and political ones, because the notion of need is strongly present as a background justification and cannot be eliminated as long as social rights are differentiated according to particular needs. Equal citizenship might be strengthened by a basic income scheme which is independent from any contributions. Yet, in contrast with political and civil rights, socially recognized needs are not so equal that they could be sufficiently covered by such universal standardization. Need is what allows for overt inequalities of entitlements in the field of social policy. People get different amounts and kinds of social welfare benefits when they are treated equally according to attributed needs. Inequality of need does not connect with equal citizenship in a straightforward way. But ultimately, both criteria can and must be linked. Once moral commands of mutual aid that aim at establishing obligations to satisfy the existential 'needs of *strangers*' (Ignatieff, 1985, my emphasis) have been satisfied, social rights ought to be oriented towards enabling *citizens* in different situations of need to recognize each other as free agents in civil society and as equal members of the polity.

Of course, the actual institutionalization of social rights is strongly influenced by other factors than equal citizenship and different social needs. The more wealthy and the more powerful groups will always try to make sure that redistribution does not damage their interests or even works in their favour. Distributive principles which confirm inequality instead of levelling it out are obviously not derived from norms of citizenship. This does not imply that any such distribution ought to be abolished (see also section 10.2). One should, for example, be cautious to dismiss compulsory social insurance schemes on the grounds that they are oriented towards the maintenance of income levels rather than towards flat-rate or needs-related benefits which certainly conform better to the idea of equal citizenship. In a market economy, universal coverage which includes the not-so-needy population will provide a more secure institutional basis for social rights than the purely needs-related schemes of what Richard Titmuss called 'residual welfare states' (Titmuss, 1963). And the better-off will only support public schemes when they also protect to some extent their own level of welfare against risks. As long as rates of economic growth in Western societies were high and increasing it seemed entirely reasonable to secure political support for the welfare state by extending its benefits to accommodate a broad middle class. But when resources get scarcer due to reduced economic growth, imbalances and perverse effects become more and more obvious. In this situation the basic justifications for social rights relating equal citizenship to needs ought to guide reorganization. Instead of reducing universal coverage and weakening thus the citizenship element one could, for example, make benefits considerably more degressive than they are in many present schemes. While the fiscal crisis of public welfare arrangements, such as retirement pensions or health services, focuses reform in many countries only on the need to save on expenditures, drawing attention to the growing gaps of social citizenship for the worst off in society should lead to a more radical questioning of vested interests and established entitlements, as well as to claiming new ones for those who have lost out during the latest phase of economic restructuring.

Neoconservative thinkers have been concerned that translating distributions according to need or desert into entitlements creates an inflation of the latter. The proposed remedy is to target resources towards the most needy but also to reconnect entitlements to obligations (Mead, 1986). Reintroducing 'workfare' arrangements is of course not a new idea in the history of public welfare in capitalism and it clearly undercuts the citizenship element of social rights. Instead of enabling them to act as autonomous citizens, welfare policies that reorient in this way towards merit and need stigmatize beneficiaries by nourishing the permanent suspicion that they may in fact be undeserving or fake their needs.

Liberal democrats should therefore be on the alert when conservatives propose to make citizenship more active. There is clearly a strong demand for reducing dependences of welfare recipients and strengthening clients' control over the services they receive. One can see a similar need for reintroducing participatory elements in politics. However, passive rights of citizenship need not be disabling in this way. An active conception of citizenship which makes the enjoyment of a right conditional upon claiming it, is in many cases just a proposal for excluding some groups who have fewer opportunities and resources to become active in this way.[12] Moreover, this exclusionary effect will be greatly strengthened if rights are tied to obligations from which they had already been separated in the historical evolution of citizenship.

8.3. NEGATIVE AND POSITIVE RIGHTS – THE CONCEPT OF LIBERTY

Rights are negative when they focus on the obligation of others not to interfere, they are positive to the extent that they specify what the bearer of the right is entitled to do or to receive. As I have explained in the preceding section, it is an error to think of negative rights as inherently active and of positive ones as necessarily passive. There is no intrinsic correlation between both dimensions. Protecting someone from interference by others implies only that these others, or the protector herself, are conceived as agents, but not necessarily the beneficiary, too. Negative rights may protect free agency and choice, but also the integrity or the mere existence of the bearer of the right. Conversely, positive rights may be passive entitlements to receive a certain share in a distribution, but the goods received may be needed as resources for autonomous action. Legitimacy is a basic resource for action in a polity governed by law. The right to do something is a positive formula which specifies actions as legitimate and thus endows an agency with this essential resource.

I will argue in this section: (1) that rather than being either negative or positive, rights are positive in different degrees; (2) that so-called negative liberties can be differentiated into two classes, which establish spheres of non-interference and of exclusive control respectively; and (3) that positive liberties also fall into two categories, those of individual self-formation and those of collective self-government.

(1) When we want to stress the autonomous agency of the bearer of a right, we call this right a liberty. (I use the term right as the most generic

one and identify the concepts of entitlement and liberty as specific kinds of rights.) There is an old debate about the contrast between negative and positive liberties. In his classic essay 'Two Concepts of Liberty' Isaiah Berlin suggested that for modern liberalism the negative aspects take priority over the positive ones (Berlin, 1979) and this point of view has been endorsed by Rawls whose principles of justice give equal liberties priority over equal opportunities and redistributive entitlements (Rawls, 1971). The liberal emphasis on non-interference, with autonomous choices and actions that do not themselves interfere with similar actions and choices of others, is partly motivated by the insight that the state, as the most powerful agent capable of providing protection, ought to remain neutral towards different individual conceptions of the good. In strongly protecting negative liberties like those of opinion, speech, religion, assembly and free transactions of property the state refrains from forcing a particular idea of the common good on its citizens.

Negative liberties have often been conceived as fundamental rights of individuals against society. As they refer to the absence of social obstacles to one's choices they seem to emphasize the idea of individual autonomy as independence from social constraints. However, negative freedom is completely empty as long as its object remains unspecified. Any answer to the question: 'freedom from what?' is necessarily relative to social conditions.

In his well-known categorization of rights, Wesley Hohfeld has distinguished liberties (which he also somewhat misleadingly calls 'privileges') from claim-rights (entitlements). The opposite of an entitlement to X is a 'no-right' and its correlate is an obligation of some other actor to provide me with X. A liberty differs from an entitlement because the opposites and correlates are reversed. The opposite of a liberty is an obligation, its correlate is a 'no-right'. If I am free to do or not to do X, it means that I am not obliged to do it or to refrain from doing it. Others have no right to demand from me the performance of, or forbearance from, X (Hohfeld, 1919). This simple but lucid definition does not at all match well with the usual distinction of negative and positive liberties. A negative liberty which focuses on non-interference is already a kind of entitlement in this sense because it puts others under an obligation. Instead of a dichotomy between negative and positive liberties one could more usefully arrange liberties and rights along a dimension of 'positivity' starting at zero.

Consider free movement for an illustration. As a liberty without any positive implication it would simply mean that I am not obliged to stay where I am. Whether others are allowed to obstruct me when I move is a different question. Only this kind of 'liberty at zero' can be imagined outside any social context. It is the liberty reigning in a state of nature or in any society with regard to those actions that the individual can perform in complete isolation. Thus it has been said that the right to commit suicide is the ultimate freedom that every human being enjoys.[13]

When we speak about the liberty of free movement in the negative sense we usually imply more than that. This second stage of liberty requires the absence of interference by other social actors. The social context is here present in the others' forbearance being a necessary condition for my enjoying a liberty. In many cases the obligation not to interfere will fall equally on any other actor, including state authorities which bind their own actions by laws and create thus the necessary space for the citizens' liberty. With some liberties non-interference is even a special obligation of the state in contrast with other social actors. Liberal states and their authorities accept, for example, a special obligation not to exercise any pressure on the citizens' freedom of religious affiliation, which is much stronger than parallel obligations of others (e.g. parents, husbands or friends) who may try to influence individuals in this respect.

The third stage of liberty defines not only which kind of interference is prohibited, but designates also third actors who are under an obligation to interfere with prohibited interference. When a woman is molested in a street, bystanders are at least under a moral obligation to intervene in order to protect her liberty. The state's monopoly of violence implies that its authorities are under a special legal obligation to interfere with unlawful interference. Here, the nature of the entitlement is clearly a positive one as far as the agency of enforcement is concerned. The role of the state as the dominant enforcement agency is closely connected to its other role as the most powerful potential intruder. In a constitutional democracy, state authorities are not only bound by law to protect the citizens' liberty against third actors but also against the state's own departments. Yet the power they need for the former task at the same time increases their power in the second regard. An authority which is, for example, able to control and sanction others who could interfere with free movement, has itself the capacity to restrict movement, too. A right of free movement therefore implies both state protection against interference by other social agents as well as guarantees of non-interference by the state itself. Paradoxically, it takes a highly developed modern state, capable of controlling movement, to enforce a right of free movement.

The fourth and final stage is reached when a liberty is defined positively, so that some external agent is under an obligation to provide means for the bearer of the right which will allow her to exercise it. In the case of free movement, the minimal interpretation along this line is that states are obliged to issue passports to their citizens which entitle them not only to leave the country but enable them also to enter others. More far-reaching

versions would insist that receiving states should not obstruct entries or
even that social rights in sending states ought to enable citizens to move out
from there.

All this shows that the boundaries between negative and positive liberty
are necessarily blurred and that the dichotomy has often been overstated for
ideological reasons. Henry Shue dismisses this distinction altogether
because 'rights ... always involve some negative duties and some positive
duties and therefore cannot themselves intelligibly be divided into negative
and positive' (Shue, 1988, p. 689, see also Shue, 1980).[14] Positive aspects
inevitably come into play not only when we consider the external
conditions and safeguards for negative liberties, but also with regard to the
definition of actions and the formation of agents capable of using liberties
to advance their own purposes. Ronald Dworkin points out that J.S. Mill's
concept of liberty was not that of licence, but of independence, which in
turn depends upon equal respect for all members of the polity (Dworkin,
1977, pp. 262–3). Charles Taylor goes much further by contrasting mere
freedom from external constraints with positive freedom, in the sense of
experiencing one's own purposes in life as authentic (Taylor, 1985).[15]
Amartya Sen, finally, opposes the juxtaposition of negative and positive
liberties on consequentialist grounds: 'If freedom *is* valuable it may have
some consequential relevance to the choice of actions. ... Why should our
concern stop only at protecting negative freedoms rather than be involved
with what people can actually do?' (Sen, 1984, p. 314, original emphasis).[16]
I do not intend to enter the philosophical questions underlying this debate.
What I want to show is that rights of liberal democratic citizenship contain
both negative and positive elements and that these correspond with different
spheres of action.

(2) I suggest that negative liberties (in the sense of the second or third
'stages of positivity' explained above) can be split into two different kinds
which ought to be analytically separated. Which of my own actions and
choices do I control because others are not allowed to interfere with them?
Which of the actions and choices of others that affect me can I control
because I am allowed to interfere with them? Answers to these questions
point to two different spheres of action which we can call those of mutual
non-interference, or autonomous control, and those of exclusive control.
The second sphere is contained within the first one, but the first one is
much wider than the second.

Let me illustrate this idea with two simple examples. When I dine out I
can choose the restaurant where I eat and as long as there are free tables the
owners have to accept me as a guest. What I cannot choose is the other
guests sitting at the table next to me. They are not allowed to interfere with
my choice but neither am I allowed to interfere with theirs. When I am the

host who invites guests for dinner, I choose them and thereby exclude other persons from joining us. In my private home I have the right to interfere with other peoples' choices. Consider as another illustration once again the paradigmatic negative liberty of free movement. A proprietor of land is free to move both on her own soil and on public roads outside. What is different is that only on her own territory is she entitled to keep others out. Negative liberty in the public spheres of civil society generally means mutual non-interference while it is mostly defined as exclusive control in the spheres of private enjoyment of property or of intimate relations. Isaiah Berlin proposed to distinguish negative and positive liberty as the answers to two questions: 'Over what area am I master?' and 'Who is master?' (Berlin, 1979, p. xliii). If being master means more than self-control over one's own actions the examples yield the following responses: *I* am master in the area under my exclusive control; and *nobody* is master in the sphere of mutual non-interference.[17]

Libertarian theorists who are insensitive to the particular qualities of the public sphere have tended to mix up these two concepts by reducing the latter to the former. David Gauthier's interpretation of the Lockean proviso[18] can be quoted as an illustration for the common confusion of the spheres of autonomous control and exclusive control. He writes that the effect of the proviso 'is to afford each person a sphere of exclusive control by forbidding others from interfering with certain of his activities. This exclusive sphere constitutes a moral space, which defines the individual in his market and co-operative relationships' (Gauthier, 1986, pp. 201–2). However, voluntary co-ordination of autonomous activities in markets and in the other institutions of the public realm require that nobody has exclusive control whereas the moral space of privacy depends on just that kind of control.

Writers who are closer to the republican tradition pay more attention to these distinctions. Hannah Arendt has characterized the private as the realm of legitimate exclusion, the social as that of legitimate discrimination and the political as that of equality (Arendt, 1977). Herman van Gunsteren similarly distinguishes the personal-private, the public-social and the public-political (van Gunsteren, 1992, pp. 48–50). Iris Young suggests that 'the private should be defined ... as that aspect of his or her life and activity that any person has a right to exclude others from. The private in this sense is not what public institutions exclude, but what the individual chooses to withdraw from public view' (Young, 1990, pp. 119–20).

While liberties that depend on non-interference require at their third stage an external actor who enforces the prohibition, rights of exclusion involve the bearer herself as an agent entitled to enforcement. They do not merely provide freedom from unwanted interference but also a positive right to interfere oneself with intruders in the private sphere. Furthermore, they strongly link up with one basic kind of positive liberty, the freedom of self-formation. A sphere of exclusive control is required in order to (re)generate the capabilities of autonomous actors in public life. Yet the right of exclusive control is only a necessary, but not a sufficient, condition for this liberty. Individuals need positive resources in order to develop into autonomous agents. These include economic means, education and intimate relations. Distributive entitlements of citizenship cannot cover intimate relations, but ought to provide some material security and public education which diminishes the dependence of individuals from family fortunes and market risks. If citizenship were reduced to the negative liberties of public life and private transactions in civil society, the less fortunate ones would be deprived of basic preconditions for substantial citizenship in modern society.

The spheres of exclusion and of non-interference are constituted in social interactions; they are not strictly identical with the spaces of the home and the market place. The traditional boundary between the home and the public world depended on the exclusion of women and children from citizenship. They have now gained independent standing in the public sphere and their relation to the state and the law is no longer only a mediated one via their husbands and fathers. This has radical implications for internal relations in the sphere of privacy. In a liberal concept of citizenship these relations are based on voluntary agreement. The realm of privacy where citizens are formed as autonomous persons is therefore not a world strictly separated from that where citizens interact as free agents. Intimacy is as much created by citizens as it (re)creates these citizens. Autonomous citizens agree among each other to construct a joint sphere of their lives from which others will remain excluded. In this sphere they will not interact as citizens but as lovers, family members or close friends. However, each of them remains protected as a citizen when their mutual dependence turns into an asymmetric one of violence and oppression, and each retains a right as a citizen to terminate the relation. The private intimate realm of the family and the household can therefore no longer be regarded as a given foundation for building the public sphere. Both spheres interpenetrate each other without dissolution of the boundary between them that is marked by the two kinds of liberties. All this is, of course, not in the same way true for children as it is for adults of both genders. Children have to grow into their role as citizens. But the attribution of citizenship status at birth symbolically confirms that they must already be respected as independent legal persons, even before they are able to step out of their family world and claim themselves all their rights.

(3) In addition to distinguishing the two kinds of negative liberties, I propose to consider two kinds of positive liberties: those related to the formation of individuals who are capable of controlling their own actions and choices, and those related to the formation of political communities that are capable of controlling the process of making collectively binding decisions. Let us call these the liberties of individual self-formation and of collective self-government. They can be conceived as answers to the questions: Can I experience myself as the author of my own life? Can I experience myself as a member of a collective which is the author of the laws it gives to itself?

Positive liberty is 'freedom to' in contrast with 'freedom from'; the former emphasizes the pursuit and realization of specific goals. Amartya Sen has proposed seeing rights in this sense not only as constraints on the actions of others, or, in Ronald Dworkin's famous phrase, as trumps (Dworkin, 1977, p. 85, 1984), but also as goals. Sen defines a 'goal right as a relation not primarily between two parties,[19] but between one person and some " capability " to which he has a right, for example, the capability of persons to move about without harm' (Sen, 1984, p. 16). While this conception does not cover all kinds of rights, it seems particularly relevant for positive liberties supported by citizenship entitlements. Substantial citizenship could be defined as rights to those capabilities that are required for autonomous agency in the public spheres of civil society and for equal membership in the polity. Legislators, state administrations and judiciaries have to assume a generalized responsibility for the fulfilment of these rights. But they need not be the exclusive providers. Entitlements clearly define an obligation involving direct transaction of the required good to the recipient, whereas in a conception of goal rights to basic capabilities the obligation is rather to secure provision by whoever is most apt to provide. Let me give three examples how this idea might be applied.

The first one is the basic social right to public education (Marshall, 1965, pp. 89–90). It implies that the state must provide the funds and a regulatory framework defining minimum standards for school education. The state need not be the sole provider. It can support private schools alongside public ones. However, the state is in the best position to provide this service. Compulsory school is not only about preparing and selecting pupils for higher education, but also the most important field of experience of common citizenship for children and adolescents across divisions of class, gender and ethnicity. A far-reaching privatization of school education would not only increase the correlation between standards of education and social class but also undermine socialization for citizenship. Liberal democratic states certainly do not have to suppress private solutions for minorities, but should make sure that the quality of education in public schools is not generally worse than in private ones and that the social composition of pupils in the former remains representative for the whole society.

A second example concerns the goal right to internal security. The state is the provider of police services and no one else can be if civil peace is to be maintained. Liberal democracy is in danger where private forces take over protection tasks in the public sphere, whether these be militias of political parties or security staff hired by wealthy individuals. However, citizens may well provide for each other additional services such as neighbourhood watch groups. More importantly, maintenance of civil peace will depend also on the actions of citizens themselves (reporting crimes, defending victims when the police are not there, etc.). The popular movement against the Mafia in Sicily has given a strong example of how citizens' civil courage can be effective in pressing reluctant or corrupt politicians and the police into action against organized crime.

A third example, again from social policies, is public assistance in the care of children and of disabled or frail elderly persons. In a comprehensive welfare state there will be state responsibility for monetary assistance or services to maintain a minimum standard of welfare for these and other vulnerable and dependent social groups. The task is not an equalization of welfare[20] across society but, again, of capabilities for citizenship. In contrast with schools and the police, the state is not necessarily the best provider of these kinds of services. Families with sufficient income will remain responsible for taking care of their relatives. Those with low income may be given monetary assistance to provide the services themselves. However, many of these persons are without a family or the family is not capable of taking care of them. State administrations will have to accept responsibility for ensuring that they will receive adequate assistance, too. Yet they need not necessarily run their own public homes. Private charities and non-profit organizations may be able to organize this task just as well or even better, and state responsibility will manifest itself in refunding and supervising them.

Asserting in this manner the ultimate responsibility of states for the maintenance of positive liberties of citizens is not the same as saying that it is the state which forms the autonomous citizens. Generalizing a suggestion already made in section 4.3, we can think of the formation of citizens as a process of self-education, i.e., of developing and maintaining intrinsic capabilities of persons to act as free and responsible members of a wider society. It is in the very exercise of rights and obligations that citizenship can be learned. However, this also requires a social environment which offers all the external resources and opportunities needed for such self-education. The role of a liberal state is much stronger in securing the provision of these external conditions than in being itself a teacher of the population.

Even if this approach allows the circumvention of Marx's critique 'that it is essential to educate the educator' (Marx, 1974, p. 121), it still leaves open the parallel questions: who will control those who control the conditions for the exercise of citizenship? Who rules the state that rules the citizens? The answer points to the second kind of positive liberty, that of collective self-government.

In democracy, citizenship becomes reflexive by enabling citizens to participate in deliberation about their own rights and obligations. Political rights of democratic participation are both positive and negative. They are negative rights in so far as citizens are free to exercise them or not. In contrast with Rousseau's notorious phrase that citizens can 'be forced [by the general will] to be free' (Rousseau, 1973, I.7, p. 195), in liberal conceptions nobody can be forced to be active in politics, even if democratic citizenship will be not be sustainable over time unless a sufficient number of citizens from all relevant social groups do become active. In Habermas's words, the code of law implies that rights of communication and participation can only be institutionalized as subjective liberties which leave their addressees free to decide whether and how to use them. The law is different from morality in being unable to *oblige* citizens to make use of their rights with a view towards rational agreement, although political rights of citizenship *insinuate* such public use (Habermas, 1992, pp. 164–5).

I have already pointed out that the pure negative liberty of not being hindered from casting a vote is of course insufficient for the right to vote. States are obliged to provide all necessary opportunities and facilities for exercising this right. Yet this still does not capture the essential character of the franchise. As a positive liberty it is a right to participation and to representation. This quality of the right depends upon the whole system of representation (the mode of aggregating votes into delegations and decisions), on the public character of deliberation before decisions are taken, and on the discursive involvement of the general public in the legitimation and critique of decisions before and after their implementation.

Even taken together all forms of public control over political decisions in representative democracy can never really amount to civil society governing itself and controlling state power. Modernity means state penetration of society. This can assume the form of totalitarian control over society or of a systemic differentiation but simultaneous interpenetration between the state and civil society in liberal democracy. The latter is not a public realm exempted from state control. It is rather a sphere in which this unavoidable control is balanced by control exercised over political authority. The libertarian notion of freedom as individual liberty to act independently from state control is profoundly anti-modern. It would make for a society without public education, social protection or broader political participation. Modern democracy implies that freedom has to be realized *within* the structural dependence of individuals from the state. We cannot become free by escaping social and political control. Nor can we individually control the institutions that rule us. But in democratic and liberal institutional arrangements we may participate in collective forms of control over the control that is exercised over us as members of a polity.

NOTES

1. The moral and legal mode of rights have been connected to the aspects of validity and facticity by Jürgen Habermas (Habermas, 1992).
2. David Lyons strongly argued the latter point, but went further in defending the view that there are rights (such as those generated by promise) which do not depend on social recognition (Lyons, 1984).
3. The right of immigrants not to be expelled after a long residence and especially the residence rights of those who have been born in the country but have been turned into aliens by *ius sanguinis*, may be mentioned as an example where legislative praxis has mostly lagged behind the evolution of a norm.
4. This is the only kind of rights which can be reduced to corresponding prohibitions and obligations. As I argue in section 8.2 the normative reference of other kinds of rights shows in the attribution of moral worth to their bearer.
5. There are two kinds of classifications of basic citizenship rights. One starts with a historical evolutionary typology. The classic example for this is T.H. Marshall's trinity of civil, political and social rights (Marshall, 1965). Some authors have proposed adding economic and 'reproductive' rights (Held, 1987, p. 285) or cultural and ecological rights (Turner, 1986). The other kind is derived from theoretical premises about normative requirements of liberal democracy. See for example Habermas (1992, pp. 155–6) or Cohen and Arato (1992, pp. 397–400).
6. Andrew Dobson has proposed calling this human-centred approach 'weak anthropocentrism' in contrast with 'strong anthropocentrism' in whose view 'the non-human world is instrumental for human well-being' (Dobson, 1990, p. 63). Even strong anthropocentrism need not necessarily be exploitative towards non-human nature. John Rawls characterizes the statement that 'Animals and nature are seen as subject to our use and wont' as the traditional view of Christian ages. Taking the good of ourselves and of future generations as the relevant values that ought to guide our behaviour could just as well support responsible policies of 'preserving the natural order and its life-sustaining properties' (Rawls, 1993a, p. 245). A theory which ascribes rights to nature takes one step beyond this traditional view in claiming that responsibility should be derived from respect for the non-human world also for its own sake. I have not presented or defended such a theory. My point has been merely to show that claims for rights of nature, as they are articulated by ecological movements today, do go beyond an instrumentalist anthropocentrism but need not confuse *rights of nature* within institutions of human societies with *natural rights*.
7. Bryan Turner suggests that the environmentalist movements' claim for rights of nature (Turner, 1986, p. 98) represents a 'fourth wave of expanding citizenship rights' (Turner, 1986, p. 98) after those questioning the boundaries of property, gender and age. He even asks whether dogs are citizens in the making (p. 100). What Turner ignores is that citizenship rights are a specific kind of rights related to political communities in which animals cannot even be passive members. The rights of animals will not be any safer if we confuse them with those of citizens.
8. Jean Cohen suggested this point to me during a discussion on animal rights.

9. The impact of scarcity on the distribution of rights will be examined in chapter 10.

10. 'Since individual and social needs almost never completely coincide, and no norm or rule applies to the former, justice stops short of the *singularity* of the person. Individual structures of needs are the *limits to justice*' (Heller, 1987, p. 32, original emphasis).

11. T.H Marshall thought that social citizenship would greatly reduce the social importance of inequality of monetary income by the extension of free services in kind to all citizens – a prediction that was highly plausible at the time of the introduction of the National Health Service in Britain but has not become the dominant trend in later developments of the welfare state (Marshall, 1965, p. 110).

12. Optional naturalization, as I have proposed it in the first part of the book, is in this sense still an active rather than a passive right. It will lead to less inclusion than automatic citizenship based on *ius domicili* would. But this rule of access will be much more inclusive than discretionary admission and the remaining exclusionary effects will be fully compensated by extending substantial rights to resident aliens.

13 I have to thank Alfred Noll for making this point in a comment on my analysis of the right of emigration as a liberty.

14. Negative duties (prohibitions) involve 'nothing more than not depriving other people of what they have rights to ... A duty's being positive, on the other hand, means that fulfilling it will require the expenditure of some resource I control'. Unlike rights, duties 'therefore range across a spectrum from the completely negative to the highly positive' (Shue, 1988, p. 689). I would rather say that on the negative–positive axis only rights can be arranged along a continuum whereas obligations are sharply distinguished into a dichotomy.

15 '[T]he subject himself cannot be the final authority on the question whether he is free; for he cannot be the final authority on the question whether his desires are authentic, whether they do or do not frustrate his purposes' (Taylor, 1985, p. 216). According to Taylor this highly contentious proposition does, however, not imply that any 'official body can possess a doctrine or technique whereby they could know how to put us on the rails, because such a doctrine or technique cannot in principle exist if human beings really differ in their self-realization' (ibid.).

16. Sen furthermore argues a point that I have already mentioned: that negative rights normally require positive action on the part of the provider: 'If the violation of negative freedom counts as a bad consequence which is to be avoided, consequential reasoning can justify – indeed require – many *positive* actions in pursuit of *negative* freedom, e.g. that one should stop A from stopping B from moving about freely' (Sen, 1984, p. 313, original emphasis).

17. Note that the distinction between the spheres of non-interference and of exclusive control is not the same as that between the second and third stages of liberty explained above. Both kinds of negative liberties can be formulated as rights on either stage.

18. Gauthier reformulates the Lockean proviso so that it 'prohibits bettering one's situation through interaction that worsens the situation of another' (Gauthier, 1986, p. 205).

19. As does Wesley Hohfeld in his typology which, apart from liberties and claim-rights, also includes powers and liabilities. Powers enable an actor to change her legal relation to another one, while liabilities characterize the position of those over whom a power can be exercised. States exercise, for example, a power over citizens who are liable to serve as jurors (Hohfeld, 1919, p. 59).

20. For a comprehensive critique of the idea of equal welfare see Dworkin (1981).

9. Special and General Rights

Rights of citizenship have been mostly regarded as special rights. They are due to citizens and to citizens only. Where this is not stated as a mere tautology the underlying idea has been to see the polity as a national community, as an association based on contract, or as a co-operative venture. I have argued in the first part of this book that citizenship rights are due to all those who have acquired social ties of membership and that they ought to include a right of access to nominal citizenship. This position must refute all three above-mentioned justifications for restricting citizenship rights to nominal citizens. In the first section of this chapter I address this task and maintain that citizenship rights are general rather than special, although this generality is a bounded one. Once that is accepted, how do general rights of citizenship then relate to human rights that are seen to be universal? This is the question raised in section 9.2. The traditional response has been to ground the universality of human rights in assumptions about human nature, i.e. to define them as 'natural rights'. I contend that this view is not only problematic from a philosophical point of view but also quite unhelpful in explaining the growing importance and the lengthening lists of human rights in the second half of this century.

9.1. CITIZENSHIP RIGHTS – BOUNDED BUT NOT SPECIAL

Rights are special or general according to how narrowly they identify their beneficiaries.[1] I propose to distinguish five types or ranges of rights with regard to their bearers: particular, group-specific, situational, bounded and universal rights. We can classify the first three as more or less special and the latter two as general.

Particular rights identify their bearer as somebody who can be called by a proper name. Such rights are typically generated by promises and contracts between specified persons or organizations. Group-specific rights are not necessarily rights of groups, but mostly those of individuals who are identified as belonging to a category of persons. These categories can be characterized ascriptively (such as gender or 'racial' groups), or as relatively stable transgenerational collectivities (such as classes or regional populations), or finally as merely temporary ones (students, unemployed, retired persons, etc.). Situational rights are those which any individual can enjoy who finds herself in a certain situation or condition. The two kinds of rights cannot always be clearly distinguished. Individuals who are in a special condition may also be characterized as a social group. Are rights of the unemployed group-specific or situational? Are the urban poor just citizens in a low-income situation or members of an underclass?[2] My purpose is not to develop a scheme for an unambiguous classification of rights. The point of distinguishing these two concepts lies in their different justification for rights. A situational definition of special rights preserves the image of an unmediated membership of the individual in the polity, whereas group-specific rights acknowledge that society also consists of different aggregates of persons and that this might be relevant for their rights of citizenship. Whether the one or the other perspective is the more appropriate one will depend on the case at hand and should not be turned into a question of ideology. As I will show in chapter 11, group-specific rights can become a starting-point for collective rights which are claimed and exercised by the group itself. In this section I want to (1) explain in which sense citizenship rights can be regarded as general, and (2) show why alternative interpretations of citizenship rights as special are either inacceptable or inconsistent.

(1) Rights are general when they are attributed to everyone within the reach of action of the institution that guarantees them. If populations have a right to the provision of some public good this is always a general right. Clean air, internal and external security, public roads and parks and other infrastructure are potential objects of general rights. However, general rights are not exclusively linked to public goods. Education is a private good but the right to public education is a thoroughly general one. A right to medical care, such as that guaranteed by the British or Canadian National Health Services, is general in the same way. Where health care depends on compulsory insurance schemes which have been extended to cover virtually the whole population, as they do in many continental countries of Western Europe, the right has been generalized in its effects although not in its form.

General rights can be bounded in various ways. Virtually all are bounded by the effective range of action of the institutional provider. Rights may be further limited within this range because they cannot be fully enforced everywhere and for everybody. Yet some rights are not only bounded in their enforceability but also in their validity. This is what essentially distinguishes universal rights from others. Rights of citizenship are either specifically valid in the polity for which they have been adopted or they are assumed to be valid in any polity and for all human beings. The latter kind of rights will still have to be institutionalized in each single state, but their validity is not seen as contingent upon a political decision. To which class a certain right belongs will be uncontested only in the extreme cases. Rights to the basic physical and moral integrity of persons (e.g. the prohibition of torture or the liberty of conscience) will always be ranked as universal human rights, while a right to a basic retirement pension, as it exists in some European states, can only be claimed where parliament has adopted such a scheme or where at least the necessary resources for such a right are available. Between these poles there is a broad range of rights which were historically seen as bounded but have been attributed universal validity in our days. A most significant development of this kind is that even though liberal democracy is far from being the dominant kind of regime on the globe, the essential political rights of democratic citizenship are today considered to be universal rather than strictly of bounded validity for those polities that have adopted democratic constitutions. Political liberties (such as those of free speech, assembly and association) or rights of participation (voting rights and access to public office) have been included in international human rights documents (see for example Articles 19, 21, 22 and 25 of the International Covenant on Civil and Political Rights). Social rights are not excluded from this tendency towards normative universalization. Free compulsory school education, for example, is today not only declared a universal human right (see Articles 13 and 14 of the International Covenant on Economic, Social and Cultural Rights), but democratic and non-democratic regimes alike generally strive towards guaranteeing it. Other social rights whose fulfilment is strongly constrained by scarce economic resources or exploitative conditions of labour will, however, remain largely declarative when they are pronounced as universal ones.

Is there any real progress in what might appear to be an inflation of human rights with elements of citizenship? Critics have attacked from opposite sides. On the one hand, universal rights have been dismissed as empty proclamations as long as there are no global institutions to enforce compliance; on the other hand, they have been seen as an ideological weapon of the West for establishing a hierarchical ranking of cultures and for justifying interference with internal political affairs of other states. I want to enter this ongoing debate only as far as necessary to answer the two questions outlined in the introduction to this chapter. Are rights of citizenship categorically different from universal rights because they are special rights for members of political communities rather than general ones? Should human rights be based on assumptions about the essential nature of human beings or can they be usefully understood as transnational elements of liberal democratic citizenship?

Answering the first question negatively does not mean that citizenship cannot contain any special rights. This could only be asserted in republican or libertarian conceptions which deny that social rights should be seen as an element of citizenship. Here I want to refute another argument which maintains that, taken as a comprehensive bundle of rights, substantial citizenship is special because it identifies the beneficiaries as members of a national or political collective. Certainly rights of citizenship are not general just because they are enjoyed by large populations. The distinction between group-specific or situational rights, on the one hand, and bounded general rights, on the other hand, does not refer to the number of beneficiaries but to their characterization. Rights belong to the former category where the characteristics of the group or situation are independent from the allocation of the right. Thus the unemployed can be described as a group or as citizens in a specific situation independently from their right to receive unemployment benefits. I will call rights general when the allocation of the right itself is what characterizes the group or situation. My contention is that citizenship rights are general in this sense.

Yet this does not seem to fit the facts. Obviously the allocation of some rights of citizenship is tied to an antecedent determination of beneficiaries as a group characterized by a shared name, i.e. as nominal citizens. It is adult nominal citizens who enjoy voting rights rather than, inversely, voting rights which define who can be called a nominal citizen. This objection might satisfy legal positivists but it is certainly not convincing for normative political theory. In the latter perspective the question is: *should* we conceive of citizenship rights as special by making membership conceptually prior to normative considerations about the distribution of the rights which it entails? On which normative grounds can citizens be said to constitute a group independently from the rights they enjoy? Making citizenship rights conditional upon nominal membership and making the allocation of nominal membership exclusive can be justified only if we can first answer these questions.

(2) What are the standard justifications for making rights special rather than general and which of these could be applied to citizenship? 'When rights arise out of special transactions between individuals or out of some special relationship in which they stand to each other, both the persons who have the right and those who have the corresponding obligation are limited to the parties' (Hart, 1955, p. 183). H.L.A. Hart identifies the following situations which can give rise to special rights: special natural relationships, promises, consent and authorization, and mutuality of restrictions.[3] These can be translated into three different arguments for seeing citizenship rights as special rather than general. The first is that citizenship is membership in a national community construed after the model of natural relationships and that its rights are grounded in the historical evolution of its political institutions; the second argument is that the social contract, just like other

contracts, creates special rights and obligations only between those who
have concluded it; the third position sees liberal democracies as ongoing co-
operative arrangements and citizens in the role of participants rather than of
signatories of a contract.

In its crudest nationalist form the first position would derive citizenship
rights from extended relations of kinship in a nation of common descent.
Quite obviously, modern nations are not 'races' of biologically related
individuals. There is a stronger argument for the cultural view. If
individuals can become autonomous persons only by being socialized in a
specific cultural environment, they might have special rights and obligations
towards the other members of this cultural group. Rights and obligations
would be derived from a principle of reciprocity – contributions which have
been received from a cultural group have to be paid back. If cultures were
perfectly congruent with national populations and if individuals were
completely locked into their cultures, this argument would be sound. But
cultures converge or diverge and individuals have the capacity of changing
their affiliations. They can learn how to communicate beyond their specific
cultures. Citizenship rights cannot be limited in their range to those who are
members of a cultural group, but must extend to actual ranges of action. A
principle of cultural reciprocity can therefore never determine the proper
range of citizenship in a mobile society with a plurality of cultural groups
and affiliations. Liberal democracy furthermore implies that people must
not be ranked according to their cultural origins. Equality of citizenship can
only be achieved where political status has become independent of such
origins.

In his critique of the French Declaration of Rights of Man and the
Citizen of 1789, Edmund Burke gave a different interpretation to the special
relationship between citizens: 'It has been the uniform policy of our
constitution to claim and assert our liberties, as an *entailed inheritance*
derived to us from our forefathers, and to be transmitted to posterity; as an
estate specifically belonging to the people of this kingdom without any
reference whatsoever to any other more general or prior right' (Burke, 1987,
p. 100, original emphasis). 'By adhering in this manner and on those
principles to our forefathers, we are guided not by the superstition of
antiquarians, but by the spirit of philosophical analogy. In this choice of
inheritance we have given to our frame of polity the image of a relation in
blood' (p. 101). For Burke, conceiving of the community of citizens as one
of descent is merely an image which supports the essential idea that a polity
is a transgenerational community in which rights of citizens will only be
safely grounded when they evolve within its historical traditions. What
Burke deliberately ignores is that the extension of citizenship rights on a
national scale has been the result of conflicts between power-holders and

social and political movements representing excluded groups, rather than of peaceful evolution. Those who claim rights that have not been established in the constitution must either refer to their particular interests and needs, or appeal to more universal principles which denounce the present distribution of rights and obligations as one of privileges and oppressive burdens. Declarations of rights in revolutionary situations represent the latter strategy. The generalization of citizenship rights in democratic constitutions, by abolishing aristocratic privilege and including women and workers, could only be achieved in the name of universalistic principles that claimed validity beyond the nation and its particular traditions.

Classic contractarian theories have already been extensively criticized in the first part of this book. Hobbes's argument from consent and authorization can give rise to special rights, but these are rights of the sovereign corresponding on the subjects' side to special obligations only. Locke's view is different in that the latter retain and protect their natural liberties in the contract of submission. Yet these are not special but universal rights. Thus the right to equality before the law in political society can be derived from the equal right of everybody to administer justice in the state of nature (Locke, 1956, II, §7, pp. 5–6). We may think that Rousseau's *contrat social* creates special rights of political participation but this is not a right of the individual citizens and their particular wills at all, but rather an obligation to abandon all special interests in the formation of a general will. The implications of a contractarian view of citizenship would be to exclude all those from entitlements to the special rights of citizenship who have not signed the contract. This is clearly spelt out in a paper by Heisler and Schmitter-Heisler: '...immigrants are not parties to the accretion of compacts among members and their antecedents that underlie the regime and the social order' (Heisler and Schmitter-Heisler, 1990, p. 11). One might certainly invent different kinds of foundational contracts where citizens grant each other special rights. But one problem would remain unresolved. As H.L.A. Hart shows, the identity of the parties is essential for special rights generated from promise and authorization (Hart, 1955, p. 184). If, as I have argued, purely contractarian theories cannot provide solid grounds for the determination of membership in a liberal democratic polity, then it follows that rights in such a state can also not be special in the sense of being naturally reserved for members as signatories to the contract.

The third position is more sophisticated in avoiding contractarian fallacies. 'When a number of persons conduct any joint enterprise according to rules and thus restrict their liberty, those who have submitted to these restrictions when required have a right to a similar submission from those who have benefited by their submission' (Hart, 1955, p. 185). Richard Dagger has followed Hart's lead in arguing that citizens of a liberal democracy are engaged in a joint enterprise of this sort. 'There is a special relationship, entailing special rights and obligations, between those who share citizenship in a political community' (Dagger, 1985, p. 143). Citizens take advantage of the opportunities a well-ordered society offers them and thereby incur an obligation to obey the laws of the state. Accepting this obligation entitles them in turn to the rights of citizenship as specially theirs.

While the nationalist and contractarian perspectives provide a clear criterion of inclusion and exclusion, the co-operative model of citizenship is inconclusive in this respect. Andrew Shacknove has asked the pertinent question: 'Yet how can we say that a criminal or revolutionary who is also a citizen participates in a joint enterprise in a way that an industrious, law-abiding refugee does not?' (Shacknove, 1988, p. 144). If the rights of citizenship are due to everybody who has accepted the duty to obey the laws of a state, then alien residents generally ought to enjoy these rights while those who break the law should be excluded whether they are foreigners or natives. Liberals may welcome the former implication but they will certainly reject the latter. Criminals may indeed (temporarily) forfeit essential liberties of free citizens, but they will still enjoy the basic right to equal protection by the law and they will not be deprived of their status as a citizen. Conceiving of a liberal democratic state as a joint enterprise of its citizens, can neither explain why compatriots ought to enjoy special rights compared to foreigners nor why the status of nominal citizenship is granted independently from voluntary acceptance of the obligations of citizenship.

Shacknove suggests that the proper answer contains two different elements.[4] First, all human beings are of equal moral worth and ought to be treated with equal respect and concern by governments. The basic normative justification for the allocation of citizenship rights is thus a universalistic one. Second, individuals' bonds to states are empirically different and this gives rise to special obligations of states to provide rights for certain groups (most obviously for those within its territorial range of administration). I would add to this that the empirical relation of individuals to states is one of power involving control and dependence. States arc obliged to grant those rights which enable citizens to regain their autonomy within this power relation.

Citizenship is therefore not primarily a tie of reciprocity between individuals in civil society but a relation between the state and each single individual. This is not at all a reciprocal relation where powers are equal and rights and obligations are mutually conditional. Hart observes that in contrast with special rights, general rights are usually 'asserted defensively, when some unjustified interference is anticipated or threatened in order to point out that the interference is unjustified' (Hart, 1955, p. 187). The paradox of democratic citizenship is that it is the same Leviathan whose unjustified interference continuously threatens the citizens' freedom who is called upon to provide the very rights that are needed to tame him.

Citizenship rights should be seen as general yet in most respects bounded because they are the democratic side of the coin whose other side is the territorial exercise of political power by the state – and not by the citizens themselves. It follows from this that such rights are fundamentally due to all who are in special relations of dependence with regard to this power, be it by living permanently in the territory or by having special relations to this society when living abroad. We might thus think of citizenship rights as special in the sense of situational rather than group-specific. But just as the group to which citizenship rights are due cannot be determined independently from the normative principles for the allocation of rights, so the situation of subjection to power is already defined as one that creates legitimate claims to rights.

The allocation of nominal citizenship is different from that of basic rights of citizenship in this regard. Its role is to highlight the distinction between membership in a polity on the one hand, and in a society subjected to state power on the other hand. Its rules ought to be derived from the contradictory requirements of inclusive but simultaneously voluntary membership. The contradiction can be resolved by adding a right to optional naturalization and expatriation to those rights of citizenship which are granted to all who have strong empirical bonds with a society or depend on a state in their existential needs. Thus, everybody who ought to be granted citizenship rights must also be considered as a potential citizen in the nominal sense of the term.

9.2. HUMAN RIGHTS AS UNIVERSALIZED CITIZENSHIP

Must human rights necessarily refer to universal features of the human existence? Or can they be usefully understood as universalized rights of citizenship that are extended to a transnational level, first discursively (as declarative rights in proclamations) and then institutionally (as subjective rights in international law supervised by international agencies)? I want to defend the latter point of view in a moderately relativistic and essentially pragmatic perspective.(1) Human rights are in my view historically but not culturally relative. They are tied to the social and political conditions of modernity but they are highly relevant for all present societies and can be defended from within each of the major cultural traditions. (2) The pragmatic part of the argument is that linking human rights to the evolution of liberal democratic citizenship seems to me the most promising way to promote their enrichment and institutionalization in the contemporary world. (3) Human rights are the cornerstone as well as the most extended application of a transnational conception of citizenship.

(1) The basic deficiency of natural rights theories is that they eliminate the very context within which the notion of rights can make sense. What is that context for human rights? Why could we not conceive of humanity as a single moral community grounded in universal features of human existence and the universal capacity of intercultural communication? This may be an adequate foundation for a moral theory. But, as I have argued in section 8.1, rights are different from moral commands. The former depend on social recognition and they appeal to institutional safeguards and enforcement. Moral rights may well be grounded in the shared moral convictions of a cultural community, and can be enforced by informal sanctions such as depriving trespassers of their social honour. In this view human rights could still be regarded as a core element of moral convictions shared by all different cultures. Yet the diversity of cultures in human history makes it impossible to conceive of human rights as firmly grounded in universally shared cultural understandings.

One might object that such a common core that is at the roots of the modern conception of human rights can be found in rights of foreigners supported by virtually all religions and premodern cultures. However, the notion of human rights goes far beyond this core. Not only do non-members enjoy special rights (like that to hospitality) but the most essential rights are *equal* for all women and men and thus *independent* of their membership in a community sharing certain moral convictions. Only the universalistic language of law can adequately express that idea and only state institutions can enforce these rights. Just like citizenship rights, human rights thus specifically appeal to political institutions. The difference is that the latter cannot only be claimed by members of polities or from inside the territorial boundaries of states. Although enforcement of human rights will strongly rely on the laws and constitutions of particular states, their validity reaches beyond all political boundaries. We must therefore define a global context of validity which does not rely on universally shared cultural understandings.

An alternative approach ties the notion of human rights to the evolution of occidental culture with its Judeo-Christian roots and the modern ideas of enlightenment and liberalism. In this view human rights are an integral element of a particular culture, and the context of universal validity has been established by conquering or outcompeting rival cultures and their ideas about rights. While ahistoric and apolitical moral universalism provides an unsatisfactory account of human rights this second approach is entirely unacceptable. It not only opens the doors for cultural relativism but gives credibility to the accusation that cultural imperialism is inherent in human rights discourse. On a theoretical level it confuses the context of origin with the context of validity. Human rights do have their particular historic origins but their validity can only be established by providing justification for them which is independent of such origins. The mere appeal to cultural tradition may be an important element in discourses of justification for rights in premodern societies. But the attempt to justify the universal validity of human rights by showing how they emerge from a particular cultural tradition is self-contradictory. This position can only lead to a wholesale rejection of the very concept of human rights.

I would like to suggest a third position. It accepts that human rights are historically relative and do indeed have their origins in modernity, which has been shaped by economic, political and cultural institutions which first emerged in Western Europe. At the same time features of modernity have become truly universal. Some of those features establish global social structures. Among these are global markets, communication and mobility. Others are just as universal but at the same time tied to particular places and populations. This is especially true for the modern nation-state as the universal form of political organization of statehood now encompassing all human populations. No matter how violently it was brought about, modernity has also created a new context for establishing the universal validity of certain rights. Rather than being tainted by their historic origins, human rights can be normatively justified as a response to the predicaments of modernity. And in this context not every substantive account of justice is a local one, contrary to what communitarians want to make us believe (Walzer, 1983, p. 314).[5]

The example of rights for aboriginal and indigenous people may illustrate the consequences of this third approach. If we thought of human rights as context-independent properties of human beings, aboriginal people should enjoy just the same kind of rights as any other citizens. Yet this view would hardly take into account their particular situation. It could even justify imposing a universal and ahistoric conception of human rights on some newly 'discovered' ethnic groups in the way Christian religions had been forced upon others in the name of a universal God. The same conception would also deny indigenous peoples specific collective rights, which are necessarily at odds with a conception of human rights that is derived from the image of the individual human being in a state of nature. But the rights indigenous peoples need and claim, refer not just to their being human but to the disastrous consequences of modernization for their traditional ways of life and often for their very chances of survival. Outside contemporary society they would hardly need such rights. If we somehow learned that there still exists an ethnic group which has never had any contact with the outside world, the only right which surely ought to be attributed to them would be a negative liberty of non-interference from our side, no matter how their internal cultural practices conform to contemporary standards of human rights. But once indigenous peoples have been dragged into the orbit of global markets their rights will have to be defined in this context. The paradox is that claiming rights within this context will accelerate political modernization. It puts ethnic groups on the path to 'nationalization'. They will codify their traditional cultures as national ones, they will develop their own national intelligentsia, and if they are strong enough they will ultimately fight for some kind of national autonomy which means abandoning the organizational structure of pre-state societies. There is no collective exit from modernity even for those who struggle against its consequences. But liberal democracy can at least create the political preconditions for a plurality of cultural and social forms of life within a single state.

This 'historicist' approach is entirely compatible with a moral core of any universalistic conception of rights. As I have pointed out above, the specific quality of rights which makes them irreducible to corresponding prohibitions and obligations is that they attribute moral worth to their targets and bearers. This quality is not related to modernity; it does not depend on any particular feature of the rights holders, neither on their membership in a group nor even necessarily on their being human. Worth is implied in the very notion of right. By proclaiming animal rights, moral worth is attributed to animals. Postulating human rights as a special kind of rights means attributing special moral standing to human beings. This is all that is necessary. Any further specification as to *which* qualities of human beings justify to attribute them rights, will be open to the challenge of cultural relativism and might lead to exclude certain men and women from the reach of these rights. Thus, if we think that human rights are derived from the capacities of communication and social interaction, the rights of people who are severely handicapped might be in danger. If, on the other hand, we ground human rights on the capacity to feel pain we will be unable to distinguish human rights from those of animals. The list of human rights, which explains what it means to attribute specific worth to their bearers as human beings, must be relative to the social conditions in which they live because this worth is itself a social attribute. If a long list of human rights can be conceived of as universal ones today, this is because modernity has dramatically universalized more and more features of the social conditions for human life.

The attribution of worth is greater the more general a right is. It can be understood as preventing the slackening of moral impulse once we no longer have special reasons for honouring a right such as promise, consent, kinship, friendship, or common membership in a wider group. The pathos inherent in the language of human rights is therefore not an entirely empty one. It is part of the attempt to mobilize compliance with moral principles in situations where the danger is especially acute that they might be ignored or violated.

Human rights are culturally neutral not because they are natural, but because they are political. They will only be securely established where political membership takes priority over cultural affiliations in the following way: a polity which supports human rights must allow for a plurality of cultural affiliations inside and also treat individuals from other cultures outside with equal respect. This enables it to attribute rights also to non-members of the polity.

(2) These arguments still do not meet one objection that can be raised against conceiving of human rights as an extended transnational form of citizenship. Libertarian writers like Friedrich von Hayek or Robert Nozick have tended to see the enrichment of citizenship with ever more rights as a development endangering the most fundamental liberties. In their view, rights of democratic participation and of social welfare do not extend the ranges for autonomous agency in modern society but actually restrain them. The reason is that these rights require ever more state interference into civil society.[6] The rather pessimistic historic perspective underlying this account could provide a starting-point for a defence of human rights as categorically different from those of citizenship, without getting too deeply involved with speculations about human nature. If the modern welfare state has indeed a tendency for extending social control in a way that undercuts individual autonomy then it might be useful to establish a list of 'natural' liberties as human rights. Rawls's theory that such liberties should be given 'lexical priority' (Rawls, 1971, pp. 42–3) over other rights, or Dworkin's view that they should be able to 'trump' majority decisions, are not entirely satisfactory in this perspective because such ranking does not fully address the *opposition* between citizenship rights and fundamental liberties. The proper strategy would be to immunize the latter against the dangerous proliferation of the former. This can be achieved by two means: first, by claiming natural status for these liberties and thus denying that they could ever be legitimately infringed for social, political or cultural reasons;[7] and second, by keeping the list of liberties as short as possible in order to avoid confusion with, and contamination by, the specific rights of modern citizenship.

Seen from this point of view, the plea for translating even more rights of citizenship into human rights seems to rely on an optimistic philosophy of history. Those who regard the accumulation of rights in liberal democracy

as an indicator for moral progress in the political evolution of humanity, would have good reasons to oppose the libertarian strategy. T.H. Marshall's thesis that in England civil rights were the achievement of the 18th century, political rights of the 19th and social rights of the 20th, can be quoted as the best-known example of a 'progressivist' theory of the evolution of rights (Marshall, 1965). Many authors have criticized the generalization of this scheme for other societies,[8] and have argued that the extension of citizenship had been a 'ruling class strategy' as much as an achievement of popular movements (Mann, 1987), that it strengthened social inequality rather than levelling it out (Waters, 1989), or that social rights are actually an alien or subordinate element in a political conception of citizenship (Roche, 1987, van Gunsteren, 1992, pp. 50–4). Some have made a strong case that the extension of citizenship depends on historically contingent outcomes of wars and social mobilization (Giddens, 1982, p. 171, Turner, 1986, 1990). Most have, however, tacitly assumed that the territorial inclusion of populations and the evolution of civil and political rights has reached a saturation point in Western democracy,[9] and that further struggles would concentrate on social rights and on new issues raised by feminism, ecological movements and 'racial' and ethnic conflicts. If this were true, a strategy of isolating human rights from those of citizenship might indeed be counterproductive because it would focus the strongest normative claims on those rights which have already been achieved and are rather safely institutionalized (at least in Western democracies). Regarding the list of human rights as open ended might therefore help to mobilize their moral weight for the new claims raised at the present stage of the historic evolution of citizenship.

The argument that I have stated above suggests once more a third view, which refrains from any strong statements about a tendency towards progress or degeneration of freedom in history. Certainly libertarians and conservative critics of comprehensive welfare policies are correct in pointing out that the ever longer list of rights is part of the story of the state's continuously widening area of social control. Yet an expanding list of rights is necessary just in order to keep pace with the erosion of individual autonomy by tighter external constraints on action and choice. These rights are not themselves inherent in the conditions of modernity. But they can be fought for and institutionalized in the constitutional framework of liberal democracy. Evolutionary views of citizenship go wrong when they confuse the expansive development of citizenship rights with a cumulative process where the newly achieved rights always rest on the safe foundation of those won in earlier struggles. Citizenship is exposed to the permanent threat of erosion in all its fundamental dimensions.

This is not because of a permanent danger of new forms of totalitarianism which would threaten civil and political rights. Today an outright reversal of fundamental constitutionally entrenched rights is not on the agenda in most contemporary liberal democracies. Well institutionalized social rights have survived even brutal attacks on the welfare state, like those of the Thatcher and Reagan administrations. They could neither achieve real reductions in overall public social expenditures nor carry privatization to the point of openly dismantling core institutions of national welfare arrangements (such as the National Health Service in Britain). The danger of erosion comes from the emergence of new forms of inequality, power and control in society which undermine the safeguards for autonomy and basic equality provided by established rights. This concerns civil and political rights just as much as social ones. New media, information and reproduction technologies provide two obvious examples. They have opened additional fields for the exercise of political and economic power, and have made possible new forms of intrusion into the spheres of privacy which undermine the integrity and autonomy of citizens. Political answers to these challenges are lagging behind. If and when they come they will be formulated as new rights of citizens. Much the same is true for the dynamic of inclusion. Hardly anybody will question voting rights for women or raise again the voting age. Yet increasing immigration combined with stagnating or falling rates of naturalization has raised the percentage of the resident adult population formally excluded from citizenship in many countries. The evolution of rights has not kept pace with that of human mobility.

Rights have to be seen as relative to social conditions and with regard to their purpose of protecting the existence, interests, needs, or autonomous agency of their bearers. In this view there is neither reason for evolutionary optimism nor for a retrograde strategy of reversing the accumulation of state power by establishing an exclusive priority for 'natural liberties' in opposition to comprehensive rights. Certain fundamental rights must indeed be immunized by specific constitutional guarantees against the threat of totalitarian abolition as well as against erosion in democracy. But it would be illusory to think that any liberties and rights can be firmly established once and for all. Constitutional entrenchment rather opens the path for reasserting these rights when new challenges arise, as well as for going beyond them by claiming additional ones. Endowed with constitutional guarantees, fundamental rights cannot be easily attacked by any occasional legislative majority. They are thus to some extent 'depoliticized', but still not 'naturalized'. Naturalizing them would not add anything to their validity and enforceability. It would not weaken any further accumulation of power but only the struggle for novel rights against novel forms of domination.

One final argument that remains to be considered is that the list of human rights ought to be fixed and kept to a minimum, because their role is to establish a basic standard of justice in the law of peoples which must allow for a plurality of regimes on the globe, just as a liberal regime ought to tolerate a plurality of cultures and forms of life within a society. John Rawls has recently defended this view (Rawls, 1993b). Extending the list of human rights seems to impose ever higher standards of liberal democracy on other kinds of regimes. But this cannot be reasonably required if the idea of international pluralism is taken seriously. For Rawls, '[h]uman rights are distinct from, say, constitutional rights, or rights of democratic citizenship ... They are part of a reasonable law of peoples and specify limits on the domestic institutions required of all peoples by that law' (Rawls, 1993b, pp. 70–1). I fully agree that a theory of justice in the relations between states ought to generate a list of human rights, and if that is the only perspective for drawing this list it will be not a very extensive one.

Still, this conception does not seem sufficient for explaining the force and urgency of claims for human rights in the present world. First, approaching human rights only from the perspective of relations between states eliminates *a priori* one of the two elements of universal conditions of modernity to which human rights must respond: the global interconnectedness of societies and their simultaneous internal modernization. Second, although theories of international law have always been concerned with justice between states, human rights have not been regarded as an indispensable element of the 'law of peoples' until quite recently. Traditionally, this law only specified rights and obligations of states rather than those of individuals in their relations to states. Contemporary developments involve changes in the conception of the community of states. They outline a still largely symbolic tie of rights and obligations between this community and the individual human being, a tie which is no longer completely mediated by her membership in a polity. Human rights are therefore more than merely limits imposed on domestic institutions that states must meet in the treatment of their citizens in order to be accepted as members of the international community of states. The law of peoples has come to encompass rights of individual human beings as obligations states not only impose on each other, but which they jointly accept as an international community towards groups of individuals whose basic rights are grossly violated. These rights can be reduced to mutual obligations only in the horizontal relations between sovereign states – in the vertical relations between the international community and individuals they confirm a special moral worth of the human being which is not derived from the requirements of justice between states. Third, Rawls builds his theory on the assumption of closed societies wherein individuals lead complete lives (Rawls, 1993a, pp. 12, 18, 40, 136, 222, 276, 301). While this is a useful starting-point for determining principles of justice within politically bounded societies, it is inadequate for a discussion of human rights in a transnational space where people are not completely tied to states by links of territorial residence or nominal membership.

(3) Combining the argument of this chapter with that of the first part of this book establishes a threefold linkage between human rights and citizenship.

First, citizenship rights include as their cornerstone a list of universal human rights that emerges from the liberal and democratic tradition, but whose validity can be established beyond that tradition. The comprehensive list is derived from the global conditions of modernity which are today shared by all societies on earth. Liberal democracy, properly understood, is only defensible if its normative political principles can be seen as responding to these universalized conditions of modernity, rather than as depending on the situation of wealthy societies or the particular traditions of occidental cultures. The rights of citizenship in each single polity will always be more comprehensive and more specific than a common list of human rights for all polities. But the 'language of rights' is the same in both cases and – given appropriate conditions – citizenship rights can be translated into universal human ones.

Second, human rights must include a basic right to citizenship, which is today only stated negatively as a right not to be deprived of one's citizenship. This right could be reformulated as a positive entitlement, i.e. as a right of access to citizenship which puts a special obligation of admission on identifiable states. It can also be stated as a right of access to substantial citizenship, i.e. a right to non-discrimination of permanently resident members of society not only with regard to their universal human rights, but also with regard to more specific rights of citizenship in their society of residence. The universalistic foundation of liberal democracy manifests in the presupposition that there are no ascriptive barriers for becoming a full member in such a polity. Although the number of actual members is necessarily limited for each particular liberal democratic polity, humanity always forms the widest circle of potential membership.

Third, human rights can be understood as a universalized form of citizenship, transcending boundaries of state membership in both nominal and territorial regard. A claim for citizenship rights always implies an appeal directed towards political institutions which could enforce the right. For universal rights these institutions cannot be only those of the separate sovereign states. Human rights enforcement clearly needs stronger instruments of international law and an international judiciary. In the global political structure such institutions are currently located at continental levels and at the level of the international community of states. The members of this community are states, not individual women and men. But if states fail to provide individual men and women with the protection of their most basic human rights, the institutions of this international community can assume direct responsibility for their fate. Hannah Arendt wrote about the refugees and stateless people in her time: 'Man, it turns out, can lose all so-called Rights of Man without losing his essential quality as man, his human dignity. Only the loss of a polity itself expels him from humanity' (Arendt, 1967, p. 297).[10] Stronger enforcement of human rights by international agencies should not be seen as a move towards 'global citizenship' but it could be characterized as the quest for a 'polity of polities' which attributes a substitute political membership to those who have been deprived of all their rights as members of particular states.

NOTES

1. I will take up the question of corresponding obligations of specified or unspecified providers of rights in chapter 12.
2. Other rights, such as employment rights of pregnant women, are both group-specific and situational.
3. Hart discusses one more kind, special liberties, which are, however, irrelevant for our discussion of equal rights of citizenship.
4. Shacknove develops this in a debate about American duties towards refugees but the same principles can as well be used to discuss the related and wider problem of whether citizenship rights are general or special.
5. Walzer concedes in a footnote that 'certain internal principles ... are reiterated in many, perhaps in all, human societies' (Walzer, 1983, p. 314). But the point about globalization is not *reiteration* based on some common features of human culture, but *connectedness* of all modern or modernizing societies that explains why certain principles apply to all of them.
6. Ralf Dahrendorf, too, argued that through the extension of rights citizenship could become self-defeating by undermining the autonomy of civil society (Dahrendorf, 1974).
7. Instead of claiming that human rights are natural, one might make the even stronger claim that they are absolute, i.e. that in contrast with other rights there is no possible moral justification for overriding them. Yet this would reduce the number of relevant human rights to practically nil. Alan Gewirth has argued that 'All innocent persons have an absolute right not to be made the intended victims of a homicidal project' (Gewirth, 1984, p. 108). He relates this to a principle according to which 'agents and institutions are absolutely prohibited from degrading persons, treating them as if they had no rights or dignity' (ibid.). But the purpose of declaring a human right is not to identify those actions which are utterly immoral. It is to protect and enlarge the space for legitimate human action against just that kind of infringement which could be justified in certain situations on consequentialist grounds.
8. This generalization of Marshall's analysis into an evolutionary scheme was actually not developed by himself but by later authors such as Reinhard Bendix (Bendix, 1964) or Talcott Parsons (Parsons, 1971).
9. Giddens does mention the new importance of civil rights but he thinks that 'There is a danger that the contemporary discussion of the significance of civil rights degenerates into the vague, and largely empty, concern with " human rights " of which President Carter made much – or at least about which he talked a good deal' (Giddens, 1982, p. 177).
10. Michael Ignatieff echoes this insight when he states the paradox that 'to treat men equally – only as men – is to deny them the respect due to their humanity' (Ignatieff, 1985, p. 36).

10. Scarcity and Alienability of Rights

How equal must the rights of citizens be if they should be able to recognize each other as equal members of a polity? In section 8.2 I have already examined one major objection against, or constraint upon, equality which says that certain entitlements of citizenship ought to be more responsive to need or desert. In this chapter I shall look at another argument asserting that rights are similar to private goods in a market economy. Such goods are fully alienable and they are normally scarce in relation to demand (or else they would not be traded). Under conditions of free markets the final distributions are in Nozick's words 'unpatterned' (Nozick, 1974, p. 158). They will be unequal even if all started with the same amount of each good because people's preferences are unequal. Let me consider whether such an argument could also be made about citizenship rights. Can rights be considered as property which can be freely alienated and will therefore be distributed unequally after a series of transactions? Are rights fundamentally scarce and does this create obstacles for an equal distribution?

10.1. ALIENABILITY OF RIGHTS

When rights are considered as a scarce and valuable resource people might be interested in trading them either for money or for some other rights. If there were a market in citizenship rights, free exchange would over a short time lead to strongly unequal distributions with some individuals accumulating rights and others retaining only a few. This outcome could not be considered as unjust in a theory like Robert Nozick's which derives all rights from those of property (including everybody's property in her own person) and maintains that voluntary transactions of justly acquired property lead by definition to just distributions.

I have argued that comprehensive citizenship in a liberal democratic welfare state is strongly disconnected from desert and defines social needs with a view towards maintaining equality of membership. With respect to the basic civil, political and social rights of citizenship, nobody can claim stronger entitlements than any other citizen because of her special merits and deserts or because of her idiosyncratic needs. Entitlements of citizenship are due equally to each member of the polity and their intended

249

effect is to confirm the equality of status and of opportunities of participation in that polity. But while these rights are due to everyone they are at the same time not the property of each individual member. Citizenship entitlements are fundamentally different from property rights because they are inalienable. Citizens are free to trade their rights to inherit or bequeath, they may buy or sell private insurance entitlements but not rights of citizenship. They cannot sell their liberty by becoming serfs or slaves and they cannot trade their votes. Neither can they sell their social rights. If they receive some public monetary assistance they may use it for buying whatever they want, but they cannot transfer their right to an unemployment benefit or to a public retirement pension to somebody who is not eligible, and they also should not be allowed to pay for jumping a queue for medical treatment or for a place in higher education. This means that citizenship rights are not only disconnected from desert and singular needs but also from the distributive principle of free individual bargaining and exchange. Furthermore, such rights are not merely exempted from exchange for money but can also not be exchanged for other rights. We cannot accept as a general rule that somebody should acquire a specific right just because she subjectively values this right more, even if she is willing to give up some of the rights that she presently enjoys.

While citizenship rights must be considered as inalienable this does not imply that citizens ought to be denied all options to claim or to waive a right. What must be equal in this respect is the right to claim or waive but not necessarily the distribution of rights resulting from a free use of such options (see Freeden, 1991, pp. 46–8). The freedom to waive a right is what characterizes it as a liberty. In many cases, this freedom is of little relevance. If I have a right to a tax exemption or a sickness benefit, which is moreover granted automatically, I will hardly make use of my liberty to waive the claim. However, it will make a difference whether I am not only entitled to vote but also obliged to do so. The right to public education is the one right of citizenship where the freedom to waive it is universally denied (see also section 12.1). Formally, we can split each liberty into two different rights: a liberty to claim or waive, and a right to whatever we get if we claim it. Distributions of citizenship rights are generally equal with regard to the first element: either all enjoy the liberty or none. If the liberty is denied to all, the subsequent distribution of that which we receive when claiming the right will be equal, too: all receive it, because nobody can waive the right. If the liberty is enjoyed by all, the resulting distribution of the second element may be unequal if some are not interested in claiming. In contrast, if a right is alienable, it is the distribution of the first element which becomes unequal.

In between full alienability and waiving there is a third possibility that people may return their rights. When a right is returned it is waived for good so that former holders also lose the right to reclaim it on another occasion. The difference with full alienability is that a right can be returned only to the actor who has granted it. In the case of citizenship rights this is of course the state. So the suggested terminology is to speak about alienability in the case of a free transfer of rights between rights holders, of returnable rights when a right can be voluntarily renounced for good without anyone else gaining it, and of waiving of rights when somebody does not make use of a right but retains an ongoing entitlement to do so in the future. It would be absurd to restrict the notion of liberty to full alienability only. All the three cases exemplify different conceptions of freedom in the use of rights. Let me illustrate the consequences of alienating and of waiving rights with a few more examples.

In the first part of this book I have argued for optional naturalization and expatriation with a possibility of acquiring multiple citizenship. At the same time I have rejected the idea that citizenships could be accumulated or sold like company shares (see section 6.2). In any case citizenship is not alienable in the sense that members could transfer their status to non-members. Granting the option of naturalization does not turn citizenship into an object of bargaining but extends its reach beyond the circle of nominal members. It is thus a move towards inclusion and equalization. At the same time the possibilities of claiming or waiving the right to nominal citizenship are constrained by objective indicators of social membership such as residence or family relations. In contrast with acquisition by naturalization or declaration the right to citizenship acquired at birth can normally not be waived. I have also supported rules that allow for optional renaturalization of former citizens. Expatriation means then that membership is waived rather than returned. Those who renounce their citizenship thereby lose their rights as citizens but remain potential citizens, endowed with the right to become naturalized.

In some cases even the right to waive a right may be controversial. Consider paid pregnancy and maternity leave and suppose that women receive their previous salary during this period. Some women might still want to continue to work because they think it will help their careers in the firm or just because they subjectively prefer the social environment of work to that of a housewife. Why should we deny them the right to waive this right, i.e. to go on working and thus to maximize their subjective welfare? The reason is obvious if we ask why this right has been introduced in the first place. It became necessary to mitigate a specific vulnerability of women in the labour market as opposed to men. Two different arguments can be made against permitting women to waive this right. The first argument is that pregnancy and the early months of maternity are a physical and psychological condition which is incompatible with most forms of paid labour. This is a paternalistic argument which maintains that women should not be allowed to work regardless of their own preferences. It might either be formulated as representing the 'objective interest' of women themselves or of the child (against the mother's wish to work). The second argument is not vulnerable to the accusation of paternalism. It says that employers are in a stronger position because there is an abundant potential supply of female labour force. Thus the price to be paid for claiming the right in terms of future chances of continued employment or promotion would probably become quite high, because pregnant women would try to stay in their jobs at almost any cost if they have to be afraid of being replaced by male workers or other women. This might even be true if we assume that women cannot be dismissed during their maternity leave and for a certain period afterwards. Allowing some women to waive their right would put an unacceptable pressure to do the same on those who would like to claim it. In this argument the objection against a liberty to waive a right is that under given social and economic conditions this would *de facto* lead to a situation of bargaining which could undermine the right as a citizenship entitlement.

Generalizing this example one could suggest that certain rights are, or should be, inalienable not only in the sense that they cannot be traded, but also in the sense that they cannot be waived because they are attached to disadvantaged positions or groups and must be protected against the potentially eroding effects of a bargaining situation. Allowing citizens in such situations or members of such groups to waive their rights might end in eliminating the factual possibility to claim the right.

However, this might be a hasty and problematic conclusion. Take as a further example rights of 'racial' and ethnic minorities under affirmative action programmes. Clearly we should not force anybody to take part, for example, in a specific training course that is offered to such minorities only in order to give them equal opportunities in job applications or internal promotion. Some individual members will want to prove that they can do better even without such assistance, and they might regard any pressure to claim the right as a diminishing of their individual achievements against the odds of social discrimination. They should have a right to waive their right in spite of the negative effect this might have on members of these groups who then might be stigmatized for claiming affirmative action that others do not need. A related example is the additional supply of instruction in the languages of ethnic minorities and immigrants, which ought to be offered optionally, but should not be made mandatory if ethnic apartheid is to be avoided. While in similar cases individuals from disadvantaged groups ought to be allowed to waive such optional rights, they cannot be compensated for waiving them. If they waive or renounce such a right, it is because they see it as disadvantageous to claim it. That means they already have found some individual compensation for giving up the right (e.g. career advantages from demonstrating that they can succeed under more difficult conditions than other competitors). They should not be entitled to any additional benefit. So one difference between waiving and alienating involves is that in the former case usually no special incentive or compensation is offered for not using one's rights.

10.2. SCARCITY AND SIMPLE EQUALITY

I will discuss in this section (1) the notion of simple equality and potential scarcity in the distribution of (2) membership status, (3) civil liberties, (4) political participation rights and, most extensively, (5) social rights. The concluding point (6) argues that the norm of equality serves as the relevant guideline for all three kinds of rights.

(1) The reference point for any normative discussion about distributive justice must be simple equality.[1] Simple equality means that each gets the same thing. For simple equality of rights the issues are therefore, first, who has to be counted among those who each get the same right, and second, how can we know that what each one gets is actually the same as what all others get? A distribution of rights can be challenged as violating simple equality if some who are not included feel that they ought to enjoy the same rights as all others, or it can be challenged if the rights of some who are included are different from those of others. Early feminists fighting for women's voting rights demanded simple equality of the vote by way of inclusion. Male workers who were enfranchised protested at that time against systems in some countries where they needed many more votes to elect a single delegate than did the wealthy classes or the aristocracy. Here, simple equality was violated because, although the liberty to cast a vote was the same, the positive right to representation in parliament was not. In this case the demand was for equalization of the right rather than for inclusion.

The quest for equal citizenship supports a general presumption in favour of inclusion and of simple equality in the distribution of citizenship rights; it permits outsiders to challenge their exclusion and insiders to fight discrimination. But there is also a certain tension between these two norms of inclusion and equality. Widening the range of membership can justify deviations from simple equality of rights for the sake of equalizing membership. As long as citizenship is confined to a socially homogeneous group, let us say adult male property owners of a single national culture, their equal standing as members of the polity will be best achieved by rights that ignore whatever group differences exist among them. But once citizenship includes the whole resident population of a highly differentiated society, some rights will have to be differentiated in order to achieve equal membership.

I will consider such arguments for inequality of rights in the following chapter. In the present one I want to focus on a different constraint which can also be linked to the inclusionary dynamic of liberal citizenship. Once it has been established who ought to be included in the distribution and what is the good to be distributed, could scarcity be a reason for deviating from simple equality? Jon Elster points out that 'Issues of distributive justice arise only when there is scarcity. The assignment of citizenship and that of the right to vote, therefore, are not properly seen as problems of distributive justice. Historically, these rights have often been granted in exchange for paying taxes or doing military service, i.e. on grounds of communicative justice' (Elster 1992, p. 122). Thus, citizenship seems to be not scarce but historically it was to some extent alienable in the sense that it could be 'bought' even if not sold by individuals.

(2) Issues of scarcity may be relevant for immigration although the view that receiving societies 'distribute' a fixed number of jobs or housing units among natives and immigrants is grossly inadequate. Apart from relieving scarcity of labour, immigration may, under favourable conditions, also contribute to the creation of more jobs and houses. In contrast with immigration, problems of scarcity are fundamentally irrelevant for the allocation of nominal citizenship once we count only the resident population as eligible. Certainly, if access to citizenship became independent from residence and every person everywhere in the world had a right to become a citizen of any other country, citizenship of the more attractive places would become a scarce good because of the immigration entitlement it entails.

Scarcity implies that not every participant in a distribution can get enough to satisfy her desires. But as long as the good is divisible and homogeneous everybody can at least get the same amount and quality of it. Constraints on simple equality are therefore considerably exacerbated when a good is not only scarce but also indivisible or heterogeneous, so that not each unit has the same desired quality (see Elster, 1992, p. 22).

As a status of membership liberal democratic citizenship is divisible and completely homogeneous. However, nominal citizenship can be, and mostly is, turned into an 'artificially scarce good'[2] by discretionary and selective rules of admission. In chapter 4 I have examined different justifications given for cutting down the supply of this good to immigrants. Some do not appeal to any principle of justice which weighs the claims of newcomers, but simply assert the right of the association to select its new members in any way it wants, or the duty of the ethnic nation to give priority to co-ethnics and family members of their nationals. Others refer to a criterion of merit (for example when immigrants are admitted because they have successfully assimilated) or utility (e.g. when priority is given to those with stable income or with special talents).

Could there also be another justification which maintains that inclusion in equal citizenship would give immigrants certain rights which are themselves scarce or imply entitlements to other scarce resources? Citizens in ancient Athens might have argued in this manner. Admitting all *metics* living within the city walls to full membership would have diluted the rights of present members. Political participation rights which were exercised in the *agora* or the rotation system for public offices might have become unworkable with a twofold or threefold increase in numbers. Maybe Kuwaiti citizens who are a one-third minority of the population think about their rights in a similar way. But this is neither the situation in any Western immigration country nor would exclusion be justifiable on the grounds of liberal democracy if such a situation ever occurred. Natural scarcity of goods, access to which depends on membership, may be a reason for inequality of entitlements among citizens but it cannot be a legitimate reason for denying resident immigrants access to citizenship.[3]

(3) Consider now the different kinds of citizenship rights and whether scarcity could count as an argument against turning them into equal entitlements. There is no such reason for the basic negative liberties. The good which they imply is that of making interference of others illegitimate and this can be made perfectly equal. What can and will be factually unequal is state interference with interference, i.e. the positive right to protection attached to the negative liberty. More precisely, it is not the right which may be unequal but 'merely' the actual level of protection provided. Every citizen has the same right that the police intervene to protect her when she is attacked, only sometimes the police are not there when they are needed. But the negative liberty will be purely formal and empty unless it implies an obligation on the part of the state to provide the essential conditions of security without any group discrimination for all citizens.[4]

Negative liberties might also be 'scarce' because not everybody can exercise them at the same time in the same place. Rights such as those of free speech or assembly concern 'activities subject to congestion' (Barry, 1992, p. 280) and therefore require some regulation for their exercise. The sole purpose of regulation is to enable citizens to make *effective* use of their liberty, and to enable – as far as possible – *all* citizens equally. Such situational regulation is, however, clearly different from a restriction of the liberty in the name of some higher good or interest.[5]

Can restrictions concerning the content of speech or the aims of associations also be justified outside 'a situation of constitutional crisis in which democratic institutions cannot work effectively and their procedures for dealing with emergencies cannot operate' (Rawls, 1993a, p. 354)? I would hesitate to say categorically 'no' as Rawls does. A ban on Nazi organizations and propaganda seems to me entirely justified, at least in the historical context of countries such as Germany and Austria, even as long as these groups do not present an acute threat to the constitutional order in the sense that they could actually overthrow it. American and European liberals are likely to disagree on this. The point of agreement is that any restriction of basic liberties can only be justified if it can be shown to be necessary in order to maintain a constitutional framework which guarantees equal liberties to all. The disagreement is about whether, for example, incitement to racial hatred is so intimately connected with violence against certain groups of citizens that its toleration would permit the destruction of the public sphere of free debate in civil society where these liberties can be exercised and would thus undermine equal citizenship. My interpretation is that a liberal democratic state can justify such restrictions if refraining from intervention would mean refusing equal respect and concern to the members of victim groups.

With these qualifications neither scarcity nor competing distributive principles can justify inequality of the communicative liberties of free speech and assembly. Much the same can be said about the rights to equal protection by the law and property rights in so far as the latter are necessary to establish an exclusive sphere of privacy. However, unconstrained ownership cannot be regarded as an element of equal citizenship if the accumulation and use of property has important external effects that concern fundamental needs and interests of other citizens or of society as a whole. Taxation, employment laws, safety regulations for production and consumer goods, and expropriation of land for the development of public infrastructure, are all indispensable restrictions on the use of property which cannot be easily justified if we start from a notion of equal ownership entitlements. The only relevant standard of equality in this respect is that interference by state authorities must follow rules, established by law, that respect the owners' rights to equal protection as citizens. This is not the same as maintaining a right to fully own and use whatever property has been acquired without violating the law or a similar right of others. Restricting ownership rights in this way can be justified by conceiving of society as a co-operative scheme (as Rawls does) where all the benefits individuals may enjoy from the acquisition and use of property are not only due to their own efforts but to those of others as well.[6]

(4) Distributive conditions for political rights of representation and participation are different from those for negative liberties. They can only be exercised in a bounded community where membership is to some extent

stable over time. However, while membership is in this way a communal good it is not inherently scarce within the community. Scarcity arises only in a republican conception of direct participatory democracy which requires that polities be not merely bounded but also very small. Representative democracy certainly reduces rights of participation but its rules allow for inclusive and equal political citizenship in large modern nation-states.

This sort of democracy creates a peculiar distribution of political power. Voting and participation rights are one kind of power which is equalized among the citizenry.[7] But from the exercise of these rights emerges a second kind of power that is highly unequal. Any system of delegation and representation leads to an accumulation of power in a hierarchical structure. Rough equality of administrative power attached to public office could be only achieved by systems of strict rotation or lotteries involving all citizens, but not in democratic representation (see Walzer, 1983, p. 306). Political power which citizens share in the form of voting rights is not a scarce resource, it is divisible and homogeneous; but the power of public office which is exercised over citizens is heterogeneous and it cannot be divided among all. It is socially scarce in the sense of being a positional good (Hirsch, 1976).

Other norms than those of inclusion and equality have to guide the distribution of this second kind of political power. In liberal representative democracy this distribution ought to be highly sensitive to ambition, talent and merit. Not everybody will be interested in public office and nobody ought to be forced to exercise it. Not every citizen who has political ambitions is also talented and by their vote citizens ought to select the better qualified politicians, just as a minister ought to give preference to the better qualified candidate for a leading position in her department. Finally, the power of office should also be sensitive to merit. Ambitious and talented politicians might still be corrupt or might have acquired a bad record in previous terms of office. They should be judged by their actual performance and not merely by their talents. The popular vote combined with publicity of democratic deliberation is meant to allow for a selection of candidates according to these concerns.

(5) Social rights provide that area of citizenship where the notion of simple equality of rights seems most obviously a rather strained one, and some rights have to be explicitly unequal for citizens in unequal social conditions. Social rights of citizenship are also most obviously affected by problems of scarcity. They involve the direct redistribution of inherently scarce economic resources or their extensive use for the organization of services such as medical or educational ones. Furthermore, problems of scarcity combine with difficulties of defining adequate standards of equality

with regard to needs that are inherently different or even unique (see section 8.2).

Under such conditions criteria of distributive justice will be necessarily controversial. What, if anything, should be equalized by social redistribution and rights? Rawls combines equality of opportunity with the difference principle. The latter starts from a position of simple equality and considers that 'the higher expectations of those better situated are just if and only if they work as part of a scheme which improves the expectations of the least advantaged members of society' (Rawls, 1971, p. 75). This is a strongly egalitarian principle. Simple equality is to be preferred unless all social groups can gain from inequality (p. 76). Ronald Dworkin argues against the idea that what is to be equalized is individual welfare, and suggests instead equality of resources as the proper criterion for redistribution. Distributive justice should be sensitive to individual ambitions and thus should accept the outcome of market allocations as far as these reflect genuine choices. However, 'Market allocations must be corrected in order to bring some people closer to the share of resources they would have had but for these various differences of initial advantage, luck and inherent capacity' (Dworkin, 1981, part 2, p. 207). While Dworkin's concern is to compensate for the distorting effect of different endowments and abilities on the outcome of voluntary transactions, Amartya Sen suggests instead that basic capabilities should be brought to a roughly equal level. Although Sen admits that there can never be an absolute standard for measuring equal capabilities, he thinks that we can still move towards more equality in this respect (Sen, 1984, p. 322).

None of these principles is meant to be used as a simple yardstick for judging a particular scheme of social policy. However, they do give us some of the basic ideas underlying discursive justification for welfare state arrangements. Instead of assessing the merits of the different formulas I suggest that social rights combine different kinds of equality in a rather fuzzy manner. First, there is a basic notion of equality of opportunity which implies that differences of initial endowments (such as those due to inherited wealth) ought to be neutralized in various ways with regard to their impact on the distribution of material wealth and social positions. Equal opportunity supports meritocratic principles for the distribution of final outcomes, but at the same time can justify far-reaching redistributive efforts in order to equalize starting positions. Equal basic education for all and free competition in access to higher positions in society without any exclusion because of class, gender, or ethnic and 'racial' origins are the major implications of this principle. The second element is a basic minimum principle: no matter how inequalities in the distribution of resources have come about, they must not be permitted to extend below a certain lower threshold which is considered to constitute the minimum of a decent life in a community of citizenship. Everybody above this threshold should contribute to its maintenance in proportion to her income and wealth. Redistribution according to this principle is not oriented towards rectification of injustice in initial acquisition or transactions (Nozick, 1974, pp. 152–3),[8] nor does it require that economic resources should be equal – no limits to inequality above the threshold are built into this principle. It is also not about creating equal opportunities in markets. But a right to a basic minimum could be interpreted as that kind of equality in society which is necessary in order to equalize opportunities for the exercise of citizenship in the polity. This principle supports universal flat rate benefits, minimum wage legislation, a basic income scheme, or extended non-market provision of services in kind, and progressive taxation in order to finance all this. The third principle is that of social insurance. Generalized risks to fall below a basic minimum of resources or capabilities due to unemployment, sickness, accident or old age should be dealt with preventively by a system of compulsory insurance, which aims at maintaining a level roughly equivalent to what it would have been had the event against which insurance had been taken not occurred. This insurance should be financed by contributions of all who profit from the scheme (employers as well as employees) and, differently from private insurance, contributions ought to be proportional to present levels of income and wealth and not to specific probabilities of risk for certain groups.

I have formulated all three ideas as normative principles. But I do not claim that any of them is derived from a universalistic conception of social justice. I see them instead as related to the idea of equal and inclusive membership in a democratic polity where capitalist market economy constantly generates social inequality. As we move from the first principle to the second and third, universalistic justification becomes weaker and specific requirements of citizenship have to sustain the argument. The basic minimum principle and, much more so, that of social insurance, originate from concerns about social peace and inclusion in a democratic polity rather than from a strictly impartial normative assessment of individual claims. This instrumental role of social citizenship in sustaining social peace in a society deeply divided by class and group interests has meant that social rights of the third kind have become the object of collective bargaining.[9] Under fair conditions, bargaining generates its own strong legitimation for rights and obligations which result from agreements. *Pacta sunt servanda* is a rule which relegates other distributive principles such as those of need and desert to the background. It broadens the range for permissible inequalities and raises the threshold for claiming adjustments of distributions. Whether the results of bargaining about social rights have been achieved under fair

conditions is difficult to establish. The relevant issue is not only inequalities
in the powers and resources of the represented groups but also whether all
groups concerned have been adequately represented.[10] As mentioned in
section 8.2, this opens the door wide for vested interests and the
establishment of special privileges which channel redistribution in their
favour just because they are powerful enough to do so. The various national
mixes of social policies which can be seen as derivatives of the three
principles have clearly underpinned the relative stability of liberal
democracies in the period since World War II. Nevertheless, current welfare
state arrangements and entitlements of social citizenship might well be
criticized as unsatisfactory on any of the liberal egalitarian accounts
mentioned above. Furthermore, many such schemes are clearly inegalitarian
or exclude relevant populations so that their relation to the norm of equal
and inclusive citizenship is a rather strained one, too.

But this does not imply that only simple equality of rights would
conform to that norm. Malcolm Waters asserts that 'citizenship is a set of
formally equal relationships between individuals and the state but which is
constitutive of substantively unequal relationships with the state, and
unequal substance of citizenship' (Waters, 1989, p. 166). This leads him to
split social rights into those which can be regarded as equal and others
which he considers to be privileges rather than rights: 'minimum wage
legislation, unemployment insurance, retirement pensions, minimum
education standards ... these benefits are generally accessible by virtue of
being a member of the state rather than being particular to membership of
an interest group. They are of a different order than schemes of progressive
taxation or positive discrimination, for example, which, while they may
ameliorate inequality, do not establish rights but rather establish systems of
differential privilege' (p. 166).[11] Although I share the view that social rights
in contemporary welfare states have become a fertile ground for the growth
of group privilege disconnected from equal citizenship, the examples given
by Waters do not at all illustrate this point. Progressive taxation does not
conform to a rule of simple equality. But paying taxes is an obligation
rather than a right of citizenship. And, as I will show in chapter 12,
obligations cannot be made equal in the same way as rights. The relevant
question is which differentiation of an obligation best allows equal rights to
be sustained. Consider two major forms of taxation of individual citizens
(rather than of capital or corporations): progressive taxation of income and
flat rate taxation of consumption (i.e. value added tax). The first is unequal
not because it establishes differential privilege, but because it flattens
privilege (seen from the normative point of view) and because only
progressive taxation can raise sufficient funds for expanding state budgets
(seen from the state interest point of view). The norm of equal citizenship

cannot determine the rate of taxation, but it lends support to shaping obligations unequally in this way rather than raising flat rate head taxes or strictly proportional ones. Equal citizenship requires neither an obligation to pay equal taxes nor even an equal obligation to pay taxes (as John Stuart Mill was still convinced it does). General income tax exemptions for those below a certain threshold of income are entirely compatible with equal rights of citizenship. They can be derived from the basic minimum principle. The taxation of current consumption by VAT is apparently equal, but this equality has no strong normative foundation. Taxing consumption rather than income is entirely a matter of efficiency in the raising of tax revenue. Seen from the perspective of social justice the tax burden which has to be carried by the buyer is equally shared by people with unequal income. In many countries this has been taken into account by lowering VAT rates for basic consumer items and increasing them for luxury goods. The norms of social citizenship in this case again supports unequal rather than equal taxation.

(6) In conclusion, what is the significance and proper range of simple equality of rights for the different elements of citizenship? With regard to civil rights it is to secure equal individual autonomy and protection for each citizen. Social rights to a minimum education, income or provision of welfare benefits can be interpreted in two complementary ways. First, as an equalization of opportunities and resources in the race for higher income or social positions, and second, as a compensation for the less lucky or less talented ones who have lost out in this race. Simple equality of the political rights of participation has a different meaning. It is not an autonomy right because it can be exercised jointly with others. Nor does it create equal resources or opportunities with regard to participation in collective decision-making and access to office. Votes would be equal resources only if each voter also stood as a candidate for election. With minor exceptions (such as a difference of age thresholds) criteria for exclusion from passive voting rights ought to be the same as for active voting. But positive opportunities to be elected can hardly be made equal in the same way as opportunities to cast a vote. Finally, equal voting rights can also not be understood as a compensation for those who have not succeeded in the race for political power. The role of equal political rights of participation is that of a power which is instrumental in restraining, and necessary for legitimating, the exercise of power. In combination with the checks and balances of an institutional division of power between the different branches of government, the citizens' rights of participation and representation serve to control the use of power by requiring holders of elective offices to mobilize popular support and consent. *Inclusive, equal* and *substantial* political rights for every citizen are necessary in order to

make legitimate the exercise of political power which *includes* the whole population, puts everyone under an *equal* obligation to obey the law and subjects all to *substantial* forms of social control.

Taken together these three interpretations of equality in civil, political and social rights form the core of what equal membership in a liberal democratic polity means in a substantive sense. None of these rights should be seen as merely instrumental for another one. Neoliberals and libertarians dismiss extensive social rights as incompatible with their idea of justice and accept representative democracy primarily because it appears to be that kind of political regime which provides the relatively best guarantees for individual liberties from state interference. Democratic socialists support political liberties because they allow for the organization of workers. They also fought for the political rights of representative democracy, assuming that this would pave the way for social redistribution because the greater numbers of the working class would give greater weight to its representatives. Republicans have tended to give priority to political rights. In their view, negative liberties can be restricted if this helps to increase participation in the search for the common good. Social rights have often been accepted only as a means for equalizing opportunities of political participation. However, democratic deliberation is just as much instrumental for implementing the requirements of social justice as social rights are necessary in order to enable citizens to participate in deliberation.

In contrast to all three views I suggest that each category of rights ought to be seen as valuable in itself, as mutually supporting the other categories, and as indispensable for equal citizenship in contemporary liberal democracy. A broad range of other rights can be regarded as instrumental for citizenship, rather than as an integral part of it. While simple equality must be secured for the core rights, rights may be unequal if such inequality contributes to equal membership. Finally, there will be also a range of rights which are perfectly alienable and where the only notion of equality that ties them to citizenship is that no category of citizens may be excluded from gaining and exercising them. Instead of starting with these latter rights and considering them as natural and fundamental ones, liberal democracy ought to see them as a broad residual category which is contrained by prior demands for equality of inalienable rights.

NOTES

1.   Michael Walzer contrasts simple with complex equality and defines the latter as the separation of distributive spheres. Social goods (such as power or wealth) ought to be distributed according to different principles and should not be convertible between spheres (so that the rich can also monopolize political power, or that power holders can also enrich

themselves) (Walzer, 1983, chapter 1). '[A] (modern, complex, and differentiated) society enjoys both freedom and equality when success in one institutional setting isn't convertible into success in another' (Walzer, 1984, p. 321). But why should separation alone lead to more equality? Walzer's argument implicitly relies on the hope that autonomous communities tend to restrain inequality in their midst and that separation of spheres is what allows for a revival of communitarian self-determination in a modern complex society. This is hardly plausible. Does the separation of the family from the public spheres of civil society make for equality between genders? Will more autonomy of markets from state interference lead to a flourishing of those worker co-operatives Walzer favours? Complex equality in liberal democracy needs more than autonomy of social spheres. It requires an overarching simple equality of membership in the polity that protects citizens against exploitative and oppressive social relations in each sphere of their lives and that can be translated into different internal standards of equality in those spheres which are essential for maintaining equal citizenship: equal votes in politics, equal liberties and basic social protection in the economy, equality in the distribution of domestic labour in the family, etc.

2. Elster distinguishes strong natural scarcity (there is nothing one can do to increase supply), weak natural scarcity (supply cannot be increased to the point of satiating every demand); quasi-natural scarcity (supply can only be increased by uncoerced actions of citizens); and artificial scarcity (the government could make the good available to everyone to the level of satiation) (Elster, 1992, pp. 21–2).

3. This does of course not mean that such arguments are never made in democracies. In the city of Vienna foreign citizens are excluded from access to public housing, which has a large share in a market where demand presently by far exceeds supply. Social Democrats, Conservatives and the right-wing Freedom Party agree that foreign immigrants should remain excluded. Now liberal naturalization is increasingly seen as a problem because it could increase the share of immigrants among the queues of applicants. The Freedom Party goes further than the other parties only in demanding publicly the securing of exclusive housing rights for natives by denying foreigners access to citizenship.

4. 'A failure in domestic protection is not merely a deficiency in coercive power: it is also a definite encroachment on the structure of good reasons on which Hobbes hoped to ground the duties of subjects. ... What implications, for example does the acute physical insecurity of many inhabitants of great American cities have for the scope of their political obligations?' (Dunn, 1991, p. 38) – an insecurity which is moreover distributed very unequally among groups of different skin colour and ethnic and class origins.

5. '[R]ules of order are essential for regulating free discussion. Without the general acceptance of reasonable procedures of inquiry and precepts of debate, freedom of speech cannot serve its purpose. Not everyone can speak at once, or use the same public facility at the same time for different ends. ... The requisite regulations are not to be mistaken for restrictions on the content of speech' (Rawls, 1993a, p. 296).

6. Rawls's interpretation that rights are generated in social co-operation is directed against the idea that rights are like property entitlements of individuals against society. It does not imply that entitlements and obligations must also be attached to participation in co-operative activities (see section 9.1). With regard to duties, Rawls distinguishes natural ones, like the duty of justice, which apply without regard to our voluntary acts and oblige us towards all persons, from those obligations which one incurs by voluntarily accepting the benefits from participation in a joint enterprise (Rawls, 1971, pp. 111–7).

7. Brian Barry has pointed out that equality of votes may also be accepted not for the sake of equalizing citizenship but because '[g]iven the competing claims to superiority of various social groups (the rich, the educated, the well-born, the old, the male, and so on), universal (and equal) suffrage was the only outcome that could command stable agreement' (Elster, 1992, p. 70, quoting Barry, 1979, p. 195). However, in an electoral system with equal individual franchise, the task of achieving equal representation – for example in determining the boundaries of constituencies – may be of considerable complexity and can still give rise to much controversy between competing claims. Compared with a hierarchical system, where every group accepts its place in the polity, egalitarianism may even enhance instability. It allows for conflicting interpretations of what equality entails. In liberal democracy, equality is therefore not only valued for its simplicity but also for its own sake.

8.   Nozick generally insists on the converse argument that rectification is different from redistribution. Yet he realizes that correcting historic injustice is a difficult matter and in the end suggests 'a *rough* rule of thumb for rectifying injustices' that comes close to Rawls's difference principle: 'organize society so as to maximize the position of whatever group ends up least well-off in the society' (Nozick, 1974, p. 231, original emphasis).

9.   Following T.H. Marshall I will show in the next chapter how collective bargaining can nevertheless pave the way towards universal social rights of citizenship.

10.   If employers and trade union representatives of employees in a firm reach an agreement about some social benefit for the latter, the question of how this would affect the position of workers in other enterprises does not arise. These might be comparatively worse off after the agreement but they can try and struggle for the same benefits. The situation is different where redistribution involves public budgets. A concession made by state authorities to some group can always be resented because it reduces the resources remaining for satisfying similarly justified demands of others.

11.   Progressive taxation lies on an altogether different level than 'positive discrimination' and can hardly be classified under a common category of 'differential privilege'. The latter is indeed about a differentiation of rights according to group membership while the former differentiates obligations according to income and wealth.

11. Collective Rights

Citizenship is a status of equal individual political membership. Yet in the society organized in such a polity there are many different groups: social classes, men and women, young and old, religious, cultural and ethnic communities. There is also a broad range of situations and conflicts in which individuals act and identify as members of social collectives rather than as equal citizens. What does this imply for the rights of citizens? Must all such rights nevertheless be individual rather than collective rights? Will equal citizenship be undermined if it ignores cultural difference and social inequality? Or will it rather become more unequal if it takes them into account by differentiating rights between groups?

I want to argue that, on the one hand, neoliberals and republicans have greatly exaggerated the dangers of this latter development and have deliberately ignored the positive contribution of collective rights to equal citizenship in societies which are not only differentiated into overlapping groups but deeply divided into mutually exclusive collectives. On the other hand, mainstream theories of interest group pluralism as well as some theories of feminism and ethnic movements seem to abandon the search for a yardstick that would allow the assessment of whether certain collective rights can still be justified as contributing to equal individual citizenship.

11.1. COLLECTIVE RIGHTS AS A DYNAMIC ELEMENT OF CITIZENSHIP

In chapter 9, I have argued that rights of citizenship are general rather than special because a liberal polity cannot be regarded as a membership group but is constituted by the very rights it establishes for its members. Similarly, the situation of being a subject of a state is generalized throughout society so that it does not give rise to specific situational rights. Yet this is only an argument about the foundations of citizenship as membership in the polity. The comprehensive structure of rights which grows on these foundations deviates from simple equality of individual rights for two reasons. First, in order to prevent the undermining of political equality some rights of citizenship will have to be differentiated according to social groups and social situations. Second, the development of general rights of citizenship itself depends upon the formation and mobilization of specifically

discriminated groups as political collectives. We can call collective rights of
citizenship those which meet the second criterion in addition to the first
one. In this section, (1) I distinguish corporate from other collective rights,
(2) examine three critiques of collective rights, and (3) argue that they can
be a motor for extending substantial citizenship.

(1) Just as with the dichotomies of special and general rights, or negative
and positive liberties, the distinction between individual and collective
rights becomes much less obvious the closer one looks at the matter, and it
seems useful to develop a further and more 'gradualist' differentiation on
top of it which is summed up in table 6.

Table 6: Individual and collective rights

type of right	group members as beneficiaries	group as collective actor	group exercising collectively the right
individual	no	no	no
group-specific	yes	no	no
collective	yes	yes	no
corporate	yes	yes	yes

I have already introduced the idea that rights can be group-specific or
situational by taking into account the different social circumstances citizens
find themselves in. Such rights are nevertheless strictly individual as long as
the group or situation serves merely to determine the entitled beneficiaries.
They only acquire the character of a collective right when a group is itself
seen as a social actor. Collective agency can mean that groups (or their
representatives) claim a right for their individual members, that they
mobilize and organize in order to gain the right or to control its
implementation. In some instances such individual rights can also be
granted without overt forms of agency on the part of beneficiaries because
the group is perceived as a powerful potential collective actor.[1] Rights
which identify a group as a collective actor can nonetheless be enjoyed and
exercised by individual members. I suggest using the term 'corporate rights'
if a right is really jointly held and exercised by a group as a whole, by its
organizations or representatives.[2] A trade union may put a decision to go on
strike to the test of a ballot among all its members. But the right to strike is
a genuinely corporate one; it cannot be exercised by individual workers but
only jointly by their association. As an illustration of the full range of
individual and collective rights consider those enjoyed by members of a
recognized national minority. The first and basic category will be perfectly
general and individual rights of citizenship such as free movement in the

whole territory of the state. A second kind of rights are group-specific without distinguishing minority members for the national majority (e.g. unemployment benefits). A third group of rights may be collective ones in referring to this membership but at the same time individual ones in the way they are exercised, e.g. a right to the use of a minority language in court. Finally, rights to regional autonomy or to special representation in parliament are collective ones in the corporate sense.

(2) Once we accept collective rights as an element of citizenship, how can we distinguish them from legal privileges that only serve particular group interests? Citizenship rights do not come with a special label so that we can immediately tell them from others. Some will be written in the constitution. But not all constitutions contain a list of citizenship rights and not all citizenship rights are necessarily constitutional ones. Characterizing a right as one of citizenship is a discursive move in a 'language game'. It raises the stakes on both sides. Those from whom the right is claimed or who are responsible for its enforcement are told that not honouring it will be regarded as a breach of the democratic promise of equality. And those who claim or reassert the right must be able to demonstrate how it is necessary for, or will contribute to, the equal standing of the group's members in the polity.

Both the republican and libertarian traditions have generally abhorred collective rights of either kind because they clearly undermine their conceptions of equal citizenship. Libertarians like Nozick do not at all oppose the formation of communities and associations with specific internal rights and obligations (Nozick, 1974, chapter 10). But no such collective or group ought to claim rights from the state, nor would a minimal state that only protects individuals by its monopoly of violence be in a position to grant these. While libertarians think that collective rights undermine individual liberty, republicans reject them for almost the opposite reason. In their view such rights dilute the undivided loyalty that citizens owe to their state. 'It is therefore essential, if the general will is to be able to make itself known, that there should be no partial society in the state and that each citizen should express only his own opinion' (Rousseau, 1973, II.3, p. 204). Yet Rousseau also saw quite clearly that the state could not simply do away with, or ignore, the political claims of social collectives, and suggested an alternative strategy of reducing their powers by multiplying their numbers: 'But if there are partial societies, it is best to have as many as possible and to prevent them from being unequal' (ibid.).

Why should a liberal democratic approach take a different view? Group-specific and situational rights can be easily justified if it is the state which defines the groups and the situations that must be taken into account in order to equalize substantial membership in the polity. But if groups themselves claim their rights from the state instead and exercise them collectively this appears to imply a threat to equality for three reasons. First and foremost, it seems to contradict the idea that citizenship rights ought to be determined by public reasoning about justice rather than being pushed by mobilization of particular interests and settled in a process of bargaining between groups. Second, the result of such bargaining will mirror the inequalities of power between groups and give those better chances to secure collective rights for themselves which are more numerous, or better organized, or have more resources at their disposal. Third, even if all collectives had equal power in this respect the result of the process would be nevertheless a structure of rights which are not only different between groups but also tie individuals to group membership rather than to citizenship in the enjoyment of such rights. When the same collective that has claimed the right will also exercise it this institutionalizes the collective as a mediator between its individual members and the polity. The political structure of feudal societies was characterized by the mediation of state membership through that of estates. Even if corporate rights in liberal democracy are different because they do not align collectives in a hierarchy, their power will be unequal to the extent that such rights are specific and this might translate into substantial inequalities of individual citizenship.

These are important arguments but they are not strong enough to justify a wholesale rejection of collective rights as an element of equal citizenship. I will raise two objections against this view. The first is that it rests on a static and overly state-centred view of democratic citizenship; the second is that collective and corporate rights are a normal feature of contemporary democracies, which can contribute to equal citizenship as long as they build upon a common structure of individual liberties and rights and improve the position of specifically disadvantaged groups.

(3) The static perspective of citizenship is that of a benevolent state whose authorities intervene in what they perceive as illegitimate discrimination and disadvantage in society, by giving rights not only to individuals but also to victim groups. This view should be able to put up with those collective rights that are claimed by groups but can only be exercised by individuals. Legislators can presumably still adopt the position of neutral arbiters in assessing whether such claims are justified. Mobilization may occasionally be necessary in order to bring the specific complaints of groups to the knowledge of parliamentarians. But when collective rights of this kind have been firmly institutionalized in the law of the state and when their administration is supervised by regular state authorities, they turn into ordinary group-specific rights which do not involve any collective decision-making powers for beneficiaries. The only relevant question, then, is whether such rights really serve to equalize

socially unequal positions or whether they have just been granted as concessions to well-organized political pressure. State authorities who think of themselves as powerful and independent enough to resist such pressure in their pursuit of the common good could easily grant collective rights but never corporate ones.

However, the statist view of citizenship is also a static one and at odds with a democratic outlook as well as with a historic account of the evolution of citizenship. The democratic perspective implies that rights are first generated as claims in the associations and public discourses of citizens before they are legislated and implemented by parliamentary and governmental bodies. The legitimacy of collective rights which are meant to equalize citizenship cannot be adequately judged from a position outside civil society. What is necessary for this judgement is the 'public use of reason' not only by judges or parliamentary delegates but by the citizens themselves (Rawls, 1993a, p. 217).

In the real world, civil society is also a battlefield of conflicting interests and ideologies where public reason generally only restrains the choice of weapons but not necessarily the pursuit of specific goals. And in historical retrospect it is obvious that the enrichment of citizenship and the inclusion of new social groups has never been the independent initiative of benevolent state authorities but the impact of popular social movements and political struggles often fighting for what they saw as *their* rights. While the general outlook of such movements has been mostly much more universalistic than that of their opponents in positions of power, they have invariably been accused by the latter of undermining equal and universal rights by raising particularistic demands. However, collective rights won in such struggles often became later accepted as, or were transformed into, elements of equal citizenship.

One example is provided by T.H. Marshall's analysis how 'industrial citizenship' in the late 19th century served as a catalyst for the development of social rights of citizenship in the 20th. Collective bargaining formed the contested core element of this industrial citizenship. The accusation raised against collective bargaining was that it infringed on the rights of individual workers and employers to conclude contracts on whatever terms they could agree upon. The right claimed by unions thus transformed an individual civil right into a corporate one, exercised by workers' and employers' associations. 'This meant that social progress was being sought by strengthening civil rights, not by creating social rights; through the use of contract in the open market, not through a minimum wage and social security' (Marshall, 1965, p. 103). 'In the case of civil rights, the movement has been in the opposite direction [to political rights], not from the representation of communities to that of individuals, but from the representation of individuals to that of communities' (p. 104). This same development later became the starting-point for the new institutionalization of social rights as an element of individual citizenship. 'Trade unionism created a sort of secondary industrial citizenship, which naturally became imbued with the spirit appropriate to an institution of citizenship. Collective civil rights could be used, not merely for bargaining in the true sense of the term, but for the assertion of basic rights. The position was an impossible one and could be only transitional. Rights are not a proper matter for bargaining' (p. 122). Ultimately, group rights originally won by collective bargaining had to be transformed into proper social entitlements of citizenship.

The case illustrates that collective rights can not only become instrumental in fighting specific exploitation or discrimination, but can also serve to integrate marginalized groups into the polity. In confronting demands of socially or politically excluded groups it is usually the position of the powerful ones which becomes exposed as merely particularistic. Transcending the perspective of particular collective interests becomes only possible when all such groups are adequately represented in political deliberation and decision-making. On the one hand, collective rights may be instrumental in achieving such representation against the odds of continued social marginalization. On the other hand, they have to be made compatible with a fundamental structure of equal individual citizenship. There is no general formula how this may be achieved. We must consider the specific impact of social discrimination, inequality and difference on membership in the polity for different kinds of collectives.

11.2. THE PERMEABILITY OF GROUP BOUNDARIES

A clearer picture of how collective rights can fit into equal individual citizenship will emerge when we look at the kinds of boundaries that divide society into groups claiming different rights. Without going into details I will briefly discuss collective rights for regional populations, age groups, social classes, ethnic and 'racial' minorities and women.[3]

(1) Let me start with the least controversial of collective rights: those which are purely regional or local. All larger contemporary democracies are territorially divided into subunits which often enjoy substantial corporate rights. Differentiated local citizenship in municipalities or federal provinces which are themselves represented as collectives at central state levels is perfectly compatible with equal membership in the polity. This is not only true where states have been formed from federal units that had retained autonomy rights in the contract of unification (as in the USA). One can also argue that substantial citizenship itself requires decentralization even where

a strongly centralized government and administration have been the dominant historical tradition (as in France until recent reforms). Giving regional and local delegates decision-making powers in affairs of regional and local concern, and representing municipalities and provinces in national decisions can be seen as a check on the concentration of power in centralized state bureaucracies. Furthermore, elections and representation at the level of territorial subunits multiply the opportunities for participatory citizenship.

A general rejection of collective and corporate rights would thus have to dismiss some basic features of contemporary democratic constitutions. But there are preconditions for reconciling corporate rights of territorial representation with individual citizenship. First, basic rights and liberties have to be the same throughout the state and the principal legislating body must emerge from direct elections based on equal individual votes. Second, individuals should be able to move and settle freely within the territory. Imagine a federal state where the liberty of free internal movement were suspended. Territorial autonomy would acquire a different character then. Not only would citizens be subject to different local laws which they could not evade by going elsewhere, but inequalities of rights and the powers assumed by local governments over citizens would also increase over time without the harmonizing effects of free entry and the corrective effects of the exit option.[4] Furthermore, with blocked mobility regional populations would become largely endogamous. After a few generations independent societies would emerge within a single state with no ties of kinship stretching across regional borders. This was in fact the situation of most rural populations in agrarian societies. It is certainly impossible to establish a common liberal democratic citizenship in societies which are regionally segregated in this way.

Consider now how demands for collective and corporate rights of young and old generations, of labour, of ethnic and 'racial' minorities and of women could be assessed by parallel criteria. Hardly any of these demands explicitly challenges the constitutional framework of equal rights and liberties. Collective rights are called for in addition to those of equal citizenship and not as a replacement. The real issues are the permeability of boundaries between each of these collectives and the claims to collective representation that can be raised in the name of the group.

(2) There is little controversy about the need for specific rights for young or old citizens who are in several respects disadvantaged when compared with economically active adult citizens. Although the transition is not voluntary in this case, it is automatic and each single individual experiences it during her life. Thus specific generational rights can be distributed equally among citizens when they remain stable over the whole

lifetime of a generation. When rights for retired persons are adopted, the present generation of economically active citizens expects that they will themselves enjoy these rights. When specific rights of children or adolescents are at stake, at least parents will be inclined to balance their own interests against those of the following generation. Yet private self-interest of citizens alone does not lead to institutionalizing generational rights. Why should economically active citizens whose parents have already died, support the present older generation instead of saving from their income in order to buy private insurance for their own old age? Why should those who possess enough resources to take care of their children's future or who are without children agree to redistribution in favour of others' children? It presupposes a stable framework of generational citizenship rights to ensure everybody that she and her children will receive the same benefits when they need them and to oblige those who will never need them to contribute nonetheless towards the welfare of others. The generalization of such obligations is inherent in citizenship of minors and of elderly people and this puts generational rights on a more solid ground than that of individual self-interest. The citizen status of minors has even stronger implications than merely securing the provision for their present needs. It underlines the claims of the next generation to sustainable political institutions, economic resources, and ecological conditions that make it not worse off than those who are now adults. Corresponding obligations do not fall only on parents but are shifted towards the polity as a whole and create a strong responsibility for legislators and governments.[5]

Generational rights may well be collective in the sense that citizens of the same age share certain historical experiences that have shaped characteristic attitudes, and also in the sense that their claims to rights may be represented by specific organizations or movements. However, generational rights are hardly ever corporate ones. They are the rights of individuals which are needed to prevent their marginalization in the polity, because of the physical and mental conditions that characterize their age or because of the social constructions of childhood and retirement. Furthermore, the inherently transitional character of generational membership prevents a stable segregation of society along these lines.

(3) Class divisions in the economy and cultural cleavages along ethnic lines pose more difficult problems. Liberal democratic citizenship responds to inequality of social class by developing social rights, and it copes with different beliefs and cultural ways of life by establishing individual liberties of opinion, speech and association. Class structures may be reconciled with equal citizenship by a policy of equalizing opportunities and levels of basic economic protection. This should increase interclass mobility and thus blur the rigid boundaries of hereditary class membership. Corporate rights for

trade unions and the specific representation of labour in economic policy, making will generally not have the effect of blocking upward mobility and may at the same time help to reduce structural inequalities in the distribution of wealth and power. We may support such rights by arguing with T.H. Marshall that they pave the way for social reform. But they can also be accepted as a permanent element of social citizenship which supplements already established social rights and maintains a constant pressure for redistributing economic growth in favour of the less well-off. As long as trade unions represent the great majority of all populations who depend on income from wage labour there is little difficulty in accepting corporate rights of 'industrial citizenship'. This situation changes with growing numbers of permanently unemployed and marginalized populations whose interests are not at all represented by organized labour. However, the task then is not to smash union power and to deprive them of their corporate rights but to extend social citizenship to the fast-growing margins of society (which will imply redistribution affecting also the well-organized and better-off employees).

Social classes strive for collective and corporate rights because they are not only statistical categories of income and employment; they are also collectives with their own organizations and distinct cultural attributes. In some societies (Britain might still be the best example) classes are almost like ethnic groups. Conversely, ethnic communities are not just groups of people who share a system of beliefs, a language, or tradition. They are often also concentrated in certain regions and specific class positions.[6] The freedom to speak their own language or to practice their religion is therefore generally not enough to integrate them into the polity as equal citizens. Membership in class and ethnic groups is to a large degree inherited rather than achieved or chosen, and both kinds of collectives are relatively stable over generations. Interlinkages between territorial, ethnic and class divisions may divide societies in a way that they turn more and more into a composite aggregate of collectives. The combination of ethnic and territorial division may blow up the unity of pluri-national states and the combination of ethnic and national identity with class often explains why social conflict turns bitter and violent.[7] The constitutional framework of liberal democratic citizenship helps to avoid this by allowing collectives to become organized political actors claiming specific rights for their members and in some cases also exercising these rights themselves on their members' behalf. However, at the end of this road the image of the polity might mirror that of society; it could turn into an aggregate of collectives that are perceived as its constituent parts.

(4) With regard to distinctions of class and ethnicity the danger is that boundaries that are not naturally given can be transformed into quasi-

natural ones. This would produce social segregation which undermines political integration through citizenship. A liberal egalitarian policy should try to make all cultural boundaries permeable so that individuals find ample opportunities to move out of their groups of origin and will also be accepted as full members when joining a different group (see Bauböck, 1994d). Cultural communities would thereby turn into relatively open associations. In addition to permitting changes of membership, the boundaries between groups can be blurred by allowing for multiple affiliations and by extending benefits of membership to those who are formally non-members. This is in fact the same dual strategy as I have outlined in the first part of the book with regard to the legal boundary separating foreign residents from nominal citizens. Increasing the permeability of boundaries of citizenship by optional naturalization, dual citizenship and denizen rights does not erase the distinction between nominal citizens and aliens, but exposes it to individual choices and makes it an internal one within a wider form of substantial citizenship that encompasses everybody with strong social ties of membership. Much the same can be said about the idea of making cultural boundaries within a liberal polity permeable in similar ways. Closed communities would become relatively open voluntary associations. But chosen membership need not be less significant for individuals than an ascribed one, and communities would not be disabled to act as collectives in the polity and to claim specific rights for their members in addition to those enjoyed individually by all citizens.

In a stable liberal democracy with a plurality of cultural and ethnic groups these may therefore enjoy collective rights such as the teaching of their languages in school, or corporate ones like some kind of territorial autonomy and the drawing of parliamentary constituencies so as to secure a mandate for minority candidates. Such rights build on the existing structure of citizenship. In addition to that, ethnicity and nationality is considered a matter of choice more than of destiny. Communication across cultural boundaries will be publicly encouraged, and people will be given opportunities to change affiliations or to adopt none at all without any diminishing of their rights as individual citizens.

And yet there seem to be specific difficulties with supporting collective rights for ethnic groups within a framework of equal citizenship. Territorial autonomy for ethnic and national groups has often been rejected by arguing that this could in the end encourage separation and lead towards dissolving the common polity itself. While this is certainly true it is no relevant objection. The borders of states are no matter of justice and, as I have argued in chapter 7, disputes cannot even always be settled by democratic decision. Democratic citizenship does not include the right to the preservation of the state in its present borders against the clear wish of a local majority to form its own state or to join another one. The challenge of how to integrate corporate rights for minorities into a framework of equal citizenship exists only as long as both parts agree on being members of the same polity. In pluri-national states this agreement might have to be achieved at the price of splitting the polity into a federation of largely autonomous national subunits which are organized in separate territories. In extreme cases comprehensive citizenship rights will be separately institutionalized within each of the parts, whereas those for the territory as a whole might be reduced to universal human rights plus those two rights which are essential for maintaining a common state: the right of free movement between all territories and direct political representation of citizens in a legislative body at the federal level. Where neither of these rights exists the polity is either under authoritarian government (as for example in the Soviet Union before the Gorbachev era) or it is a confederation of democratic states which cannot be characterized as one single polity. When assessed by these criteria the European Union is close to guaranteeing free internal movement but still very far from full political representation of individual citizens in legislation at the Union level.

Around 1900 the Austrian social democratic theorists Karl Renner and Otto Bauer proposed a solution different from regional autonomy for the ethnic and national conflicts that plagued the Hapsburg monarchy. They suggested that the numerous nationalities and minorities of the empire should enjoy national-cultural autonomy instead of, or in addition to, a purely territorial one. Each citizen would declare her national affiliation in an electoral register, and national groups would then be represented in a second chamber of parliament that should take over matters like language education in schools from the federal body of legislators (Renner, 1902, Bauer, 1907). This may seem an attractive idea for organizing the representation of dispersed minorities and it could help to provide a platform for a temporary truce in ongoing national conflicts. But it also implies an uneasy compromise between the representation of individuals as members of national communities and as citizens of the common polity which in the long run must become incompatible with equal citizenship.[8] Rather than wither away, national conflict would be institutionalized as a permanent feature of politics. Territorial autonomy provides at least a frame within which national leaderships become exposed to claims for full rights of citizenship for the whole population, whereas national-cultural autonomy encourages them to play the national card in each political conflict.

Individuals can neither choose the place where they are born nor the primary culture into which they will be socialized. But in mobile and liberal societies they can change both facts later in their lives if they so wish. Where then is the difference between a merely regional form of autonomy and one referring to ethnic and national divisions? Seen from the perspective of individuals, the difference is that the kind of person they are, and even more so the kind of person they are seen to be by others, is much more determined by the cultural than by the purely local environment of their childhood. At least in modern society it is more difficult to fully identify with, and be accepted by, an ethnic or national group different from that of one's origins than to settle in a different place. Seen from the perspective of state interest, ethnic groups have a much stronger potential for challenging the common political framework than merely regional ones. The cultural homogenization of diverse ethnic and territorial populations into national ones is at the origins of modern states (Gellner, 1983). Unlike religious affiliations, cultural ones cannot be simply declared a private matter. A national culture permeates the public sphere of civil society and for its maintenance and development it requires public resources and the institutions of a nation-state. Some pluri-national states have achieved an unstable equilibrium between different collectives that relies on entrenching the latter's corporate rights in a constitutional order. In many other states ethnic minorities which have survived waves of repression or assimilation claim their own collective rights. There are a few successful models for resolving ethnic conflict by granting corporate rights. But these invariably involve some kind of power-sharing in politics rather than a clear separation between a strictly neutral state and the free formation of cultural associations in civil society, as the liberal model of religious tolerance would suggest. Each such solution implies the danger of excluding third groups, especially those who change or combine affiliations, such as families of mixed ethnic origins and immigrants who form new minorities. These are generally perceived as a threat to an established national culture or to an equilibrium among several national groups. The best test for the democratic sustainability of ethnic representation is whether those who are newcomers from outside, who change their affiliations, or who combine several, will also be fully represented as citizens (see Bauböck, 1993b).

Will Kymlicka has formulated a liberal position on minority rights that strongly supports collective and corporate rights but does not share the view that liberties and opportunities of individual change or combination of cultural memberships are crucial. For Kymlicka 'cultural membership is not a means used in the pursuit of one's ends. It is rather the context within which we choose our ends, and come to see their value, and this is a precondition of self-respect, of the sense that one's ends are worth pursuing' (Kymlicka, 1989, p. 192). Minorities have special rights to the protection and promotion of their culture (and, I would add, to political representation in order to achieve this goal) because they are collectively disadvantaged compared with majorities who receive as a free public good the cultural resources they need in order to become self-respecting persons and autonomous citizens. Kymlicka insists that the right of cultural minorities to the protection of their communities does not imply the preservation of particular features of those cultures, as this would limit the members' choices with regard to those features (pp. 167–9). Yet he considers the desire of individuals to leave their cultures and to join different ones only as an effect of enforced assimilation: 'respecting people's own cultural membership and facilitating their transition to another culture are not equally legitimate options' (p. 176).

In a consistently liberal view cultures should not only be seen as a context of choice but also as themselves exposed to two different kinds of choices by their members: those of voice and of exit. Assimilation in the sense of a complete change of cultural affiliation ought to be neither enforced nor promoted, but should be regarded as an individual option by both groups involved. As with naturalization, assimilation will only become optional under fair conditions of choice, i.e. when neither decision generally diminishes social opportunities and the political status of citizenship. This presupposes public recognition and a redistribution of resources in order to enable individuals from a minority background to gain access to the same social positions as the majority and to equal representation in the polity. As long as ethnic minorities are socially and politically discriminated against, there will be a strong incentive for individual members to assimilate into the majority which may ultimately destroy the cultural community. But not all means to preserve a cultural community can be regarded as legitimate.

The most effective ways to ensure the survival of, for example, aboriginal minorities as cultural communities might be to deny them the right to leave their native territory or to institutionalize racist discrimination against those who migrate to the cities. Once these minorities are regarded as citizens of a liberal state both answers are equally unacceptable. While there is little difficulty in supporting the rights of aboriginal people to restrict immigration of others into their territories, it would be quite unacceptable to encourage or permit them to restrict the emigration of their own members. The former right is only a very minor restriction on the equal liberty of free movement for majority citizens who are guaranteed sufficient opportunities to move to other places, while the latter would restrain the liberty of minority members in the most drastic way. In a classical utilitarian calculus the small disadvantage for a large number might outweigh the total denial of free movement for a minority. However, an egalitarian theory of citizenship ought to guarantee for all the most comprehensive level of a basic right that is feasible. As I have already argued in section 10.2 when defending a legal ban on Nazi propaganda, deviations from this norm must be justified and constrained by an overriding concern to secure equal respect for all citizens. It can be easily demonstrated that free immigration into Indian reserves would in fact mean denying Indians living there equal protection for their culture and ways of life.[9] A less than perfect equality of liberty in this case seems to conform perfectly with the general requirements of equalizing membership for people in substantially different social positions.

The problem I see in Kymlicka's stance is not his defence of territorial autonomy for aboriginal minorities, but the fact that he has very little to say about the collective rights of people of aboriginal origins who have moved to the cities where they are discriminated against because of these origins. I suggest that a liberal view ought to combine both kinds of rights. Certain corporate rights may well be tied to a specific territory but collective rights of individuals, including cultural rights and protection against discrimination, ought to be provided throughout a state wherever members of minorities live in sufficient numbers. Dispersed and diaspora minorities are just as much entitled to grow up in a cultural environment where they can develop into self-respecting citizens as territorially concentrated ones. This requires not only protection against discrimination but also public recognition and respect for their cultural choices – not segregated education in a traditional culture of origin as it is defined by the majority's ethnographers, but the necessary resources for creating a sustainable cultural way of life from their diverse migrant and minority experiences.[10] These kinds of minorities cannot be shielded from opportunities to assimilate except by collective discrimination and exclusion. Cultural rights for ethnic minorities should thus be generally provided within a structure of equal citizenship that keeps open the full range of individual choices.

(5) Although we do not choose our cultural affiliation at birth we may change it later in our lives. But people generally cannot change their sex or the colour of their skin. So it seems that the criterion of optional transitions cannot be applied in order to reconcile collective rights for women and for racially discriminated minorities with equal individual citizenship. Of course, both gender roles and 'racial categorization' are social constructs just as ethnicity or class. But in the case of 'race', natural markers are used (or invented as with the invisible Jewish 'race') in order to establish that the distinction is completely unaffected by individual choice or cultural interpretation. While liberal democracy can accommodate ethnic and gender difference and even endorse their public expression, 'racial' distinctions combine two factors fundamentally at odds with a liberal idea of citizenship. First, 'racial' boundaries are sealed against individual choice, transition, or multiple affiliation. 'Races' are perceived as transgenerational and biologically self-reproducing human populations which ought to remain 'pure' and not to mix with each other. This central imperative of purity

construes the boundary between two groups as a clear-cut dichotomy, which is in stark contrast with the actual broad statistical variation of the usual phenotypic markers. Racism creates mutually exclusive categories so that, for example, in the USA any recognizable African American ancestry can lead to being classified as 'black' in contrast with 'white'. Second, the distinction is inherently a vicious one, designed to establish a natural ranking between groups or to exclude a whole population from a polity as naturally unfit for membership.

The ultimate goal must clearly be to erase the social significance of 'racial' distinctions. However, there are two major difficulties in achieving this target. First, a policy which is 'colour blind' in a way that would deny the victim groups specific protection against discrimination and positive support in order to improve their opportunities of access to better positions in society will not come closer to this goal. Equal negative liberties can be established for every citizen without using ascriptive characterizations of groups and collectives. But positive rights have to operate with their own categorization of the group they are meant to protect. That raises the dilemma of how to this without reinforcing the general significance of 'racial' distinctions in society. Antiracist guidelines may, for example, ask employers to show that they do not discriminate against certain groups which will induce firms to register the 'race' of job applicants and employees. In order to monitor discrimination in society, some states have included a question about 'racial' self-categorization in their census.

Second, even distinctions that are racist in their origins can be transformed into ethnic ones in the victim groups' self-definition, when they respond by not only claiming equal rights but by also asserting their own distinct culture. Liberal democracy which abolishes racist exclusion from citizenship promises them equal respect. But ongoing social exclusion undermines the credibility of that pledge. The transformation of racial boundaries into ethnic ones should be understood as a response to this discrepancy. It is a struggle for recognition (Taylor et al., 1993) that can only be waged from within a framework of equal citizenship. Prominent US liberals like Arthur Schlesinger Jr. have accused the movement for African American curricula in schools and universities of reintroducing the same segregation which the civil rights movement had fought against (Schlesinger, 1992). This critique misrepresents the fundamental difference between involuntary exclusion from citizenship and claims for autonomy and corporate representation.

A shift of this struggle to the cultural terrain can certainly undermine common conceptions and institutions of citizenship, especially with regard to school education. But the liberal critique of multiculturalism and minority ethnocentrism has often reacted by defending the 'values of occidental culture' as a national heritage that must be accepted by all minorities without realizing that its own stance mirrors the very image of fundamentalism that it perceives among minority leaders. There is no need or justification for denying these minorities the potential to develop their own high cultural traditions from their peculiar social experience and ways of life. The ethnicization of 'racial' boundaries is not simply their cultural reassertion but potentially also a step towards blurring and undermining them as '*racial*' ones. It means that affiliation can in principle become a matter of choice rather than of destiny. Black culture has influenced the life-style of white middle-class youths everywhere in the Western world while US middle-class professionals of African American origins are certainly strongly assimilated into mainstream white society. Expanding the range of individual choices and encouraging the development of syncretic culture can in itself become an important contribution towards undermining the salience of 'racial' distinctions. Rather than preserving the hegemony of national cultural traditions, the important task is to preserve common and non-segregated educational and cultural institutions by offering minorities adequate representation and responses to their complaints about exclusion. Segregation is the easy way out for both sides when cultural conflicts escalate, but it destroys the commonality of citizenship which is the basis for finding solutions acceptable to all.

The most penetrating critique of an ethnocentric response to racist exclusion among minorities is that it creates opportunities only for small intellectual elites in the educational system but does not address the issues of poverty and social exclusion for the bulk of affected populations. The answer must be a comprehensive programme of inclusion in social citizenship. Collective and corporate rights will have to be an element of any such strategy. Racism cannot be overcome without mobilizing and specially representing victim groups.

(6) Equality of membership excludes neither attention to gender difference nor specific rights against gender discrimination. A large discrepancy between women's share in the electorate and in parliaments or governments manifests an obvious gender bias in the political right to representation. The concentration of female labour in unstable and low-paid jobs requires a gender-specific social policy as a contribution towards equalizing social citizenship. The unequal division of domestic labour undermines women's chances to equal participation in public life and persistent violence against women in the family as well as in streets or places of work threatens their integrity as persons. In all these regards it is not difficult to specify how current patterns of discrimination ought to be changed in order to comply with a norm of equal respect and concern for

citizens of both genders. The difficulty lies in saying how the attribution of individual or collective rights could bring about such changes.

Gender and 'racial' boundaries share in common the notion that individuals cannot choose to which side they want to belong. Gender, generation and ethnic distinctions are similar in that they are not inherently discriminatory. Societies are composed of persons, of men and women belonging to different generations, grown up in, and affiliated to, different cultures, rather than of sexless, ageless and culturally 'disembedded' or 'unencumbered' individuals.[11] There can be no doubt that liberal democratic citizenship includes a 'right to difference' in the sense of not only tolerating but also promoting a plurality of identities and ways of life. A concept of substantial citizenship that combines equality of fundamental rights and differentiated collective rights for socially unequal groups allows for ample representation of these differences in the public political sphere.

Both gender and 'race' are socially constructed categories using biological or phenotypic differences. But of the two only gender difference is built into the conditions of human society as well as into the formation of identity of each individual person. Human beings are gendered just as they are endowed with the faculty of language. What they share with regard to language is not merely the capacity to articulate a range of different sounds, but to build grammatical sentences in different languages. Similarly, as members of societies men and women are not just defined by their biological sexuality, but in a much more complex way by the gender interpretation given to sexual difference in their cultures. While from within modern culture any particular aspect of gender roles may be challenged, the recognition of the difference itself is unavoidable.

In this regard gender is also different from ethnic and cultural boundaries. Societies can be culturally homogeneous or heterogeneous in varying degrees. In different periods of history ethnic distinctions have split societies internally or have defined their external boundaries. Modern societies are shaped in this respect by the opposing forces of the nationalist quest for homogenization and the drive towards territorial expansion and economic integration. But gender difference is always an internal one within each society and within each social community or collective. So how could it be irrelevant to the public identity of citizens as members of a polity?

This does not imply that the expression of such difference requires corporate rights. The very variability of gender roles means that they can become the object of individual choice. Although very few people use modern medical techniques to change their biological sex, quite a number of men and women may develop different sexual orientations and many more may combine in their own lives activities that have been historically strictly divided between genders. Consistent liberalism wants to increase the range of choice in this regard, too, and pledges to protect those from social discrimination or political exclusion whose choices deviate from those of majorities. This would not lead to a vanishing of gender difference, but to seeing it as a polarity inherent in every person that can be developed in different ways.

Group representation inevitably restrains the range for individual difference by homogenizing the image of the represented group. Corporate rights do not address those who deviate from common identities or interests of the collective which exercises them. Our previous discussion has shown that such rights may nevertheless contribute to equal citizenship in three different situations. First, when a cultural or 'racial' boundary that characterizes the group is also a stigma that keeps members in marginalized social positions; second, when corporate rights help to counterbalance specific disadvantage in exchange and bargaining as in the case of trade union rights; and third, when a corporate right improves all citizens' opportunities of participation as in regional representation. As a general social fact gender discrimination does not seem to fit any of these conditions. While I think that there are many reasons for group-specific and collective rights of women, the idea of corporate representation of women's as women at the level of the polity is much less attractive. Once women have overcome exclusion and gender selection in access to representative bodies it becomes obvious that their interests and perspectives are no longer those of a social group that defines itself primarily via the discrimination to which it is subjected. Addressing them only as representatives of women's issues or female views has in fact become a more subtle form of denying women the full range of autonomy and diversity of interests that men have always claimed for themselves. Women will need corporate representation within minorities where 'racial', ethnic or class discrimination combines with that of gender and reinforces the latter. However, at the level of society as a whole the task is rather to free gender perspectives from the rigid divisions of labour and cultural attributes that have their origins in the history of male domination.

11.3. GROUP REPRESENTATION AND INDIVIDUAL CITIZENSHIP

Contemporary feminist theorists have raised a challenge that goes beyond the question of how to fight overt discrimination. They have argued that the alleged gender-neutrality of liberal citizenship actually supports a male vision of the democratic polity and have suggested that an alternative concept of citizenship should represent persons in their different collective identities rather than as individuals. Iris Marion Young has elaborated the latter argument (Young, 1989, 1990). A critical appraisal of her approach will help to point out in which way collective rights ought to remain subordinate to individual ones.

Young attacks the liberal idea that citizenship is rooted in the norms of individual equality. In her view this relies on an idea of justice as impartiality that abstracts from the situated experience of individuals as members of groups (Young, 1989, p. 257, 1990, chapter 4). The impossible ideal of impartiality serves as a liberal cover for the reinforcement of privilege by denying oppressed groups collective rights. Against this Young asserts a strong version of corporate rights of group representation:

> A democratic public, however that is constituted, should provide mechanisms for the effective representation and recognition of the distinct voices and perspectives of those of its constituent groups that are oppressed or disadvantaged within it. Such group representation implies institutional mechanisms and public resources supporting three activities: (1) self-organization of group members so that they gain a sense of collective empowerment and reflective understanding of their collective experience and interests in the context of the society; (2) voicing a group's analysis of how social policy proposals affect them, and generating policy proposals themselves, in institutionalized contexts where decision makers are obliged to show that they have taken these perspectives into consideration; (3) having veto power regarding specific policies that affect a group directly, for example, reproductive rights for women, or use of reservation land for Native Americans (Young, 1989, pp. 261–2).

I will sum up my critique in five points: first, Young's call for group veto rights does not pay attention to the different kinds of group boundaries which require different kinds of rights for inclusion in citizenship; secondly, she remains ambiguous as to whether collective representation compensates for group discrimination or sustains group difference which is constitutive for a democratic polity; third, she avoids the problem that individuals also need rights against the groups which represent their interests; fourth, she creates a myth of groups as comprehensive ways of life which is at odds with a liberal emphasis on choice of affiliations; fifth, her vision of a democratic polity whose members are groups rather than individuals lacks a credible account of what the parts have in common and how cohesion could be achieved without group dominance.

(1) The two kinds of rights mentioned at the end of the above quotation are fundamentally different in how they mediate group membership and individual citizenship. The power of American 'Indians' to veto decisions on the use of reservation land is a clear case of an inherently corporate right. However, the right of women to decide about abortion is, in the terminology I have suggested, a strictly individual group-specific right. It is a negative liberty of non-interference by either the state or the male partner

with an individual choice. At the same time, the right is group-specific in identifying women as the sole bearers of the right to decide. An equal right to decide by both men and women would not allow the resolution of conflicts between them and it is clearly the woman who is more strongly affected and who is also most likely to constrain her own decision for the child's sake. This right is about individual self-determination rather than a group veto power against collective decisions. But probably that is not what Young has in mind. Women's group veto could come into play, for example, when parliaments take a decision on abortion laws or when courts of justice interpret the relevance of constitutional provisions on this issue. Should female members of parliament take a block vote across all party lines which can veto decisions by an overall majority? Should courts of justice not only give a hearing to representatives of women's groups but actually revoke their own decisions when they are vetoed by such groups?

I contend that the proper answer consists of two elements none of which involves a group veto. First, in a democratic polity it is important that the groups most affected by a collectively binding decision are adequately represented among the decision-makers. (An all-male parliament or judiciary is highly likely to take a biased view on a question like abortion.) But in these bodies decisions still ought to be taken by individuals rather than by groups. Second, no matter how decision-making bodies are composed, each individual member is under a moral obligation to consider not only the interests of a group which he or she represents but those of all affected by the decision. This moral imperative becomes stronger when fundamental rights are at stake. In its light, decisions which override the interests of affected but underrepresented groups are illegitimate even when they are taken according to democratic procedural rules. The call for veto power undermines both the claims for adequate representation in the primary decision and the appeal to moral standards in democratic deliberation. It may be justified in a situation of bargaining where interests of the weaker group have to be specially protected. Or it may be necessary when a group needs segregation within the polity for its survival as a distinct group. Group vetoes in decisions about basic rights of citizenship would either turn rights into a matter of bargaining or split the polity into segregated collectives whose own internal rights take precedence over those of citizenship. Inclusion of American 'Indians' in citizenship requires territorial autonomy and group veto rights are implied in this; in contrast, inclusion of women has to be achieved by strengthening their specific individual rights and their participation and representation in all arenas of a democratic public.

(2) Young calls for special representation only of oppressed groups, because 'privileged groups are already represented' (Young, 1989, p. 262).

This suggests that corporate rights are but an instrument for overcoming oppression and are only justified as long as it persists. But Young also believes 'that group difference in modern complex societies is both inevitable and desirable, and that wherever there is group difference, disadvantage or oppression always looms as a possibility' (ibid.). Should group rights in an ideal democratic polity, then, express desirable difference or should they prevent potential discrimination? Maybe Young would answer that there is no need to choose between these two interpretations. However, in a liberal democracy desirable difference which needs the backing of communities can be cultivated in voluntary associations with no claim to special corporate rights, whereas group discrimination and disadvantage may require such rights. We can, for example, say that a plurality of religious and political views is a desirable feature of a liberal society. But this hardly justifies granting congregations or political parties special group rights of the sort suggested by Young. I have also argued above that, independently of gender discrimination, gender difference is significant for social life and for the formation of persons. However, a rigid structure of group representation would reify the distinction by tying it to biological sex. Only one kind of difference is both desirable for a liberal vision of democracy and tied to corporate rights. This is the internal subdivision of a polity into a plurality of regional quasi-polities and the external confederation of polities into transnational quasi-polities. Cultural difference of an ethnic kind and autonomy rights of indigenous groups can be permanently sustained in such a structure. But gender, generational, class, and 'racial' distinctions should not be tied to the formation of separate quasi-polities. In these cases, corporate rights ought to be related to manifest (not merely potential) discrimination.

(3) There is a tension between group representation and individual choice of affiliation. How are those represented who dissent from the majority of the group or who leave the group? Seeing collectives rather than individuals as the constituent parts of a democratic polity deprives individuals of the security that their status as citizens will remain unaffected when they change their collective affiliation and identity. Young rightly emphasizes that self-organization and representation reduces the danger of negative stigmatization. But she ignores the other danger that those who cannot avoid being categorized with a group do not feel represented by its representatives. In a polity composed only of self-organizing groups, all rights would become collective ones and boundary transitions would be excluded or discriminated against.[12]

Democracy works best when groups within civil society organize as internally democratic associations. This strengthens the legitimacy of group representation. But liberal states cannot interfere with the internal rules of voluntary associations in order to make them more democratic. All they can and must do is ensure that membership itself is, in the appropriate way, voluntary in entry and in exit (see chapter 6). No association can legitimately speak on behalf of individuals who have never had a say in whether they want to be represented by the group. Religious congregations are rarely internally democratic, and yet they are perfectly entitled to voice the concerns of their faithful members as long as these have not been forced to convert or are not prevented from leaving. Similar constraints must also be accepted by associations which represent ascriptive social groups such as women or 'racial' minorities. Representatives can only speak on behalf of members but not for those who share the ascriptive trait and yet refuse to support the association. Moreover, for each group there will be normally a plurality of associations of this sort which compete with each other for members. They may enhance the weight of their voice in the public by forming umbrella organizations. But such an association of associations must again be voluntary in the same way.[13]

By insisting that groups should be represented by voluntary associations, liberal democracy gives priority to the rights of individuals over those of groups and confirms that it is individuals rather than groups who are the constitutive members of the polity. The foundation of citizenship is rights which individuals have towards the state and towards each other as members of the polity. Some of their rights will be tied to specific group memberships and a few among these will require collective agency and exercise of rights by associations representing groups. But as citizens they also retain rights against associations which claim to represent their interest. The most fundamental of these are the rights of voluntary entry and exit.

(4) 'A social group is a collective of persons differentiated from at least one other group by cultural forms, practices, or ways of life' (Young, 1990, p. 43). Young's image of groups as 'comprehensive identities and ways of life' is certainly different from that of the closed and self-sufficient rural communities of agrarian society. She asserts that the specific social location of oppressed groups gives them 'a distinctive understanding of all aspects of the society and unique perspectives on social issues' (Young, 1989, p. 267). I agree with that part of her argument. I disagree where she explicitly contrasts social groups not only with aggregates but also with associations. 'The association model also implicitly conceives of the individual as ontologically prior to the collective, as making up, or constituting, groups' (Young, 1990, p. 44). 'Groups, on the other hand, constitute individuals' (p. 45). It should be noted that Young's claim here goes far beyond that raised by liberal communitarians. Saying that the self is constituted by the totality of its social experiences and affiliations at least makes sense as a philosophical position. But claiming that groups within society constitute

the individual seems a completely indefensible statement. In which way, for example, are women 'constituted as individuals' by the group of women? It does not really clarify the issue when Young immediately asserts that individuals are only partly constituted by their group affinities. Let us leave aside that individuals are obviously first shaped by relations to other individuals, namely their parents, brothers and sisters (the family does not fit Young's definition of groups). Even if we could characterize an individual by the multiplicity of her past and present affinities and affiliations to groups we would thereby still say that it is the capacity of combining and transcending group affinity which characterizes her as an autonomous person. No single group can create the individual capacity of being a member of a *different* group from which the group differentiates itself as a comprehensive way of life. Nor could the ensemble of such groups generate that capacity.

From the perspective of a theory of citizenship it is the priority of individual membership over collective rights which has to be asserted in a similar way. No group within a society can claim to be a form of life so comprehensive that it represents as a collective all its members' interests. And the individual rights of citizenship constrain any such claims that might be raised by groups. Nor can a liberal polity pretend to be itself such a collective. Optional emigration and expatriation constrain this claim even in the most perfect democracy. Neither the social groups Young has in mind, nor liberal states, are voluntary associations in the sense that they are founded by consent among individuals and that all members have individually consented to their affiliation. Individuals do not choose to be male or female, white or black, or a citizen of the state where they were born. But each of these unchosen collectives can in different ways be represented by voluntary associations or itself become to some extent associational. This is also the essential precondition for an unfolding of all the virtues Young discovers in the comprehensive perspective of oppressed groups. Only when individuals learn that being a member of that group is not a matter of destiny but can become their own social choice will they be inclined to transcend particularistic group interests and attempt to address 'national' or even global problems from their situated position within society.

(5) Young replaces the republican vision of the democratic polity where citizens share a common past and future and strongly experience their bonds of mutuality[14] with an almost identical image of groups within the polity. But this leaves the question unanswered that troubles contemporary republicans' minds. How can democracy achieve cohesion in a plural society where private interest or loyalty to groups prevails over the search for the common public good?

In contrast with republican or communitarian views, liberal democratic theory does not rely on strong assumptions about what citizens must have in common to form a sustainable polity. They need not share a common past. Newcomers can easily become full citizens without completely assimilating and accepting the national history as their own. What they have to accept is the specific constitutional framework of politics that is a result of past political choices by the citizens and their representatives. Citizens also need not share a common vision of the future. They may pursue different utopias or none at all. Some may also plan to leave and have only a temporary interest in the future of this society. What sustainable democracy requires is, again, a constitutional framework that allows for continuity and creates rational expectations about its continued existence among all citizens, including the inactive or fundamentally dissenting ones.

Citizens share with each other a present status of membership that is embedded in this institutional continuity. Their situation is characterized, on the one hand, by common and, in their core elements, equal rights of citizenship, and, on the other hand, by a common dependence on the state which guarantees these rights. The commonalty of rights and dependence may not make for strong emotional bonds but it allows an integration of the diverse affinities and affiliations to groups and collectives into the broader framework of the polity without overriding them. At the same time it 'constitutes the individual', not as a person, but as a citizen, and protects her to some extent from the effects of economic exploitation, of social oppression, and from the pressure of groups which could restrain her autonomy.

Citizens share not only rights but also dependence. Republicans have tended to glorify this dependence by calling it freedom. They conceive of political dependence as a mutual one among citizens rather than as an asymmetrical one of each citizen on the state. Recent feminist theory has shown a different understanding of relations of dependence. Referring to the findings of moral psychologist Carol Gilligan about a female ethics of care which supplements a male ethics of justice (Gilligan, 1982), Annette Baier criticizes liberal morality for 'its inattention to relations of inequality or its pretence of equality', and for 'its exaggeration of the scope of choice, or its inattention to unchosen relations' (Baier, 1987, p. 54). The relation of citizens to the state is an unequal one characterized by existential dependence, and it is also unchosen from their side. Indeed, in these respects it resembles the first social relations which we have all experienced, that between child and parents (p. 55).

However, the implications of this analogy are far from obvious. Little children who are dependent and even at the mercy of their parents need more than rights. They require attention, care and love, and parents are under a corresponding moral obligation to satisfy their children's emotional needs as well as their physical ones. But are the citizens' needs in their relation of dependence on the state similar to those of children? Should state authorities provide citizens not only with rights but also with attention, care and love? This is not so far-fetched as it may sound. The imagery of the family has been used again and again to characterize the ideal state, and not only by authoritarian regimes. The social democratic founders of the welfare state have frequently interpreted it as a 'peoples' home', a caring institution for the nation.[15] This is not the liberal democratic view. Social citizenship is a matter of rights rather than care; the holders of these rights are individual citizens and in some cases social groups but not the nation as a collective. A bureaucratic state is also not a good provider of care. It can and should provide a *right* to care for abandoned children, for the sick, the disabled and frail elderly who need it. However, the relation of dependence of citizens from the state is not that of helpless children but of autonomous individuals facing an overwhelming power on which they depend for protecting their autonomy. And most of the benefits of civil, political and social citizenship are rights that reinforce the autonomy of citizens within society and towards the state. What is normatively required in relation of dependence between parents and child is care, what is required in the relation of dependence between state and citizens is rights. Care which is not oppressive and possessive will turn the child into an autonomous person; rights presuppose individual autonomy as much as they protect it.[16]

Citizens generally do not choose their membership in a polity but inherit it from their parents or receive it as a gift of birth from the state in whose territory they are born. In this respect citizens may even seem to be much less autonomous than individuals are in relation to their parents. Most children leave their parents' home when they have grown up and if they found a family they themselves choose their partners. Few citizens ever change their relation to their state of birth in this way. However, liberal citizenship extends the scope of choice both with regard to entry and exit and to internal democratic participation so that the relation may come to be affirmed as a voluntary one.

Feminist theories have launched a quite successful critique of liberal theories for turning a blind eye on justice in the world of privacy and the family. At the same time the debate about the ethics of care has shown that in intimate relations there is a 'need for more than justice' (Baier, 1987). However, in my view feminist critique has failed to undermine Rawls's claim that 'justice is the first virtue of social institutions' (Rawls, 1971, p. 3) if only one replaces the term 'social' with 'political'. The requirements of political justice in liberal democracy are not those which would hold among equal but socially unconnected individuals in a state of nature. Nor do they refer primarily to justice between social groups. They are the conditions for a legitimate exercise of political power in modern societies where all permanently depend on protection by this power. The basic requirement of political justice is to provide all members of society with a comprehensive bundle of citizenship rights that takes into account their different social positions and group affiliations but enables them to see themselves as equal individual members of the polity.

Without this baseline of individual equality, a vision of the polity as composed of a plurality of groups would not only perpetuate the struggle for dominance between groups but also reinforce their control over members as their most important source of political power.

NOTES

1. The introduction of social insurance in the 1880s by the conservative governments of Bismarck in Germany and of Taaffe in Austria can be interpreted in this way. Rather than complying with the demands of the socialist and trade union movements, this policy was meant to undermine their autonomous organizations. The beneficiaries of the newly created collective social rights were present as potential actors whose movements had to be controlled.

2. Will Kymlicka points out that minority rights need not be collective in the sense that I call corporate: 'on many definitions of a " collective right", a measure only counts as a collective right if it specifies that the community itself exercises certain powers. But some of the measures which define the special status of aboriginal peoples in Canada do not involve such collectively-exercised rights. Instead, they simply modify and differentially distribute the rights of individuals'. Minority rights 'typically involve both individual and collective rights' (Kymlicka, 1989, p. 139).

3. For an attempt to address the specific paradoxes and dilemmas of collective rights for immigrant, ethnic, and 'racial' minorities see (Bauböck, 1993b, 1994c).

4. The system of closed cities and internal passports in the Soviet Union supported not only the general power of the nomenclatura but also helped to underpin the emergence of strong local and national factions within this bureaucracy. Once the disciplining force of the Communist Party was shaken a nationalist reorientation became a quite natural way for many of these factions to preserve and enhance their power.

5. Generational rights become a much more difficult matter when we are asked to take into account those of future generations yet unborn. When assessed by a criterion of social ties of communication, the rights of generations to come would rest on less firm foundations than those of animals. Equal citizenship is no guideline here either as it can only be realized among contemporaries, but obligations of justice may nevertheless stretch to later generations (see Rawls, 1971, pp. 284–93).

6. The Marxist thesis has been that the working class develops from a class-in-itself to an organized and self-conscious class-for-itself. John Rex parallels this with a movement of ethnic groups towards the same goal but from an opposite starting-point: they move from consciousness of kind towards awareness of their common social interests: 'Classes become like ethnic communities. Ethnic communities become classes' (Rex, 1986, p. 82).

7. 'Classes, however oppressed and exploited, did not overturn the political system when they could not define themselves " ethnically ". Only when a nation became a class, a visible and unequally distributed category in an otherwise mobile system, did it become politically conscious and activist. Only when a class happened to be (more or less) a " nation " did it turn from being a class-in-itself into a class-for-itself, or a nation-for-itself. Neither nations nor classes seem to be political catalysts: only nation-classes or class-nations are such' (Gellner, 1983, p. 121).

8. Otto Bauer was consistent in his theory which saw nationalities as historical communities of fate and culture. His concern was to defuse nationality conflicts so that common class interests could be more easily organized but not to make democratic citizenship a political identity disconnected from, and more important than, national membership.

9. This argument agrees with Kymlicka's conclusions on that point but differs in the emphasis on a framework of equal citizenship, which is dismissed by Kymlicka in his discussion of the problem as a fetish (Kymlicka, 1989, p. 228).

10. Kymlicka regards as the typical minority situation 'a stable and geographically distinct historical community with separate language and culture rendered a minority by conquest or immigration or the redrawing of political boundaries' (p. 258). This leads him to assert that 'in fact, it is the situation of Indians, not blacks, in America which is most relevant for understanding questions of the protection of minorities. It is the special circumstances of American blacks which are anomalous in the international arena' (p. 257). Such remarks only show that Kymlicka's discussion of concrete minority rights does not live up to his own important theoretical contribution to liberal justice concerning cultural membership. A general theory of minority rights ought to take into account the situation of all different kinds of minorities. In North America today these are aboriginal people just as well as French Canadians, Afro-American blacks or Latino and Asian immigrants.

11. The terms are from Michael Sandel's critique of liberal theories of justice (Sandel, 1982).

12. In his only half-satirical description of a communitarian utopia, Stephen Lukes writes perceptively: 'Not all Communitarians fit well into the subcommunitarian categories. Recalcitrant individuals have been known to reject the category by which they are identified or to pretend that they don't belong to it. Some cross or refuse to acknowledge identifying boundaries, and some even reject the very idea of such boundaries. Non-, ex-, trans-, and anti-identifiers are not the happiest people in Communitaria' (Lukes, 1993, p. 25).

13. In exceptional cases group rights might be exercised by organizations with automatic membership. In Austria trade union membership is voluntary but all workers and employees are automatically members in the Chambers of Labour. Such a scheme can only be accepted when there is a broad consensus about the benefits of membership and when the task of the organization is the representation of narrowly specified interests related to social positions rather than of comprehensive identities or ideologies. While the Chambers of Labour more or less meet the latter condition, the broad consensus about automatic membership among their clientele has recently been challenged.

14. See Young's critique of Benjamin Barber (Young, 1989, p. 256, 1990, pp. 116–7).

15 'Maternal thinking' in feminist theory has produced its own versions of the desire for the caring state. See Dietz (1985) for a critique from a republican view of citizenship.

16. Baier concedes that the liberal pretence of equality among *de facto* unequals may lead to 'a desirable protection of the weaker, or more dependent' (Baier, 1987, p. 53). But she criticizes liberal theory for masking the question of moral relations among superiors and inferiors: 'Citizens collectively become equal to states, children are treated as adults-to-be, the ill and dying are treated as continuers of their earlier potent selves, so that their " rights " could be seen as the rights of equals' (ibid.). I would object that citizens have to be regarded and treated as equal *individual* members of the polity rather than as *collectively* equal to states. The latter idea, which is derived from contractarian theory, can be rightly dismissed as a mere ideological mask for the exercise of power. Equality is a norm that applies between the 'inferiors' in this relation of dependence just in the way that Baier says it does for minors, for the ill or dying. It is not merely equality of dependence and subjection but equal membership of individuals who are seen as autonomous agents. Rights (including those to material resources or medical treatment) cannot turn minors or dying persons into autonomous agents. But they are all a state can provide for them and they might facilitate the provision of care by individuals.

12. Rights and Obligations

I have written a lot about rights but very little about obligations. Rights talk of this sort has met two critiques. One is that those who call for more rights must also be willing to accept more obligations because rights and obligations necessarily correspond with each other. I will try to show that this is conceptually misconceived and explain why rights and obligations of citizenship are increasingly disconnected. The second critique maintains that focusing on rights threatens to overburden liberal democracy with calls for ever more state provision, whereas emphasizing obligations would encourage self-reliance on the part of citizens as well as a sense of commitment towards the political community. However, a rights-based political conception of citizenship can inspire civic courage and responsibility, whereas the inverse priority on citizens' obligations generally serves to press for conformity and to justify exclusion or inequality of membership. In the first section I compare obligations with rights; in the second I examine the allocation of obligations which correspond with citizenship and transnational rights.

12.1. RIGHTS, OBLIGATIONS, AND AGENCY

Among the characteristics of obligations which distinguish them from rights are the following: (1) obligations address their bearer as a moral agent; (2) there are no collective obligations, strictly speaking – institutional obligations must specify individual responsibility; (3) neither liberties nor passive rights can be at the same time obligations of the same bearer; (4) obligations narrow the scope for choice by determining actions while rights expand it; (5) positive legal obligations cannot be equalized and generalized in the same way as rights of citizenship; (6) moral and legal obligations are discontinuous whereas moral and legal rights form a continuum.

(1) Rights and obligations refer in different ways to human agency. As I have already explained in section 8.2, rights do not necessarily presuppose that their bearer is an autonomous agent capable of rationally determining her own interests. What is implied in a right is some intrinsic moral worth of the recipient or bearer. The attribution of an obligation, on the other hand, presupposes even more than merely instrumental rationality. Persons who incur an obligation are conceived as moral agents capable of acting

according to generally binding rules. These rules may be moral ones which are assumed to be universally binding, ethical ones which are valid within a specific culture or society, or legal ones valid within a state. The implication of moral capacities explains why obligations are the foundation of moral philosophy, whereas rights are the building blocks of normative political theory that deals with just institutional arrangements.

This might seem too strong as a general statement about obligations. Is the motivation to comply with obligations not reduced to the fear of sanctions in many cases? Are tax payers really conceived as moral agents who have to accept that paying taxes is necessary for the common good or that they are obliged to if others have already complied with their obligation? However, fear of sanctions alone is not sufficient to speak about an obligation. Would we say that a prisoner who performs compulsory labour has an *obligation* to work hard, or that a dog which has been trained to bring back the stick is *obliged* to do so? As with the attribution of moral worth to the bearers of rights, what is essential for an obligation is the attribution of moral capacities rather than the actual motivation of actors. Calling an action an obligation means that there is some generalizable norm according to which the action should be performed by someone who has the moral capacity of accepting this norm as valid.

This does not mean that all obligations are moral ones (just as the attribution of intrinsic moral worth to a bearer of rights does not mean that all rights are moral ones). Paying taxes is primarily a legal obligation. But we will not call it an obligation when it is the naked enforcement of tribute by some occupying power. The code of law assumes generalized validity for norms which have been adopted according to the requisite procedures. If these procedures are those of democratic rule, the assumption is, moreover, that citizens have been adequately represented in the decision and can rationally accept that the law binds their own actions. By presupposing a generalized moral legitimation for the laws that determine their legal obligations, such a political system relieves citizens from the difficult cognitive, motivational and organizational demands they would have to meet if they had to decide autonomously in each single case what their moral duty is (Habermas, 1992, pp. 146–51).

(2) If we focus on the presumption of moral agency, another apparent problem is whether we do not thereby exclude obligations of institutions and organizations. Corporate actors can develop their own interests which are irreducible to those of their individual members, but they cannot be regarded as moral agents. Only individual human beings are capable of moral reasoning. But certainly states, governments, parliaments, enterprises, voluntary associations, etc. can incur obligations? The answer is that moral responsibility is always that of individual representatives, but as

representatives, not as private individuals only. States may, for example, have interests to intervene in, or to stay out of, a foreign conflict, while moral considerations, which take into account the fate of the population in the affected area, could support a course of action contrary to these interests. Considering the impact of state actions on non-members of the state is not an obligation of the state but of the individual ministers or members of parliament who are called upon to take a decision.

This is an example of moral obligations. How about legal ones? Citizenship rights require corresponding institutional legal obligations rather than individual moral ones. The law might, for example, hold the government responsible for providing enough resources for public education and for distributing them so that every child finds a place in a local compulsory school. As this is a legal obligation, the ministries for finance and for education are asked to comply rather than to make their own moral judgement whether this is appropriate. But although the obligation is not a moral one, it is yet an individual one. Institutional obligations always presuppose that there are some individuals who represent the institution, association or organization and can be addressed as moral agents. An unorganized group which has no spokespersons cannot incur an obligation. If a male, white, heterosexual adolescent living in neighbourhood X commits a crime, none of the social groups defined by these markers can be held responsible for this and punishing anybody other than him would be immoral. However, if the ministry of education does not take provisions for building enough schools the minister is responsible for failing to meet the institutional obligation (even if she can identify the subordinate department whose civil servants have caused the failure). A comprehensive bundle of citizenship rights therefore requires a well-organized state administration as the principal addressee of the corresponding obligations so that any institutional responsibility can be located with certain individuals.[1]

If there is any area where the notion of corporate obligations seems to be almost unavoidable it is obligations of states in the international arena emerging from contractual bonds and international law. The Hobbesian image of the sovereign as an artificial person endowed not only with interests but also with a will and moral capacities of his own, conforms to the traditional view of international law and politics. It is not governments but states which incur obligations when they sign a treaty, and future governments will have to honour these obligations (whereas a new parliament may, within the bounds of the constitution, undo the laws of its predecessors or also change the constitution itself). And yet, it is only in a shorthand way that we may speak of the obligations of a state towards other states. We still refer to obligations of persons in positions of power who represent the state in its external relations. These persons are normally obliged to respect that states have a continuity of their own in the international order which ought to be generally maintained as an element of stability conducive to peace. In honouring the obligations of a state they do not submit to its autonomous will but interpret what is required from them as holders of a public office.

In contrast to obligations, corporate rights may be genuinely exercised by a collective rather than by its individual members. Of course, claims for such rights will also be articulated by individuals who are the authorized representatives of a group, association or organization. But the right is not individually theirs in the way an institutional obligation obliges the institution's representatives as individuals.

(3) Rights and obligations refer not only in different ways to human agents but also to the actions themselves. Rights are resources for relatively undetermined action. If I have a right to do *x* I may do *x* or not. This alternative is the liberty aspect of rights which is only absent when a right is simultaneously formulated as an obligation. The right to public education is tied to compulsory schooling. The right to vote is sometimes coupled with a legal obligation to go to the polls. As I have explained in section 10.2, rights need not be alienable in order to be understood as liberties. Liberty is only absent when there is an obligation not to waive the right, as in the two examples just mentioned.

In a liberal perspective these should be evaluated differently. T.H. Marshall characterized compulsory education as 'a personal right combined with a public duty to exercise the right' (Marshall, 1965, p. 90). 'The right to education is a genuine social right of citizenship, because the aim of education during childhood is to shape the future adult. Fundamentally it should be regarded, not as the right of the child to go to school, but as the right of the adult citizen to have been educated' (p. 89). As a child the future adult is not in a position to take her own decision whether she should use or waive this right. She is addressed as a passive holder of an entitlement. Her right requires a corresponding obligation of parents to send her to school, i.e., to claim the right on the child's behalf.[2]

There is no such justification for compulsory voting because citizens should not be treated as children. It is also somewhat inconsistent to think that citizens are mature enough in their political judgement to know for which party or candidate they should cast their vote, but to deny that they could decide for themselves whether they should go to the polls.

In a republican view this argument may be rejected by claiming that the political community has a collective right to the active vote of each of its citizens: 'no person can have a right (except in the purely legal sense) to power over others: every such power which he is allowed to possess, is morally, in the fullest force of the term, a trust. But the exercise of political

function, either as an elector or as a representative, is power over others ...
His vote is not a thing in which he has an option; it has no more to do with
his personal wishes than the verdict of a juryman. It is strictly a matter of
duty; he is bound to give it according to his best and most conscientious
opinion of the public good' (Mill, 1972, 'On Representative Government',
p. 324).[3] This interpretation will be hardly plausible for contemporary
liberals. However, as long as a right is in this way combined with a purely
moral duty to make responsible use of it, its character as a liberty is not yet
jeopardized. Liberty is endangered when the obligation is backed up by
social sanctions and is destroyed when the obligation turns into a legal one.

   Jon Elster notes about this combination: 'It is not always clear whether
something is a good or a burden. Are voting and jury service rights or
obligations? ... the formal right easily turns into an informal obligation'
(Elster, 1990, p. 122). A non-utilitarian normative theory should be able to
characterize rights and obligations without referring to individual
preferences that define something as a good or a burden. Goods and
burdens are not always clearly delimited and may overlap or turn from one
into the other. While the object itself may remain the same, the individual's
attitude towards it can shift or even change signs. Somebody who has given
up smoking may regard a prohibition to smoke in some public place as a
good whereas before she thought of it as a burden. A shift can also be due
to a change in circumstances that turns a former good into a burden, or vice
versa. The obligation to serve in a jury may be seen as a good by the
ambitious citizen, who wants to demonstrate her value to the community,
but it may turn into a burden when she has to deal with a Mafia case in
which jurors receive death threats. The distinction between a right and an
obligation is, however, not tied to this possible change in situations or
individual utilities. Whether something is a right or an obligation can be
exhaustively defined by looking at the relevant norms and rules. If an action
is commanded by moral, social, or legal norms, it is an obligation regardless
of whether the individual enjoys performing it. The test is that only the
actual performance of the required action will be regarded as compliance
with the norm. If an action is within the discretion of the individual and
both performing and not performing it are regarded as satisfying the norm,
then this norm is a liberty right. Both kinds of norms cannot be merged into
a single one without contradiction.

   An obligatory franchise may, however, without contradiction combine
the right to vote, which refers to a free choice of candidates or of alternative
options in a referendum, with an obligation to take part in a vote, which
denies voters the liberty not to go to the polls. This combination preserves
the positive liberty of representation, while it takes away the negative one of
exercising the franchise. The positive right is endangered when citizens are

under pressure to declare publicly their political preferences, and it is destroyed when there is no free choice between competing candidates. Liberal democracy can endorse a moral obligation to go to the polls and it can put up with informal social obligations as long as these do not lead to discrimination of non-voters. But it rejects legal enforcement of this obligation of participation and supports extensive liberty in representation.

(4) In contrast with rights, obligations determine actions. Positive obligations command certain actions, and prohibitions, i.e. negative obligations, tell us what we should not do, or are not allowed to do. Prohibitions translate norms into rules that are intended to restrain the range of human choices and actions to those which are regarded as legitimate. Positive obligations select within this range of permissible choices and actions those which are normatively commanded. 'Determining' is here used in a sense different from 'specifying'. Obligations can be very unspecific, such as the Kantian imperative never to treat other human beings only as means. Conversely, rights may be very specific about the actions they enable or the interferences they prohibit. Nevertheless, the action supported by a right is indeterminate because it is not required whereas obligations determine actions by commanding them. Although obligations may be unspecific, moral reasoning about them will lead to the selection of one single right answer in standard cases. In contrast with moral obligations, legal ones have to be specific enough to serve as a reference for non-arbitrary judicial sentences.

The graphic image of obligations discourse is an initial universe of unrestrained options. Because 'ought implies can' a first line is drawn that eliminates those which can be regarded as impossible and then a second one excluding everything prohibited from consideration. The remaining possible courses of action will be located in a circle that is successively drawn narrower until we finally find the solution to what we should do.

Rights discourse pursues the opposite goal. Its target is to extend the range of choice and action.[4] The starting-point is not a universe of possibilities but human beings as social animals whose existential needs can only be satisfied by other human beings. In a first step, they are attributed positive rights to those resources they need in order to become autonomous agents. Positive rights thus expand a space of concrete possibilities which is extremely narrow for the rightless outcast of society. In a second step, this range is widened by specifying negatively which of their actions may not be prohibited or interfered with and the performance of which actions may not be commanded, thus leaving the actors free to do whatever they like outside the no-go areas demarcated by others' rights.

The shrinking space of obligations and the expanding space of rights can neither be thought of as completely separate from each other nor do they combine so that both tendencies simply cancel each other out. In deontological philosophy the individual is seen as an autonomous moral agent from the very start. Moral rights are derived from, and constrained by, moral duties, so as to promote justice rather than merely respect for the others' rights. In post-contractarian political theory of liberal democracy this sequence is reversed. We may have moral obligations before we have moral rights, but we do not have any political obligations unless we enjoy rights. Nobody can be autonomous in a polity without being attributed fundamental rights by the institutions of this polity. Individuals must first be turned into citizens in the substantial sense, i.e. they must be addressed as bearers of rights that establish their freedom of choice and agency. This is the precondition for addressing them also as moral agents.

In this latter role, citizens are not only expected to comply with legal prohibitions and obligations to which they could rationally consent, but also to introduce their own judgements into deliberations about collectively binding decisions for the polity. But this essential obligation of citizenship is a moral, not a legal one. It is different from the combination discussed above, where a right is no longer a liberty because there is a legal prohibition against waiving it. The political obligation to form an independent judgement on the issues concerning the polity as a whole is combined with a legal right not to do so or to remain silent about one's opinions. This obligation cannot be enforced by translating it into a legal one, without interfering with individual autonomy that is presupposed in liberal justification of democratic participation.

(5) The norms of equality and inclusiveness apply in different ways to rights and obligations. Equal and generalized rights form the core of human rights and substantial citizenship, but only negative or highly unspecific obligations can be equalized and universalized. Moral commands and those legal prohibitions which correspond to a negative liberty are generally addressed to all. People are equally obliged to save the lives of others if they can do so with little risk for themselves, or to stay out of other persons' homes if they are not invited in. But as we reach the narrower core of positive obligations which determine specific actions, we must increasingly take into account the agents' positions and resources.

In previous chapters I have also argued for a limited differentiation of rights. But this differentiation builds upon a strong core of equal rights and is entirely instrumental for achieving a more comprehensive form of equality. In a complex and divided society some rights have to be unequal in order to equalize the worth of citizenship. Most legal obligations of citizenship no longer convey this sense of belonging to a community of equal members. They are rather perceived as necessary burdens, as a tribute that must be paid to the state and that ought to be distributed fairly and without diminishing citizens' rights.

A fair allocation of obligations among individual members of a group will be equal and inclusive if all are equally situated with regard to their opportunities to perform the required action. An association may to some extent disregard inequalities of resources by creating a kind of 'situational equality' among its members with regard to the activities they share. The members of a club may have perfectly equal obligations to pay membership fees or to perform some duty for the club, although they have different resources of income and leisure time. However, in order to maintain equality of obligations, clubs will also be selective in admissions so that the distribution of relevant resources from which members make their contributions does not become too unequal. In combination with selective admission, equal positive obligations support the idea of equal membership and strengthen loyalty and cohesion in voluntary associations.

Republican conceptions of citizenship see the polity as a voluntary association or a joint enterprise of this sort. They have tended to combine equal rights with equal obligations, arguing sometimes that the former entail the latter (which is logically mistaken, as I will show in the following section). The emphasis on equal obligations in turn provides a legitimation for excluding those who do not possess the requisite resources in order to perform these duties. If all citizens should perform military service in order to be equally involved in the defence of the state, and if women are presumed to be unfit for the army, then the latter must remain excluded from citizenship as well. If foreigners cannot be drafted because they are subject to another sovereign they should not be given citizen rights. If all citizens ought to pay taxes so as to have an equal stake in the economic success of the community, it makes sense to deny low-paid workers access to active citizenship. Moreover, preferably taxes should be equal lump sums per head or proportional to income, because these schemes will strengthen the general awareness of equal obligations. In their desire to justify equal obligations, republicans have not only reinterpreted rights as obligations (as John Stuart Mill did with regard to the franchise) but also obligations as rights. For the patriotic citizen, military service ought to be conceived as a right as well as an obligation. There are limits to the plausibility of this *quid pro quo*. Although tax paying is a lighter burden than risking one's life in a war, it has rarely been seen as a right because income is just too strongly tied to private interest.

Liberal democratic citizenship supports a very different conception of what equal membership implies. It gives priority to inclusion and to equalization of basic rights and accepts that this will lead to unequal positive legal obligations. As I have already explained in section 10.2,

taxation of income ought to be progressive rather than equal and those
below the poverty line should be exempted without any negative impact on
their status as citizens. So this obligation is neither equal nor inclusive.
Military service is a question of justifiable requirements for defence
policies. Whether a state has a professional army or relies on general
conscription will depend on a number of contingent circumstances. If there
is a need for conscription there should also be a possibility for
conscientious objection. Apart from situations of a just war of defence that
affects the territory of the state, military service should never be an
obligation which is required for citizenship, or is enforced under the threat
of denaturalization.[5] This does not mean that considerations of equality are
irrelevant for the allocation of obligations. Neither the rules for taxation nor
for military drafts can be arbitrary or only determined by considerations of
efficiency from the point of view of state budgets or defence. However, it is
attention to equal rights and equal respect rather than the equalization of
obligations themselves which restrains policies in these areas. In other cases
it is important to equalize obligations but only because they are intimately
tied to equal rights. Compulsory schooling is, once again, the obvious
example. For a still largely agrarian population which traditionally relies on
child labour this will imply considerable burdens. General enforcement of
an equal obligation may require special compensation for those who can
hardly afford to comply.

If political legitimation in a democracy were achieved by the individual
consent of each citizen to membership, this would strongly back demands
for equal rights as well as obligations. Those who do not wish to incur the
obligations, or who feel unable to bear them, could simply remain as
foreigners outside the polity (see section 5.2). And those who join would
share equally in all the specific benefits and burdens of membership. They
could well remain unequal in their private possessions and with regard to
those rights and obligations that result from private transactions and
contracts, but they would rationally expect to have equal obligations in a
polity which they have all entered as equals because of their own free
choice. Equality of obligations is not only supported by this Lockean notion
of social contract but also by republican models of direct democracy where
citizens really share in ruling and being ruled. Political legitimation of
power which citizens themselves exercise mutually over each other requires
equal obligations as well as equal rights.

A liberal democracy is not a voluntary association or a joint enterprise of
its citizens. It holds a territorial monopoly of power over society and most
citizens are attributed membership at birth. Their conditional right of exit
does not offset their existential dependence on the state as long as they stay.
In an inevitably asymmetric relation of state power over individual citizens,

rights and obligations assume a contrasting role. Obligations confirm the grip of power and its alienation from the individual who is unable to determine herself what her appropriate duties towards the community would be. Legal obligations become in this way opposed to moral ones. Citizens are not only relieved of the burden of making their own moral decisions, but also experience the loss of individual autonomy in a modern state. Rights of citizenship, on the other hand, are what recreates autonomy within this iron cage. Political legitimation of power can therefore only be legitimated by substantial rights (including those of exit), but not by obligations. The contractarian idea of equality derived from individual consent *to* membership is replaced by the democratic idea of equal rights *of* membership. Equal rights indirectly restrain the permissible inequality of obligations. No obligation may undermine the citizen's status as a bearer of rights (soldiers, too, must be treated as citizens rather than as subjects) and those obligations which are necessary contributions towards maintaining the institutions of the state have to be adjusted to citizens' capacities to contribute.

(6) The tendency of contemporary liberal citizenship to make rights independent from duties parallels a second one to disconnect moral from legal obligations. Both were registered by T.H. Marshall although he did not give a full explanation for them. Marshall noted 'the changing balance between rights and duties. Rights have been multiplied, and they are precise. Each individual knows just what he is entitled to claim' (Marshall, 1965, p. 129). The duties to pay taxes and social insurance, of compulsory education and military service are mentioned as determinate ones. 'The other duties are vague, and are included in the general obligation to live the life of a good citizen, giving such service as one can to promote the welfare of the community' (ibid.).

Interpreting Marshall as deploring this disconnection,[6] Morris Janowitz presents an extended list of obligations[7] and restates the classical republican view: 'Citizenship is a pattern and a rough balance between rights and obligations in order to make possible the shared process of ruling and being ruled' (Janowitz, 1980, p. 3). The basic error resulting from an Aristotelian definition of citizenship is to identify civic virtues and responsibilities with legal obligations imposed by the state. In modern democracy legal obligations primarily specify what is implied in being ruled, but are no longer connected to ruling in turn (exemplified by rotation in public office). The balance of rights and duties of the ancient city-state is no longer possible or even desirable. With the exception of randomly selected juries, the legal obligations of citizens towards the state (of tax paying, military service, and generally observing the law) are those of citizens being ruled and not those of citizen-rulers. They do not depend on the democratic character of the political system and remain more or less the same in authoritarian regimes. This is also true for obligations to participate in elections, which are more common in authoritarian than in democratic regimes.

In addition to legal obligations towards the state, citizens have different kinds of private obligations towards others resulting from contract or special relationship, which may be enforced by the state. Some of these obligations are not of a legal kind but may still be backed up by informal social enforcement. In the small worlds of face-to-face communities, malicious gossip, dishonour, or simply being no longer talked to may be very efficient sanctions for enforcing social obligations.

Towards the wider society of fellow citizens we have moral obligations of a different kind. The locus of these obligations is the public realm of civil society. This is neither an ensemble of organized and powerful institutions nor a closed national community which mirrors the smaller ones of families and peer groups, but an open social space where citizens meet as strangers rather than as subjects, relatives or friends. The others towards whom we are morally obliged have no formal legal instruments and only weak informal social means for imposing sanctions.

In republican polities the competitive nature of the distribution of honour creates its own rewards and sanctions which spur individual efforts. Those who stand in the spotlight of public attention can therefore be easily punished if they fail to meet their moral obligation to do the best they can for the community. (In a modern republican polity it might be enough just to stop reporting about them.) The problem is that direct democracy is hardly superior to representative democracy in promoting the selection of candidates according to their political virtues. Even in classical Athens it was mostly not excellence in this regard which brought individuals into prominent positions.

In contrast with an Aristotelian or Arendtian idea of the polity, civic virtue in liberal democracy does not show in the striving for excellence but rather in the decency and honesty of ordinary citizens who are confronted with political and moral choices in the public realm. John Rawls characterizes one aspect of this obligation very well: 'the ideal of citizenship imposes a moral, not a legal duty – the duty of civility – to be able to explain to one another those fundamental questions how the principles and policies they advocate and vote for can be supported by the political values of public reason. This duty also involves a willingness to listen to others and a fairmindedness in deciding when accommodations to their views should reasonably be made' (Rawls, 1993a, p. 216). Rawls discusses this duty under the ideal conditions of a nearly just society where 'the political conception of justice and the ideal of honoring public reason mutually support one another' (p. 252). Under non-ideal conditions, civic duty implies a second obligation, which in contrast with the first kind requires the virtue of civic courage.[8] That is the obligation to maintain the conditions for civility by resisting unjust and tyrannical exercise of political power. It may involve hard choices and severe sacrifices such as those citizens had to make when hiding Jews from the Nazis or when refusing to denounce their friends to Stalin's police. Yet there are enough occasions for practising this kind of civic virtue in Western democracies, too. Giving shelter to refugees who have received deportation orders can be mentioned as an example that has become relevant again in many Western European countries and in the USA.

A duty of resistance seems to be at odds with the core obligation of citizenship in political theory: the duty to obey the law. As a legal obligation this is beyond dispute; it is implied in the very concept of law and it is a mere tautology to say that the law obliges us to obey the law. Whether there is also a general moral obligation to obey the law is a matter of considerable disagreement among liberal theorists. The test case is, of course, when the legal obligation collides with our moral convictions. Is there a right or even a duty to disobey a law that we think is unjust? Ronald Dworkin asserts that 'In our society a man does sometimes have the right, in the strong sense [of a moral right], to disobey the law' (Dworkin, 1977, p. 192). 'Both conservatives and liberals suppose that in a society which is generally decent everyone has a duty to obey the law, whatever it is ... But this general duty is almost incoherent in a society that recognizes rights' (ibid.). John Rawls agrees that 'There is ... no political obligation, strictly speaking, for citizens generally' (Rawls, 1971, p. 114) which could be derived from consent or voluntary acceptance of benefits in a scheme of co-operation. But he thinks that 'in a situation of near justice anyway, we normally have a duty to comply with unjust laws in virtue of our duty to support a just constitution' (Rawls, 1971, p. 354).[9] Rawls considers this as a 'natural duty' which nevertheless leaves sufficient scope for a justification of civil disobedience or conscientious objection (pp. 363–91).[10] John Dunn discusses several possible explanations for how citizens could acquire a moral duty to obey the law: from prudence, fidelity, gratitude, fairness, or consent. Prudence would have to rely 'on real advantages for each and every subject in his own subjection' (Dunn, 1991, p. 41), fidelity on actually given promise. 'Duties of gratitude and fairness may be conceptually well-shaped to restrain the hastiness and self-righteousness of an ultra-individualistic political culture. But within such a culture they can only appear as moralizing external reasons and of correspondingly questionable moral force. Only the eminently individualistic criterion of consent retains comfortable force in the face of this culture. But its political significance is sharply restricted by the severely limited presence of anything that could readily be mistaken for consent in the practical political life of modern societies' (p. 46).

I do not wish to take a strong position in this debate. All states operate on the assumption of a general obligation to obey the law. This is, again, not a specific obligation of democracy. Whether this claim to obedience can also find support in normative theory will of course depend on the nature of the regime. Any theory which derives generalized legitimation for this command from a fictitious social contract, presumed natural bonds of community, or the utility of submitting to state power, regardless of its benign or malign character must certainly be rejected. The factual legal obligation to obey the law under any regime ought to be clearly distinguished from whatever normative justification we can give for generally obeying laws in a 'nearly just' liberal democracy.

The discontinuity between moral and legal duties of citizenship contrasts with the continuity between moral and legal rights explained in section 8.1. A claim to a right is always directed at social recognition that can be translated into a legal provision without contradicting or fundamentally changing the intention of the appeal. Turning certain moral rights into legal ones may not be desirable. Calling for courts to be arbiters in minor conflicts between individuals can be destructive for the generation of trust in social relations, and for the development of social skills to settle conflict by fair agreement. But claiming a moral right implies the appeal to an external arbiter, protector, or judge, be it God, elders, group leaders or the state. All that is required in the transformation to legal rights is to reformulate the right so that it can be administered as a general law within a polity. The moral obligations of citizenship are not translatable into legal ones in this way. An obligation is an appeal to the bearer of the obligation as a moral being. A legal obligation is addressed to citizens by the legislator, but a moral obligation they have to address to themselves. Calling on external agents to enforce it would profoundly alter or distort the nature of the command. The duties of civility and the virtues of civic courage are moral obligations but cannot be prescribed by the law. And the debate about a political obligation to obey the law is of course not concerned with introducing a corresponding legal obligation that exists anyway, but inversely with specifying the conditions under which the legal obligation could also be justified as a moral one.

12.2. THE ALLOCATION OF OBLIGATIONS

Who has to fulfil the obligations that are necessary in order to maintain the provision of citizenship rights? I will argue (1) that the corresponding obligations are institutional ones whereas those of citizens are indirect and supportive; (2) that liberal democratic citizenship provides an institutional framework for solving the problems of imperfectly allocated obligations; that it need not undermine the motivation of citizens to comply with their legal (3) and moral (4) obligations; and (5) that a transnational conception of citizenship can help to address the problem of unallocated obligations in issues of transnational justice. Finally, (6) I will apply this rights-based approach to the case of refugees and asylum seekers.

(1) A right and an obligation correspond with each other if an actor A's enjoyment of the right depends upon an actor B's performance of a commanded action or forbearance from a prohibited one. Correspondence must be distinguished from conditionality, which means that one and the same actor is granted a right only if she complies with an obligation. Authors who want to derive citizenship rights from prior obligations often seem to confuse both relations or assume that the former implies the latter.

This would be true if citizenship could be understood as membership in a voluntary scheme of mutual assistance similar to those developed by early workers, movements or small peasant co-operatives. If a number of farmers jointly buy a tractor, the right of farmer A to use it corresponds with an obligation of all others to pass it on when it is A's turn, and A's right is conditional upon contributing a monthly fee for the costs of purchase and maintenance of the machinery. When the co-operative turns into a larger enterprise it becomes a corporate actor which concludes separate contracts with each individual farmer. The right to borrow a tractor will still be conditional upon an obligation to pay fees. However, this right no longer corresponds directly with obligations of other members of the association. The obligation to lend out machinery on the terms specified in the contract has become that of the co-operative itself rather than of its individual members.

Citizenship is one further step removed from the model of mutual assistance. Not only are the obligations that correspond with membership rights clearly those of state administrations rather than those of the other citizens, but rights are also no longer conditional upon meeting obligations, as they are in the contract model of private economic transactions. Liberal democratic citizenship makes the allocation of rights as unconditional and inclusive as the exercise of state power over resident populations. The obligations of citizens towards one another are primarily moral ones. They are important for sustaining a democratic political system but they do not correspond with their rights guaranteed by the constitutional order. Their obligations towards the state are primarily legal ones but their rights as citizens are not strictly conditional upon fulfilling these obligations. They may be punished for refusing or evading them but they will thereby neither lose their basic rights as citizens nor their status of nominal membership.

The priority for rights in a liberal democracy means that generally obligations are conditional upon rights but not vice versa. The North American revolution started with the rallying cry 'no taxation without representation'. At that time the inverse rule was taken for granted, too: 'no representation without taxation'. Today the demand for local voting rights of resident foreigners has often been expressed in terms similar to the former slogan[11] while property qualifications for the franchise are no longer considered acceptable. However, even the conditionality of obligations upon rights is a rather loose one in many respects. It is not a relation between specific rights and obligations but a general condition of democratic legitimation for obligations. The obligation to pay taxes depends not on the right to vote but, on the one hand, on the general legitimacy of a democratic constitutional order and, on the other hand, on a fair allocation of necessary burdens.

Citizenship rights correspond directly with institutionalized obligations of states and state authorities. The common obligations of individual citizens towards the state can be regarded as necessary contributions for maintaining a state's capacity to meet its institutional obligations to provide citizens with a comprehensive bundle of rights. In an important statement on transnational obligations, Henry Shue has pointed out that many rights can be better fulfilled by institutional rather than individual obligations for two reasons: efficiency and respite. Organizations make it possible to pool resources and to use them more economically than unorganized individuals ever could. And the performance of no individual's duties is improved 'by his being so preoccupied with them that the remainder of his life is deprived of satisfaction ... We are all entitled to some off-duty time' (Shue, 1988, p. 697). When institutions are the best providers of rights and bear the corresponding obligations, individuals may have indirect obligations: 'duties to create, maintain, and enhance institutions that directly fulfil rights' (p. 696).

Shue argues from the example of positive obligations to provide for basic welfare where charitable donations by individuals could never lead to adequate safeguards for rights. With regard to other rights, states are often not only comparatively better equipped to fulfil obligations but the only possible providers. Collective internal security cannot be maintained in a state of nature where everybody has the right to defend herself with all means available and to be a judge in her own case. It requires a state monopoly of legitimate violence to guarantee a right to security for all. In contrast with welfare rights, efforts by individuals to relieve the state of its institutional obligation by taking care of their own right to security or volunteering to assist others to maintain theirs will undermine efforts to maintain civil peace. The indirect obligations of citizens are legal and enforceable ones to comply with commands of a power that is meant to protect them. More generally speaking, for a theory of citizenship rights states cannot be regarded merely as *mediating* institutions (Shue, 1988) for the duties of individuals so that their rights can be fulfilled. The polity is the only framework within which rights of citizenship can be generated in the first place, and the corresponding obligations fall therefore 'naturally' upon the state.

(2) There are rights without corresponding obligations and obligations without corresponding rights. The first are of lesser importance for a theory of citizenship. These are what Wesley Hohfeld called privileges or what I have analysed as liberties at 'zero positivity' (see section 8.3). Obligations without corresponding rights are called imperfect duties. In John Stuart Mill's words they mark off justice from morality: 'duties of perfect obligation are those duties in virtue of which a correlative right resides in some person or persons; duties of imperfect obligation are those moral obligations which do not give birth to any right' (Mill, 1972, 'Utilitarianism', p. 51). '[A] right in some person, correlative to the moral obligation ... constitutes the specific difference between justice, and generosity or beneficence' (p. 52).

As many other dichotomies in moral philosophy that of perfect and imperfect obligation is much less clear-cut than it appears at first sight. At the one extreme end of the spectrum there are virtues rather than duties: a disposition for supererogatory actions which are beneficial for others towards whom we have neither universal nor special obligations and which may involve substantial costs or risks for ourselves. These actions are praiseworthy, but optional (O'Neill, 1991, p. 287), and an optional obligation would be a contradiction in terms. At the other pole, obligations perfectly correspond with rights in that both the commanded action and the responsible agents are determined by the very nature of a right. Such perfect obligations may be special or universal in the same way as rights (see section 9.1). Negative liberties normally correspond with universal obligations of non-interference, but they may in certain cases imply special obligations, e.g. a court injunction for a husband who has beaten his wife not to contact her again after they have divorced. Positive rights quite often correspond with general rather than special obligations: everybody who is in a position to save a life without risk to her own is obliged to do so.[12] When a duty is formulated as a legal obligation there will normally be a corresponding right of someone who is the beneficiary of the performance of the obligation, or who is entitled to enforce the obligation on behalf of a potential beneficiary. The difficult cases lie in the middle range between virtues of supererogation and perfect obligations. Obligations can be 'imperfect' in two different ways: either because we cannot identify the bearers of a corresponding right or because we cannot identify the bearers of the obligation themselves. Extending a useful terminology suggested by Onora O'Neill, we might speak of unallocated rights in the former case and of unallocated, or rather of imperfectly allocated, obligations in the latter.

But what would be an unallocated right? Suppose we maintain that the rich have an obligation of being generous by giving some of their wealth for non-profit purposes, but they are free to spend it on any of a large class of different tasks (ranging from famine relief to arts donations for public museums). Generosity of this kind is not supererogatory but can be well expected from everyone in that position. As the duty is only to give none of the potential recipients has a right to the donation, and because it is a voluntary rather than a legal obligation the state has no right to enforce it even on behalf of all the potential recipients taken together. Who else, then, could then be attributed a corresponding right? Religious views might see it as a right of God, humanistic philosophies as a right of humanity and nationalist ones as a right of the national community. Yet none of these views really needs the notion of rights. They reduce them to the mere correlate of obligations and eliminate thereby the most important characteristic of rights: their attribution of intrinsic moral worth. Defining rights in the terms I have suggested in section 8.1 presupposes that we can identify their bearers or targets, and that either they themselves can claim their rights or some other persons or institutions can do this on their behalf. This is different with imperfectly allocated obligations where we can clearly identify the right and its bearers, but not who has to comply with the corresponding obligation. Table 7 sums up these categories of obligation in a two-by-two scheme.

Table 7: Perfect and imperfect obligations

| | | corresponding rights | |
		yes	*no*
bearer of obligation	*determinate*	perfect	imperfect
	indeterminate	unallocated	supererogatory

The examples explored by Shue and O'Neill are basic welfare rights, or more specifically the right to food in a world where there is enough to feed everybody (Shue, 1980, 1988, O'Neill, 1986, 1991). In contrast with imperfect duties it makes sense to speak about an individual human right not to be exposed to starvation. This right is not reducible to the correlate of an obligation of those who are well fed to be generous. Normally this universal right correlates with special obligations. Different from universal obligations not to interfere with negative liberties, food must be provided by specific agents. But if a local structure of obligations such as those of kin, neighbourhood, regional administration and the state has broken down or is no longer willing or capable of maintaining adequate levels of provision, who will then be responsible for complying with the obligation? We might think that it then turns into a universal one so that everybody with sufficient resources would be obliged to take action to secure the right. But this is no answer to the question of how to get food to the single starving family. The problem obviously requires an allocation of obligations with international institutions and organizations. The duties of individuals and also of individual states will then become mediated and indirect ones, in the same way as explained above for obligations of citizenship.

That suggests a more general proposition that polities are institutional ensembles for resolving the problem of imperfectly allocated obligations within a territorially limited population. The generalized responsibility of state agencies for citizenship rights makes it possible to assign direct and indirect duties so that rights can be guaranteed which would otherwise remain empty declarations. At the same time this framework creates incentives to transform imperfect duties into unallocated ones, i.e., to claim rights where before there had been only moral obligations, in the expectation that it is the task of states to solve the allocation problems. The evolution of citizenship is in this way driven by claims for rights within political communities. This is a development very different from a general moral improvement of humanity by educating people to acknowledge their (imperfect) obligations towards one another. If we derive obligations from rights we will adopt another kind of policy than if we aim merely to motivate and enable people to comply with their imperfect obligations.[13] The former path leads towards institutional solutions, whereas the latter points towards moral pedagogy.

A theory of this kind has to face three relevant critiques. First, the framework of liberal democracy with its emphasis on rights might seduce citizens to 'invent' rights which overburden the state's capacity to meet them. and to avoid indirect obligations necessary to sustain the framework of rights. Second, institutional solutions for unallocated obligations might crowd out private initiative driven by a sense of moral obligation. Third, if such solutions can only be found within the framework of a polity, they might be unworkable for the most urgent problem of how to secure basic human rights on an international scale, and we could be forced to rely on the language of imperfect duties in this area.

(3) Unquestionably the disconnection of rights from obligations and of legal from moral obligations in liberal democracy has its drawbacks. Citizens develop a free-rider attitude with regard to rights, and simply try to avoid obligations when they no longer feel that their legal obligations are justified, either because they are preconditions for their enjoyment of rights, or because they are immediately derived from moral obligations which they acknowledge. This will increase the costs of enforcement. Excessive enforcement against broad reluctance or resistance will, however, diminish consent about the legitimacy of obligations because then they appear not only disconnected from, but directly opposed to, citizenship rights. This vicious circle can only be broken if liberal democracy also has an impact on citizens' preferences and motivations. Republicans and communitarians ask too much from citizens in requiring them to subordinate their individual good to the common one. Neoliberals ask too little when they assume that legal obligations could ever be reduced to those that correspond to the task of maintaining security. The socialist tradition has suggested that extensive redistribution of wealth will lead to a profound change in preferences, or in fact, to the emergence of community-oriented new men and new women. None of these approaches has given a convincing account of basic human and citizen rights, and of the institutional arrangements that could legitimate the exercise of political power in modern societies (see Lukes, 1993). The liberal democratic tradition does somewhat better in this regard. However, it relies on a rather messy combination of ideas from all these rival traditions with regard to the question how these institutions can shape individual preferences so that they will support their maintenance.

Liberal democrats expect that a combination of basic negative liberties, of substantial welfare rights and of political rights of participation and representation will create motivations to comply with obligations that are necessary in order to sustain political institutions guaranteeing all these rights. They can point to empirical cases where a lack of one or more of these elements of citizenship has tended to undermine necessary compliance with legal obligations as well as a sense of civic duties towards other citizens. But they have rarely succeeded in explaining how institutional arrangements actually shape individual preferences. Claus Offe and Ulrich Preuß suggest that addressing this task could point the way towards further institutional reforms. They propose that the focus of such reform is on the micro-contexts of civil society. In this sphere, a radicalization of democracy may still be possible that puts a premium on the formation of 'reflective preferences' that can be defended in democratic deliberation. Institutional designs based upon a principle of reciprocity (as can be found in voluntary associations, co-operative ventures and social movements) could stimulate such preference learning and preference formation among citizens (Offe and Preuß, 1991, pp. 167–71). The approach I have defended in this book focuses on the macro-context of democracy and the unresolved tasks of inclusion in membership and extension of rights. Perhaps continuous reform on both levels with a clear differentiation of principles that apply to each sphere is the essential precondition for sustainable liberal democracy.

I have argued that conservative and libertarian worries about a proliferation of rights are misconceived when we look at the many areas where citizenship rights are undermined by new social, economic, and technological developments (see section 9.2). However, I have also conceded that, especially in the area of social welfare, many rights have become group privileges that are difficult to reconcile with an egalitarian concept of citizenship (see sections 8.3 and 10.2). Liberal democratic citizenship creates an institutional setting favourable to the articulation of claims for public rights with corresponding obligations or generalized responsibilities of state agencies. The question, then, is how citizens and social movements can be motivated to argue for their rights within a framework of citizenship that devalidates those claims which divert from the norms of equality and inclusiveness. The answers suggested by Offe and Preuß could also be relevant for this problem. Representatives of corporate actors who lobby the government and bargain behind closed doors for their clients' interests are unlikely to defend their claims with reference to the norms of citizenship. Social movements which have to rely on broad public support in civil society to gain their cause are much more likely to appeal to these norms. This is not an argument against the professional organization of interest, but for the involvement of a maximum number of citizens in activities and movements where they can practice their 'duties of civility' and learn the 'public use of reason'. It is also not a moralizing approach that directs this appeal towards inactive citizens, but a call for an institutional reform of democracy that encourages such participation by increasing the opportunities of active citizens to make an impact on political decisions. In this way a rights-based approach which focuses on institutional obligations could also pay attention to the motivational conditions necessary for sustaining institutional guarantees of rights.

(4) O'Neill develops the second point of critique mentioned above. Claiming rights and 'doing the right thing' may be at odds with each other: 'those who claim rights view themselves within an overall framework of recipience. Rights are demands on *others*' (O'Neill, 1991, p. 286, original emphasis). In O'Neill's view the perspective of the claimant is even

narrower than that of the recipient. 'This suggests that the rhetoric of rights is not the fundamental idiom of action-centred reasoning, but a derivative (and potentially rancorous) way of thought in which others are seen as the primary agents and rights-holders as secondary agents, whose action depends on opportunities created by others' (ibid.). I would object that claiming a right is itself an activity that goes beyond recipience and that enjoyment of citizenship rights is enabling rather than disabling. However, O'Neill's basic point is undoubtedly correct. Only obligations always presuppose moral agency and appeal to it, whereas rights may also refer to passive receivers. The question is, which perspective is the more appropriate one in which context. I suggest that rights are the proper answer to situations of dependence which are in themselves disabling. Citizenship rights answer to the existential (Hobbesian) dependence of men and women on state power. Rights for human beings mostly aim at generating capabilities of autonomous actions where they do not yet exist (as with minors), or restoring them where they have been impaired. In a context of dependence the problem is mostly how to institutionalize and enforce the corresponding obligations, but rarely how to allocate them. Knowledge of relevant circumstances and moral intuition tell us who the people and institutions are that are obliged to grant rights. My above argument suggested that the problems of initially unallocated obligations can often be solved within the wider context of a democratic polity and that this is generally preferable to regarding them as imperfect obligations without corresponding rights.

I disagree, therefore, with O'Neill's view that unallocated obligations disappear within a rights framework, but I concede that imperfect duties cannot be addressed. 'Since the discourse of rights requires that obligations are owed to all others or to specified others, unallocated right action, which is owed to unspecified others, drops out of sight' (O'Neill, 1991, p. 286). Rather than ignoring the areas of unallocated obligations, rights discourse aims at reducing them, but it cannot answer the problem of unallocated right action. However, this latter problem arises in different contexts from the former. It is a context of deprivation rather than of relations of power and inequality. The characteristic situation to which imperfect duties respond is not that of the oppressed, exploited, or powerless but that of the needy stranger who has no claims to rights and therefore must appeal to generosity and benevolence.[14]

There are such situations within the most egalitarian, democratic and wealthiest polities. Not even the most comprehensive bundle of rights can satisfy all those needs which appeal to a sense of obligation in other human beings. And in the extended public space of liberal democracies all citizens confront one another as strangers. It is a price of their freedom that relations between anonymous citizens are not special enough for allocating obligations to assist one another beyond the elementary duties of mutual aid. So there is a need for such a sense of obligation even without corresponding rights. An extended framework of citizenship rights and corresponding institutional obligations in a wealthy and strongly individualistic society might indeed weaken public awareness of this duty. But it also puts, for the first time in history, a majority of citizens, rather than a small privileged elite, in a position where these obligations appeal to them. This might after all be a better starting-point for strategies of regenerating solidarity in civil society.

(5) A liberal democratic polity might not resolve the moral issues of how to motivate people to comply with imperfect obligations that do not correspond with rights. But it establishes a general solution for problems of how to allocate obligations that correspond with rights, and also provides the instruments for enforcing obligations once they have been formulated as legal ones.[15] But what solution is there for unallocated obligations beyond the fences of the polity?

Henry Shue explores different kinds of special relations between two individuals, Al and Benny, which could give rise to special obligations: Al might have caused harm to Benny and be obliged to rectify or compensate for this; Al and Benny might share a community membership in which implies a promise of mutual co-operation and assistance; finally, Al could have obligations corresponding indirectly to Benny's rights because both are citizens in a polity that institutionalizes rights and obligations. But what if Al and Benny live in different countries and have never met? 'There is a considerable danger of building a catch-22 here. Al and Benny cannot have reciprocal rights and duties because they do not share community or institutions, but they do not share community and institutions, at least in part, because they do not acknowledge rights and duties to each other' (Shue, 1988, p. 701). Communitarians and republicans generally resign to the difficulties of allocating obligations beyond the polity by postulating that these are imperfect moral duties only because there are no rights outside the polity anyway. For others '[t]he evident rights of distant strangers, like the right to food, suggest that we must have some positive duties across national borders' (Shue, 1988, p. 702). Could a transnational concept of citizenship provide some positive guidelines on how to allocate obligations outside the polity? I would suggest the following elements of an answer.

In contrast with a theory of natural rights, building upon a theory of citizenship means that the rights of distant strangers can only become *evident* ones within a global political context. If societies were cut off from one another a claim for rights could not resonate beyond borders. But not any connection makes for a 'spider web' (Shue, 1988, p. 693) of corresponding rights and institutional obligations that stretches across continents. Global society is an institutional reality, an ever denser network of organizations and institutions that operate beyond all national borders, rather than a 'life-world' within which moral obligations can be felt to be ethical ones towards those with whom we share cultural and social communities. Information, trade, visits and even the shared attributes of 'global culture' do not provide solid ground for the motivation to accept transnational obligations. Extensive media coverage about the situation in other countries is certainly not sufficient. The images of starving people in Africa may appeal to compassion, but it is paradoxically their global dissemination which weakens their appeal. They can hardly kindle the same sense of moral obligation and rights as when we are immediately confronted with misery in a social setting where we know that somebody's survival could depend on us rather than on millions of others who also watch TV. Market transactions create and dissolve special rights and obligations. They do not generate permanent moral or political ties between economic agents. Nor can the fact that people travel more and visit other countries, or meet those who visit theirs, account for the imperative force of duties beyond borders.

The only social phenomenon which strongly appeals to such obligations is migration. Migrations are targeted movements between countries and they involve shifts in social ties of membership. If there is a right on the side of the migrants it is usually not difficult to point out where corresponding obligations must lie. Ongoing migration expands societies beyond territories not only in their institutional interactions but also with regard to individual membership. It creates a wider social space within which people become accustomed to move. And even if political restrictions of immigration can be justified we cannot feel unconcerned by the people who try to move into our country, in the same way that most people feel unconcerned by the plights of distant strangers. Hostile reactions towards immigrants reflect a sense of guilt from denied obligation more than merely a defence of rational interest. Those who 'apply' even for only temporary membership in our country are no longer distant strangers, although it is a matter of considerable controversy what their rights towards receiving societies are. I shall discuss this in the concluding chapter.

And yet there are reasons to recognize transnational obligations also towards those who have no chance to leave. Human rights do not appeal so much to the vision of a global society as to a global fear of the fate that hits those who have lost their state's protection of rights, or whose state actively persecutes them. The strongest experiences which make claims to universal human rights resonate are the collective traumata of wars, totalitarian regimes and refugee flows in this century. And as Kant already knew, the need for a confederation of states emerges from the threat of war that does not permit any polity to regard itself as a definitely safe place for its citizens (Kant, 1984, second article). The global political context that provides incentives and justification for translating human rights into institutional obligations is thus in two essential ways still related to the framework of separate polities, rather than to that of either a natural moral order or of global society. On the one hand, it is the self-interest of each stable and peaceful state to fend for its own security by supporting international efforts that promise to promote stability elsewhere, and, on the other hand, the threat of being deprived of substantial citizenship requires an internationally recognized substitute membership in a 'quasi-polity of polities' that allows for the attribution of rights independently of nominal citizenship (see section 9.2). The second task, especially, makes it necessary to fill the institutional vacuum of the international order of states with organizations and agencies that are capable of accepting obligations towards those whose basic rights would otherwise find no response anywhere.

However, the unalterably plural structure of the global political system renders rather futile any hope that international organizations might ever become as powerful and effective in dealing with unallocated obligations as the institutions of liberal democratic states. Shue argues that international agencies are necessary to mediate the duties of individuals who fully enjoy their citizenship rights towards those unfortunates who don't, because individuals would simply be overburdened with this task. Given the scope of deficits of rights and the lack of prospect for much stronger global institutions, these institutions will be constantly overburdened as well. They might be able to alleviate some of the worst plights, but they will hardly ever be able to *guarantee* human rights in the way a democratic state guarantees the rights of citizenship. A perspective of transnational citizenship would therefore focus first on the underused capacities of states to accept obligations that reach beyond those towards their own citizens or their resident population.

This approach would recognize special obligations of each government towards specific populations that may result from active involvement in the affairs of another country, from geographical proximity, or from historic ties. Such relations explain why a population expects a particular foreign state to assist in the protection of its human rights.

Often, such obligations can be argued for in the same way as those of citizenship. Relations of power and dependence reach beyond national borders. Even where they are primarily of an economic kind they involve governments as responsible agents who take decisions about trade policy, the enforcement or cancellation of foreign debts, etc. But special obligations of this sort cannot be derived only from a principle of rectification of injustice or restitution for harm.[16] This principle is both too strong and too weak to provide a solid ground. It is too strong because not even the most comprehensive transnational obligations could ever compensate for injustice committed during the history of European colonialism and Western imperialism. It is too weak because rectification is past-oriented and aims at creating a situation where all obligations end after claims have been satisfied. However, duties that result from present involvement and a future-oriented commitment to create conditions for the provision of basic human rights, will generally receive stronger support among those who are asked to contribute than past-oriented ones. In the wider perspective of transnational citizenship we can become aware that not only harmful intervention, but also beneficial assistance, strengthens the ties between societies and thus also the claims for institutionalizing transnational rights in this common social space. The recognition of rights beyond borders creates corresponding obligations. However, the fulfilment of these obligations does not dissolve the rights but anchors them durably in international relations.

Between the area of rights where special obligations can be assigned to states and the scope of responsibility of international agencies there will remain a broad space that can be filled by joint obligations of states. These can be derived from the capabilities of states to assist in the maintenance of rights beyond their borders rather than from their particular ties or involvement. Obligations of this kind are not clearly allocated, but they might be formulated as a duty of each single state to co-operate with others in joint efforts to respond to urgent claims for human rights, and to be willing to accept a fair share of burdens.

(6) Before turning to the general issue of migration rights let me illustrate how this multilayered theory of obligation might be applied to the special case of refugees and asylum seekers.[17]

The rights of displaced people in a country where famine, war, civil strife or dictatorship have made it impossible to stay, create unallocated obligations rather than special ones for most other states.[18] For ordinary citizens in Western countries, the appeal of these rights is a rather weak one. They are called upon to assist in relief efforts by way of charitable donations, i.e., to recognize that they have an imperfect duty towards people with whom they share no other social ties than the fact of being human and being potentially exposed to the same plight. For governments and international governmental organizations this perspective is not sufficient. They cannot be motivated to act out of 'generosity and beneficence'. It requires a perspective of unallocated, rather than imperfect, obligations to get them to work. The recognition of rights must become internalized as a constraint on their pursuit of interest in external affairs just as it is in domestic ones. If they have not been involved in the area so far their obligations will not be special ones towards the people of the catastrophe-stricken country, but general ones to participate in international efforts which share burdens. This obligation refers primarily to the capacities of states to improve others' basic rights and it is proportional to these capacities. Not doing anything, although one could easily do something, is morally wrong.

As long as the main task is to establish refugee camps and to fly in food and medicine, Non-Governmental Organizations may be in a better position to help because they can avoid the impression of pursuing foreign policy interests. NGOs can also appeal directly to citizens' sense of imperfect duties in order to collect the necessary resources for their operations. When the situation in the area also requires military and police operations to ensure that assistance reaches its targets or even to stop ongoing fighting, the rights perspective becomes an imperative one. Imperfect duties can never justify intervention of this sort; only the defence of human rights of specifiable victim populations can provide justification for this move.

States that have been involved have special obligations, and even those which had first only entered the scene as part of an international effort will thereby become involved in a way that could entail future special obligations. These obligations may include not only provisions for displaced persons in the area, but also taking out contingents of refugee, who simply cannot stay or who have already left and cannot be accommodated in neighbouring countries. Geographical proximity does make for special obligations towards refugees because their right of exit in order to save their lives will only be fulfilled when they can cross land borders without being pushed back. However, special obligations of this sort must be counterbalanced with the general ones of fair burden-sharing among states that have not themselves been causally involved in the catastrophe. As the countries which generate displacement and refugee flows are generally located in corners of the world other than those which have the best capacities to accommodate refugees, this is a stronger obligation for the latter.

Bringing displaced people actively out of their own countries will only be a policy of the last resort. However, a smaller number of the world's refugee population are also asylum seekers who themselves try to reach a country where they could find protection. They usually do not choose their destination randomly. Apart from the country's reputation with regard to economic opportunities, political stability and its treatment of immigrants, their decision may be influenced by subjective reasons (knowing the language, having relatives or friends among immigrants living there) or by the receiving state's special ties to the country of origin. Most of these reasons have to count as relevant for assigning special obligations to the state so chosen. The obligation is not to admit all who want to come but to consider claims referring to the context of emigration (i.e. the well-founded fears of refugees) as well as those concerning the choice of a specific country of immigration.

There is, nevertheless, still an element of imperfect duties in the admission of asylum seekers.[19] We might describe it as an excess of obligations over corresponding rights. For the citizens of receiving states this is the more convincing perspective. While state administrations who process asylum claims must treat applicants primarily as bearers of rights, the wider population has an obligation of hospitality and generosity which goes beyond what can be claimed from them in the name of these rights. A government's respect for the rights of asylum seekers and the citizens' honouring of their imperfect obligations mutually reinforce each other. Conversely, if governments treat refugees generally as a threat to national security, this will undermine the citizens' willingness to comply with obligations which cannot be based on rights.

The rights perspective becomes much stronger once asylum seekers have been admitted and have stayed in the country for some time. The social ties they have acquired will then count in addition to the claim not to be sent back where they could be persecuted or where their lives will be in danger. What states do when they accommodate refugees (independently of whether they give them official refugee status or just admit that they cannot be sent back) is to provide them with that basic right of citizenship of which they had been deprived: to be protected in one's existence by the state on whom one depends for this protection. Refugees are therefore potential citizens of receiving states in a much stronger sense than other immigrants who retain this element of their citizenship of origin. The claims of refugees directly translate universal human rights into special obligations of states towards non-members.

NOTES

1   John Stuart Mill argues along these lines against boards as decision-making bodies within the executive: 'What " the Board" does is the act of nobody; and nobody can be made to answer for it' (Mill, 1972, 'On Representative Government', p. 361).

2.   Because minors are seen as passive receivers of the right to public education, they will need representatives to defend their right when it is in jeopardy. These representatives may either be state administrations which enforce the parents' obligation, or parents themselves who claim their children's rights. As an illustration for the latter case, suppose a decision is taken to introduce a maximum quota for children of immigrant origin. If a child is denied admission in the local compulsory school because of this rule her parents may

defend their right in court. Yet in doing this, they still act as the trustees of the child's right. Even in this example right and obligation are not identical.

3. Mill suggests a second argument for compulsory voting which rests upon the common confusion between alienating and waiving a right: 'If it is a right, if it belongs to the voter for his own sake, on what ground can we blame him for selling it, or using it to recommend himself to any one whom it is his interest to please?' (Mill, 1972, 'On Representative Government', p. 324).

4 Ronald Dworkin has explained very well the implications of choosing the one or the other approach. In joint opposition to goal-based theories, rights-based and duty-based theories 'place the individual at the center, and take his decision or conduct as of fundamental importance. But the two types put the individual in a different light. Duty-based theories are concerned with the moral quality of his acts ... Rights-based theories are, in contrast, concerned with the independence rather than the conformity of individual action. They presuppose and protect the value of individual thought and choice' (Dworkin, 1977, p. 172).

5. See also Walzer (1970, chapter 5, pp. 99–119).

6. A similar position is taken by Heisler and Schmitter-Heisler: 'Citizenship has become increasingly unidirectional: it emphasizes rights or entitlements deriving from the state and no longer stresses the obligations or duties traditionally expected of individuals.' The authors would not like to concede the 'inevitability, irreversibility or normative justifiability of this trend' (Heisler and Schmitter-Heisler, 1990, p. 7). This has implications for their discussion of immigration and citizenship. While they play down existing differences of rights between aliens and nominal citizens, they strongly emphasize what they see as inequality of duties. 'Minimally, the formal distinction between citizens and non-citizens may impede the latter's integration along various dimensions of social relations – although there is no clear evidence that it does. On the other hand, non-citizens have fewer obligations to the political community in which they reside than citizens.' Their whole approach illustrates well how a conception of the polity which emphasizes obligations can justify exclusion from rights.

7. Apart from a duty to make responsible use of the vote, Janowitz adds to Marshall's list a duty to participate in voluntary associations, which is almost a contradiction in terms. Both Marshall and Janowitz also discuss somewhat inconclusively a general duty to work (Marshall, 1965, pp. 129–31, Janowitz, 1980, p. 22).

8. Agnes Heller and Ferenc Fehér give a more extensive list of civic virtues which includes 'radical tolerance [except towards force, violence or domination], civic courage, solidarity, justice and the intellectual virtues of *phronesis* and discursive rationality. The practice of such virtues makes the " city" what it is meant to be: the sum total of its citizens. Whatever other virtues men and women develop in addition to these civic virtues, contributes to their own good life. Civic virtues contribute to the good life of all' (Heller and Fehér, 1988, p. 88).

9 Rawls makes a significant exception for 'permanent minorities that have suffered from injustice for many years' (Rawls, 1971, p. 355).

10 See also Cohen and Arato (1992, p. 572).

11 This argument is profoundly misconceived if it is not derived from the foreigners' general obligation to pay taxes and social security contributions but from a surplus of their contributions over the benefits they receive. The entitlements of citizenship cannot depend on a cost-benefit analysis of this kind.

12. This obligation is situational and therefore not strictly universal. Only those who are in a position to help are obliged to do so. On the other hand, it is also not really special because it does not presuppose any prior relation between the bearers of the right and of the obligation.

13 This difference exists already with strictly corresponding rights and obligations and becomes only more pronounced with non-corresponding ones: 'In many cases ... corresponding rights and duties are not correlative, but one is derivative from the other, and it makes a difference which is derivative from which' (Dworkin, 1977, p. 171).

14. O'Neill thinks that 'for the more powerful, who could end or reduce others' needs, concentration on rights and recipience could mask recognition of power and its obligations, and so constrict moral vision and concern' (O'Neill, 1991, p. 286). But power emerges within relations of dependence and creates claims to equality and rights. The powerful can well develop a moral vision by considering the rights of those who depend on

them, and the powerless would be not be wise to rely on paternalistic motivations within a relation of dependence. Imperfect moral duties are addressed to the resourceful rather than to the holders of power.

15. This still leaves open the problem of scarce resources which are needed in order to meet these obligations. A right to food might be perfectly allocated with all the requisite instruments for enforcement, but when a drought has affected the whole country it could be impossible to guarantee this right even with extensive internal redistribution. However, the causes of famines are rarely purely natural ones and egalitarian systems of entitlements can prevent as well as relieve them (see Sen, 1981).

16. See Gibney (1986) for a normative argument about immigration rights that gives priority to a 'harm principle' over a 'basic rights principle'. In Gibney's presentation, basic rights create strictly universal obligations while special obligations are only derived from the infliction of harm. This dualistic reasoning dismisses special obligations which result from extended social ties of membership, such as immigration rights of close family members. A theory of transnational citizenship need not give absolute priority to such claims, but it will rank them very high and define them as individual rights with corresponding obligations rather than merely as discretionary favours granted by an immigration state.

17. I refer here only to what can be seen as moral obligations corresponding to human rights of refugees. I do not discuss the legal rights and obligations of national asylum laws or the Geneva Refugee Convention. For an analysis that pays attention to the legal, political and moral aspects see Zolberg, Suhrke and Aguayo (1989).

18. In 1994, the situation in Somalia and Ruanda presents dilemmas of this kind.

19. Sibylle Tönnies has strongly argued that *only* the perspective of imperfect duties is adequate. Asylum 'is a duty beyond all state laws to which no right corresponds, that results, just on the contrary, only from the rightlessness of the others' (Tönnies, 1992, p. 43, my translation). As a moral argument this is indefensible. Rightlessness cries for the attribution of rights and not merely for mercy. Human rights are retained as claims towards the international community of states when they are violated by the state of one's citizenship, and it is this claim that is addressed to a specific state of asylum.

13. Migration Rights[1]

Until recently, and with a few significant exceptions, political and moral philosophers have not had much to say about migration. It was mostly taken for granted that state sovereignty implied the right to control movement of persons across borders (and quite often also within these borders). Free internal movement and choice of residence within a state and the freedom to leave any state have become accepted as universal human rights only after World War II (see Article 13 of the 1948 Declaration of Human Rights). Whether there is, or ought to be, a symmetric right of free immigration is generally denied by scholars of international law but has become a controversial issue in a rapidly growing number of essays in normative political theory.

13.1. ARGUMENTS FOR FREE MOVEMENT

If free movement were a human right it ought to be guaranteed by states even if its consequences would affect negatively some collective interests. So arguments that appeal to universal principles of justice should be examined first before turning to consequentialist reasoning about the likely effects of such a right. In the second part of this section I examine whether a right to immigration can be derived from other rights that are generally acknowledged to be universal.

(1) In his short treatise of 1795 'On Perpetual Peace', Immanuel Kant proposed a world citizen right of free movement which he grounded in humanity's common property of the earth (Kant, 1984, third article, pp. 21–4). Originally nobody has a stronger right to be in any place than anybody else and the limited surface of the earth makes it impossible for humanity to avoid contact between societies by spreading ever more over the globe. So all human beings must have a right to offer themselves for social contact with established inhabitants of any territory. Yet from these strong premises Kant derives only a right of 'hospitability', i.e. not to be treated in a hostile manner upon arriving. He seems to advocate a universal right of travel and peaceful trade rather than of immigration. For Kant, the right to reject unwelcome immigrants is illustrated by the experience of societies invaded, colonized and exploited by Europeans. There is, however, one important proviso which reads like an early formulation of the

non-refoulement principle of Article 33 of the Geneva Refugee Convention: aliens can only be turned away if this does not lead to their perishing. Kant's vision seems deeply embedded in preindustrial capitalism. When trade is the major motive of people moving abroad, a right of visiting will be perfectly sufficient for their purposes and anything more than that must seem threatening for potential hosts. But when people migrate because they have to seek employment outside their societies of origin this will clearly not do. A right of immigration and of permanent residence will become necessary to secure their autonomy and to meet their needs. Yet such a right can hardly be derived from the fiction of original common property in the earth's territories. Immigration rights of this kind cannot be conceived ahistorically as natural human rights but have to be grounded in the specific forms of mobility of modern society.

In a spirit of Kantian universalism, Bruce Ackerman has gone much further in defending a *prima facie* right of immigration. For Ackerman, citizenship in a liberal state is a valuable and scarce resource. People who claim that they want to share in enjoying such a resource can only be rejected if their exclusion can be defended in a dialogue under constraint of neutrality: no contestant is allowed to base her case on asserting that her conception of the good, or she herself, is morally superior. Contrary to communitarian philosophers like Michael Walzer (1983, pp. 40–1.), Ackerman insists that a liberal state is not a private club. In ideal theory '*all* people who fulfill the dialogic and behavioral conditions [that their actions conform to their words] have an unconditional right to demand recognition as full citizens of a liberal state' (Ackerman, 1980, p. 8, original emphasis). Ackerman concedes that in the real world there may be justifiable limits to free access. Beyond a certain threshold, immigration could provoke a backlash of anxiety among the native population and fascists could seize political power. But 'the *only* reason for restricting immigration is to protect the ongoing process of liberal conversation itself' (p. 95, original emphasis). This raises a number of puzzling questions. If, *prima facie*, citizenship is a resource which requires bounded political communities for its generation, how can there be a *prima facie* case for free access to such communities? When some association defends special entitlements of its members against claims of outsiders can it only do so by asserting the *moral inferiority* of non-members? If immigrants are admitted on a purely first-come first-served basis until a critical threshold has been reached, how can we make sure that special moral claims for entry, such as those of refugees and family members, will be given priority? Finally, if the threshold is determined by the threat of a political backlash, will this not give opponents of liberal democracy a chance to pressurize liberal regimes into restricting immigration below levels that might be perfectly acceptable when measured by other criteria?

Although Ackerman does not fully succeed in arguing for free immigration, one can use his approach in defending an essential ethical principle of admission policy: even if states may be entitled to restrict entry they may not reject immigrants *arbitrarily*. They must be able to provide reasons for non-admission which do not violate equal respect for immigrants as autonomous human beings. Reasons which imply a moral inferiority of individuals or of their conceptions of the good cannot be accepted. All immigrants who have not shown by their personal deeds that they are hostile to a liberal democratic order must be attributed the *capacity* of being citizens of a liberal state, independently of their 'racial' or cultural origins.

Instead of arguing positively for a right of immigration, one may as well deny that states are entitled to control it. The libertarian framework of justice developed by Robert Nozick (1974) seems to support this approach. Free movement is the prototypic negative liberty. Liberals generally share John Rawls' view that justice requires the most extensive system of liberties compatible with equal liberties for all (Rawls, 1971).[2] Libertarians only accept restrictions of liberty incurred from voluntary contractual obligations, but not in the name of state or collective interests. While justly acquired property in land gives owners the right to deny entry to other persons, states in this view would not be legitimated to do the same. Nevertheless, as O'Neill observes poignantly, 'libertarians are known for advocating free trade, but not for advocating the dismantling of immigration laws. This may be because their stress on property rights entails an attrition of public space that eats into the freedom of movement and rights of abode of the unpropertied, even within national jurisdictions' (O'Neill, 1991, p. 290). In spite of this inconsistency, libertarian reasoning could support the following conclusion: in a world of minimal states which use their monopoly of force only to defend basic civil rights but develop neither democratic forms of collective decision-making nor extensive social redistribution, there would indeed be no good moral reason for state restrictions of immigration.

If one attributes some ethical importance to political and social citizenship rights there is another challenge to be answered. Why should the achievements of democratic welfare states be the exclusive property of those lucky enough to be born there? Some authors have suggested a global application of Rawls's theory of justice (Barry, 1973, Beitz, 1979). Behind a global veil of ignorance, representatives in the 'original position' would vote for a right of free movement, because it extends the overall system of liberties and because it seems to follow from the difference principle that social inequalities are to be arranged so that they are to the greatest benefit of the least advantaged (Carens, 1987a, Barry, 1989, p. 189).[3] The same inspiration has led many to demand free access in the first world for third world immigrants as a compensation for the failures of development aid. If the global distribution of resources is unjust and if resources cannot be brought to where people are, people should be allowed to go where the resources are (Lichtenberg, 1981, pp. 92–3, Goodin, 1992, p. 8). This is an argument from consequences rather than from natural liberty. But will the effects of free migration be really redistributive in this way? Research shows a rather ambiguous pattern of benefits and burdens. Sending countries might benefit during an initial period from remittances but will often suffer long-term costs because of losing the most active parts of the population. Instead of leading to a flow of resources towards sending states, free labour immigration mostly opens the scissors of inequality within receiving countries. Overall, consumers would gain modestly from free immigration because of cheaper labour costs. Employers of immigrant labour will clearly profit and native workers competing within the same economic sectors will lose, while the distribution of benefits will be inverse in other sectors of the economy. Immigrants themselves will benefit in economic terms but at the same time the system of social protection for workers, which they enter, will be gradually eroded. One may with good moral reason say that this is price worth paying when confronted with global poverty. But then this cure might worsen the disease. Enforcing social redistribution within bounded political communities might be a more promising strategy to deal with the causes (van Parijs, 1992).

(2) Arguing for free movement as a natural right or as a demand of universal justice is not the only strategy available. One can defend a disputed right which has not been widely granted by appealing to other well, established rights and claiming that they imply the novel right by way of analogy, symmetry or causal relation. A frequently heard analogy is that if money and goods can move freely between countries then people should be entitled to do so, too.[4] Another argument says that immigration and emigration are symmetric phenomena, and so should be rights corresponding to both kinds of movements. A third consideration, which appeals both to analogy and symmetry, observes that states are not entitled to restrict internal movement across administrative boundaries (e.g. of federal states) even when collective policy goals are affected negatively. So they should also not be allowed to control movement across international borders for similar reasons.

Mere analogy or symmetry can be criticized by showing that there is some morally important difference between both sides of the equation. Goods and money do not have the same moral standing as people. Unlike people, goods are legitimately treated as mere means for satisfying the needs of other people. The analogy between both could be used to argue for free slave trade as well as for free migration. There is a utilitarian variation of this theme, based on liberal economic theory: free movement for capital and labour will lead to the most efficient allocation of factors of production and will optimize aggregate wealth and welfare.[5] In this view migrants are conceived as guest workers who come voluntarily in search of economic opportunities. Yet in liberal democratic states individuals who are admitted into the country must be treated not only as economic agents but as bearers of fundamental rights, and if they stay they ought to be treated as potential citizens. Thus immigrants can raise substantial claims to status and resources in receiving societies. If they are accepted as moral beings with morally relevant ties and rights towards both sending and receiving societies, considerations about aggregate economic welfare are insufficient to determine rights and duties of states as well as of individuals involved.

The argument that emigration and immigration rights ought to be symmetric seems a much stronger one in these respects. However, there are again some morally important differences. Voluntary associations generally allow their members to leave but do not admit anybody who wishes to become a member. States might not be voluntary associations but the analogy holds at least for emigration rights: freedom of exit is a minimum test for consent in government (see section 5.2). If states are seen as political communities which are entitled to redistribute resources and benefits among their members they seem to have good reasons for restricting access from outside. So, unless one can show why states *should* be different from voluntary associations in their admission policies, Walzer's conclusion that 'immigration and emigration are morally asymmetrical' (Walzer, 1983, p. 40) seems to hold. Resident aliens may have a right to naturalization which is grounded in their social membership, but how could migrants who have never before set a foot on the ground have a right to enter?

However, even if there is no strict symmetry, the right of emigration may *imply* corresponding immigration rights. From the point of view of international law the right of emigration might be no more than a mere negative liberty, i.e., the corresponding obligation is only that of the state of origin not to prohibit or obstruct somebody's attempt to leave.[6] But in political theory the essential role of exit rights lies in the possibility of escaping from tyrannical power. For refugees it does not matter whether their state closes its borders for emigration, or all neighbouring states close their borders for entry. Liberalism has extended this idea towards a right to choose a different society for residence. We cannot choose our place of birth but we should be able to leave it if we wish. Only the positive freedom to go somewhere else will compensate for the arbitrariness of our initial membership. In order to enjoy the right of emigration in any of these substantial intepretations, there must be other countries where one can go (Zolberg, 1987, p. 270). This is an important argument for immigration rights, but not for universal ones. While the obligation for permitting emigration falls always on a single state of present residence, a corresponding right of immigration has to be guaranteed by no particular other state. It is not obvious at first sight how this paradigmatic case of unallocated obligations could be solved by redefining them as universal or special duties.

The argument from internal freedom of movement draws attention to the fact that the establishment of zones of free migration has been an important achievement within modern liberal states. A general right of mobility becomes important only in a mobile society. In premodern society, mobility was mostly attached to the life either of social outcasts or of highly specialized elites. Neither the big majority of the population, i.e. agricultural producers, nor the inhabitants of walled cities enjoyed or required mobility as a right. In an economy with a generalized labour market, the right of mobility becomes an urgent one. This does not mean that it is a functional necessity of the economic system. Mobility need not be voluntary. If labour does not, or can not, move freely to places of production, its mobility can also be enforced by evictions, slave trade, indenture and other forms of unfree labour (Cohen, 1987). Invariably, those who have been moved rather than themselves have chosen to move, lack basic rights. However, political and union struggles of workers have set constraints on these forms of labour, and industrial development within these constraints has made the forceful allocation of labour not only morally inacceptable but also more and more inefficient. Whereas the walls around ancient or late medieval city-states were a necessary condition for maintaining the liberties and privileges of urban citizenship, restrictions of mobility make for unequal citizenship in modern society. Internal freedom of movement has contributed to the equalization of citizenship within nation-states, but state control over transnational movement has reinforced distinctions between aliens and citizen. Those who have to move across borders will only become full citizens when they also enjoy the *liberty* to move. Increasing transnational mobility in societies which are politically organized as territorial states thus provides a strong case for freedom of movement.

Yet the very achievement of substantial and equal rights of citizenship within a space of free movement might also require some form of external closure.[7] If objections along this line stand the test of moral scrutiny, this will mean that universal freedom of movement has to be seen as a target for liberal democratic policies rather than as a moral right which constrains all present political options. Adopting a universal immigration right as a long-term target will still have an impact on the evaluation of today's policies. It means that immigration rights ought to be extended rather than restricted wherever possible. Extending citizenship rights beyond national memberships and territories creates the necessary preconditions for this.

13.2. IDEAL WORLDS AND PRESENT DILEMMAS

This line of argument only makes sense if one agrees that in an ideal world of modernity, freedom of movement would be established as a universal right. Brian Barry has recently opposed this view. He argues first that 'an ideal world would be one in which the vast majority of people were content with conditions in their own countries' so that few would wish to migrate anyway (Barry, 1992, p. 279). If, however, too many people used this right for crowding in the same places, migration would still have to be regulated like any other activity subject to congestion. So it appears that free movement were either of little importance or restricted in similar ways as today. Second, in a world like ours people are induced to migrate by economic incentives and deterred from doing so by cultural attachment to their societies of origin. Barry suggests 'a rule that people will migrate from a place so long as there is at least one other place with a material standard of living higher enough to offset the cultural differences between the two places' (p. 281). However, as immigrants tend to form their own cultural communities in receiving societies, the cultural barrier can be overcome and mass immigration would go on until 'conditions would be no better in these countries than in the rest of the world' (ibid.).

Would the right of immigration be nearly irrelevant in an ideal world because people would have no incentives to move? Even if all countries were equally rich and democratic they need not contain in themselves a complete opportunity structure for all desires and needs that individuals should be free to satisfy. The principality of Luxembourg is too small to have its own university and therefore sends its students abroad. Is there something wrong with the existence of such states or with their inhabitants' wishes to get access to other countries' resources? Only the world can be regarded as a complete opportunity structure for all the needs of humanity. Global markets, communication and mobility in modern society have turned the vision of economically self-sufficient and socially closed nation-states into a backward-looking idea. A world could be called ideal with regard to territorial mobility if all people found roughly equal levels of resources in the places where they are born, but also if everybody also had the right to search for better opportunities elsewhere without being impeded by the circumstances of their origins. The amount of migration in this utopian world would result from a market-like co-ordination of individual preferences with regard to places of residence, inhibited by a strong moment of inertia. Most people would stay where they are; not because men and women are naturally sedentary creatures – it seems they were rather nomadic in their early history (see Davis, 1974) – but because being a fully integrated member in a liberal democratic society has its own rewards and the efforts of resocialization when we go elsewhere are normally high. Furthermore, there would be some state regulation in case of 'market failure' in certain specially attractive places. The fact that an activity requires regulation because not everybody can engage in it at the same time in the same place is not an argument against asserting it as a liberty (see section 10.2). With a few areas closed because of congestion or damage to the ecology, and some queuing for access to permanent residence, this would still be a very different world compared to the present one where states defend their sovereign right of controlling, selecting or rejecting immigrants without a corresponding right of being admitted on the latter's part.

The goal of liberal democracy is not to create states so perfect that people could only wish to leave for idiosyncratic reasons, but to create a world in which movement is generally voluntary rather than enforced by adverse social and political conditions. This utopia of free movement would still be compatible with a global political system consisting of a plurality of states. In liberal democracy the primary role of territorial boundaries of states is not to control human mobility but the organization of local populations as polities which democratically control the political power to which they are subject. This requires a criterion of residence for the exercise of political rights of representation.[8] But, by and large, states could leave the decision of who are to be their residents to the self-regulating forces of social interaction in a free society.

If arguments for free immigration are not strong enough to succeed in the present world, why is it still important to assert such a long-term goal? The best justification for utopian thinking is that it could be a relevant guide for present political decisions. A catastrophic scenario of the consequences of deregulation, as it seems is implied in Barry's comment, is meant to discourage such considerations. If one looks at the combined effects of population growth, political instability and economic catastrophes in some regions of the world it is not at all difficult to find this convincing. However, some relevant facts and questions are omitted from this bleak picture.

A first one is that we do notknow nearly enough about the social forces that shape migratory flows when they are politically uninhibited. There are self-perpetuating chain migrations, but there are also many cases where the real puzzle is why people do not leave although they have all the relevant incentives and opportunities. Even more interesting is the observation that unrestrained migrations also tend to be self-limiting; they build transnational economic networks which sustain populations in the sending countries or allow people to travel back and forth without settling in the destination country. The idea that migrations are primarily determined by wage differentials and tend to go on until these have been levelled out is not supported by much empirical evidence.[9]

A second consideration is that the gap between demographic and industrial development which today creates huge emigration potentials outside the OECD world has also characterized much of 19th century Europe. Open gates in the New World were part of the success story of industrial capitalism in Europe. It is not only poverty and wars, but also a take-off in economic development that can trigger emigration flows in the most densely populated countries of the global South. Policies which try to fight the root causes of involuntary mass emigration must take into account the paradoxical effect that their very success may stimulate additional outflows. Keeping open some doors in the North will be a necessary element of a global strategy.

Both points are certainly not enough to justify the lifting of all restrictions on territorial movement in the present world. But they could strengthen liberal intuitions that these restrictions must be subject to moral and political constraints which direct policies towards the long-term target of removing them altogether. Although I have found none of the arguments for universal freedom of movement here and now entirely convincing, each of them can provide us with normative guidelines for present policies. Let me sum these up in five points.[10]

(1) Individuals who can be considered as members of a society represented in a state ought to enjoy the right to enter this state and to stay in it without threat of expulsion. Where societal membership does not coincide with nominal citizenship of a nation-state, these rights must be extended to aliens, too. This principle serves as a foundation for the rights of family reunification and of permanent residence.

(2) The universal right of emigration implies a right to be admitted for those who have lost the protection of their states. States specially responsible for admitting refugees are those who share some responsibility for the causes of flight, to whom refugees have already some personal or collective ties, or who are in the best position to provide shelter. Ultimately, the universal right of exit implies a joint obligation of the community of states for refugees and therefore a more specific obligation for each state to contribute towards international solutions for refugee crises.

(3) The primary reason which can legitimate restrictions on immigration is the maintenance of a comprehensive system of civil, democratic and social rights of citizenship. Policies of protecting such systems within nation-states ought to go hand in hand with extending them to transnational levels and removing thereby the major normative justification for immigration control.

(4) For those who are not exempted from control or who cannot claim priority in access there ought to be fair and non-discriminatory procedures for distributing places to applicants. Paying equal respect to non-entitled immigrants means that quantitative limitation should be more important in organizing such a scheme than qualitative selection.

(5) The costs of admitting more immigrants than criterion (3) would permit must be balanced against the costs of deterring or rejecting those who want to come, and of detecting and deporting those who have come illegally. Confronted with a big immigration push, a liberal democratic state may face a dilemma in choosing which costs to minimize. If this dilemma is to be mitigated, policies of two different kinds must be combined: one kind has to address the root causes of poverty, unemployment, ecological disaster, mass disease, war and repression in sending states, and the second kind should co-ordinate a gradual extension of receiving capacities among target states.

Controlling immigration raises intricate moral dilemmas for liberal democracy. Egalitarian liberalism generally tries to create a social order in which the arbitrary facts of birth will be neutralized as far as this is possible by giving people resources and opportunities that enable them to change their social position. What stronger indicator of injustice in the present world order than the fact that people born in Central Africa have vastly fewer resources and opportunities than those born in Western Europe, Northern America or Japan? If one takes liberal values seriously it is impossible to regard the claims of people who cross international borders in search of protection or opportunities as irrelevant. More than anything else, immigration control seems to confirm that citizenship in liberal democracy is after all a protection of relative privilege rather than a bundle of rights that appeal to universalistic values.

However, the other horn of the dilemma is not less high. Such rights do not exist in a state of nature and they would be endangered in a global state. Only democratic polities in a world of many states are a relatively safe place where rights can be claimed as well as enjoyed. The rights of citizenship equalize individuals as members of a polity and limit the extent and effects of social and economic inequalities. Any redistributive system which tries to keep internal inequalities smaller than those in its environment cannot keep access completely open for further participants.

The redistributive effects of free movement with regard to wages and consumer prices on a world scale may be a matter of dispute. But free movement would certainly not lead to a global redistribution of those social rights that depend on the state's capacity to regulate territorial labour markets and employment conditions.

The principles I have suggested above do not offer any simple formula for how to avoid the dilemma. It will stay with us for the coming decades. Normative theory cannot do much more than reduce inconsistency in our reasoning and provide us with good arguments for our strongest intuitions. The underlying idea of this book has been that, in the increasingly mobile societies of modernity, citizenship must be transnationalized in order to retain its significance as equal membership in territorial polities. There are two policy implications of this idea: the first is to extend the polity as a community of citizenship rights by giving resident aliens a right to citizenship in the substantial as well as the nominal sense; the second is to extend the nominal citizens' traditional right of re-entry by establishing special immigration rights for refugees and for immigrants who have already acquired social ties of membership, by introducing fair procedures for other new admissions, and by a gradual opening of borders as far as the internal sustainability of substantial citizenship rights permits.

NOTES

1.   This chapter is an extended version of an essay published in Robin Cohen (ed.) (1994), *The Cambridge Survey of World Migration*, Cambridge University Press, Cambridge, UK.
2.   Rawls now suggests instead the requirement of 'a fully adequate system of liberties' (Rawls, 1993a, pp. 331–4).
3.   As I have already mentioned in section 9.2, Rawls argues in a recent essay against these conclusions and for establishing only basic human rights as the standard of justice in international relations (Rawls, 1993b).
4.   This analogy structures the most comprehensive overview of political theory approaches to free movement so far, edited by Brian Barry and Robin Goodin (1992).
5   As discussed above, in the real world an increase in aggregate utility achieved in this way will be hardly Pareto-optimal; there will be many losers.
6.   Alfred Noll reminded me that this is the standard interpretation in international law.
7.   Hannah Arendt and Michael Walzer have strongly argued this point: 'Freedom, wherever it existed as a tangible reality, has always been spatially limited. This is especially clear for the greatest and most elementary of all negative liberties, the freedom of movement; the borders of national territory or the walls of the city-state comprehended and protected a space in which men could move freely. Treaties and international guarantees provide an extension of this territorially bound freedom for citizens outside their own country, but even under these modern conditions the elementary coincidence of freedom and a limited space remains manifest' (Arendt, 1963, p. 279). In Walzer's view, states cannot be as open as neighbourhoods: 'If states ever become large neighborhoods, it is likely that neighborhoods will become little states. ... Neighborhoods can be open only if countries are at least potentially closed' (Walzer, 1983, p. 38).
8   I want to leave open the question, whether it also requires nominal membership. On the one hand, if access to citizenship were optional in the way that I have suggested in Part 1 of this book, voting rights for foreigners in parliamentary election could well remain tied

to naturalization without thereby becoming excessively exclusive. On the other hand, this is an unreasonable requirement for local elections because local membership depends on residence in a much more straightforward way (see section 6.2). Furthermore, the granting of a quite extensive parliamentary franchise to non-citizens in Britain or New Zealand has not really caused a break down of democracy in these countries.

9.   There are recent contributions to economic theory that explain some of these observations within a rational choice framework, see for example Stark (1991).

10.   I have tried to defend these principle, at greater length in Bauböck (1994b).

References

Ackerman, Bruce A. (1980), *Social Justice in the Liberal State*, Yale University Press, New Haven.

Anderson, Benedict (1983), *Imagined Communities. Reflections on the origins and spread of nationalism*, Verso Editions and New Left Books, London.

Andrews, Geoff (ed.) (1990), *Citizenship*, Lawrence & Wishart, London.

Archdeacon, Thomas (1992), 'Reflections on Immigration to Europe in Light of US Immigration History' *International Migration Review*, vol. xxvi, no. 2.

Arendt, Hannah (1958), *The Human Condition*, University of Chicago Press, Chicago.

Arendt, Hannah (1963), *On Revolution*, Faber and Faber, London.

Arendt, Hannah (1967), *The Origins of Totalitarianism* (revised edition), George Allen & Unwin, London.

Arendt, Hannah (1970), *Men in Dark Times*, Harvest Books, San Diego.

Arendt, Hannah (1977), 'Little Rock' in *Zur Zeit. Politische Essays*, München DTB-Verlag.

Aristotle (1981), *The Politics*, Penguin Books, London.

Axelrod, Robert (1984), *The Evolution of Co-operation*, Basic Books, New York.

Baier, Annette C. (1987), 'The Need for More than Justice' *Canadian Journal of Philosophy*, supplementary vol. 13.

Barry, Brian (1973), *The Liberal Theory of Justice*, Clarendon Press, Oxford.

Barry, Brian (1979), 'Is Democracy Special?' in Laslett, P. and Fishkin, J. (eds), *Philosophy, Politics and Society*, 5th series, Blackwell, Oxford.

Barry, Brian (1989), *Theories of Justice, A Treatise on Social Justice*, vol. I, Harvester-Wheatsheaf, London.

Barry, Brian (1992), 'The Quest for Consistency: A Sceptical View' in Barry, Brian and Goodin, Robert E. (eds), op. cit.

Barry, Brian and Goodin, Robert E. (eds) (1992), *Free Movement. Ethical Issues in the transnational migration of people and of money*, Pennsylvania State University Press, Pennsylvania.

Barth, Fredrik (ed.) (1969), *Ethnic Groups and Boundaries. The Social Organization of Culture Difference*, Universitetsforlaget, Oslo.

Bauböck, Rainer (1991), 'Migration and Citizenship' *New Community*, vol.

18, no. 1.

Bauböck, Rainer (1992a), *Immigration and the Boundaries of Citizenship*. Monograph in Ethnic Relations no. 4, Centre for Research in Ethnic Relations, University of Warwick, Coventry.

Bauböck, Rainer (1992b), 'Optional Citizenship: Articulation of Interests and Identities in Naturalisations' *Innovation*, vol. 5, no. 2.

Bauböck, Rainer (1992c), 'Zur Zukunft des Nationalismus in Europa' in *Das Kriegsjahr 1991: Unsere Zukunft? Friedensbericht 1992*, VWGÖ-Verlag, Wien.

Bauböck, Rainer (1993a), 'Einbürgerungen. 29 Thesen über Immigration, Staats- und Stadtbürgerschaft' *Migration*, no. 17.

Bauböck, Rainer (1993b), 'Integration in a Pluralistic Society' in *Rescue–43. Xenophobia and Exile*. Articles from the Conference at the University of Copenhagen 3–5 October 1993, Munksgaard, Copenhagen.

Bauböck, Rainer (1993c), 'Nationalismus und Selbstbestimmungsrecht' *Zukunft*, no. 1, Wien.

Bauböck, Rainer (1993d), 'Staatsbürgerschaft und Immigration' *Journal für Sozialforschung*, vol. 33, no. 1.

Bauböck, Rainer (ed.) (1994a), *From Aliens to Citizens. Redefining the Legal Status of Immigrants*, Avebury, Aldershot, forthcoming.

Bauböck, Rainer (1994b), 'Legitimate Immigration Control' in Adelman, Howard (ed.), *Legitimate and Illegitimate Discrimination: New Directions in Migration*, York Lane's Press and UNESCO, Toronto, forthcoming.

Bauböck, Rainer (1994c), 'Drei Multikulturelle Dilemmata' in Ostendorf, Bernd (ed.), *Die multikulturelle Gesellschaft. Modell USA*, Fink-Verlag, München, forthcoming.

Bauböck, Rainer (1994d), Kulturelle Integration von Einwanderern, *Journal für Sozialforschung*, vol. 34, no. 1.

Bauböck, Rainer, Çinar, Dilek, Gächter, August and Riegler, Henriette (1994), *Rechtliche und politische Aspekte der Einbürgerung von Einwanderern in ausgewählten OECD Staaten*. Eine vergleichende Studie im Rahmen des Projekts 'Ausländerpolitik und ethnische Grenzziehung' Institut für Höhere Studien, Wien.

Bauer, Otto (1907), *Die Nationalitätenfrage und die Sozialdemokratie*, Wien.

Beitz, Charles R. (1979), *Political Theory and International Relations*. Princeton University Press, Princeton, New Jersey.

Bendix, Reinhard (1964), *Nation-Building and Citizenship. Studies of our Changing Social Order*, John Wiley & Sons, New York.

Bentham, Jeremy (1987), 'Anarchical Fallacies' in Waldron, Jeremy (ed.), op. cit.

Berlin, Isaiah (1979), *Four Essays on Liberty*, Oxford University Press, Oxford.

Bodin, Jean (1981), *Sechs Bücher über den Staat*, Buch I–III, Verlag Beck, München.

Brubaker, Rogers W. (ed.) (1989a), *Immigration and the Politics of Citizenship in Europe and North America*, University Press of America, Lanham and London.

Brubaker, Rogers W. (1989b), 'Introduction' in Brubaker, Rogers W., (ed.), op. cit.

Brubaker, Rogers W. (1989c), 'Citizenship and Naturalization: Policies and Politics' in Brubaker, Rogers W. (ed.), op. cit.

Brubaker, Rogers W. (1992), *Citizenship and Nationhood in France and Germany*, Harvard University Press, Cambridge, Mass.

Brubaker, Rogers W. (1993), 'National Minorities, Nationalizing States, and External National Homelands in the New Europe. Notes towards a Relational Analysis' *Institute for Advanced Studies Research Memoranda, Political Science Series*, no. 11, Vienna.

Bruschi, Christian (1988), 'Le Droit de cité dans L'Antiquité: un questionnement pour la citoyenneté aujourd'hui' in Wihtol de Wenden, Cathérine (ed.), op. cit.

Burke, Edmund (1987), 'Reflections on the Revolution in France' in Waldron, Jeremy (ed.), op. cit.

Carens, Joseph H. (1987a), 'Aliens and Citizens: The Case for Open Borders' *The Review of Politics*, vol. 49, no. 2.

Carens, Joseph H. (1987b), 'Who Belongs? Theoretical and Legal Questions about Birthright Citizenship in the United States' *The University of Toronto Law Journal*, vol. 37, pp. 413–43.

Carens, Joseph H. (1989), 'Membership and Morality' in Brubaker, Rogers W. (ed.), op. cit.

Carens, Joseph H. (1994), 'Cultural Adaptation and Integration: Is Quebec a Model for Europe?' in Bauböck, Rainer (ed.), forthcoming, op. cit.

Çinar, Dilek (1994a), 'From Aliens to Citizens. A Comparative Analysis of Rules of Transition' in Bauböck, Rainer (ed.), forthcoming, op. cit.

Çinar, Dilek (1994b), 'Einbürgerungspolitik im internationalen Vergleich' in Bauböck, Rainer et al., op. cit.

Cohen, Jean and Arato, Andrew (1992), *Civil Society and Political Theory*. MIT Press, Cambridge, Mass.

Cohen, Robin (1987), *The New Helots. Migrants in the International Division of Labour*, Avebury, Aldershot.

Constant, Benjamin (1988), 'The Liberty of the Ancients Compared With that of the Moderns' in *Political Writings*, Cambridge University Press, Cambridge.

Dagger, Richard (1985), 'Rights, Boundaries, and the Bonds of Community: A Qualified Defense of Moral Parochialism' *The American Political Science Review*, vol. 79.

Dahl, Robert (1989), *Democracy and Its Critics*, Yale University Press, New Haven.

Dahrendorf, Ralf (1974), 'Citizenship and Beyond: The Social Dynamics of an Idea' *Social Research*, vol. 41.

Davis, Kingsley (1974), 'The Migrations of Human Populations' *Scientific American*, vol. 231, no. 3.

de Groot, Gerard-René (1989), *Staatsangehörigkeitsrecht im Wandel. Eine rechtsvergleichende Studie über Erwerbs- und Verlustgründe der Staatsangehörigkeit*, Carl Heymans Verlag, Köln.

de Rham, Gérard (1990), 'Naturalisation: The Politics of Citizenship Acquisition' in Layton-Henry, Zig (ed.), op. cit.

DeSipio, Louis (1988), 'Social Science Literature and the Naturalization Process' *International Migration Review*, vol. xxi, no. 2.

Dietz, Mary G. (1985), 'Citizenship with a Feminist Face' *Political Theory*, vol. 13, no. 1.

Dobson, Andrew (1990), *Green Political Thought*, Allen & Unwin, London.

d'Oliveira, Hans Ulrich Jessurun (1990), 'Tendenzen im Staatsangehörigkeitsrecht' *Zeitschrift für Ausländerrecht und Ausländerpolitik*, no. 3.

d'Oliveira, Hans Ulrich Jessurun (1992), 'Plural Nationality and the European Union' paper presented at the conference 'Plural Nationality: Changing Attitudes', European University Institute, Florence.

Dowty, Alan (1987), *Closed Borders. The Contemporary Assault on Freedom of Movement*, Yale University Press, New Haven.

Dummett, Ann (1994), 'The Acquisition of British Citizenship. From Imperial Traditions to National Definitions' in Bauböck, Rainer (ed.), forthcoming, op. cit.

Dummett, Ann and Nicol, Andrew (1990), *Subjects, Citizens, Aliens and Others. Nationality and Immigration Law*, Weidenfeld & Nicolson, London.

Dunn, John (1991), 'Political Obligation' in Held, David (ed.), op. cit.

Dworkin, Ronald (1977), *Taking Rights Seriously*, Harvard University Press, Cambridge, Mass.

Dworkin, Ronald (1981), 'What is Equality?' part 1: 'Equality of Welfare' part 2: 'Equality of Resources' *Philosophy and Public Affairs*, nos 3, 4.

Dworkin, Ronald (1984), 'Rights as Trumps' in Waldron, Jeremy (ed.), op. cit.

Dworkin, Ronald (1985), *A Matter of Principle*, Harvard University Press,

Cambridge, Mass.

Dworkin, Ronald (1986), *Law's Empire*, Harvard University Press, Cambridge, Mass.

Elster, Jon (1984), *Sour Grapes. Studies in the Subversion of Rationality*, Cambridge University Press, Cambridge.

Elster, Jon (1990), 'Local Justice' *Archives Européenne de Sociologie*, vol. 31, no. 1.

Elster, Jon (1992), *Local Justice: How institutions allocate scarce goods and necessary burdens*, Cambridge University Press, Cambridge.

Elster, Jon (1993), 'Majority Rule and Individual Rights' in Shute, Stephen and Hurley, Susan (eds), op. cit.

Evans, M.D.R. (1988), 'Choosing to be a Citizen: The Time-Path of Citizenship in Australia' *International Migration Review*, vol. xxii, no. 2.

Fehér, Ferenc and Heller, Agnes (1994), 'Naturalization or Culturalization' in Bauböck, Rainer (ed.), forthcoming, op. cit.

Fleischer, Henning (1987), 'Entwicklung der Einbürgerungen seit 1983' *Wirtschaft und Statistik*, no. 1.

Freeden, Michael (1991), *Rights*, Open University Press, Milton Keynes.

Friedrich-Ebert-Stiftung (1986), *Situation der ausländischen Arbeitnehmer und ihrer Familienangehörigen in der Bundesrepublik Deutschland*, Bundesminister für Arbeit und Sozialordnung, Bonn.

Gauthier, David (1986), *Morals by Agreement*, Clarendon Press, Oxford.

Gellner, Ernest (1983), *Nations and Nationalism*, Blackwell, Oxford.

Gewirth, Alan (1984), 'Are There Any Absolute Rights?' in Waldron, Jeremy (ed.), op. cit.

Gibney, Mark (1986), *Strangers or Friends. Principles for a New Alien Admission Policy*, Greenwood Press, New York.

Gibney, Mark (ed.) (1988), *Open Borders? Closed Societies?*, Greenwood Press, New York.

Giddens, Anthony (1982), *Profiles and Critiques in Social Theory*, Macmillan, London.

Giddens, Anthony (1984), *The Constitution of Society*, Polity Press, Oxford.

Gilligan, Carol (1982), *In a Different Voice*, Harvard University Press, Cambridge, Mass.

Goodin, Robert E. (1992), 'If people were money...' in Barry, Brian and Goodin, Robert E. (eds), op. cit.

Grawert, Rolf (1973), *Staat und Staatsangehörigkeit. Verfassungs-geschichtliche Untersuchungen zur Entstehung der Staatsangehörigkeit*, Duncker & Humblodt, Berlin.

Habermas, Jürgen (1981), *Theorie des kommunikativen Handelns*, 2 volumes, Suhrkamp, Frankfurt am Main.

Habermas, Jürgen (1991), *Erläuterungen zur Diskursethik*, Suhrkamp, Frankfurt am Main.

Habermas, Jürgen (1992), *Faktizität und Geltung*, Suhrkamp, Frankfurt am Main.

Habermas, Jürgen (1993), 'Anerkennungskämpfe im demokratischen Rechtsstaat' in Taylor, Charles B. et al., op. cit..

Hailbronner, Kay (1989), 'Citizenship and Nationhood in Germany' in Brubaker, Rogers W. (ed.) (1989), op. cit.

Hailbronner, Kay (1992), *Rechtsfragen der doppelten Staatsangehörigkeit bei der erleichterten Einbürgerung von Wanderarbeitern und ihren Familienangehörigen*. Rechtsgutachten im Auftrag des Ausländerbeauftragten des Senats der Freien und Hansestadt Hamburg, Hamburg.

Hammar, Tomas (1990), *Democracy and the Nation State. Aliens, Denizens and Citizens in a World of International Migration*, Avebury, Aldershot.

Hart, H.L.A. (1955), 'Are There Any Natural Rights?' *Philosophical Review*, vol. 64.

Heisler, M.O. and Schmitter-Heisler, B. (1990), 'Citizenship – old, new, and changing: Inclusion, Exclusion, and Limbo for Ethnic Groups and Migrants in the Modern Democratic State' conference paper, published in Fijalkowsky, Jürgen et al. (eds) (1991), *Dominant National Cultures and Ethnic Minorities*, Freie Universität Berlin, Berlin.

Held, David (1987), *Models of Democracy*, Polity Press, Oxford.

Held, David (1990), 'Between State and Civil Society' in Andrews, Geoff, (ed.), op. cit.

Held, David (ed.) (1991a), *Political Theory Today*. Polity Press, Oxford.

Held, David (1991b), 'Democracy, the Nation-State and the Global System' in Held, David (ed.), op. cit.

Held, David and McGrew, Anthony (1993), 'Globalization and the Liberal Democratic State' *Government and Opposition*, vol. 28, no. 2.

Heller, Agnes (1987), *Beyond Justice*, Basil Blackwell, Oxford.

Heller, Agnes (1991), 'The Concept of the Political Revisited' in Held, David (ed.), op. cit.

Heller, Agnes and Fehér, Ferenc (1988), *The Postmodern Political Condition*, Polity Press, Oxford.

Hendrickson, David C. (1992), 'Migration in law and ethics: A realist perspective' in Barry, Brian and Goodin, Robert E. (eds), op. cit.

Hindess, Barry (1993), 'Citizenship in the Modern West' in Turner, Bryan S. (ed.), op. cit.

Hirsch, Fred (1976), *Social Limits to Growth*, Harvard University Press, Cambridge, Mass.

Hirschman, Albert O. (1970), *Exit, Voice, and Loyalty*, Harvard University

Press, Cambridge, Mass.

Hirschman, Albert O. (1978), 'Exit, Voice, and the State' *World Politics*, vol. 31, no. 1.

Hobbes, Thomas (1973), *Leviathan*, Everyman's Library, London.

Hobsbawm, Eric and Ranger, Terence (eds) (1983), *The Invention of Tradition*, Cambridge University Press, Cambridge.

Hohfeld, Wesley (1919), *Fundamental Legal Conceptions as applied in Juridical Reasoning*, Yale University Press, New Haven.

Hume, David (1953), *Political Essays*, The Library of Liberal Arts, Bobbs-Merrill, Indianapolis and New York.

Ignatieff, Michael (1985), *The Needs of Strangers. An essay of privacy, solidarity, and the politics of being human*, Viking, New York.

Ignatieff, Michael (1990), 'Citizenship and Moral Narcissism' in Andrews, Geoff (ed.), op. cit.

Isaacs, Harold R. (1975), 'Basic Group Identity. The Idols of the Tribe' in Glazer, Nathan and Moynihan, Daniel P. (eds), *Ethnicity. Theory and Experience*, Harvard University Press, Cambridge, Mass.

Janowitz, Morris (1980), 'Observations on the Sociology of Citizenship: Obligations and Rights' *Social Forces*, vol. 59, no. 1.

Jordan, Bill (1989), *The Common Good. Citizenship, Morality and Self-Interest*, Basil Blackwell, Oxford.

Kant, Immanuel (1984), *Zum Ewigen Frieden*, Reclam Universal-Bibliothek, Stuttgart.

Kittel, Bernhard (1993), 'Die Selbstbeschreibung der Gesellschaft. Der Begriff der Nation als missing link der Systemtheorie?' *Institute for Advanced Studies Research Memoranda, Political Science Series*, no. 4, Vienna.

Kymlicka, Will (1989), *Liberalism, Community, and Culture*, Clarendon Press, Oxford.

Layton-Henry, Zig (ed.) (1990), *The political rights of migrant workers in Western Europe*, Sage, London.

Lichtenberg, Judith (1981), 'National Boundaries and Moral Boundaries: A Cosmopolitan View' in Brown, Peter and Shue, Henry (eds), *Boundaries. National Autonomy and its Limits*, Rowman & Littlefield, Totowa, NJ.

Lichtenberg, Judith (1983), 'Mexican Migration and U.S. Policy: A Guide for the Perplexed' in Brown, Peter and Shue, Henry (eds), *The Border That Joins. Mexican Migration and U.S. Responsibility*, Rowman & Littelfield, Totwa, NJ.

Locke, John (1956), *The Second Treatise of Government and A Letter Concerning Toleration*, Edited with an Introduction by J.W. Gough, Macmillan, New York.

Locke, John (1987), 'For a General Naturalization: 1693' in Reznick, David, 'John Locke and the Problem of Naturalization', *The Review of Politics*, vol. 49, no. 3, pp. 368–88.

Lovelock, James E. (1979) *Gaia*, Oxford University Press, Oxford.

Luhmann, Niklas (1984), *Soziale Systeme. Grundriß einer allgemeinen Theorie*, Suhrkamp, Frankfurt am Main.

Lukes, Steven (1993), 'Five Fables About Human Rights' in Shute, Stephen and Hurley, Susan (eds), op. cit.

Lyons, David (1984), 'Utility and Rights' in Waldron, Jeremy (ed.), op. cit.

MacIntyre, Alasdair (1981), *After Virtue*, University of Notre Dame Press, Indiana.

MacIntyre, Alasdair (1989), *Whose Justice? Which Rationality?*, University of Notre Dame Press, Indiana.

Makarov, Alexander N. (1962), *Allgemeine Lehren des Staatsangehörigkeitsrechts*, second edition, Berlin.

Mann, Michael (1987), 'Ruling Class Strategies and Citizenship' *Sociology*, vol. 21, no. 3.

Marshall, T.H. (1965), 'Citizenship and Social Class' in *Class, Citizenship, and Social Development. Essays by T.H. Marshall*, Anchor Books, New York.

Marx, Karl and Engels, Friedrich (1974), *The German Ideology*, Lawrence & Wishart, London.

Maturana, Humberto R. and Varela, Francisco J. (1980), *Autopoiesis and Cognition*, D. Reidel Publishing Company, Dordrecht.

Mead, Lawrence M. (1986), *Beyond Entitlement. The Social Obligations of Citizenship*, The Free Press, New York.

Mill, John Stuart (1972), *Utilitarianism, On Liberty and Considerations on Representative Government*, Everyman's Library, London.

Miller, David (1976), *Social Justice*, Clarendon Press, Oxford.

Ministère des Communeautés culturelles et de l'Immigration du Québec (1990), *Visions. A Policy Statement on Immigration and Integration*, Montréal.

North, David S. (1987), 'The Long Grey Welcome: A Study of the American Naturalization Program' *International Migration Review*, vol. xxi, no. 2.

Nozick, Robert (1974), *Anarchy, State, and Utopia*, Basil Blackwell, Oxford.

Offe, Claus und Preuß, Ulrich (1991), 'Democratic Institutions and Moral Resources' in Held, David (ed.), op. cit.

Oldfield, Adrian (1990), *Citizenship and Community. Civic Republicanism and the Modern World*, Routledge, London.

O'Neill, Onora (1986), *Faces of Hunger. An Essay on Poverty,*

Development and Justice, Allen & Unwin, London.

O'Neill, Onora (1991), 'Transnational Justice' in Held, David (ed.), op. cit.

Pachon, Harry P. (1988), 'An Overview of Citizenship in the Hispanic Community' *International Migration Review*, vol. xxi, no. 2.

Parsons, Talcott (1971), *The System of Modern Societies*, Prentice-Hall, London.

Pateman, Carole (1988), *The Sexual Contract*, Polity Press, Oxford.

Patterson, Orlando (1982), *Slavery and Social Death*, Harvard University Press, Cambridge, Mass.

Plant, Raymond (1990), 'Social Rights and the Reconstruction of Welfare' in Andrews, Geoff, (ed.), op. cit.

Plato (1961), 'Crito' in *The Collected Dialogues of Plato*, Princeton University Press, Princeton, NJ.

Portes, Alejandro and Curtis, John W. (1988), 'Changing Flows: Naturalization and its Determinants Among Mexican Immigrants' *International Migration Review*, vol. xxi, no. 2.

Rawls, John (1971), *A Theory of Justice*, Harvard University Press, Cambridge, Mass.

Rawls, John (1993a), *Political Liberalism*, Columbia University Press, New York.

Rawls, John (1993b), 'The Law of Peoples' in Shute, Stephen and Hurley, Susan (eds), op. cit.

Renan, Ernest (1882), 'Qu'est-ce qu'une nation?' in *Discours et Conférences par Ernest Renan*, Calman-Lévy, Paris.

Renner, Karl (1902), *Der Kampf der österreichischen Nationen um den Staat*, Franz Deuticke, Leipzig, (published under Renner's pseudonym Rudolf Springer).

Rex, John (1986), *Race and Ethnicity*, Open University Press, Milton Keynes.

Richmond, Anthony (1988), *Immigration and Ethnic Conflict*, St. Martin's Press, New York.

Riegler, Henriette (1994), 'Zwischen Rechtserwerb und Identitätsbedrohung – Einbürgerung aus der Sicht von MigrantInnen' in Bauböck, Rainer et al., op. cit.

Roche, Maurice (1987), 'Citizenship, social theory, and social change' *Theory and Society*, vol. 16, no. 3.

Rousseau, Jean-Jacques (1973), *The Social Contract and Discourses*, Dent, Everyman's Library, London.

Sandel, Michael (1982), *Liberalism and the Limits of Justice*, Cambridge University Press, Cambridge.

Scarry, Elaine (1992), 'Consent; Place, Right, and Body' Paper presented at the Urban Forum Conference 'Place and Right' Harriman, NY,

September 1992.

Schlesinger, Arthur M., Jr. (1992), *The Disuniting of America. Reflections on a Multicultural Society*, Norton, New York.

Schuck, Peter H. (1989), 'Membership in the Liberal Polity: The Devaluation of American Citizenship' in Brubaker, Rogers W. (ed.) (1989), , op. cit.

Schuck, Peter H. and Smith, Rogers M. (1985), *Citizenship without Consent. Illegal Aliens in the American Polity*, Yale University Press, New Haven and London.

Schumpeter, Joseph A. (1950), *Capitalism, Socialism and Democracy*, third edition, Harper Torchbooks, New York.

Sen, Amartya (1981), *Poverty and Famines: An Essay on Entitlement and Deprivation*, Clarendon, Oxford.

Sen, Amartya (1984), 'Rights and Capabilities' in *Resources, Values and Development*, Basil Blackwell, Oxford.

Shacknove, Andrew E. (1988), 'American Duties to Refugees. Their Scope and Limits' in Gibney, Mark (ed.), op. cit.

Shue, Henry (1980), *Basic Rights: Subsistence, Affluence, and U.S. Foreign Policy*, Princeton University Press, Princeton, NJ.

Shue, Henry (1988), 'Mediating Duties' *Ethics*, no. 98.

Shute, Stephen and Hurley, Susan (eds) (1993), *On Human Rights*, Basic Books, New York.

Sidgwick, Henry (1897), *The Elements of Politics*, second edition, Macmillan, London.

Sørensen, Georg (1993), *Democracy and Democratization. Processes and Prospects in a Changing World*, Westview, Boulder.

Stark, Oded (1991), *The Migration of Labour*, Blackwell, Oxford.

Taylor, Charles (1985), 'What's Wrong with Negative Liberty?' in *Philosophy and the Human Sciences. Philosophical Papers*, vol. 2, Cambridge University Press, Cambridge.

Taylor, Charles, Gutman, Amy, Habermas, Jürgen, Rockefeller, Steven, Walzer, Michael, Wolf, Susan (1993), *Multikulturalismus und die Politik der Anerkennung*, S. Fischer, Frankfurt am Main.

Titmuss, Richard (1963), *Essays on the Welfare State*, Allen & Unwin, London.

Tönnies, Sibylle (1992), 'Kann Asyl ein Recht sein?' *Zeitschrift für Rechtspolitik*, no. 2.

Turner, Bryan S. (1986), *Citizenship and Capitalism. The Debate over Reformism*, Allen & Unwin, London.

Turner, Bryan S. (1990), 'Outline of a theory of citizenship' *Sociology. The Journal of the British Sociological Association*, vol. 24, no. 2.

Turner, Bryan S. (ed.) (1993), *Citizenship and Social Theory*, Sage,

London.

Ueda, Reed (1982), 'Naturalization and Citizenship' in Thernstrom, Stephan (ed.), *Immigration, Dimensions of Ethnicity, A series of Selections from the Harvard Encyclopedia of American Ethnic Groups*, Harvard University Press, Cambridge, Mass.

van den Bedem, Ruud (1994), 'Towards a system of plural nationality in the Netherlands: changes in regulation and perceptions' in Bauböck, Rainer (ed.) (1994a), forthcoming, op. cit.

van Gunsteren, Herman R. (1988), 'Admission to Citizenship' *Ethics*, no. 98, July.

van Gunsteren, Herman R. (1992), *Eigentijds Burgerschap*, Wetenschappelijke Raad voor het Regeringsbeleid, Den Haag.

van Parijs, Philippe (1992), 'Commentary: Citizenship exploitation, unequal exchange and the breakdown of popular sovereignty' in Barry, Brian and Goodin, Robert E. (eds), op. cit.

Waldron, Jeremy (ed.) (1984), *Theories of Rights*, Oxford University Press, Oxford.

Waldron, Jeremy (ed.) (1987), *Nonsense upon Stilts. Bentham, Burke and Marx on the Rights of Man*, Methuen, London.

Wallerstein, Immanuel (1983), *Historical Capitalism*, Verso, London.

Wallerstein, Immanuel (1988), 'La construction des peuples: racism, nationalisme, ethnicité' in Balibar, Etienne and Wallerstein, Immanuel *Race, Nation, Classe. Les Identités ambiguës*, Editions la Découverte, Paris.

Walzer, Michael (1970), *Obligations. Essays on Disobedience, War, and Citizenship*, Harvard University Press, Cambridge, Mass.

Walzer, Michael (1983), *Spheres of Justice: A Defense of Pluralism and Equality*, Basic Books, New York.

Walzer, Michael (1984), 'Liberalism and the Art of Separation' *Political Theory*, vol. 12, no. 3.

Walzer, Michael (1987), *Interpretation and Social Criticism*, Harvard University Press, Cambridge, Mass.

Waters, Malcolm (1989), 'Citizenship and the Constitution of Structured Social Inequality' *International Journal of Comparative Sociology*, vol. 30, no. 3–4.

Whelan, Frederick G. (1981), 'Citizenship and the Right to Leave' *American Political Science Review*, vol. 75, no. 3.

Wihtol de Wenden, Cathérine (ed.) (1988), *La Citoyenneté et les changement de structures sociale et nationale de la population française*, Edilig, Fondation Didérot, Paris.

Wihtol de Wenden, Catherine (1994), 'Citizenship and Nationality in France' in Bauböck, Rainer (ed.), forthcoming, op. cit.

Young, Iris Marion (1989), 'Polity and Group Difference. A Critique of the Ideal of Universal Citizenship' *Ethics*, no. 99.

Young, Iris Marion (1990), *Justice and the Politics of Difference*, Princeton University Press, Princeton.

Zolberg, Aristide (1987), 'Keeping Them Out: Ethical Dilemmas of Immigration Policy' in Myers, Robert J. (ed.), *International Ethics in the Nuclear Age*, University Press of America, Boston.

Zolberg, Aristide, Suhrke, Astri and Aguayo, Sergio (1989), *Escape from Violence. Conflict and the Refugee Crises in the Developing World*, Oxford University Press, Oxford.

Index